THE BALLET LOVER'S COMPANION

THE

Ballet
Lover's

COMPANION

ZOË ANDERSON

YALE UNIVERSITY PRESS
NEW HAVEN AND LONDON

Published with assistance from the Nancy Batson Nisbet Rash Publication Fund

For information about this and other Yale University Press publications, please contact:
U.S. Office: sales.press@yale.edu   www.yalebooks.com
Europe Office: sales@yaleup.co.uk   www.yalebooks.co.uk

Typeset in Adobe Caslon Pro by IDSUK (DataConnection) Ltd
Printed in Great Britain by TJ International Ltd, Padstow, Cornwall

Library of Congress Cataloging-in-Publication Data

Anderson, Zoë.
    The ballet lover's companion / Zoë Anderson.
        pages cm
    Includes bibliographical references and index.
    ISBN 978-0-300-15428-3 (hardback)
1. Ballet.   2. Ballet—History.   I. Title.
    GV1787.A469 2015
    792.809—dc23

                                                                2014047020

A catalogue record for this book is available from the British Library.

10 9 8 7 6 5 4 3 2 1

This book is dedicated to my parents,
Gavin and Maggie Anderson.

CONTENTS

PREFACE

B ALLET MAY BE venerable, but it isn't a museum art form. In the twenty-
first century it has found a fresh lease of life, with excitement generated
by new works and new choreographers. There's another chapter to add
to the existing story of ballet's roots in sixteenth-century European courts,
its development on the gaslit stages of the Romantic era, its reflections
of the grandeur of Imperial Russia, and the adventures of the twentieth
century. By the end of that century, there were fears of ballet's decline:
a generation of major choreographers had died, leaving its future uncer-
tain. Since then, however, there's been a burst of energy, with the emergence
of leading names such as Alexei Ratmansky, Christopher Wheeldon,
and even newer names such as Justin Peck and Liam Scarlett. Ballet is
busy again.

So this is a good time for an overview of the art form, a time in
which current works can be added to ballet's long history. That history is
complicated. Where theatre or opera can confidently resurrect works from
the sixteenth and seventeenth centuries, ballet has not been so lucky. For
much of its history, dance works have been passed down from dancer
to dancer in a movement equivalent of an oral tradition: there was no
standardised, universally accepted notation, such as that for music. If ballets
were neglected for a generation, their choreography was lost. If they were
adapted or updated, the update was usually what survived. All art forms
look at their past through the lens of the present; ballet does this more than
most. In recent years there's been an attempt to reverse this, with companies going back to the roots of celebrated works, paying new attention to
notation systems and recording works on film. The repertory is expanding
in two directions: as new works are created, ballet is also rescuing and
reconstructing apparently 'lost' works. If I had written this book fifteen

years ago, I wouldn't have included Frederick Ashton's *Sylvia* or Vasily Vainonen's *The Flames of Paris*. Both have now made successful returns to the stage.

The book is designed as a guide to ballet as it is now. Choosing which works to cover, I've focused on those I think readers are most likely to see onstage. That will vary around the world: though ballet is an international art form, it's also a local one, with choreographers often attached to particular companies. Over time, other companies will take up some of their best-known, most admired works. For instance, while New York City Ballet's repertory includes as many as seventy-five works by George Balanchine, its founder choreographer, some of those pieces are rarely performed, and are unlikely to be danced elsewhere. I have entries on Balanchine masterworks such as *Apollo* and *Agon*, which are danced by almost every major company, but not for the quirky *Variations pour une porte et un soupir*, which is fairly rare even at New York City Ballet.

With prolific choreographers, I've tried to pick a representative sample of their works – choosing the most popular, certainly, but also giving some sense of the artist's range: are they known for short works as well as those lasting a whole evening, for plotless and for story ballets? I've also aimed to cover ballet's history. Léonide Massine's 'symphonic' ballets, which were hits in the 1930s, have since fallen out of fashion. However, I've included an entry on *Les Présages*, the best known of these works, both because it is still revived and also because the genre of symphonic ballet does have a lingering influence, notably on the work of present-day choreographer Alexei Ratmansky. As the twentieth century progressed, the boundaries between ballet and 'modern' or 'contemporary' dance began to blur. Since many classical companies now dance works by Jiří Kylián, Nacho Duato and others, I've included those, too.

This book is arranged chronologically. Each chapter has an introduction, describing the development of the art form in a particular period, giving a broader context for the individual ballet entries that follow. The book is designed to be read either as a continuous history, or to be dipped into for particular ballets.

In some cases there are multiple versions of a ballet: scores such as Felix Mendelssohn's music for *A Midsummer Night's Dream* or Sergei Prokofiev's *Cinderella* have been staged by many different choreographers. In most cases, I have written a single entry on what I consider to be the most influential staging of the work (often the earliest surviving production), ending with some discussion of other versions of the ballet. In a few cases I have written separate entries. Balanchine's *A Midsummer Night's Dream* and Ashton's *The Dream* are both danced to Mendelssohn's music and based on

Shakespeare's play, but they have different titles: it's simpler to keep them separate. Prokofiev's *Romeo and Juliet* actually has three separate entries. The productions, by Leonid Lavrovsky, John Cranko and Kenneth MacMillan, all had huge international success, helped shape or develop the companies for which they were created, and took a distinctive approach to the score and story. Their contexts, and their influence, are different and significant enough to earn individual entries.

Entries include details of choreographer, music, designs and first performances, with discussion of the ballet's context, theme or subject matter, choreography and impact. Russia did not adopt the Gregorian calendar until 1918, so its dates were out of sync with the western calendar, falling twelve days behind during the nineteenth century. For nineteenth-century Russian ballet premieres, I have used the local, 'old style' date.

Story ballets have a plot synopsis. A word about spoilers: ballet is usually relaxed about giving away the plot, with companies often including a synopsis in programme notes. What happens to the characters of Romeo and Juliet is unlikely to be a surprise to audiences, though the way the ballet is staged may still be unexpected. I will summarise and discuss plots – though, particularly with comedies, I've tried not to give away surprises or I've added warnings on individual entries where you might want to go in unspoiled.

ACKNOWLEDGEMENTS

'M GRATEFUL TO many people who have helped me in the writing of this book.

The staff of dance companies and venues have found and confirmed all manner of details for me. I'd like to thank Deborah Moe of Boston Ballet, Katya Novikova of the Bolshoi Ballet, Erica Espling of Cullberg Ballet, Cindy Koopman of Dutch National Opera & Ballet, Sarah Lam of Houston Ballet, Kina Poons of New York City Ballet, Catherine Heuls, Jérôme Maurel and Thierry Messonnier of the Opéra national de Paris, Anna-Katerina Gravgaard of the Royal Danish Ballet and Abigail Desch and Eugénie Dunster of Sadler's Wells.

I'm grateful to my agent, Michael Alcock of Johnson & Alcock, for his encouragement, energy and gentle prodding. At Yale University Press I thank my very supportive editor, Robert Baldock; also Candida Brazil, Rachael Lonsdale, Lauren Atherton and my eagle-eyed copy-editor, Richard Mason.

For discussion, facts, suggestions and moral support, I thank Leo Anderson, Erik Aschengreen, Gerald Dowler, Judith Flanders, Beth Genné, Robert Greskovic, Veronica Horwell, Clare Jackson and Michael Firbank, David Jays, Andrea Lyons, Alastair Macaulay, Fiona Mountford, Claire Peposhi, Giannandrea Poesio, Nicola Rayner, John Snelson, Nicholas Southwell, Ivy Sparks, Emilia Spitz, Roslyn Sulcas (Forsythe detective extraordinaire), Graham Watts and Lisa Wells-Turner. I'm particularly grateful to Jonathan Gray for reading my manuscript and making invaluable suggestions and corrections.

A GLOSSARY OF BALLET TERMS

adagio or *adage*. Slow, sustained movement: a section of the dancer's traditional ballet class will focus on movements of this kind. It can also refer to the opening section of a formal *pas de deux*, and to partnering in which the male dancer supports and displays his ballerina.

allegro. Quick, lively movement, often with jumps and quick footwork. A section of the ballet class will focus on movements of this kind.

arabesque. One of the best-known ballet positions. The dancer stands with his or her weight on one leg, the other stretched out behind with straight knee and pointed foot. In an *arabesque penchée*, the dancer leans down towards the ground, forming a diagonal line of torso and raised leg.

attitude. The dancer stands on one leg, the other leg lifted with bent knee and stretched foot. One arm is curved above the head, the other to the side. The pose is based on the statue of Mercury by Giovanni da Bologna.

ballerina. A principal female dancer. The terms prima ballerina and even prima ballerina assoluta are sometimes used to suggest higher ranks.

battement. A beating movement of the leg. In *battement tendu*, the dancer starts with both feet together, slides one foot until it is fully pointed, then slides it back.

beats, or beaten steps. Beating the legs together, or crossing and uncrossing the legs, while jumping (or while being lifted into the air).

bourrée, pas de. The dancer takes very small, fast steps, shifting his or her weight quickly from one foot to the other and back again. This can be a linking or a travelling step. Performed on *pointe*, a series of *pas de bourrées* can suggest the dancer is gliding across the stage.

character dancing. Term used for other dance styles, such as folk and national dances, performed within ballet. It can also refer to comic dances, or to roles focused on drama and mime rather than classical technique. Ballet dancers used to be divided into three categories: the 'noble', most elegant dancers, 'character' dancers who specialised in folk or comic dances and, in between these two extremes, the 'demi-caractère' dancer. These distinctions are now rarely used.

corps de ballet. Group of dancers who perform as a chorus to the soloists.

divertissement. A self-contained set of dances, sometimes inserted into a larger work. *Divertissements* can have a loose connection to the ballet's main plot – such as the dances in act 3 of *The Sleeping Beauty*, where fairytale characters come to dance at Aurora's wedding.

enchaînement. A sequence of steps, created for the classroom or the stage.

extension. The dancer's ability to raise and hold a leg high in the air. In the late twentieth century, dancers developed high extensions that were nicknamed 'six o'clock positions' – because one leg pointed down and the other straight up, like the hands of a clock.

feet, five positions of. The basic positions of the feet in ballet. The dancer stands with legs turned out from the hip, so that the toes point to the sides rather than to the front. In first position, the heels are together, toes pointing out. In second, the dancer stands with the feet a step apart. In third, the feet are placed one in front of the other, so that the heel of the front foot rests against the instep of the back foot. In fourth position, one foot is placed in front of the other, the feet a step apart. In fifth position, the feet are placed one in front of the other, so that the toe of each foot is by the heel of the other. Some systems, such as Serge Lifar's, have added extra positions to the standard five.

fouetté. A turn in which the dancer raises one leg to the side, then whips the foot into the knee while turning. In the coda of the 'Black Swan' *pas de deux* in *Swan Lake*, Odile spins thirty-two *fouetté* turns.

mime, or pantomime. Dramatic gestures, often used in story ballets. Nineteenth-century ballets use a formal mime language, with recognised gestures, such as pointing to the ring finger to indicate 'marriage'.

pas d'action. A setpiece that moves the story forward through both dance and mime, such as the Rose Adagio in *The Sleeping Beauty*.

pas de deux. A dance for two people. In the nineteenth century, a formal structure developed for the classical *pas de deux*: an *adagio* or entrée in which the male and female dancer perform together, usually in slow tempo, a variation (or solo) for each and a final coda, in which they dance together, usually in fast tempo. This structure could be expanded into a grand *pas de deux*, in which the central couple are supported by other dancers, who perform group dances or more solos.

plié. Bending the knee or knees, often in preparation for a jump. As an exercise in itself, it is usually the opening exercise of the traditional ballet class.

pointe. To dance on *pointe* is to dance on the extreme tips of the toes. Dancers wear specially made *pointe* shoes which help to support the foot.

sissone. A jump in which the dancer takes off from both feet, and lands on one foot.

terre-à-terre. Ground-skimming dancing, with few jumps.

variation. Solo dance.

BALLET'S BEGINNINGS

BALLET STARTED AT court. Today's theatre style has its roots in the pageantry of Renaissance Italy, when rulers used lavish entertainments, including music and dancing, to proclaim their own magnificence. In the fourteenth and fifteenth centuries, when ballet began to develop, Italy was divided into many small city states, ruled by dukes and princes who competed in war, politics and in the splendour of their courts. The classical past was being rediscovered, leading to an outpouring of new developments in the arts and sciences. Powerful families, such as the Medici in Florence, the d'Este in Ferrara and the Sforza of Milan, turned to artists to design, improve and embellish their palaces. The earliest ballets were part of this flourishing of art. Staged to celebrate special occasions, such as dynastic marriages, they carried political messages, glorifying rulers with images and allegories. Princes and courtiers took part in the performances: for the nobility, dance was a pleasure, but it was also a form of training that developed poise and grace.

The earliest surviving dancing manual was written shortly after 1400 by Domenico of Piacenza, who served the d'Este court. Written before the invention of printing, it survives as a handwritten manuscript, *De arte saltandi et choreas ducendi (On the Art of Dancing and Conducting Dances)*. The manual lays down elements of technique and describes some of the dances Domenico created. It also distinguishes between a *danza*, performed to a single rhythm, and a *ballo*, which had varied rhythms. Skilled dancing masters, like other skilled artists, were prized: one of Domenico's followers, Guglielmo Ebreo (also known as William the Jew), was in demand across Italy, creating dances for rulers such as Lorenzo de' Medici (the Magnificent) and Galeazzo Sforza, Duke of Milan. Dance had become an established part of Italian court life.

When the Italian noblewoman Catherine de' Medici married Henri II of France in 1533, she brought these entertainments with her. A lover of the arts and of pageantry, Catherine was also skilled in making political points through such spectacles, which were often staged to celebrate alliances, treaties and dynastic marriages. The most famous entertainment was created in 1581 at the court of the widowed Catherine, to celebrate the marriage of Marguerite de Lorraine to the Duc de Joyeuse; Marguerite was the sister of Catherine's daughter-in-law Louise, the queen of Henri III. The *Ballet comique de la Reine Louise* lasted five and a half hours, combining poetry, music and dance. It showed the escape of Ulysses from the enchantress Circe, who was a symbol of division. France had been riven by wars of religion, so the defeat of Circe promised unity and happier times. Choreographed by the Italian ballet master Balthasar de Beaujoyeulx, this spectacle was a huge, and hugely expensive, success, recorded in an illustrated book that was circulated to many European courts.

Now firmly established on French soil, the court ballet flourished. Catherine's grandson, Louis XIII, was another enthusiast. He performed in court ballets and used the 1617 ballet *La Délivrance de Renaud* to announce that, at sixteen, he was now ready to take power into his own hands, rather than relying on the regency of his mother, Marie de' Medici. His son Louis XIV, another admired dancer, appeared in his first court ballet at the age of twelve. Two years later he danced Apollo, the god of the sun, in *Le Ballet de la Nuit*. Cardinal Mazarin, his first minister, was a statesman who understood the value of court art as a political tool. He promoted the young king as an absolute monarch, a figure of unquestioned power and authority. The ballet provided Louis XIV with his enduring nickname, 'Le Roi Soleil' (the Sun King).

The Académie royale de danse, founded in 1661 under Louis XIV with the aim of 're-establishing the art of dance in its perfection', was focused on noble, courtly dance: it organised the teaching of social dance for aristocrats. It was the Académie royale de musique, founded eight years later, that would encourage the development of theatrical dancing. Its director, the composer Jean-Baptiste Lully, developed the opera-ballet, an extravagant spectacle combining singing and dancing. Since the court ballet lost importance when Louis XIV stopped dancing, the opera-ballet became the most significant platform for dancing. The balance shifted from aristocratic to professional performance, from the court to the theatre.

This created a new need for professional dancers. The Académie royale de musique recruited more dancers, directed by the court ballet master

Pierre Beauchamp, who is credited with the invention of the five positions of the feet. At first, female roles were performed by boys – as they had been in Shakespeare's theatre, earlier in the seventeenth century – but in 1681 women began to dance in Académie performances. By 1713 a permanent, professional dance school was founded, laying the foundation of today's Paris Opéra Ballet. This organisation of training, so characteristic of the centralising French state, gave dancing a sense of continuity and tradition. Systems of training were developed, codified and passed down. The language of ballet is still French. Its steps have French names, while the formal mime scenes of the nineteenth century follow French grammar: a dancer will gesture 'I – you – love', or 'Je t'aime'.

Now established as a theatre form, the opera-ballet continued to develop as an extravagant spectacle, while dancers made breakthroughs in technique. Ballet's earliest stars were men, such as Louis Dupré (1697–1774) who was nicknamed 'The God of the Dance'. Male costume allowed freer movement than women's long, heavy skirts. Marie Camargo (1710–1770) shortened her skirts to show off her brilliant footwork. Her rival, Marie Sallé (1707–1756), was known for the dramatic qualities of her dancing: 'it was not by leaps and frolics that she went to your heart,' wrote the ballet master Jean-Georges Noverre.[1] Sallé made her most daring experiments in London. In *Pygmalion*, her own miniature dance-drama of 1734, Sallé wore draperies instead of panniers, and moved with a blend of dance and mime. London had already seen the work of John Weaver, whose 1717 ballet *The Loves of Mars and Venus* told its story through movement and music alone, without singing or speech.

As the old opera-ballet became increasingly artificial, dancers and choreographers across Europe experimented with a form that would become known as the *ballet d'action*. These dramatic works saw dance as an art in itself, rather than a subsidiary part of plays or operas. In 1760, Noverre published his *Letters on Dancing and Ballet*, arguing for a form of ballet that was serious and expressive rather than merely spectacular. Dance and music should work closely together to convey the chosen theme, with steps that looked natural and appropriate to the dramatic situation. Costumes should be simpler and less restrictive, abandoning the hoops and heavy headdresses that were a leftover from ballet's court past. 'Poetry, painting and dancing are, or should be, no more than a faithful likeness of beautiful Nature,' he wrote.[2]

Noverre was not alone: ballet masters such as Gasparo Angiolini and Franz Hilferding experimented with similar developments. Jean Dauberval, who danced with the company that Noverre created in Stuttgart, was particularly praised for the way he wove dance and action together. His most celebrated ballet was *La Fille mal gardée* (1789), a village comedy with appealing, believable characters. For Dauberval, mime and gesture 'explains with rapidity the movements of the soul; it is a universal language, common to all times ... I do not want just to please the eyes, I must interest the heart.'[3] Dauberval's own choreography for *La Fille mal gardée* is lost, but the sense of down-to-earth communication survives in Frederick Ashton's lovely 1960 production.

Gaétan Vestris, a superlative dancer born in 1729, also appeared with Noverre's company and was a star across Europe. He was the exemplar of the 'noble style', which looked back to the grace and dignity of court ballet, while also working with the new choreographers. His son Auguste, born in 1760 to the ballerina Marie Allard, was smaller and slighter than his father: according to the genre divisions of the time, he was a *demi-caractère* dancer, halfway between the grandeur of the noble style and the character *comique* dancer. Auguste and the dancer Pierre Gardel were credited with inventing pirouettes – which had been danced by the acrobatic performers of popular theatres, but only now reached the formal ballet stage. When Gaétan and Auguste appeared together in London in 1781, Parliament interrupted its sessions so that members wouldn't miss the performances.

Auguste Vestris was a star in his own right, but was to have even greater influence as a teacher. After his retirement in 1816, he taught at the Paris Opéra, passing on the principles of French style to a new generation. His pupils included the ballerinas Marie Taglioni, Fanny Elssler and Lucile Grahn, and the choreographers Charles-Louis Didelot, Jules Perrot, August Bournonville and Marius Petipa. The thread of his teaching runs through the major achievements of nineteenth-century ballet. Auguste Vestris made his last appearance onstage in 1835 partnering Marie Taglioni, the icon of the Romantic era, in a minuet, the dance associated with the eighteenth century.

The early history of ballet is dominated by Paris, but the art form developed in many different centres: London, Stuttgart, Vienna and Bordeaux. In Italy, where ballet had its earliest roots, it was overshadowed by opera. Yet Italian dancers and teachers still influenced ballet across the world. Carlo Blasis (1797–1878) was born in Naples but spent his early career in France, where he worked with Dauberval. *The Elementary Treatise*, the technical manual Blasis published in 1820, laid down the principles of dance technique. (One of its illustrations shows the *attitude* position and its original model, the statue of Mercury by Giovanni da Bologna.) From 1837, Blasis directed the ballet school of La Scala, Milan, developing a system of training that produced generations of virtuoso dancers. Italian ballerinas would help to inspire the greatest phase of Petipa's career, starring in *Swan Lake* (1895) and *The Sleeping Beauty* (1890), both composed by Tchaikovsky. Before that, however, Parisian ballet was to have its Romantic golden age.

2

THE ROMANTIC BALLET

W HEN MARIE TAGLIONI made her debut at the Paris Opéra in 1827, ballet changed, almost literally overnight. Her style was hailed as something new and revolutionary. 'It is Romanticism applied to the dance,' wrote Le Figaro's reviewer. 'There is a vaporous, voluptuous quality in all her movements.'[1] Within weeks, other dancers were 'taglionising'.

What was so different about Taglioni? The Irish novelist Marguerite, Countess of Blessington, wrote:

> Hers is a totally new style of dancing, graceful beyond all comparison, wonderful lightness, an absence of all violent effort, or at least the appearance of it, and a modesty as new as it is delightful to witness in her art. She seems to float and bound like a sylph across the stage, never executing those *tours de force* that we know to be difficult and wish were impossible . . .[2]

Taglioni's apparently effortless dancing was the result of gruelling practice. Born in Stockholm in 1804, the daughter of the Swedish ballet dancer Sophie Karsten and the Italian dancer and choreographer Filippo Taglioni, she was not considered promising as a child. Fellow dance pupils mocked her round shoulders, saying, 'Can this little hunchback ever learn to dance?'[3] In preparation for her Viennese debut in 1822, she trained with her father for at least six hours a day: two hours' work on her suppleness, two on slow *adagio* work, two on jumping. She would hold challenging positions while she counted to a hundred, or make careful complete turns in a held pose, making sure that every angle, every transition, was without strain. Throughout her career, Marie Taglioni would remain fiercely disciplined. She paid attention to every detail, from her facial expressions to her fingers, so that everything would contribute to a harmonious whole. Conscious of those shoulders and her unusually long arms, she found poses that would flatter them, her torso softly tilted.

Taglioni was not the first to use *pointe*work, which began to be developed before 1820, but her use of this technique made it look natural. Like her other feats, it was part of her dancing, rather than an extra trick or display. Adding to her impression of weightlessness, *pointe*work would heighten Taglioni's ethereal quality in supernatural roles. She seemed to defy gravity, becoming an elusive sprite rather than a merely human woman.

Taglioni's revolution in style was to be matched by a revolution in staging, one that was already brewing when she made her first steps on the Paris stage. This was heralded by Romanticism, a movement that had already transformed other art forms with its revolt against the academic schools of the eighteenth century. It was a time of huge upheaval: the revolution in America and then in France thrust forward liberty and equality as the new ideals. In France, political and social systems were swept away by revolution and the Napoleonic wars that followed it. Across Europe, the Industrial Revolution was also gathering pace, transforming daily life and creating a new urban population – which in turn created a new demand for entertainment. Tastes, values and the arts were all radically altered. The Age of Reason was over.

The first generation of Romantics responded ardently to personal emotion, the natural world, to ideas of the sublime and the transcendent. Johann Wolfgang von Goethe's novel *The Sorrows of Young Werther*, first published in 1774, dwelled on its hero's emotional states: his delight in the simple peasant life he sees on his travels and his hopeless love for Charlotte. A generation of readers sensed their own feelings reflected in those of young Werther. In 1798, William Wordsworth and Samuel Taylor Coleridge published *Lyrical Ballads*, which expressed a vivid response to the natural world. Ten years later Beethoven's 'Pastoral' sixth symphony would celebrate it in music. This new movement in the arts prized depth of feeling over formal clarity. Shakespeare's free-ranging genius was in vogue, as artists turned away from the strict rules imposed by classical drama and classical forms. In fashion, rich women switched from stiff corsets and heavy panniered skirts to soft, clinging draperies: in 1800 the painter Jacques-Louis David painted the socialite Madame Récamier in plain draperies, with tousled curls and bare feet, an effect of apparent simplicity.

By the time ballet caught up with Romanticism, the tone of the movement had already darkened. The delight in nature expressed by Coleridge and Wordsworth was followed by the brooding anti-heroics and exotic settings of Lord Byron. In 1819, Géricault's painting *The Raft of the Medusa* showed the anguished and contorted bodies of the few survivors of a recent shipwreck, who in the aftermath of the wreck had taken to cannibalism. Berlioz's *Symphonie fantastique* of 1830 is full of visions of damnation, with an execution and a witches' sabbath. The Romantic movement had always valued intensity of feeling and expression; now it sought more extreme situations and emotions.

In Paris popular, melodramatic theatre led the way with supernatural stories, feeding a taste for the sensational with adventures complete with bandits, monsters and special effects. These techniques appeared at the Opéra in the ballet scene of *Robert le Diable*, the grand opera written by Meyerbeer in 1831. Robert, one of Romanticism's doomed anti-heroes, goes to a haunted cloister to steal a magic branch. Led by their abbess, danced by Marie Taglioni, the ghosts of sinful nuns surround him, luring and tempting him.

The scene was originally planned as mythological ballet, of the kind the Opéra had been churning out for decades. The designer Henri Duponchel refused, creating instead a spooky moonlit cloister, helped by recent advances in stage lighting. The footlights and the chandelier in the auditorium were extinguished, and – in a brand-new stage effect – gaslights were suspended from the flies, casting an eerie light over the scene. The cloister itself was lovingly realised in elaborate, naturalistic scenery, part of the new vogue for local colour. Rising from their tombs, the nuns wore gauzy white draperies. This would become the essential uniform of the Romantic ballerina: *pointe* shoes and a long white tutu.

Robert le Diable was a sensational success. Meyerbeer worried that his opera might flop without Taglioni, but the Ballet of the Nuns was a longlasting triumph; it was still being staged in the 1870s, when Edgar Degas painted it twice. With its vision of white-clad women dancing in the moonlight, it launched a new dance fashion, the '*ballet blanc*'. Older operas, such as Mozart's *Don Giovanni*, suddenly acquired spectral ballet scenes. Yet the impact of the *ballet blanc* went beyond supernatural shudders. It could be both dramatic and near-abstract: its ghosts might be gothic, but they also gave choreographers an opportunity to create lucid dance patterns.

Taglioni herself, who disliked the ballet's seduction scene, soon withdrew from *Robert le Diable*. Like Lady Blessington, critics and audiences had noted Taglioni's 'modesty' as a rare and unusual quality. Dancers, who showed off their bodies on the public stage, were not considered respectable. Many had rich protectors. Louis Véron, director of the Paris Opéra from 1831 to 1835, took advantage of this situation by opening the *foyer de la danse*, formerly a plain rehearsal room, to rich patrons. It came to operate as a fashionable club, where well-heeled men could pick up mistresses. In 1833 the Jockey Club was set up close to the theatre; officially concerned with racing, the club's members were just as interested in pursuing ballet dancers.

Ballets made the most of the female dancers' allure: the dancers in *Robert le Diable* were naughty nuns, after all, tempting the hero into sin. Alongside its technical and dramatic strengths, nineteenth-century ballet was frankly an opportunity to ogle pretty women. The poet, critic and librettist Théophile Gautier was characteristically blunt:

> A woman who appears half-naked in a flimsy gauze skirt and tights to pose before your opera glasses in the glare of eighty footlights with no other purpose than to display her shoulders, bosom, arms and legs in a series of *attitudes* that show them off to best advantage, seems amazingly impudent if she is not as beautiful as [the Graces].[4]

For *Giselle*, one of the greatest Romantic ballets, composed by Adolphe Adam and premiered in 1841, Gautier as the librettist was said to have insisted that only the most attractive girls in the *corps de ballet* should appear as peasants and as the ghostly wilis (supernatural women who dance men to death).

At the same time, interest in male dancing flagged. Although the Romantic era produced impressive male stars, including Lucien Petipa, Jules Perrot and August Bournonville (son of Antoine), men were increasingly edged offstage in favour of women. The development of *pointe*work gave female dancers a new technical edge, particularly in the fashionable supernatural ballets. The *pointe* shoe sets up a fundamental division between male and female roles in ballet: with very, very few exceptions, men are not expected to dance on *pointe*. Some critics shuddered that men should dance at all, particularly once more women began dancing male roles *en travesti*, disguised as men. Gautier would admit that Lucien Petipa – whose brother Marius would go on to a career of choreographic splendour at St Petersburg's Mariinsky Theatre – was 'not too repulsive for a man'.[5]

By 1840 the critic Jules Janin was contrasting 'a pretty dancing girl who displays the grace of her features and the elegance of her figure, who reveals so fleetingly all the treasures of her beauty' with:

> a man, a frightful man, as ugly as you and I, a wretched fellow who leaps about without knowing why, a creature specially made to carry a musket

and a sword and to wear a uniform. That this fellow should dance as a woman does – impossible! That this bewhiskered individual who is a pillar of the community, an elector, a municipal councillor, a man whose business it is to make and above all unmake laws, should come before us in a tunic of sky-blue satin, his head covered with a hat with a waving plume amorously caressing his cheek, a frightful *danseuse* of the male sex, come to pirouette in the best place while the pretty ballet girls stand respectfully at a distance – this was surely impossible and intolerable. . . .[6]

In Janin's description, ballet becomes a safe, frivolous, feminine space. Men looked ludicrous to him in ballet because they were meant to be doing something important in the real world, wielding power in the community rather than seeking to amuse onstage. Women, who in nineteenth-century Paris didn't have the option of making and unmaking laws, could safely reign supreme over this pretty, made-up kingdom.

Yet if Romantic ballet appealed to the male gaze, it also gave women great theatrical power. The ballerina was the most important, most interesting and – not incidentally – the best-paid person onstage. Thrust into the limelight, female performers were given the space to show off their skills and personalities along with their bodies. (For all Gautier's insistence on physical beauty, it's worth remembering that Taglioni, the supreme ballerina of the age, wasn't considered pretty.) Women as well as men flocked to the ballet; Taglioni, who combined seductiveness and modesty, had a particularly enthusiastic female fan base. From *Giselle* to *Swan Lake*, ballet became the ballerina's story, told from her perspective. Whereas nineteenth-century plays and operas were full of fallen women, lamenting and self-sacrificing, ballet plots were more likely to focus on male infidelity and its catastrophic consequences. Giselle forgives her faithless lover, but not until we've seen a whole act of vengeful female ghosts. Later plots would be even more blatant; in Marius Petipa's 1877 ballet *La Bayadère*, the gods punish Solor's broken vow by dropping a palace on him.

That said, men continued to dominate behind ballet's scenes. Many leading male dancers, including Perrot, August Bournonville and Arthur Saint-Léon, had important careers as choreographers. This was much rarer for women. Ballerinas created solo material – Fanny Elssler's sister Thérèse, for instance, choreographed many dances for Fanny and herself – but women weren't often entrusted with entire productions. The ballerina Fanny Cerrito choreographed two successful ballets: *Rosida* in 1845 and *Gemma* in 1854. Neither survives. In 1860, after her retirement as a dancer, Taglioni created *Le Papillon*, starring her pupil Emma Livry. This had a much longer life: a version of *Le Papillon* was still being danced in Russia into the twentieth century, and its *pas de deux* is still performed. *Le Papillon*'s success was an exception. Although ballerinas ruled the stage, they had fewer opportunities for creative influence beyond their own performances.

The ballet that gave Taglioni her own defining role features an early example of the faithless-lover plot. The tenor Adolphe Nourrit, who had sung the title role in *Robert le Diable* opposite Taglioni's abbess, wrote the libretto for *La Sylphide*, choreographed by Filippo Taglioni in 1832 to music by Jean Schneitzhoeffer. *La Sylphide*'s erring hero, a Scottish Highlander, was tempted away by Taglioni's enchanting sylph on his wedding day. This story brought together the two strands of Romantic ballet, the charm of the supernatural and a delight in local colour. Scotland was an exotic location for Paris audiences, already primed by the hugely popular Scottish romances of Walter Scott – he was Marie Taglioni's own favourite novelist. *Walterscottomanie*, as it was called, brought tartan into fashion; in France, people held fancy-dress parties on Scott themes, or redecorated their drawing rooms to evoke his novels. National dances, real and imagined, were woven through Romantic ballets: Scottish reels in *La Sylphide*, Italian tarantellas in August Bournonville's *Napoli* (1842), and evocations of India in François Auber's *Le Dieu et la Bayadère* (1830), another opera-ballet production starring both Taglioni and Nourrit.

Romantic ballet itself, though most strongly associated with Paris, was an international movement. Indeed, dancers from one country came to be associated with the dances and style of another: Gautier would describe the ballerina Carlotta Grisi as 'an Italian who has the air of a German, just as the German [sic] Fanny [Elssler] had the air of an Andalusian from Seville . . .'[7] Filippo Taglioni's version of *La Sylphide* is lost, but the Danish dancer and choreographer August Bournonville, having seen the ballet in Paris, went home to Copenhagen to create his own enchanting version, which survives in repertory today. The fashion for Romantic ballet spread quickly, as dancers travelled and found new audiences across Europe, Russia and even America. Many of these dancers shared a history. Critics might exclaim that Taglioni had banished the formal poses and technical display of the old *danse noble*, but the training of dancers still had its roots in the eighteenth-century school. Dancers flocked to Paris as a cultural capital, a city in which they could earn international fame – but also as a place to learn, to put the final touches to their technique, often under the eye of Auguste Vestris, the hero of an earlier era.

If Marie Taglioni was acclaimed as the ideal sylph, her greatest rival was to embody the more grounded joys of national and character dancing. The Austrian ballerina Fanny Elssler joined the Paris Opéra in 1834, having already achieved great success in Berlin and London. Her most famous dance was the *cachucha*, a Spanish dance with castanets that she first performed in *Le Diable boiteux* in 1836. 'She seems to shake down clusters of rhythm with her hands,' wrote an enraptured Gautier. 'How she twists! How she bends! What fire! What voluptuousness! What ardour! Her swooning arms flutter about her drooping head, her body curves back, her white shoulders almost brush the floor . . .'[8] Elssler, a superb dramatic ballerina, was also to bring new emotional insight to *Giselle*, though the ballet was created for another dancer.

Giselle, the archetypal Romantic ballet, combined the human and the ethereal. As noted, the libretto was written by Gautier, who was inspired by the poet Heinrich Heine's writings on the supernatural. Betrayed in love, the village heroine dies and dances with the wilis, vengeful female spirits – giving the ballerina a chance to show her skill in both local colour and the ghostly. The atmospheric, dramatic score by Adolphe Adam showed how far ballet music had come by the 1840s. At the start of the century, ballets had been full of borrowed tunes. Familiar arias would prod the audience's memory, giving them a key to the new ballet's character or situation. There were even complaints as ballet music became more ambitious, telling its own stories.

The title role was danced by the rising star Carlotta Grisi, and her dances were arranged by Jules Perrot, a dancer and choreographer who was also her lover. The rest of the production was left to Jean Coralli, the Paris Opéra's ballet master. Despite the triumph of *Giselle*, Perrot was not welcome at the Opéra, where he had quarrelled with the management over his salary. Instead, he turned to London. From 1843 to 1848 he was ballet master at Her Majesty's Theatre on Haymarket, an incredibly fertile period that made London the second home of Romantic ballet, rivalling and even surpassing the Paris Opéra in these years.

Most of Perrot's ballets have now been lost, but his skill was to influence later generations of choreographers. He was particularly admired for his storytelling, with strong characterisation and a sense of realism. The dancing carried the story forward: from the star ballerina's numbers to the crowd scenes, Perrot's dances were an expressive part of a complete stage picture. He had a vivid gift for atmosphere, from the medieval Paris evoked in *La Esmeralda* – based on Victor Hugo's *Notre-Dame de*

Paris – to the Oriental fantasy of *Lalla Rookh*. Perrot's *Ondine*, created in 1843, with music composed by Cesare Pugni, was another supernatural ballet, presenting the Neapolitan dancer Fanny Cerrito as a water sprite who becomes human. In one of the ballet's most famous scenes, Ondine sees her shadow for the first time, and dances with it. It is a moment that encapsulates many aspects of Romantic ballet: the supernatural and the everyday, the expression of each onstage enhanced by advances in stage lighting.

Alongside these grand examples of Romantic storytelling, Perrot created showpieces for particular dancers, leading to one of the era's most famous images of ballet. The Romantic ballet was star-led, with ballerinas gaining passionate followings. Queen Victoria had asked to see Elssler and Cerrito dance together. Perrot arranged a very tactful display, showing both ballerinas to equal advantage. In 1845 this was followed by the *Pas de quatre*, starring the four greatest ballerinas of the moment: Taglioni, Cerrito, Grisi and Lucile Grahn. It was a sensational success, followed by more multi-starred divertissements. Although the dancer Arthur Saint-Léon scornfully referred to Perrot's 'steeplechases' – diversions that sent rival performers over technical hurdles – they showed off Perrot, as well as his various ballerinas, as a choreographer who could celebrate the individual gifts of his dancers.

Fanny Cerrito, who had starred in many of Perrot's major works, married Saint-Léon in 1845. A violinist and choreographer as well as a dancer, he created several ballets for his wife – including in 1849 the remarkable *Le Violon du Diable*, to music by Pugni, in which Saint-Léon danced and played the violin to accompany Cerrito's dancing. Like Perrot before him, Saint-Léon worked in Russia, where he was particularly praised for his national dances. He commuted between Paris and St Petersburg, and returned to France for good in 1869. A year later he created *Coppélia*, his last and most celebrated ballet, to the music of Léo Delibes.

Lucile Grahn, the youngest of the four *Pas de Quatre* ballerinas, was born and trained in Denmark, where August Bournonville had created his version of *La Sylphide* for her. Bournonville staged other supernatural ballets, including *A Folk Tale*, and had an irresistible gift for local colour. With a tradition of continuous performance in Denmark, Bournonville's works represent an unusually authentic image of Romantic choreography. Whereas Perrot's *Giselle* was revised by Marius Petipa, Bournonville remained in charge of his own ballets for decades, and set up a strong tradition in Copenhagen. It's a distinctive, Danish take on Romanticism.

A virtuoso dancer himself, and loyal to his training with Auguste Vestris, Bournonville maintained a balance between the sexes, creating fine roles for both; he was less swept away by ballerina mania.

That quality of moderation is an important Bournonville characteristic. When he stages the supernatural, he avoids doom-laden gothic; in *La Sylphide* tragedy occurs due to human error as much as to magical vengeance. That sense of human behaviour comes through in Bournonville's naturalistic mime scenes; the lemonade and macaroni sellers of *Napoli* were based on real street life the choreographer had observed in Naples. In addition to presenting plays and operas, the Royal Theatre in Copenhagen staged many of his ballets. Henrik Ibsen's play *A Doll's House* had its premiere there; Betty Hennings, Ibsen's first Nora, was trained by Bournonville.

There's a warmth and intimacy to Bournonville's style: the footwork is speedy, with many beaten steps, and jumps are high but not explosive. Instead of making a huge leap that demands a moment for recovery, Bournonville dancers dart from step to step, constantly moving. The friendly, modest demeanour is linked to Bournonville's celebration of domestic virtue. The dancer Lloyd Riggins, who trained in this style at the end of the twentieth century, says: 'Just think of Bournonville's pirouettes: you always end up with your feet neatly together in fifth position and your arms nicely down – it is so hard to cover up mistakes! Bournonville is simply a very honest style – very revealing.'[9]

Although Bournonville flourished, he did so away from what had been the mainstream of European ballet. In his visits to other cities he was frequently shocked by what he found. Romantic ballet reached and passed its high tide in the 1850s, fading from popularity in what had been its great centres. The love of ballet survived in Denmark and Russia, but the fickle London public switched its attention to opera, while French ballet slid into decadence.

By the 1860s the golden age of Romantic ballet had ended. The ballerinas of the *Pas de quatre* generation had left the stage. Some of their most promising successors died tragically young: Taglioni's pupil Emma Livry died after her costume caught fire from a gas jet, while Giuseppina Bozzachi died of smallpox. Bournonville aside, the choreographers died or retired; their replacements failed to create the same impact. Ballet continued, adding spectacle to operas and music-hall bills, but its heyday seemed to be over. It was in Russia that the art found fresh energy and a new beginning. Under Marius Petipa, Romantic softness would develop into Imperial grandeur.

La Sylphide

Choreography: Filippo Taglioni
Music: Jean Schneitzhoeffer
Libretto: Adolphe Nourrit
Premiere: 12 March 1832, Paris Opéra, Paris
Original cast: *The Sylph* Marie Taglioni; *James* Joseph Mazilier

Choreography: August Bournonville
Music: Herman Løvenskjold
Libretto: Adolphe Nourrit
Premiere: 28 November 1836, Royal Theatre, Copenhagen
Original cast: *The Sylph* Lucile Grahn; *James* August Bournonville

Choreography: Pierre Lacotte
Music: Jean Schneitzhoeffer
Libretto: Adolphe Nourrit
Premiere: 1 January 1972 (television broadcast)
Original cast: *The Sylph* Ghislaine Thesmar; *James* Michaël Denard

In 1832, Paris was already enchanted by Scotland. Walter Scott's historical novels were best-sellers across Europe: two characters in *La Sylphide*, Madge and Effie, have names that would have been familiar to readers of Scott's *Heart of Midlothian*. The ballet's story was created by the tenor Adolphe Nourrit, drawing on Charles Nodier's *Trilby, ou le lutin d'Argail* (*Trilby, or the imp of Argyle*). In Nodier's tale a male sprite woos the wife of a Scottish fisherman, but Nourrit switched the genders. By combining Scott's and Nodier's romanticised Scotland with the ethereal women who had proved such a success in *Robert le Diable*, Nourrit and his collaborators created the first full-length Romantic ballet.

James, the hero of *La Sylphide*, is torn between these two worlds: between everyday life and the unattainable, between his flesh-and-blood fiancée and the ungraspable sylph. James is a strong role, with clear characterisation and opportunities for both classical and Scottish dancing, but the star part is the sylph. It was to be a defining role for Taglioni, a perfect vehicle for her floating jump and ease of movement.

Filippo Taglioni's original 1832 staging hasn't survived, so we know the ballet through Bournonville's restaging, created just four years after the Paris premiere. Bournonville kept Nourrit's story, but commissioned new music from the Norwegian composer Herman Løvenskjold rather than using the more expensive original Schneitzhoeffer score. This version has been kept in repertory by the Royal Danish Ballet, and has achieved international popularity since the second half of the twentieth century.

Synopsis

Act I. A Scottish manor house. It is the morning of James' wedding to Effie. The curtain rises on James, a young Highlander, asleep by the fire. The Sylphide kneels beside him – in an image that was widely reproduced in prints. She kisses James' forehead and wakes him. Fascinated and charmed, he chases after her, but she vanishes up the chimney. He wakes his companions, but none of them have seen her. Gurn, who is also in love with Effie, realises that James has become infatuated with someone else.

Effie, James' mother and their companions prepare for the wedding. An old woman, Madge, slips into the hall to warm herself by the fire. James tries to throw her out, but Effie persuades him to let Madge stay and tell the fortunes of some of the guests. She prophesies that Effie will marry Gurn. Furious, James threatens Madge, who curses him. Effie runs off to change for the wedding, leaving James alone. The Sylphide comes in through the window (another image popular with printmakers) and declares her love for James. Gurn sees them, and tries to warn Effie that James is unfaithful – but the Sylphide has disappeared again.

The wedding celebrations begin with a Highland reel. During the dancing, James keeps seeing the Sylphide, distracting him from the dance and taking the wedding ring meant for Effie. At last he runs into the forest after her. When his absence is discovered, all are horrified, while Effie weeps.

Act II. A glade in the forest. In the heart of the forest, Madge is planning her revenge. With her fellow witches, she prepares a spell in a cauldron, and produces an enchanted veil. They leave.

As the mist lifts, James enters with the Sylphide, who shows him her forest realm. She brings him berries and water, but won't allow him to touch her. She calls on her sisters and the forest fills with sylphs, who dance for him. Though he tries to catch his Sylphide, she evades his embrace. They leave.

James' friends and companions come looking for him. Gurn finds his hat, but Madge persuades him to say nothing. Gurn proposes to Effie and, encouraged by Madge, she accepts. Everyone returns home to prepare for a new wedding.

Madge convinces James that he can capture the Sylphide using the magic veil. When the Sylphide sees the veil, she is delighted, and allows James to place it around her shoulders. In Bournonville's production, he winds the veil around the Sylphide's arms, as if tying her down, as he kisses her. This is fatal: the Sylphide loses her sight and her wings drop off. Dying, she returns the wedding ring to James. The other sylphs prepare a funeral: surrounded by her grieving sisters, the Sylphide is floated into the heavens. As this procession disappears, James sees another in the distance: the wedding of Effie and Gurn. By pursuing the unobtainable, he has lost both the Sylphide and his human love. Madge triumphs over him.

Bournonville's staging preserves some of the nineteenth century's supernatural stage machinery. The sylph vanishes up the chimney or melts into the furniture, using traditional and often charming special effects. In this ballet the human women do not wear *pointe* shoes. *Pointe*work becomes another special effect, setting the sylphs apart from ordinary mortals. Madge and her fellow witches are often danced by male dancers.

The choreography blends dance and drama, with clear characterisation in both steps and mime scenes. Alongside the airy dances of the heroine and her sisters, there are lively character dances for the hero James, his fiancée Effie and the Highland villagers. The exhilarating Highland reel of the first act is a portrait of the whole community, from a little girl who joins the dancing to the bravura solos for James and another male dancer. The story, with its moral, is woven through this set piece. As James keeps chasing after the sylph, the pattern of the dance breaks down behind him: he is missed, first by his partner Effie and later by the rest of the dancing group. Pursuing his sylph, breaking his promise, James has an impact on everyone around him, something embodied in the dance itself.

Other Stagings

In 1972, Pierre Lacotte's production of *La Sylphide* was broadcast on French television, and taken into the repertory of the Paris Opéra Ballet later that year. Lacotte's production attempts to recreate the lost Taglioni ballet, drawing on contemporary records. To evoke 1830s style, Lacotte asked female dancers to wear corsets, which give a slight forward tilt to the torso. He also puts the Highland village women on *pointe*, reducing the contrast between humans and sylphs.

In 1994, Matthew Bourne staged *Highland Fling*, a contemporary dance version of *La Sylphide*. Danced to the Løvenskjold score, it fastforwarded the action to modern Scotland, with nightclub scenes, drugs and feral, barefoot sylphs. In 2013, Scottish Ballet became the first ballet company to dance Bourne's production.

In 2014, Nikolaj Hübbe staged a controversial new production of Bournonville's *La Sylphide* at the Royal Danish Ballet. Designer Bente Lykke Møller does away with the Scottish manor and the forest glade in favour of abstract settings, though a few celebrated pieces of scenery, such as the armchair and the window, remain. Hübbe also gave the plot a homoerotic twist: Madge (a role often traditionally danced by men) becomes James' cast-off male lover, who plots revenge.

Giselle

Choreography: Jean Coralli and Jules Perrot
Music: Adolphe Adam
Libretto: Théophile Gautier, Jules-Henri Vernoy de Saint-Georges and Jean Coralli
Premiere: 28 June 1841, Théâtre de l'Académie Royale de Musique, Paris
Original cast: *Giselle* Carlotta Grisi; *Albrecht* Lucien Petipa; *Myrtha* Adèle Dumilâtre

Giselle is the quintessential Romantic ballet. A story of love, betrayal, death and ghosts, it offers the ballerina a role that combines Romanticism's two major themes, local colour and the supernatural. In the first act, we see Giselle as a villager, a human woman who loves Albrecht and loves dancing. In the second, she becomes a wili, the ghost of a woman who has died before her wedding day. Giselle is ballet's first great dual role.

The ballet got its start when one Romantic poet was inspired by another. 'My dear Heinrich Heine,' wrote Théophile Gautier:

while leafing through your excellent book, *De l'Allemagne* ... my eyes rested on a charming passage ... in which you speak of the white-robed elfs whose hems are ever damp, the nixes who display their little satin feet on the ceiling of the nuptial chamber, the pallid wilis and their piti-less waltz, and all those delightful apparitions which you encountered in the Harz mountains and on the banks of the Ilse in the velvety mists of German moonlight – and involuntarily I said to myself, 'What a lovely ballet that would make!'[10]

Gautier's first idea was to start the ballet in a ballroom, with the wilis joining the dancers. Dissatisfied, he turned to Saint-Georges, an experienced librettist, who developed the village tragedy of the first act.

Synopsis

Act I. A Rhineland village. Albrecht, a nobleman, is interested in the peasant girl Giselle. To spend time with her, he has disguised himself as a villager, Loys. Attended by his squire, Wilfred, Albrecht arrives in his own nobleman's clothes, then retreats into a hut to change into his peasant disguise. He knocks on the door of Giselle's cottage, then hides. She steps out and – finding nobody there – starts to dance, until she hears the sound of Albrecht blowing kisses. She is charmed by him, but doubtful when he promises to love her forever. She plays 'he loves me, he loves me not' with the petals of a daisy, and is disappointed with the outcome. Albrecht cheats, secretly tearing off a petal then asking her to count again. Hilarion, a forester who is in love with Giselle, warns her not to trust Albrecht. Village girls come in from the harvest and invite Giselle and Albrecht to join their dance.

Berthe, Giselle's mother, is worried to find her daughter dancing – Giselle has a weak heart. To warn her, Berthe tells the stories of the wilis, the ghosts of young women who have died before their wedding days. If they find any man between midnight and dawn, the wilis will force him to dance until he dies. Giselle shrugs off her mother's warning. Hunting horns are heard in the distance. Wilfred warns Albrecht that a courtly hunting party is approaching, so he leaves. Hilarion, left alone, breaks into Loys' hut.

The hunting party arrives, led by the Prince of Courland and his daughter, Bathilde. They call for refreshments, and Giselle brings them wine. Amazed by Bathilde's rich clothes, Giselle creeps up behind her to touch the velvet of her dress. Bathilde is charmed by Giselle's admiration, and gives her a gold necklace. In mime, Giselle explains that she is engaged, though her lover is nowhere to be seen. Bathilde explains that she, too, is engaged. The hunting party go into Giselle's cottage to rest, leaving the hunting horn hanging up outside.

The villagers return with the harvest, and Giselle is crowned Queen of the Vintage. During the celebrations, Hilarion appears with Albrecht's sword and cloak, denouncing him as an impostor. Albrecht makes as if to attack him. Hilarion snatches the hunting horn and blows it, summoning the hunting party. Emerging from the cottage, Bathilde and the Prince recognise Albrecht and exclaim over his peasant clothes. Giselle breaks in, insisting that Albrecht is her lover.

Told that Bathilde is engaged to him, Giselle goes mad. She falls, letting down her hair; when she stands up, she has lost her reason. She seems to see spirits in the air, and relives moments she spent with Albrecht: the test of the flower, fragments of steps they danced together. She stumbles over Albrecht's sword, left on the ground, and snatches it up, trying to stab herself. Albrecht drags the sword away. She rushes to her mother, then on to Albrecht, and drops dead. The villagers lament over her body.

Act II. The forest at night. Hilarion grieves by Giselle's grave. (In some productions, Giselle dies of her weak heart, but the fact that she was buried in the forest, in unhallowed ground, suggests that she committed suicide, stabbing herself with Albrecht's sword.) Fearful of the sounds and lights of the forest, Hilarion leaves. Myrtha, the queen of the wilis, appears. She crosses the stage in a gliding *bourrée*. With its flat-footed hops in *arabesque* and its whirling jumps, Myrtha's solo shows that the wilis are both earth-bound and ghostly. Picking up a branch, she summons the wilis. After their dance, Myrtha calls Giselle from her grave, and initiates her as a wili. Released from the ground, Giselle turns in a driven, hopping spin, before bounding in freedom.

The wilis exit, and Albrecht enters, wrapped in a cloak and carrying an armful of lilies for Giselle's grave. She appears to him, and they dance together. The wilis find and pursue Hilarion, forcing him to dance and driving him to his death in a pool of water. Then they find Albrecht. Myrtha condemns him to dance until he dies. He is protected by the cross on Giselle's grave, so Myrtha orders Giselle to dance, luring him into danger. Giselle dances with him, trying to protect him, keeping him alive until dawn breaks, when the wilis lose their power. The ghostly dancers fade away. Giselle returns to her grave, leaving Albrecht grieving.

The choreography for *Giselle* was entrusted to Jean Coralli, the ballet master of the Paris Opéra. He was regarded as a competent rather than an inspired producer, but *Giselle* brought out the best in him. 'Coralli has recaptured, for the ballet, a freshness of ideas of which I no longer thought him capable,' wrote Léon Pillet, the director of the Paris Opéra.[11] The wili scenes of *Giselle* are superb, evoking Heine's ghost stories. Where the sylphs in *La Sylphide* were airy and innocent, mischievous rather than cruel, the wilis dance with dark power.

With her sliding hops and gliding bourrées, the queen of the wilis commands and defines the stage. 'Myrtha's stage-skimming crosses, her re-entries at unexpected points, the weighty incantation of her dance along the ground were all intended to describe her authority in that space, on that spot of earth, and under it,' wrote the critic Arlene Croce in 1981. 'These are graves on which she dances, and they are, as we see in a moment, the graves of dancers. Myrtha prepares the drama. Anyone who has not experienced the thoroughness of her preparation has not felt the icy breath of *Giselle*.'[12] The *corps de ballet* patterns are stark: lines of dancers hop with implacable rhythm, both weighted and weightless. Driving Hilarion and then Albrecht to dance, they line up in a sharp diagonal, a pitiless wall.

Although Coralli was in charge of rehearsals, the dances and scenes for Carlotta Grisi, who danced Giselle, were created by Jules Perrot, her lover. An emerging star, Grisi was praised for combining the virtues of the aerial Marie Taglioni and the more grounded Fanny Elssler. In the first act, Giselle has skimming *terre-à-terre* steps; in the second, she takes on the qualities of a wili. As a human woman, she links arms with Albrecht to skip and bound. As a ghost, she floats insubstantially in his arms. Throughout this act, she is torn between her love for Albrecht and her wili nature – which itself draws on the love of dancing she has shown in the ballet. The second act is the heart of *Giselle*, the core idea that inspired Gautier and his collaborators. When Elssler danced the ballet in 1843, she shifted the balance of the work. Grisi's mad scene had been more danced than mimed; Elssler's was acclaimed as an acting triumph. This range has made Giselle one of the most coveted and challenging ballerina roles.

Like all surviving nineteenth-century ballets, *Giselle* has been revised over time. Perrot produced it in St Petersburg in 1848 with Elssler as Giselle and Marius Petipa as Albrecht. As ballet master, Petipa kept it in repertory, though he updated it over several revivals. A waltz was added to the first act, and he also revised the 'peasant' *pas de deux*, a first-act showpiece that had been added to the ballet in Paris. Sometimes this becomes a peasant *pas de six*. The variation Myrtha now dances was choreographed by Petipa, to substituted music. These revisions also took account of developments in technique, particularly in *pointe*work, but keeping the spirit of the ballet: the rustic charm of the first act, the supernatural chill of the second.

Napoli, or The Fisherman and his Bride

Choreography and libretto: August Bournonville
Music: Holger Simon Paulli, Edvard Helsted, Niels Wilhelm Gade, Hans Christian Lumbye
Premiere: 29 March 1842, Royal Danish Ballet, Royal Danish Theatre, Copenhagen
Original cast: *Teresina* Caroline Fjeldsted; *Gennaro* August Bournonville

'If you love the warmth of the sun,' Bournonville wrote in his memoirs, 'the sea and the clear air, flowers and lively people picturesquely posed . . . then do not waste time reading but go to Italy and study nature.'[13] Northern European audiences were enchanted by the idea of the warm south, buying travel memoirs and flocking to exhibitions of genre paintings. Long before he went to Italy, Bournonville was making successful ballets on this theme, such as *The Festival in Albano* (1839). But it was *Napoli*, which he created after his first visit to Italy, that became Denmark's national ballet, the biggest success of Bournonville's career.

In 1841, Bournonville made the mistake of appealing to the king of Denmark during a performance, trying to settle a theatrical dispute. This counted as *lèse-majesté*; after being placed under house arrest, he was given unpaid leave of absence, which he spent travelling. Naples delighted him: his letters home are full of delighted detail, with many incidents that found their way into the ballet *Napoli*. Lodging by the fishmarket, he saw people of all classes: fishermen in picturesque shorts and religious amulets, macaroni cooks, monks, beggars and lemonade sellers. In half an hour, he would later write, he could collect more groupings than he could use in ten ballets. Most of these images found their way into *Napoli*.

Synopsis

Act I. Naples, by the bay of Santa Lucia, evening. Crowds gather on the wharf of Santa Lucia. Peppo, a lemonade seller, and Giacomo, a macaroni seller, hope to marry Teresina, the daughter of the widow Veronica. They ask Veronica for encouragement, but Teresina is not interested: she is in love with the young fisherman Gennaro, who arrives and embraces Teresina. Veronica reluctantly agrees to their betrothal.

The monk Fra Ambrosio begs for alms. Gennaro and Teresina give him money, and he blesses them. Peppo and Giacomo try to make Teresina jealous of a young woman who buys fish from Gennaro, without success. When Gennaro gives Teresina an engagement ring, Peppo and Giacomo spread rumours that he is in league with the devil.

The lovers set out for a moonlit sail in the bay. Back on the quayside, the crowds are entertained by a street singer and puppeteer, until a violent storm breaks. The fishermen go to help. Gennaro is rescued, unconscious, but Teresina is missing. Veronica accuses Gennaro of drowning her daughter, and the townsfolk reject him. He prays to the statue of the Madonna. Fra Ambrosio urges him to go to sea in search of Teresina, giving him an image of the Madonna for protection.

Act II. Capri, the Blue Grotto. Teresina has been rescued by naiads and brought to the Blue Grotto, home of the powerful sea sprite Golfo. She asks Golfo to let her go home. Fascinated by her beauty, he refuses, and pours the magical water of the grotto over her. In an onstage transformation scene, she becomes one of the naiads, her peasant dress whisked away to reveal a sea-creature's skirts. Golfo's slaves celebrate. Although the spell has made Teresina forget her mortal past, she still rejects the sea sprite.

Gennaro's boat enters the grotto. Golfo orders his naiads and tritons to leave so he can deal with the intruder. Gennaro spots Teresina's guitar, and realises she is still alive. The naiads bring her to him, but since she is no longer human she does not recognise him. Remembering the image of the Madonna, Gennaro prays that Teresina's memory may be restored. She becomes human again, and the lovers embrace. Furious, Golfo tries to prevent them leaving. Teresina holds up the image of the Madonna and he is vanquished. The sea creatures bow to the Madonna and give the young couple treasures before they leave.

Act III. The shrine of the Monte Virgine, near Naples. Teresina and her mother have gone with the people of Naples on a religious pilgrimage. When Gennaro arrives, Peppo and Giacomo again spread rumours that he is evil. Teresina insists that Gennaro rescued her, but her mother separates the lovers, and the townsfolk flee in fear. Fra Ambrosio arrives and explains that Teresina was saved through the power of the Madonna. Everyone gathers around the happy couple to celebrate their reunion. The ballet ends with a marvellous suite of dances, with a *pas de six* and tarantella.

Napoli was an immediate triumph. According to one eyewitness, the first audience, 'for want of castanets, accompanied the tarantella unceasingly with clapping and cheers, and there was a gaiety throughout the whole house which could waken the dead'. The tarantella, the ballet's most famous number, was another of Bournonville's Neapolitan memories. Writing to his wife, he described his trip to Baia, a fishing village that had once been a Roman pleasure resort. By the ruined temple of Mercury, peasants sold mosaic fragments and shells to tourists. Bournonville bought souvenirs from one pretty girl, who then led her companions in a dance:

> Along came Rosa, as the girl was called, with several other lads and lasses. One banged the tambourine, another sang; and now Rosa and another girl began the tarantella. It was no masterpiece; it was performed in bare feet, and the steps were rather monotonous. But the location,

the air, the delicious scent of flowers from the surrounding gardens made it extremely poetic. It was a changing dance; a young chap called Rafaelle took the place of the second girl and performed many comical movements. Encouraged partly by my [travelling] companions and partly by my own irresistible urge, I tossed aside coat and neckerchief and joined in the dance. Rafaelle stepped aside, and I now performed all the figures I could remember. Everyone joined in the singing, the tambourine's tempo was doubled, Rosa laughed and shrieked. I danced until I could no longer stand it, and we ended the dance to universal cries of 'Bravo!', which rang through the lofty vault of the ancient temple.[14]

Bournonville's own tarantella is danced in shoes, with the women on *pointe*, and a much greater variety of steps. It keeps the atmosphere, and even some of the details, that Bournonville had described. Gennaro pulls off his coat and hat to join the dance, replacing another man. More dancers join in, with little rivalries and flirtations woven through their dances, while the onstage crowd watches and marvels. Traditionally, pupils from the Royal Danish Ballet school watch from the bridge at the back of the stage, gaining stage experience and familiarity with the ballet.

In 2009 artistic director Nikolaj Hübbe and leading Bournonville ballerina Sorella Englund staged a new production of *Napoli* for the Royal Danish Ballet. The first two acts were updated to the 1950s, a Federico Fellini-tinged milieu in which *corps de ballet* members smoke cigarettes and the hero and heroine return on a motor scooter rather than a bridal cart. The second act was restaged with a new score by Louise Alenius. (It was always the least popular, even nicknamed 'the Bronnum act', because Copenhagen ballet-goers would sit it out in the Bronnum restaurant close to the theatre, returning to see Act III.) As in Hübbe's staging of *A Folk Tale*, the religious element was toned down, so that Gennaro now wins Teresina back with a love token she has given him, rather than a religious amulet. The last act remained essentially unchanged. Inevitably, the production was controversial, but it has also been acclaimed at home and abroad. The Royal Danish Ballet's dancers proved to be equally vivid as 1950s Neapolitans as they had been playing nineteenth-century peasants.

Le Pas de Quatre

Choreography: Jules Perrot
Music: Cesare Pugni

Premiere: 12 July 1845, Her Majesty's Theatre, London
Original cast: Marie Taglioni, Carlotta Grisi, Fanny Cerrito, Lucile Grahn

Benjamin Lumley, the manager of Her Majesty's Theatre in the 1840s, had a sharp eye for both art and business. He was well aware of the box office power of star dancers, and in Jules Perrot he had a ballet master who could make the most of them. The clever result was *Le Pas de quatre*, which brought together four of Romantic ballet's greatest stars in a single divertissement.

Marie Taglioni, Carlotta Grisi and Fanny Cerrito were all to be in London at the same time: publicity immediately dropped hints that they might 'appear in one single ballet – a collision that the most carelessly managed railroad could hardly hope to equal'.[15] By the time Perrot came to create his ballet, Lucile Grahn had been added to the list. (Fanny Elssler, the other great ballerina of the age, was missing: she and Taglioni had been fierce rivals since Elssler had danced *La Sylphide*, Taglioni's most celebrated role.)

In his memoirs Lumley joked that governing a state was an easy job compared to ruling these four ballerinas. 'Every twinkle of each foot in every pas had to be weighed in the balance, so as to give no preponderance. Each danseuse was to shine in her peculiar style and grace to the last stretch of perfection; but no one was to outshine the others – unless in their own individual belief.'[16] When it came to arranging the solos, it was agreed that Taglioni was more equal than others and so was given the final variation. But how were the others to be ordered? When Cerrito and Grisi quarrelled, poor Perrot was in despair. Lumley had the answer: the oldest ballerina should dance last. It worked. 'The ladies tittered, laughed, drew back, and were now as much disinclined to accept the right of position as they had before been eager to claim it.'[17] The final order of solos was Grahn, Grisi, Cerrito and Taglioni.

The ballet begins with the three younger dancers kneeling around Taglioni, all four with roses in their hair. It became one of Romantic ballet's most cherished images. The opening dance was full of soft groupings, Taglioni always at their centre. Then Grahn danced a brilliant solo, followed by a brief duet for Cerrito and Grahn, ending with flying jumps from Taglioni. In their main variations, Grahn was light and vigorous, hopping lightly on *pointe*, Grisi was coquettish, Cerrito was buoyant and spectacular, while Taglioni showed her gentle authority. In the coda, all four dance, finally coming back to their original grouping.

Other Stagings

The *Pas de quatre* was a triumphant blend of artistry, rivalry and substantial financial profits. It was performed just four times with its original cast, and successfully revived in 1847 with Carolina Rosati replacing Grahn. In 1941, Anton Dolin staged his own version of the work, based on contemporary descriptions and reviews. His four ballerinas were Nana Gollner, Alicia Alonso, Nina Stroganova and Katherine Sergava. In 1957, Dolin created *Variations for Four*, a companion work showing off four male virtuosi, starring John Gilpin, Flemming Flindt, Louis Godfrey and André Prokovsky.

Konservatoriet (originally subtitled A Proposal by Advertisement, also known as Le Conservatoire)

Choreography: August Bournonville
Music: Holger Simon Paulli
Premiere: 6 May 1849, Royal Danish Ballet, Royal Danish Theatre, Copenhagen
Original cast: Juliette Price, Pauline Funck, Ferdinand Hoppe, Sophie Price

Konservatoriet was originally a two-act ballet, with a comic plot about the inspector of the Conservatoire who advertises for a fashionable wife but is brought to see that he will be happiest with his devoted housekeeper. At its heart, however, there was a sparkling classroom scene, in which Bournonville paid homage to Auguste Vestris, recalling his own studies with the great teacher. The ballet was also the debut of Juliette Price, who would become one of Bournonville's greatest ballerinas. In 1941, Valborg Borchsenius and Harald Lander staged this opening scene as a one-act *divertissement*, a view of dancers at work.

The setting is Paris in the 1820s, the time of Bournonville's youth. Even the set suggests behind-the-scenes pragmatism: there's a glittering chandelier, but it's muffled up in a dustsheet. The dancers wear practice uniforms of the period, the women with bows of black ribbon tied around their necks. Just as class pianists will use familiar tunes to accompany the exercises, Holger Simon Paulli's score draws on existing material. He includes most of J. P. Rode's seventh violin concerto which, as historian Ole Nørlyng points out, was used as an examination piece for young violinists at the time Bournonville was living in Paris.[18]

A ballet master oversees the studies of adult dancers and a handful of children. The scene begins and ends with a *grand plié* – both a basic, fundamental step for the classroom and, onstage, a test of the whole company's balance. In rows, the dancers bend their knees deeply, sinking towards the floor with their torsos held upright, and rise smoothly up again. It's both challenging and modest. As the class progresses, the exercises build up speed and complexity. The cast ranges in age from child students to two ballerinas and a male soloist.

Bournonville first studied with Vestris at the age of fourteen, and again when he lived in Paris four years later. During Vestris' lifetime, Bournonville would return to his classes each time he visited Paris. He was a devoted student, noting down Vestris' *enchaînements* and using them in his own lessons. His students included Per Christian Johansson, who took his schooling with him to St Petersburg, where his own pupils would include Anna Pavlova and Tamara Karsavina. 'The Russian school is the French school, only the French have forgotten it',[19] Johansson would say later. *Konservatoriet* celebrates and demonstrates the school of Vestris.

Today the ballet is best known in its one-act divertissement form. In 1995 the Royal Danish Ballet staged the two-act version, reconstructed by Kirsten Ralov – who had danced in the two-act version as a child – with Niels Bjørn Larsen and his daughter Dinna Bjørn.

Konservatoriet is the first of a number of classroom ballets. Lander went on to create his own *Etudes* in 1948. In Russia, Asaf Messerer's *Class Concert*, staged for the Bolshoi Ballet in 1963, is another *divertissement* in classroom form.

A Folk Tale (Et folksagn)

Choreography: August Bournonville
Music: Niels W. Gade and J. P. E. Hartmann
Premiere: 20 March 1854, Royal Danish Ballet, Royal Danish Theatre, Copenhagen
Original cast: *Hilda* Juliette Price

A Folk Tale was Bournonville's favourite among his own ballets, his 'most perfect and finest choreographic work, especially as regards its Danish character'.[20] It drew on a distinctly Danish version of Romanticism, from the Danish folk tales collected by Just Mathias Thiele in the eighteenth century to Hans Christian Andersen's 1845 tale 'The Elfin Hill'. For music, Bournonville turned to two composers with a similar interest in Scandinavian mythology and themes. The bridal waltz that Niels Gade wrote for the last scene is still one of the most popular pieces of wedding music in Denmark.

Synopsis

Act I. The park of a medieval estate. A hunting party from the noble house of Holgarden stops to rest and eat. Birthe, the bad-tempered heiress, is rude to her cousin and fiancé, Junker Ove, and flirts with Sir Mogens, a neighbour. As the party returns home, Ove lingers, even though he has been warned that trolls live inside a nearby hill.

As darkness falls, the troll hill magically opens, to reveal trolls at work in a forge, hammering gold. Hilda, a beautiful young woman, steps out of the hill. She offers Ove a golden goblet, trying to lure him back into the hill with a magic drink. Ove refuses, and the drink is spilled. The troll sorceress Muri, who lives in the troll hill, calls Hilda back and summons a group of elf maidens. She summons up a group of elf maidens who whirl and dance around Ove, driving him mad.

Act II. Inside the hill. Muri's sons, Diderik and Viderik, are both courting Hilda. Muri has decided that Diderik, as the elder brother, should be the one to marry her. Viderik protests, and they squabble. Hilda falls asleep and dreams of young trolls stealing a human baby, leaving a troll child behind. They also take a golden cup. In her dream Hilda is fascinated by the sight of a crucifix. When she wakes, she makes a cross from two twigs, which frightens Muri.

The trolls assemble for Hilda's wedding to Diderik. At the celebrations, Hilda dances and the trolls become drunk. She takes the opportunity to escape, with Viderik's help.

Act III. Scene 1. On the edge of the forest. Hilda and Viderik are asleep in the forest, by a holy spring where sick people come to be healed. Waking up, Hilda gives alms to the poor. Ove arrives, carrying the golden cup, still spellbound by troll magic. Hilda takes him to the spring, where the water cures him. He recognises her. Estate workers arrive and try to chase Viderik and Hilda away.

Scene 2. Birthe's manor. Birthe, full of bad temper, bullies her servants. Hilda appears, carrying the golden cup. She is recognised as the rightful heiress, while Birthe is the troll changeling.

Scene 3. The gardens. Muri arrives with Viderik and Diderik, who all recognise Birthe as part of their family. Offered riches and gold, Sir Mogens agrees to marry Birthe. Hilde is united with Ove. The final celebration takes place on midsummer's eve, with garlands, a maypole dance and joyful divertissement dances, including the festive *Pas de Sept*, often staged separately.

Coppélia, or The Girl with the Enamel Eyes

Choreography: Arthur Saint-Léon, later restaged by Marius Petipa, Enrico Cecchetti and others
Music: Léo Delibes
Libretto: Arthur Saint-Léon with Charles Nuitter
Premiere: 25 May 1870, Théâtre National de l'Opéra, Paris
Original cast: *Swanilda* Giuseppina Bozzachi; *Franz* Eugénie Fiocre

Coppélia is a ballet of dolls and disguises, music box charms and more naturalistic lovers' quarrels. The libretto, written by the choreographer Arthur Saint-Léon with Charles Nuitter, is based very loosely on the E. T. A. Hoffmann story *The Sandman* – a creepy tale, full of images of stolen eyes, that was to inspire Sigmund Freud's essay 'The Uncanny'. Like Tchaikovsky's *The Nutcracker*, another ballet based on Hoffmann, *Coppélia* sweetens its source material. It pushes aside the author's nightmarish visions to create a village comedy with an assertive heroine and her flighty boyfriend. Where earlier Romantic ballets were dominated by the supernatural, *Coppélia*'s dancing dolls are animated by clockwork or human trickery. The delightful score is by Delibes, who had written two scenes for *La Source*, an earlier Saint-Léon ballet. As well as sparkling 'clockwork' dances, *Coppélia* has a famous waltz and eastern European character dances, including a mazurka and a *czárdás*.

Synopsis

Act I. The square of a small town in eastern Europe. Dr Coppélius, a mysterious toy-maker, has made a life-sized clockwork doll, Coppélia, which he sets up on the balcony of his house, apparently reading. Swanilda greets the doll, taking her for a human girl, and is indignant when Coppélia ignores her. She's even crosser when her sweetheart Franz, enchanted by the doll, blows her kisses – and Dr Coppélius makes the doll kiss her hand to him. The town's burgomaster announces celebrations for the dedication of a new bell, adding that dowries will be given to betrothed couples. Franz expects to marry Swanilda, but they quarrel over his flirting. In a set-piece dance, with a *pas de deux* and dances for Swanilda's friends, she tries to test Franz's

fidelity with an ear of corn. If it rattles when shaken, she will marry him –
but she can't hear anything.

As night falls, Coppélius sets out to the inn for a drink, locking up his
house. In the ballet's nastiest scene, the loutish young men of the village
mock and threaten the elderly outsider, but he is rescued by the innkeeper.
In the skirmish Coppélius drops his key. Returning to the square, Swanilda
and her friends find the key, and decide to investigate Coppélius' workshop.
Franz then appears with a ladder, also planning to seek out Coppélia. The
curtain falls as he starts to climb to her balcony.

Act II. Dr Coppélius' workshop. Swanilda and her companions find the
workshop is full of automata – and discover that Coppélia is also a doll.
Coppélius returns and drives the girls out, except for Swanilda, who hides.
Franz climbs in through the window. Coppélius confronts him, then real-
ises he can make use of him and gives him drugged wine. He plans to steal
Franz's life force, using it to bring Coppélia to life.

The doll seems to respond – because she is actually Swanilda, who has
disguised herself as Coppélia. Coppélius is delighted, but soon she starts
disobeying her creator, asking about Franz. Coppélius tries to distract her,
making her dance a Spanish and a Scottish dance. Finally Swanilda wakes
Franz, and wheels out the dummy Coppélia. The young couple escape,
leaving Coppélius sorrowing over his doll.

Act III. The square. The townsfolk celebrate the new bell. The local lord
gives dowries to betrothed couples, who now include Swanilda and
Franz. Coppélius is given compensation for his damaged workshop. The
celebrations include a dance of the hours, solos representing dawn and
prayer, a *pas de deux* for Swanilda and Franz, and a final galop. In the
third act there is a noticeable change of tone: less mime, less story and
grander, more formal dancing. Many productions dress Swanilda in a short,
high tutu for this act, whereas she wears longer, softer skirts in the rest of
the ballet.

The Paris production of *Coppélia* came at the end of an era, this being
Saint-Léon's final work and the last gasp of French Romantic ballet. By
this point, the Opéra had a powerful male audience who liked to
watch pretty female dancers; nine years earlier, there had been a riot
when Richard Wagner tried staging his opera *Tannhäuser* with the ballet
scene in the first act rather than in the third. Ballets had mostly female
casts, to the point where male roles were played by women – the first

Franz was danced by Eugénie Fiocre. The first Swanilda was Giuseppina Bozzachi, a very gifted sixteen-year old who achieved great success in the role.

Some seven weeks later, in July 1870, the Paris Opéra closed with the outbreak of the Franco-Prussian War. In the same year Saint-Léon died of a heart attack, while Bozzachi died of smallpox on her seventeenth birthday. After the war, the ballet returned to the Paris Opéra where, until the 1950s, the role of Franz was once again danced by a woman.

Although Saint-Léon created *Coppélia*, most modern productions are based on the St Petersburg staging by Marius Petipa, choreographed in 1884 and revised by Enrico Cecchetti a decade later. Petipa's Swanilda is characterized by strong, bold dancing: speedy footwork, a wonderful sideways bend in her first solo, buoyant steps for a confident village girl. Mime and dancing in *Coppélia* have an appealing down-to-earth quality, as when Swanilda and her friends sneak hand-in-hand into the workshop, only to reveal that their knees are shaking with fear.

Dr Coppélius is a substantial role for a character dancer, a mysterious figure who can be played as eccentric, comic or with a sinister edge. His delight when Swanilda comes to life, and his disappointment when the truth comes out, can be very touching. At the same time, we can see why Coppélius spends more time with automata than with people: when Swanilda-Coppélia gets out of hand, he tries to put her back in the cupboard.

Other Stagings

Alexandra Danilova, a celebrated Swanilda, and George Balanchine staged *Coppélia* for New York City Ballet in 1974, when Balanchine re-choreographed the third-act celebrations and created his own *czárdás* and mazurka. (Balanchine loved *Coppélia*: he once said that all his choreography sprang from the 'ear of corn' dance in the first act, with its theme and variations format.)

In 1975, Roland Petit choreographed a new version for his Ballet de Marseille, dancing the role of Coppélius himself. Petit's Coppélius is in love with Swanilda; the doll is his fantasy of her, while the townsfolk are reduced to doll-like figures. In 2009, Sergei Vikharev staged a new production for the Bolshoi Ballet, a 'new/old' reconstruction of the 1894 version by Petipa and Cecchetti, using contemporary notations and costume and decor sketches. More lavish than many Western productions, it is choreographically very similar.

3

IMPERIAL BALLET

W HEN MARIUS PETIPA arrived in Russia in 1847, he joined a long line of imported dance professionals. By the time of his death in 1910, the situation had reversed: it was the dancers and choreographers of Russia who would revive ballet in Europe and beyond.

Ballet in Russia began as a court art form, as it had in Italy and France. The first recorded Russian ballet performance took place in 1673 when Tsar Alexei, who had heard of the danced entertainments of European courts, ordered something similar for his summer seat in Preobrazhenskoye village, near Moscow. He was delighted with the results, but it was not until the eighteenth century that ballet training became established in Russia. Peter the Great brought French and Italian dancing masters to Russia as part of his westernising programme, but not to prepare stage dance: they were to train the children of Peter's aristocracy in ballroom dancing and etiquette. The first Russian ballet school had its roots in this courtly training. In 1736, during the reign of the Empress Anna, more than a hundred pupils from the Cadet Corps appeared in the finale of Francesco Araja's opera-ballet *La Forza dell'amore e dell'odio*, dancing 'a most pleasant ballet'.[1] Their teacher, the French ballet master Jean-Baptiste Landé, started a ballet school in St Petersburg two years later. His twenty-four students were the children of palace servants. From the beginning, until the revolution of 1917, Russian ballet was dependent upon the Tsar.

When Catherine the Great came to the throne in 1762, she turned St Petersburg into an important theatrical centre, establishing state theatres for French drama, Russian drama and French and Italian ballet and opera. Italian and French teachers and choreographers came to work in St Petersburg, including Charles-Louis Didelot, Jules Perrot, Arthur Saint-Léon, Bournonville's student Per Christian Johansson and Marius Petipa.

They were joined by a steady stream of guest artists. Marie Taglioni visited for five years running, to enormous acclaim; on one occasion, devoted balletomanes ate a pair of her shoes, cooked and served in a sauce.

For foreign artists, money was a large part of Russia's appeal. The Imperial Theatres had a reputation for lavish generosity, paying heavy fees to visiting stars. 'The present situation in Europe means that artists can only be thinking of our theatres,' Count Guedeonov, the director of the Imperial Theatres, wrote in 1848, as a wave of revolution spread across Europe – though not Russia – with closed theatres and interrupted seasons as one of its side effects. He continued hopefully: 'Consequently their demands must be less excessive than in the past . . .'[2] There were other reasons to be thinking of Russia. If the ballet of western Europe was affected by political events, it was also suffering a decline in popularity. In Russia, where ballet had the support and patronage of the court, Petipa was to maintain and develop a tradition that was failing elsewhere.

Petipa came from a dancing family. Born in Marseilles in 1818, he joined his father's travelling company at the age of nine. At sixteen he joined the theatre in Nantes, where he also created his first dances. His early career included a disastrous visit to America where a theatre manager absconded with the box office takings a period of study with Auguste Vestris in Paris, and four years as a dancer and choreographer in Madrid. He left Spain in a hurry, after being challenged to a duel by a marquis, but came away with an affection for Spanish dancing, setting several ballets in Spain and including Spanish character dances in many more.

Although he was a reliable partner and a fine mime, Petipa the dancer was overshadowed by his starrier brother Lucien, who was the first to dance Albrecht in *Giselle*. Marius went to St Petersburg in 1847 as a *premier danseur*, but couldn't command the kind of fees that Jules Perrot or Fanny Elssler could demand from the Imperial Theatres. He worked his way up through the Russian ballet system; it would be a long, slow process. Petipa made his St Petersburg debut in *Paquita*, a restaging of a Spanish-themed ballet by Joseph Mazilier. He acted as assistant on Jules Perrot's restaging of *Esmeralda* in the winter of 1849, but Perrot's arrival in 1848 and his position as chief choreographer put back any choreographic ambitions Petipa might have cherished.

When Perrot left St Petersburg in 1859, Arthur Saint-Léon replaced him as chief choreographer. Nevertheless, Petipa began to find more opportunities to create works. His big chance came in 1861, when a new full-length ballet was needed for the guest ballerina Carolina Rosati. This was a tricky commission: Rosati, who was on the point of retirement, had had little success in her Russian debut. Although she had been promised a new ballet, the director of the Imperial Theatres put off authorising it, delaying until there were just six weeks left to create the production. But Petipa was well prepared. He had already gone back to Paris to consult Vernoy de Saint-Georges, who had worked with Théophile Gautier on *Giselle*. In fact, they turned to Gautier again, using his Egyptian-themed romance *The Mummy's Tale* as the basis for *The Pharaoh's Daughter*. On his way back to St Petersburg, Petipa stopped off in Berlin to visit the Egyptian Museum; Egypt was in the news, both for its antiquities and for the building of the Suez Canal, on which work had begun in 1859.

The Pharaoh's Daughter, which had its premiere in 1862, was a monster hit, a vast and extravagant spectacle in which an English aristocrat falls in love with the Egyptian princess he sees in an opium dream. Crammed with dancing and special effects (including a scene in which dancers were suspended over the stage, apparently lifted by jets of water), *The Pharaoh's Daughter* was an immediate success. It remained in repertory until the 1920s, and was a favourite for artists' benefit performances because, the ballet librettist Sergei Khudekov remembered, 'having *The Pharaoh's Daughter* on the bill would produce perpetually full houses'.[3] (It disappeared from the repertory in the 1920s, although Pierre Lacotte staged his own version in 2000.) After such success, Petipa was named second ballet master – with Saint-Léon still in first place.

Saint-Léon answered *The Pharaoh's Daughter* with *The Little Humpbacked Horse*, which turned to Russian fairy tales for its material. This was a period of political change and increasing Russian patriotism. Alexander II, who came to the throne in 1855, launched radical reforms, including the emancipation of Russia's serfs in 1861. In the arts, there was a new focus on native Russian material: the 'mighty handful' of composers – Mily Balakirev, César Cui, Modest Mussorgsky, Nikolai Rimsky-Korsakov and Alexander Borodin – rejected European models in favour of Russian folk forms, while architects, writers and painters shifted their attention to Russian life and culture. Russian ballet, which had relied on imported stars, was starting to produce its own leading dancers. The French-born Saint-Léon hardly qualified as a Russian artist, but he spoke fluent Russian and interested himself in Russian subjects – unlike Petipa, who never fully mastered the language of the country he lived in for sixty-three years, and who preferred far-off locations for his ballets.

For the rest of the 1860s, Petipa and Saint-Léon created ballets in alternation, with eager balletomanes taking sides in the fierce competition. Saint-Léon was most admired for individual numbers, especially those created to show off individual dancers, and for his national dances. He was weaker when it came to planning ballets as a whole, their large-scale structure and dramatic content. 'In his ballets, pantomime and story – the soul of a complete choreographic work – were always missing,' grumbled Khudekov, a Petipa fan. 'They were simple divertissements, collections of dances', compared to Petipa's more dramatic productions.[4]

The rivalry ended in 1870 when Saint-Léon left Russia, leaving Petipa as chief ballet master. Over the next thirty years he staged forty ballets, as well as revising and restaging existing works. The early ballets followed the template set by *The Pharaoh's Daughter*: large-scale spectaculars, with foreign settings affording local colour, special effects and big dance set pieces. It was a decisive shift away from the shorter, more direct stories of Romantic ballet.

Petipa liked to keep his eye on the news, too, giving his grand spectacles a topical hook. In 1877, during the Russo-Turkish War over the Balkans, he staged *Roxana, the Beauty of Montenegro*. Indeed, the ballet itself became part of contemporary events: the grand march that Ludwig Minkus wrote for *Roxana* proved popular with Tsar Alexander II, and this music played as the Russian army stormed the Ottoman town of Plevna (now in Bulgaria). *La Bayadère*, one of the earliest Petipa ballets to remain in the repertory, was in part prompted by the visit of the prince of Wales, Queen Victoria's son and the future Edward VII of Britain, to India in the winter of 1875–6. Looking at *La Bayadère* now, it's hard to imagine anybody taking any aspect of Petipa's Indian-themed pageantry as documentary realism. Yet to at least one contemporary it wasn't far off. The *Journal de Saint-Pétersbourg* reported:

> Everything necessary to render the *couleur locale* exactly has been taken from engravings appearing in the *Graphic* and the *Illustrated London News* on the occasion of the Prince of Wales' journey. As a result we see a series of scrupulously exact tableaux of the mores and costumes of the Indians, which naturally give the ballet an ethnographic interest quite exceptional and singularly fascinating.[5]

The *Graphic* and the *Illustrated London News* had been packed with spectacular images that do indeed look like scenes from *La Bayadère*: a torchlit procession with dancers performing in front of the prince's elephant, the prince fighting off a tiger, views of dawn over the Himalayas, all drawn in a style that is both naturalistic and highly romantic. The Prince of Wales' trip was a diplomatic mission, designed to promote Britain's imperial policy in

India. In 1876 the London *Times* argued that the tour had won over the British public, counterbalancing 'troublesome financial problems' by presenting India's 'dazzling accumulation of natural marvels, great traditions, wealth and historic influence', and persuading Indian princes that they were now 'members of an organised Empire'.[6] Exotic spectacle is never apolitical. This was an imperialist century, when the far-off places of travelogues were likely to be valuable colonial possessions. When the *Graphic* and the *Illustrated London News* romanticised India, they were supporting the colonial project.

In ballet, the scenery and dances of foreign lands were a familiar theme. They were also becoming more fantastic, more exoticised. The fantasy East of *Le Corsaire*, choreographed by Joseph Mazilier in 1856 and later revised by Petipa and others, is full of racist stereotypes, from a miserly Jewish slave trader to the foolish, lecherous Pasha. (The Mariinsky's 1987 production has the Pasha outwitted by false 'pilgrims', who take advantage of the Muslim evening prayer to rescue women from his harem.) Western productions have tried to cut or rewrite the most offensive aspects of such scenes, but the stereotypes linger. Local colour is built into many nineteenth-century ballets, which delighted in the folk and traditional dances of different countries. Whatever their other differences, both Saint-Léon and Petipa loved national dances. In his memoirs, Petipa boasts of the authenticity of his Spanish fandango; when he needed to stage a *lezghinka* for an opera, he sought out Caucasian dancers who could show him the original dance. At their best, ballet's national dances are a celebration of different dance cultures. The fact remains that stereotyping is much more likely to crop up in Chinese or Arabian numbers than in Russian *trepaks*.

In the early 1870s, August Bournonville visited Russia, where he was shocked by the ballets he saw, disapproving of their spectacle and 'lascivious' dancing. Petipa and Johansson admitted privately that he had a point, explaining 'with a shrug of the shoulders that they were obliged to follow the current of the times, which they charged to the blasé taste of the public and the specific wishes of the high authorities'.[7] The audience was indeed becoming blasé: the number of ballet performances was reduced, suggesting declining interest. Petipa's career was re-energised by two new factors: in 1881, Ivan Vsevolozhsky was appointed director of the Imperial Theatres; then four years later, a group of Italian dancers visited St Petersburg, winning audiences back by displaying fresh technical and dramatic skill.

Vsevolozhsky was an intelligent and charming director, a former diplomat and playwright who had spent five years in Paris and was knowledgeable about European theatre. He had a talent for caricature, sharp enough that it was said to have ended his diplomatic career. As director, he would draw sketches for new productions, helping to create a unified concept. He was particularly attentive to ballet, which was very popular with the tsar and his family. Vsevolozhsky's reforms included higher salaries for artists and workers, setting up a new ballet teaching syllabus and the encouragement of private theatres. He abolished the post of ballet composer after the retirement of Ludwig Minkus in 1886, bringing in new composers who would include Tchaikovsky and Glazunov. Vsevolozhsky's reforms were enormously expensive and didn't always pay off; the quality of the new ballet composers varied enormously. Nevertheless, the director's support elevated Petipa and the Imperial ballet to new heights.

In 1885 a troupe of Italian dancers appeared at one of St Petersburg's summer theatres. They danced an extravagant ballet called *A Flight to the Moon*, based on a science fiction novel by Jules Verne. Italy was the home of virtuoso dancing: the teacher Carlo Blasis and his pupils had developed new technical feats, particularly in *pointe*work and turns. The 1885 troupe featured the ballerina Virginia Zucchi, who combined impressive technique with extraordinary dramatic power. She was quickly invited to dance at the Imperial Theatres. The artist Alexandre Benois, a smitten fifteen-year old, went to her debut, 'ready, in case of need, to fight the gang of nationalistic ballet lovers who had, so we heard, threatened to sabotage the foreign star. But the enthusiasm with which Zucchi was greeted . . . was enough to discourage any opposition.'[8]

Petipa at first resisted 'this unruly Italian virtuosa', but was soon won over.[9] When he restaged *Esmeralda* for her, he added a new *pas de six* that gives some idea of her technique and passionate personality. Her career at the Imperial Theatres was short, however; after two years the tsar forbade her the stage because of her affair with an aristocrat. She was followed by a wave of Italian stars: Pierina Legnani, Carlotta Brianza, Antonietta dell'Era and Enrico Cecchetti, who as a teacher would strengthen the next generation of Russian dancers. New training, and the edge of competition, would spur Russians to new heights. Petipa added thirty-two *fouettés* to the 'Black Swan' *pas de deux* of *Swan Lake* because Legnani was the one ballerina in Russia who could do them; there was rejoicing when the Russian Mathilde Kschessinska mastered the feat.

Italian technique changed Petipa's choreography. Romantic ballerinas had skimmed and flitted rather than holding long balances on *pointe*. Critics exclaimed over Carlotta Grisi's hops on *pointe* in the 1846 ballet *Paquita*, suggesting that these steps were not part of the original choreography for *Giselle*, which had been created for her in 1841. As earlier ballets were restaged, they were usually updated, taking advantage of dancers' new skills. In his ballets of the 1890s, Petipa also used these skills dramatically. When Aurora balances on *pointe* in the Rose Adagio of *The Sleeping Beauty*, she reveals to us her independence as well as the dancer's steadiness: she is partnered by four princes, but chooses none of them.

Developments in *pointe*work led to a further shift in the hierarchy of male and female roles, affecting relations between the sexes onstage as well as the attention paid to each one. With long balances, partnering becomes a drama of support and self-reliance. The ballerina-worship of Romantic ballet had tended to sideline male dancers; in Petipa's classical choreography, they become the ballerina's devoted cavaliers. The shift was heightened because Petipa was more interested in making dances for women than for men. When Petipa watched Johansson's classes for men, he would take notes; Johansson would wink and say, 'The old man's pinched some more.'[10] In the 1890s, Petipa responded to the technical prowess of guest ballerinas, but leading male roles were still created for Pavel Gerdt, a dancer of great presence who was by then well into his forties.

Petipa's classical *pas de deux* had an established format: an entrée or *adagio* in which the ballerina and her partner dance together, variations (solos) for each dancer, and a coda that brings them back together. The *pas de deux* is often the climax of a larger divertissement: Aurora and her Prince conclude a series of fairy-tale dances in the last act of *The Sleeping Beauty*, for instance. The *pas de deux* or the divertissement can be performed separately, out of context, as a suite of dances. Petipa, admired in his own time for his sense of structure and drama, had a command of dance architecture that makes his self-contained scenes satisfying in themselves. In the twentieth century, choreographers would develop the formal divertissement as an end in itself: George Balanchine's *Theme and Variations* was commissioned as a companion-piece to the last act of *The Sleeping Beauty*. The formal *divertissement* also heightened ballet's sense of hierarchy: the ballerina at the top, supported by her cavalier, followed by ranks of soloists and *corps de ballet*.

The Nutcracker, commissioned as a follow-up to *The Sleeping Beauty*, was choreographed by Petipa's assistant Lev Ivanov. Born in St Petersburg in 1834, Ivanov trained and then danced at the Imperial Theatres. As a dancer he had an usually wide range, performing classical, character and mime roles, but he doesn't sound dazzling. The ballerina Ekaterina Vazem remembered that 'he managed all his dances equally well, never spoiling anything'; he was overtaken as a dancer by the more brilliant Pavel Gerdt.[11] Although Ivanov was known as a good partner, he was extremely short-sighted, and worried that he might drop his ballerina; fortunately, his fears were never realised. If Ivanov came second to Gerdt as a dancer, he also spent his choreographic career in Petipa's shadow. He had a diffident personality, lacking drive in an aggressively competitive organisation. His greatest breakthrough came after Tchaikovsky's death, when he created the lakeside dances for *Swan Lake*. This was a different approach to classicism, softer and less formal than Petipa's grand architecture, and one that influenced later choreographers such as Mikhail Fokine. In his memoirs, Ivanov mentions neither *Swan Lake* nor *The Nutcracker*, apparently unaware of their significance. He died in 1901.

The 1890s were the last flowering of Imperial Russian ballet. Not all its directors were as sympathetic as Vsevolozhsky; in 1903, Vladimir Telyakovsky pushed Petipa into retirement after the failure of his ballet *The Magic Mirror*. Petipa left behind him an extraordinary legacy, not just of individual ballets but of an entire style – ballet polished to crystalline brilliance.

Le Corsaire

Choreography: Marius Petipa and others
Music: Adolphe Adam, Cesare Pugni, Léo Delibes, Riccardo Drigo, Pyotr Oldenburgsky, Ludwig Minkus, Julius Gerber, Baron Boris Fitinhof-Schnell and Albert Zabel
Libretto: Jules Henri Vernoy de Saint-Georges and Joseph Mazilier
Premiere: 13 December 1868, Mariinsky Theatre, St Petersburg
Original cast: *Medora* Marie Surovshchikova Petipa

Le Corsaire is a very silly ballet, a lurid confection of pirates, shipwrecks and set-piece dance numbers. It is loosely based on Lord Byron's 1814 poem *The Corsair*, a best-seller with a moody hero and a huge readership. Ballet masters were quick to adapt the story, with stagings in Milan in 1826 and London in 1837. Joseph Mazilier's 1856 production for the Paris Opéra was more influential. With Saint-Georges, the co-librettist of *Giselle*, Mazilier streamlined the plot and included a spectacular shipwreck scene. It was an international hit, with stagings as far away as Boston and St Petersburg, where Jules Perrot restaged it with a cast that included Marius Petipa as the hero. Petipa revived it in 1868, adding the 'Jardin animé' scene to frothy, sweet music by Delibes. Modern stagings are based on his 1899 revival, which made more tweaks.

For a sense of how much tinkering *Le Corsaire* has gone through, you only need to look at the number of composers credited with the score. The

1987 Mariinsky production credited the score to five composers (the first five listed above). When the Bolshoi Ballet reconstructed the 1899 staging in 2007, it had six (dropping Adam, adding Zabel and Gerber). English National Ballet's 2013 staging has nine.

Synopsis

Act I. A crowded bazaar. The slave trader Lankedem has slave-girls for sale. A band of corsairs (pirates) appear in the square, led by Conrad, with his slave Ali and his friend Birbanto. Medora, Lankedem's ward, throws Conrad a flower from the balcony of her guardian's house. He is delighted.

The Pasha, the governor of the time, arrives to buy slave-girls. He rejects some, but buys a beautiful young woman called Gulnara. Then he catches sight of Medora, and insists on buying her. Lankedem reluctantly accepts, to Medora's horror. At Conrad's signal, the corsairs overrun the village, carrying off Medora and the other slave-girls, along with Lankedem.

Act II. The pirates' cave. The corsairs rejoice at their success. Medora dances with Conrad and Ali, and begs Conrad to free the slave-girls. He agrees, despite protests from Birbanto and the other pirates, who wish to keep the women. Birbanto is angry and humiliated, so when Lankedem suggests a plot against Conrad, he agrees. A flower is drugged with a sleeping potion and given to Medora, who innocently gives it to Conrad. Smelling the flower, Conrad swoons. When the plotters rush in to abduct Medora, she stabs the disguised Birbanto in the arm before fainting. She is carried off by Lankedem and the pirates. Birbanto is about to kill Conrad, who wakes up just in time. Birbanto then explains that Medora has been abducted, and swears loyalty. Conrad and his corsairs set off to rescue her.

Act III. The Pasha's palace. The odalisques dance and play games. Gulnara is the most admired woman in the harem. Lankedem brings more slave-girls, including the captured Medora. Delighted, the Pasha buys her, and celebrates by smoking opium.

In his dream, he sees a fantasy garden – this scene is known as the 'Jardin animé – filled with beautiful women, including Medora and Gulnara. This garden fantasy is staged as a garland dance, the *corps* creating arches and avenues. In her solo, the ballerina playing Medora dances over garlands laid on the floor, in a kind of floral obstacle course.

The Pasha is woken by the arrival of Conrad and his corsairs disguised as pilgrims (or, depending on the production, as entertainers). They throw off their disguises to rescue Medora and chase away the Pasha and his men. Medora recognises Birbanto by the stab wound on his arm. Conrad, Medora and the corsairs escape to their ship.

At sea, a storm blows up, with thunder, lightning and rough seas. The ship is wrecked. As the storm calms, two survivors climb onto a rock – Conrad and Medora, who are united in each other's arms.

The most popular number in *Le Corsaire* is its *pas de deux*, which the virtuoso dancer Vakhtang Chabukiani developed from an Act II *pas d'action* for Medora, Conrad and Ali. Although Conrad is the ballet's hero, it is Ali who appears in the *pas de deux*, with showstopping steps and glittering lamé trousers. In the West, this *pas de deux* was popularised by Margot Fonteyn and Rudolf Nureyev, who first danced it in 1962.

Le Corsaire goes all out on pyrotechnics: the dancing and the storytelling are about flash rather than depth. From the ballet's beginnings with Mazilier, it has had plenty of special effects: 'all Paris will go to see the scene of the ship sinking beneath the waves,' predicted *La France musicale* in 1856. Tamara Karsavina, a celebrated Medora in Petipa's revival, remembered the shipwreck finale as:

> ever such fun . . . What the stage directions were I never quite knew, but we took them to be *ad libitum*, and, in the heat of make-believe, rather overacted this scene and played at shipwreck like excited children. Guerdt [Pavel Gerdt] shouted orders through the megaphone; when the caravel split and sank in two tidy halves, my female attendants and I screamed. But screams, cannon, megaphone, and orchestra were all drowned by the thunder and howling wind . . .[12]

The first full-length Western production of *Le Corsaire* was staged by the Zagreb Ballet in 1975, incorporating chunks of *La Bayadère*. Anna-Marie Holmes staged *Le Corsaire* for Boston Ballet in 1997, in a production closely based on the Kirov Ballet's version by Pytor Gusev. Holmes' production has since been restaged, with revisions, at American Ballet Theatre and English National Ballet.

Don Quixote

Choreography: Marius Petipa, later revised by Alexander Gorsky
Music: Ludwig Minkus
Libretto: Marius Petipa, after Miguel de Cervantes

Premiere: 26 December 1869, Bolshoi Theatre, Moscow
Original cast: *Kitri* Anna Sobeshchanskaya; *Basilio* Sergei Sokilov; *Don Quixote* Wilhelm Vanner

Although most of Petipa's productions were created in St Petersburg, *Don Quixote* had its premiere in Moscow. Aiming to please Muscovite taste, Petipa emphasised the comedy and character dancing of the ballet; when he restaged it in St Petersburg, two years later, he revised it as a more formal spectacle, including new classical ensembles. This was also Petipa's first collaboration with Ludwig Minkus, the house ballet composer for the Bolshoi Theatre. Minkus moved to a similar position in St Petersburg in 1871, and worked closely with Petipa on many more ballets.

Alexander Gorsky, who revised *Don Quixote* in Moscow in 1900, had a more realistic approach. Influenced by the methods of Konstantin Stanislavsky, who was developing a naturalistic acting style at the Moscow Art Theatre, Gorsky presented the *corps* dancers as individuals, with different costumes and personalities, rather than having them dance in unison. His revision was such a success that, two years later, it was put on in St Petersburg, under the offended Petipa's nose. Later productions are descended from Gorsky's staging, with its mix of classical dance and character comedy.

The ballet's plot is loosely based on an episode from Miguel de Cervantes' *Don Quixote*, adding a few of the picaresque novel's more famous scenes along the way. Don Quixote is a non-dancing role, a benevolent chivalric figure who blesses young lovers and has mishaps of his own.

Synopsis

Prologue. Don Quixote dreams in his study, reading his books of chivalry. In a vision, he sees Dulcinea, the woman of his dreams. Sancho Panza enters, chased by angry shopkeepers: he has stolen a goose. Don Quixote rescues him and appoints him his squire. Together, they set out on adventures.

Act I. A square in Barcelona. Kitri, the pretty daughter of the innkeeper Lorenzo, flirts with the handsome barber Basilio, but her father hopes she will marry the rich, foppish Gamache. The toreador Espada struts with other bullfighters and his girlfriend, the street dancer Mercedes. When Don Quixote and Sancho Panza arrive, the old knight mistakes the beautiful Kitri for his adored Dulcinea. Sancho Panza is teased by the townsfolk, who toss him in a blanket. In all the bustle, Kitri and Basilio sneak away. Lorenzo and Gamache hurry after them, while Don Quixote and Sancho Panza follow.

Act II. Scene 1. The tavern. Kitri and Basilio meet at a tavern. Lorenzo follows, and tries to bring Kitri away. In a comic mime sequence, Basilio insists that he will die without Kitri, and appears to stab himself, collapsing in a heap. (He usually throws down a cloak first, to give himself a soft landing.) Kitri weeps over the apparently dying Basilio, and persuades her father to let her marry him before he dies. Her father accepts, and Basilio springs back to life.

Scene 2. A gypsy encampment. Outside the town, gypsies have set up camp near some windmills. Don Quixote and Sancho Panza arrive, and sit down to watch a puppet show with the gypsies. Swept up by the action, Don Quixote starts to fight the puppets, disrupting the performance. He then mistakes the windmills for giants, and attacks them with his lance, until he is caught on one of the sails and carried through the air. Battered by the encounter, he faints at Sancho Panza's feet.

Scene 3. The unconscious Don Quixote dreams. He sees a vision of his beloved Dulcinea – the dancer who plays Kitri – surrounded by nymphs, with Amor (Cupid) and the Queen of the Dryads. They dance a classical ensemble for the delighted knight.

Act III. The local duke is giving a fiesta, which becomes the setting for Kitri and Basilio's wedding. The celebrations include a *grand pas* performed by Kitri and Basilio with other soloists. At the end of the ballet, Don Quixote and Sancho Panza set off in search of new adventures.

Petipa loved Spanish dancing. In his memoirs, he fondly remembers dancing the fandango and other traditional dances, saying with pride that 'I danced and played the castanets no worse than the best dancers of Andalusia.'[13] *Don Quixote* was one of several ballets he created on Spanish themes. The ballet is also known for its big, bravura steps. The last-act *pas de deux* is a popular gala number, with overhead lifts, big jumps and a variation with a fan for Kitri, who snaps it open or shut with one hand, or flutters it as her feet brush the floor in teasing footwork. The variation for the Queen of the Dryads is also celebrated, particularly in Russia. The flying leaps that the heroine dances in the first act are sometimes called 'Kitri jumps': she arches her back as she leaps, with her back leg bent so that her foot almost touches her head.

Other Stagings

Recent productions have followed Gorsky in trying to strengthen the ballet's storytelling. When Alexei Ratmansky staged it for Dutch National Ballet in 2010, he went back to Petipa's 1869 libretto, focusing on the drama and working with the dancers on acting and characterisation. Carlos Acosta's 2013 production for The Royal Ballet in London has Spanish guitarists playing onstage in the gypsy scene, and cries of *olé* from the dancers. Acosta's Don Quixote rides a puppet horse, inspired by the remarkable horses of the National Theatre's production of *War Horse*. Where real horses are used, casting Don Quixote's lean steed has proved tricky. The critic Cyril Beaumont reported that 'the horses hired locally for the Pavlova Company's production of the ballet were much too well-fed for the part of Rosinante and had to be made up accordingly'[14] – often so successfully that there were visits from the Royal Society for Prevention of Cruelty to Animals.

La Bayadère

Choreography: Marius Petipa
Music: Ludwig Minkus
Libretto: Sergei Khudekov
Scenery: Ivan Andreyev, Mikhail Bocharov, Piotr Lambin, Andrei Roller, Matvey Shishkov and Heinrich Wagner
Premiere: 23 January 1877, Mariinsky Theatre, St Petersburg
Original cast: *Nikiya* Ekaterina Vazem; *Solor* Lev Ivanov; *Gamzatti* Maria Gorshenkova; *Rajah* Per Christian Johansson

La Bayadère is the extravagant tale of a warrior's love for a temple dancer, complete with jealous rivals, staggering procession scenes and a collapsing palace. At the centre of this grand spectacle, Petipa created the 'Kingdom of the Shades', in which the *corps de ballet*'s dancing conjures a vision of eternity.

Bayadères are Indian dancing girls, particularly those associated with Hindu temples. They had been floating around the Romantic imagination since Goethe wrote his poem 'Der Gott und die Bajadere' ('The God and the Bayadère') in 1797, in which a god visits a humble bayadère while disguised in human form. Schubert set the poem as a song; Auber turned it into an opera-ballet, with the god sung by Adolphe Nourrit – the librettist of *La Sylphide* – and the bayadère danced by Marie Taglioni. In an early draft of *Giselle*, ghostly dancers from around the world appeared in the second act: a bayadère was among them, displaying 'her Indian poses'. 'The very word bayadère evokes notions of sunshine, perfume and beauty even to the most prosaic and bourgeois minds,'[15] wrote the ever-excitable Théophile Gautier, reviewing real Indian dancers in Paris in 1838. So when Marius Petipa chose an Indian setting for his latest spectacular ballet, a temple dancer was the obvious heroine.

Like *The Pharaoh's Daughter*, Petipa's great hit of 1862, *La Bayadère* was a grand, leisurely spectacle. The exotic setting was timely, following the visit of Britain's Prince of Wales to India in 1875–76, which had been widely reported, with colourful artists' impressions of Indian scenes. For the Kingdom of the Shades, Petipa also drew on Gustave Doré's illustrations of *Paradise* from Dante's *Divine Comedy*, with its groups of ethereal angels. The Mariinsky Theatre's team of designers conjured up spectacular scenery, including jungles, temples and palaces. In her memoirs, Ekaterina Vazem, the first Nikiya, particularly praised Andrei Roller, 'who also distinguished himself as the machinist of the masterful destruction of the palace at the end of the ballet'.[16]

Act I. Scene 1. A temple in the jungle, with a sacred flame and a pool. Led by Solor, a group of young warriors are on a tiger hunt. Solor meets the fakir Magdaveya by the temple walls, and asks him to arrange a meeting with Nikiya, one of the bayadères. The High Brahmin and the priests leave the temple and gather at the sacred flame for a ceremony. Fakirs and bayadères perform dances. Nikiya appears, veiled. When she removes her veil, all are struck by her beauty, particularly the High Brahmin. Although he has taken a vow of celibacy, the High Brahmin confesses that he loves her. Shocked, she rejects him. While Nikiya and the other bayadères carry water from the sacred pool to the fakirs, Magdaveya gives her Solor's message. She is delighted.

Night falls, and the two lovers meet secretly, unaware that the High Brahmin is eavesdropping on their conversation. Solor asks Nikiya to flee with him, and swears by the sacred flame that he will be faithful. She agrees. The High Brahmin plans revenge: clenching his fist, he lowers it slowly in a mime gesture of vengeance.

Scene 2. The Rajah's palace. The Rajah Dugmata tells his daughter Gamzatti that she is to be married to a brave warrior, and shows her his portrait. It is

Solor. When Solor arrives, he is overcome with confusion: he is promised to Nikiya, but cannot refuse the Rajah's command. Dancers entertain the royal family, including the D'Jampe dancers, who each have a long scarf tied to one knee, and wave the fabric as they dance. In some productions, Nikiya performs a *pas de deux* with a slave.

The High Brahmin arrives, and asks to speak to the Rajah in secret. Although the Rajah sends everyone away, Gamzatti hides and eavesdrops. The High Brahmin tells the Rajah about Solor's love for Nikiya. The Rajah, furious, decides that Nikiya must die. The High Brahmin is horrified, warning him that the gods will be angry if he kills a bayadère, one of their servants. The Rajah does not relent.

When the Rajah and the High Brahmin leave, Gamzatti orders her slave to bring in Nikiya. Struck by the bayadère's beauty, Gamzatti realises she is a serious rival. She tells Nikiya about her forthcoming wedding – then shows her the portrait of Solor. Nikiya protests: Solor loves her, and has made a vow of fidelity. Gamzatti tries to bribe her with jewels, but Nikiya throws them aside. As Gamzatti shakes her, Nikiya picks up a dagger in rage. The slave stops her, and Nikiya leaves. Gamzatti is furious: she will never give Solor up. Using the same mime gesture for vengeance, she swears that Nikya must die.

Act II. Outside the Rajah's palace. Celebrations are held for the betrothal of Solor and Gamzatti. Dancers enter in a spectacular procession. (In some productions, such as Rudolf Nureyev's 1992 staging for the Paris Opéra Ballet, this includes a stage elephant.) There are many group and solo dances, including the 'Manu' dance for a woman balancing a pot of water on her head, a drum dance, and a virtuoso solo for the 'Bronze idol', a male dancer painted bronze. Solor and Gamzatti dance a grand *pas de deux*.

At last, Nikiya appears to dance. She dances sorrowfully, until a servant gives her a basket of flowers, telling her that they are a gift from Solor. Nikiya's dance becomes happier and faster, until suddenly a deadly snake crawls from the basket and bites her. The High Brahmin offers her an antidote, but knowing that Solor will marry Gamzatti, she refuses it, and dies.

Act III. Solor's room. Filled with remorse for Nikiya's death, Solor smokes opium. Hallucinating, he imagines himself in the Kingdom of the Shades, where Nikiya dances among the other ghostly bayadères. When he wakes, Solor is told that he must prepare for his wedding.

Act IV. A hall in the Rajah's palace. Preparations are underway for the wedding of Solor and Gamzatti. During the dances, Solor keeps seeing Nikiya's ghost, which reminds him of his vow. When Gamzatti is given a basket of flowers, she recoils, reminded of her rival's death. As the High Brahmin begins the wedding ceremony, a storm breaks. When he joins the hands of Solor and Gamzatti, an earthquake shakes the palace. The great hall collapses, covering everyone.

Apotheosis. Solor's ghost follows Nikiya into the afterlife.

The plot of *La Bayadère* has echoes of many other works. Like the heroine of *Esmeralda*, Nikiya dances at her rival's betrothal party, and like *The Pharaoh's Daughter*, the ballet moves from exotic processions to a supernatural kingdom. It also recalls Giuseppe Verdi's 1871 opera *Aida*; Petipa had choreographed the dances for the opera's St Petersburg production in 1875. Like Aida, Nikiya is in love with a warrior who is promised to the ruler's daughter. Where the opera ends with self-sacrifice (Radamès dies rather than break his vow to Aida, who chooses to join him in death), the ballet has a less rigorous hero. He accepts Gamzatti as his bride, only to die when the gods destroy the palace in fury.

The Kingdom of the Shades has become *La Bayadère*'s best-known and most admired scene, sometimes staged as a stand-alone set piece. The first entrance of the Shades is a stern test for the *corps de ballet*. One by one, in single file, they descend a zigzag ramp, each woman repeating the same sequence of steps – an *arabesque* that reaches forward into space, then a pose with arched back and raised arms, followed by two steps forward for the next *arabesque*. The line of ghostly women winds down the ramp and across the stage, repeating this phrase in unison. The repetition becomes hypnotic: like the reflections of a hall of mirrors, the Shades' dance reaches to infinity. Minkus, often mocked for his danceably rum-ti-tum tunes, produced an ethereal melody for the Shades' entrance, its own repetitions adding to the effect. After this mesmerising beginning, Petipa created distinctive dances for three solo Shades. The dances for Nikiya and Solor include a *pas de deux* with a long scarf, which stretches between them as they dance.

Other Stagings

The Kingdom of the Shades was first seen in the West in 1961, when the Kirov Ballet performed it on tour. Two years later, Kirov defector Rudolf Nureyev staged the scene for The Royal Ballet, challenging and showing off the company's *corps de ballet* and soloists. Natalia Makarova staged the scene for American Ballet Theatre in 1974, and went on to stage the full ballet for the company in 1980. In Russia, the last act had been dropped, so that the ballet ended with the Shades scene. Makarova created her own version of Act IV, with its collapsing palace and apotheosis. Nureyev hoped to do the same in his spectacular 1992 Paris production, but ill health meant that he had to abandon this plan. In 2002, Sergei Vikharev reconstructed the four-act version of *La Bayadère* for the Kirov Ballet, drawing on sources from Petipa's four-act revival of 1900.

Pas de Trois and Grand Pas from Paquita

Choreography: Marius Petipa
Music: Ludwig Minkus
Premiere: 27 December 1881, Mariinsky Theatre, St Petersburg
Original cast: Ekaterina Vazem

The original *Paquita*, created in 1846 by Joseph Mazilier, was the tale of a Spanish gypsy who saves the life of a French officer during the Napoleonic wars. Carlotta Grisi and Lucien Petipa starred in a ballet packed with Spanish dances and unlikely incident, including plotters making secret entrances through a revolving fireplace. The next year Lucien's brother Marius made his debut in St Petersburg dancing the hero of *Paquita*.

When he revived the ballet in 1881, Petipa revised it considerably, asking the composer Minkus for a new *pas de trois* and *grand pas* to add to Edouard Deldevez's original score. Although Petipa's set pieces survived, the rest of the ballet fell out of repertory. Pierre Lacotte created a version for the Paris Opéra in 2001, however, and Alexei Ratmansky and Doug Fullington staged an enchanting reconstruction for the Bayerische Staatsballet in 2014.

The *grand pas* is a Spanish-tinted classical ensemble, danced by a ballerina and her partner with six first soloists and eight second soloists. Although the opening march, *adagio* and coda stay the same, the six *Paquita* soloists can bring their own variations, drawn from other ballets. It's a very *grand pas*, demanding virtuosity, authority and style from its dancers.

The *grand pas* sometimes includes a *pas de trois*, which has also been staged separately: Balanchine choreographed two versions of it, for the Marquis de Cuevas company in 1948 and for New York City Ballet in 1951. The *grand pas* has been staged in the West by dancers including Alexandra Danilova, Rudolf Nureyev, Galina Samsova and Natalia Makarova. Leading dancers are often cast in all six soloist roles.

Esmeralda (also known as La Esmeralda)

Choreography and libretto: Jules Perrot
Music: Cesare Pugni
Premiere: 9 March 1844, Her Majesty's Theatre, London
Original cast: *Esmeralda* Carlotta Grisi; *Gringoire* Jules Perrot; *Quasimodo* Antoine Louis Coulon

Esmeralda was one of Jules Perrot's biggest successes, a danced retelling of Victor Hugo's *Notre-Dame de Paris*. Perrot worked closely from the novel, but also narrowed the focus, from the sweep of medieval Paris to the figure of the gypsy dancer Esmeralda. He also drew on the opera libretto that Hugo himself had prepared – which, like the ballet (and the 1996 Disney cartoon), gives the story a happy ending. Perrot's *Esmeralda* was a triumph.

When he came to St Petersburg in 1849, Perrot restaged the ballet for Fanny Elssler, with the assistance of Marius Petipa, whom Perrot cast in several of his ballets. As ballet master, Petipa kept several of Perrot's works in regular repertory, including *Giselle* and *Esmeralda*, preserving the narrative structure but updating the choreography to show off new dancers. He revised *Esmeralda* several times, most importantly in in 1886, when he added a *pas de six* to show off the dramatic ballerina Virginia Zucchi. In 1935 it was revised again by Agrippina Vaganova, who choreographed a new 'Diana and Actaeon' *divertissement*, with a bravura *pas de deux* that is often danced separately.

Synopsis

Act I. Scene 1. The ballet opens in the Cour des Miracles, a dangerous slum district of Paris, inhabited by beggars and criminals. The poet Gringoire is caught by a group of thieves. Since he has no money, they sentence him to death, but he will be saved if a woman chooses to marry him. As he is about to be hanged, the gypsy Esmeralda arrives. After a high-spirited solo, she asks about Gringoire, takes pity on him, and agrees to marry him. Following the custom of the district, Gringoire smashes a jug to determine how long their marriage is to last. It breaks into four pieces, meaning four years of marriage.

Claude Frollo, the archdeacon of the cathedral of Notre Dame, is obsessed with Esmeralda. He orders Clopin to abduct her, telling the hunchback Quasimodo to help. A group of soldiers interrupt the kidnap. Their captain, Phoebus, orders the rescue of Esmeralda and the arrest of

Quasimodo. She is grateful, and charmed by the captain's good looks. Phoebus gives her his scarf as a memento. At her request, he frees Quasimodo, but she slips away when he tries to flirt with her.

Scene 2. Esmeralda's room. Esmeralda admires Phoebus' scarf, and spells out his name in ivory letters. Gringoire, her new husband, enters and tries to embrace her. She refuses, explaining that she only wished to save him from death. He accepts this, and plays the tambourine for her as she dances. As night falls, she sends him to sleep in a separate room.

As Esmeralda dreams of Phoebus, Frollo and Quasimodo sneak into her room. She orders Frollo to leave, but he begs her to accept his love. She rejects him, explaining that she loves Phoebus. When he persists, she fends him off with a dagger. Quasimodo, who has accompanied Frollo, stops Esmeralda from stabbing him. Remembering her kindness to him, he helps her to escape. Frollo picks up the dagger Esmeralda has dropped, vowing revenge.

Act II. A mansion. Fleur-de-Lys, a wealthy young woman who is engaged to Phoebus, is preparing for their betrothal celebrations. She and her companions embroider a banner and make garlands. After the bustle and character dances of the first act, Fleur-de-Lys and her friends are a classical ensemble, dressed in tutus and performing a suite of formal dances with Phoebus and his companions. Yet Phoebus is distracted, lost in thought of Esmeralda. Fleur-de-Lys notices he is not wearing the scarf she gave him, but her suspicions vanish when he gives her a ring. Fleur-de-Lys' mother announces that she has prepared a present, the allegorical ballet 'Diana and Actaeon'.

As a final entertainment, Esmeralda enters, with Gringoire and her friends. She tells Fleur-de-Lys' fortune, then dances for the guests – a scene that is sometimes performed as a gala *pas de six*. As all the gypsy girls dance, Esmeralda sees Phoebus, and realises he is engaged to Fleur-de-Lys. Devastated, she decides to leave, putting on the scarf. Recognising the present she gave to Phoebus, Fleur-de-Lys is horrified and throws down Phoebus' ring. In the confusion, Esmeralda leaves, and Phoebus hurries after her.

Act III. Scene 1. An inn. Clopin shows Frollo a hiding place, from which he observes a meeting between Esmeralda and Phoebus. Furiously jealous, Frollo leaps out and attacks Phoebus, using Esmeralda's dagger. Phoebus falls to the ground.

When a crowd gathers, Phoebus tells a judge that the dagger is Esmeralda's. The judge accuses her of murder. She protests her innocence.

Frollo whispers that he will save her if she will accept his love. She pushes him angrily away. The judge breaks his staff over Esmeralda's head, and throws a veil over her: she is to be executed. Frollo gloats.

Act III. Scene 2. The square outside the Cathedral of Notre Dame. A procession, led by Frollo, takes Esmeralda to the prison. A crowd watches. Gringoire, looking through the prison window, realises that Esmeralda is being tortured.

A crowd of beggars and tramps enter, celebrating the Festival of Fools. Quasimodo, who has been elected their king for the day, holds court, dressed in royal robes. Angry at this mockery of authority, Frollo tears off Quasimodo's robe.

Esmeralda is brought out and led to execution. She says her goodbyes, and asks Gringoire to bury her with Phoebus' scarf. Frollo again offers to save her, but she rejects him, and prays. Phoebus appears – he was only wounded, and has recovered. He accuses Frollo of attacking him, proclaiming Esmeralda's innocence. Frollo draws a dagger, but Quasimodo disarms him and throws him off the bridge. Esmeralda and Phoebus are happily united.

Esmeralda was an influential work in Russia. In many of Petipa's early ballets the dances for the heroine blend classical and character qualities. The *pas de six* he created for Virginia Zucchi in his restaging of *Esmeralda* has parallels with his own ballet *La Bayadère*, in which Nikiya must dance at her lover's betrothal to another woman. In *Esmeralda* the heroine finds out during her performance that the man she loves is engaged to another woman. She is devastated, but must dance on, sinking into despair or pulled up again by her own love of dancing. The poet Gringoire – the role originally created by Perrot for himself – partners Esmeralda through use of a tambourine. Rather than his taking her hand, they both hold onto the instrument, suggesting both her emotional distance from him and the way they are linked by artistry. In her variation, Esmeralda dances a long, zigzag bourrée that takes her gliding across the stage, alternating between sorrow and revived energy. It's a moment that blends the latest technical developments with expressive drama.

Petipa cherished *Esmeralda*, and was careful in casting it. The ballerina Mathilde Kschessinska, known for her virtuoso technique more than her acting, was eager to dance it. 'You love? You suffer?' Petipa asked her.[17] The ballet needs emotional depth as well as strength. Kschessinska finally got her wish in 1899; it remained her favourite role.

Other Stagings

Roland Petit's 1965 ballet *Notre-Dame de Paris* returned to Victor Hugo's original, tragic storyline, in a staging full of pop sensibility. (See separate entry in Chapter 7.)

The Sleeping Beauty

Choreography: Marius Petipa
Music: Pytor Ilych Tchaikovsky
Libretto: Ivan Vsevolozhsky
Premiere: 3 January 1890, Mariinsky Theatre, St Petersburg
Original cast: *Princess Aurora* Carlotta Brianza; *Prince Désiré* Pavel Gerdt; *Lilac Fairy* Marie Mariusovna Petipa; *Carabosse* and *Blue Bird* Enrico Cecchetti; *Princess Florine* Varvara Nikitina

The idea for *The Sleeping Beauty* came from Ivan Vsevolozhsky, director of the Imperial Theatres. In 1888 he proposed the subject to Tchaikovsky, suggesting 'a mise-en-scène in the style of Louis XIV' and fairy-tale dances in the last act. *The Sleeping Beauty* was criticised for being a '*ballet-féerie*', a genre of extravagant spectacle and very little sense. Yet this would prove to be a ballet of extraordinary richness, its music and choreography full of layered meanings.

Vsevolozhsky's choice of Louis XIV was intended as a celebration of the Tsarist court, linking Russia's imperial rule with the Sun King, whose reign also lies at the roots of ballet itself. The plot literally turns on a point of court etiquette: the wicked fairy Carabosse is angry because she wasn't invited to the christening of baby Aurora. Yet this monarchist fable also shows images of rebirth, of the changing day and the turning seasons: the Lilac Fairy is named for a flower associated with springtime, while the heroine herself, unnamed in Perrault's original fairy tale, becomes Aurora, named for the dawn.

The ballet was planned in great detail. As Roland John Wiley has shown in his study *Tchaikovsky's Ballets*, Petipa would prepare the stage action at home, working out scenes and patterns using little papier-mâché figures. He would give his composer detailed instructions, laying the scenario out with requests for numbers of particular length and tempo, sometimes suggesting orchestration. 'Mutual caresses, miaowing, and scratching with their claws,' he wrote to Tchaikovsky for the cats' duet from *The Sleeping Beauty*. 'For the beginning love music in ¾. At the end, accelerated ¾ and miaowing. (This *pas* must not be long.)'[18]

This method explains why some nineteenth-century ballet music feels by-the-yard. By contrast, Tchaikovsky – who took a free hand with some instructions, discussing the score with Petipa – created an extraordinary score, creating brilliant melodies for the many short numbers and building them all into a radiant whole.

Prologue. The Christening. The palace of King Florestan XXIV. Celebrations are held for Aurora, the baby princess. Courtiers and guests arrive, supervised by the court chamberlain Catalabutte. A fanfare announces the arrival of the King and Queen.

A group of fairies enter with their cavaliers, followed by pageboys carrying gifts. They are Aurora's godmothers, who each dance a solo and give the child a gift. The fairy Candide gives her beauty and openness; Fleur de Farine (Wheatflower) gives her grace; Miettes Qui Tombe (Falling Breadcrumbs) gives her generosity; Canary gives her eloquence; Violente gives her temperament. (These are Petipa's and Vsevolozhsky's titles: they are renamed in some productions.) The Lilac Fairy, the most important, dances last. All the fairies dance together; cavaliers lift the Lilac Fairy, who pours down blessings over Aurora's cradle.

A clap of thunder sounds, and an attendant runs in, warning of the approach of the fairy Carabosse. She is brought in, drawn in a carriage by her attendants, in a furious rage because she was not invited to the party. The king and Catalabutte check the list, and find that she has indeed been overlooked. She rounds on Catalabutte, pulling off his hat and wig, and plucking out tufts of his hair. Then she announces her gift to Aurora: a curse. She will grow up, she will have all the gifts the other fairies have promised her – but then she will prick her finger on a spindle and die. The Lilac Fairy steps forward to soften the curse. Aurora will prick her finger, but instead of dying she will fall asleep for a hundred years, to be woken by the kiss of a prince.

Act I. The spell. The palace gardens. Peasants and courtiers gather to celebrate Aurora's twentieth birthday. Three women are knitting, despite the royal ban on pointed objects. Horrified, Catalabutte seizes the needles. The King orders that the knitting women should be hanged, but the Queen pleads for them, and they are pardoned. (In some productions, a disguised Carabosse is one of the knitting women.) The peasants now dance a garland waltz, and four princes arrive, suitors for Aurora's hand.

The orchestra heralds Aurora's entrance with gathering excitement, like a quickening heartbeat. She runs on in a quick, joyful solo. Her four suitors then partner her in the Rose Adagio – a sustained test, not just of the balle-rina's balances, but of her classical line, presence and musicality. She dances with her princes, accepting roses from them but choosing none of them. When she steps into an *attitude* on *pointe*, each prince in turn takes her hand to support her, and then lets go, leaving her to balance alone. At last she opens out her pose, balancing in *arabesque*, unsupported and inde-pendent. At the end of the Rose Adagio, she bows deeply, acknowledging her partners and the audience: Aurora is a courteous princess, with good manners built into the bones of her choreography.

As Aurora dances with her friends, they are interrupted by a tapping in the score: Carabosse attracts Aurora's attention by tapping with her stick, then gives her a spindle. The princess is fascinated, never having seen such a thing, and pricks her finger and swoons. Her parents and the court rush to help her. Shrugging off the injury, she starts to dance, moving in fast, dizzy circles until she falls unconscious. The Lilac Fairy appears, reassuring the court and casting a spell that sends the whole castle to sleep.

Act II. The vision. Prince Désiré is hunting near the enchanted forest. The costumes of the royal hunting party show that a hundred years have passed. The prince is withdrawn and melancholy: when a countess approaches him, he politely rebuffs her. She starts a game of blind man's buff with Gallison, the Prince's tutor. Hunting horns sound again: the quarry has been sighted. The hunting party sets off in pursuit, but the Prince chooses to stay behind.

The Lilac Fairy appears in a magical boat, and shows the Prince a vision of Aurora. Amazed by her beauty, he begs to meet her, and the vision of Aurora now appears to dance with him, surrounded by a group of nymphs. This vision scene has echoes of the supernatural ballets of the Romantic era. Although the Prince partners Aurora, she seems intangible and remote – the nymphs move to separate them when he tries to embrace her. Aurora's dances are softer and more withdrawn than the brilliant, happy dances of Act I. At last she vanishes, and the Prince asks to follow her.

The Prince and the Lilac Fairy set sail, travelling to the castle as the scenery changes around them and Tchaikovsky's 'Panorama' music plays. Carabosse's theme is heard as a memory – originally she did not appear in this act but some productions include her, to add a confrontation to this scene. Arriving at the cobwebbed palace, the prince finds Aurora asleep. Prompted by the Lilac Fairy, he kisses Aurora, waking her up. The court comes back to life and the King and Queen bless the marriage of Aurora and the Prince.

Act III. The wedding. Fairy-tale characters join the court to celebrate the wedding of Aurora and her Prince. The scene opens with a grand polonaise, followed by many divertissements. These include dances for jewel fairies, for Puss in Boots with the White Cat, Little Red Riding Hood with the Wolf, Cinderella and her slipper. The most famous is a virtuoso *pas de deux* for the Bluebird and Princess Florine. At last, Aurora and the prince dance a formal *pas de deux*. The finale is a joyful mazurka, which shifts into the Tsarist hymn 'Vive Henri Quatre' for the final tableau, in which the Lilac Fairy blesses the marriage.

In most media, it's an uphill struggle to make the heroine of *The Sleeping Beauty* interesting. She could almost be the definition of a passive character: she's given her virtues at birth, has most of her fate decided for her by curses and counterspells, and then spends half the story unconscious. On paper, there seems to be little opportunity for characterisation. But not in ballet: Petipa's Aurora is full of life and energy, the centre of the stage world, a rich and varied challenge for any ballerina.

The symphonic qualities of Tchaikovsky's score are matched by the architecture of the choreography. In the fairy solos of the prologue, we see Aurora's 'gifts' danced for us: qualities of movement that the ballerina must come to embody. The heroine's virtues are not passive or bland: they are dance qualities, alive and active onstage. We watch Petipa's Aurora grow up, from the speedy brilliance of Act I to the romantic quality of the vision scene in Act II and the new grandeur she shows as a married woman in Act III.

In 1890 the ballet had a mixed reception. 'Very nice,' the tsar said coolly to the composer:[19] Tchaikovsky was crushed. Critics worried that the score wasn't suitable for dancing, that it was too rich and densely coloured, encroaching on the more highbrow territory of operas and symphonies. Audiences responded more warmly.

Alexandre Benois, utterly smitten with the music, thought the choreography was 'the magnificent crown' of Petipa's work. As for the dancers, 'their collective personal mastery and the charm of each artist flowed together in the beauty of the ensemble. Thus I had at that time the good fortune to see a genuine *Gesamtkunstwerk* [total work of art].'[20] He saw it again and again, bringing his friends, turning his circle into 'genuine balletomanes'. This circle was the group of artists who would work with Serge Diaghilev on the Ballets Russes, which would become known for its blending of the arts in productions that, in their turn, were hailed as *Gesamtkunstwerks*. In 1921, Diaghilev would revive *The Sleeping Beauty* itself, converting a new generation to the wonders of Petipa's classicism.

Over ballet's later history, *The Sleeping Beauty* would itself become a symbol of rebirth, a source of classicism to which later choreographers returned. In a powerful gesture, this was the ballet that reopened London's Royal Opera House after the Second World War. *The Sleeping Beauty* has had an enduring impact on choreography. Frederick Ashton, who saw the ballet 'literally hundreds of times', called watching it 'having a private lesson'.[21] The geometries of the group dances, the rigour and charm of the individual variations, echo down through classical ballet.

The Nutcracker

Choreography: Lev Ivanov
Music: Pyotr Ilych Tchaikovsky
Libretto: Ivan Vsevolozhsky and Marius Petipa, after E. T. A. Hoffmann
Premiere: 16 December 1892, Mariinsky Theatre, St Petersburg
Original cast: *Sugar Plum Fairy* Antonietta dell'Era; *Prince* Pavel Gerdt; *Nutcracker* Sergei Legat; *Clara* Stanislava Belinskaya; *Drosselmeyer* Timofei Stukolkin

If *Swan Lake* is the world's most famous ballet, *The Nutcracker* has a popularity that goes far beyond dance. It has become a holiday tradition, as much a part of Christmas as red-nosed reindeer and decorated trees.

After the success of *The Sleeping Beauty*, Tchaikovsky was commissioned to create a double bill for the Mariinsky Theatre: the one-act opera *Iolanta* and the two-act ballet *The Nutcracker*. Petipa drafted the scenario, based on Alexandre Dumas *père*'s version of *The Nutcracker and the Mouse King*, originally by E. T. A. Hoffmann. The story has a Christmas setting and an element of spooky fantasy. The creation was difficult: Tchaikovsky was unhappy with the theme, while Petipa was taken ill, so the work of choreographing the ballet was passed to his assistant, Lev Ivanov. In 1892 the first production was severely condemned by critics, jeered at for its perceived childishness, weak storyline and over-elaborate scenery. As Tchaikovsky wrote to his brother Anatole after the first performance, the staging was 'magnificent, even too magnificent. The eyes weary from this luxury.'[22]

Although it was given comparatively few performances, *The Nutcracker* kept a foothold in the repertory. After Ivanov's death, it was revived by Nikolai Sergeyev, who brought the notation of this and many other ballets with him when he left Russia after the revolution of 1917, and restaged it in the West. George Balanchine, who had danced in the ballet when he was a student at the Imperial Ballet School, created his own production for New York City Ballet in 1954. Based on the original scenario, it established *The Nutcracker* as a holiday tradition in America.

Synopsis

Act I. Scene 1. The drawing room of the Stahlbaum house. The Stahlbaums are giving a Christmas party. With their guests, they are decorating a Christmas tree, before calling their children to see it. Another guest arrives, the mysterious Drosselmeyer. As he arrives, the Stahlbaums' owl clock chimes, the owl flapping its wings. Drosselmeyer brings mechanical, dancing toys for the children, and a special Nutcracker doll for the Stahlbaums' daughter, Clara. Her brother Fritz breaks the Nutcracker doll; Drosselmeyer comforts Clara and mends the doll. The children play with their Christmas presents, and there is a gentle lullaby for the girls with their dolls, interrupted by the whistles, trumpets and martial toys of the boys. The guests dance a traditional 'grandfather' dance – the traditional end to a party – and leave. The family goes to bed.

Clara comes downstairs in the night, looking for her new toy, but is frightened by mice. When the owl clock strikes twelve, Clara sees that the owl has turned into Drosselmeyer. Mice appear, and the Christmas tree grows to enormous size. A battle breaks out between the toy soldiers, led by the Nutcracker, and the mice, led by the Mouse King. To save the Nutcracker, Clara throws her slipper at the Mouse King, who falls dead. The Nutcracker turns into a handsome prince and leads Clara on a magical journey.

Scene 2. A fir forest in winter. Clara and the Nutcracker Prince arrive in the forest. Snow falls, and snowflakes dance in swirling patterns.

Act II. The palace of the Sugar Plum Fairy in the Kingdom of Sweets. Clara and the Nutcracker Prince are welcomed by the Sugar Plum Fairy. The Nutcracker explains how Clara saved him. The Sugar Plum Fairy orders a divertissement in her honour: chocolate, which is a Spanish dance, an Arabian dance for coffee, a Chinese dance for tea and a Russian *trepak* dance. More dancers appear, with flutes (the 'Dance of the Mirlitons'). The fairy-tale character Mother Ginger appears, with children climbing out from under her skirts, followed by a grand waltz of flowers. At last the Sugar Plum Fairy and her prince dance a grand *pas de deux*, followed by an ensemble for all the characters. Many productions end with Clara waking up; others, including Balanchine's, show her setting off on a new journey.

Tchaikovsky's score is irresistible, from the wintry thrill of the overture to the invention of the toy battle. The ballet's big scenes have a heart-catching grandeur: the growing Christmas tree, the adagio for the Sugar Plum Fairy and her cavalier. Tchaikovsky's inventive orchestration included a new instrument for the Sugar Plum Fairy's variation, the tinkling celesta. Petipa had asked for music that sounded 'as if drops of water were shooting out of fountains'.[23] On a visit to Paris, Tchaikovsky heard the celesta, invented just six years earlier by Auguste Mustel, 'something between a small piano and a glockenspiel with a divinely marvellous sound'. He had one brought to St Petersburg in secret, telling his publisher: 'I would prefer it to be shown to nobody, for I am afraid that Rimsky-Korsakov and Glazunov will get wind of it and use its unusual effects sooner than me.'[24]

It is the score that has made *The Nutcracker* a worldwide hit. Some of the early criticism of the ballet was justified. It's dramatically lopsided, with all the story in the first act, and most of the dancing relegated to the second. The ballerina does not appear until the second act, and dances only briefly. Yet Ivanov's contemporaries also praised his snowflake scene as one of his finest creations, a waltz in which dancers eddy and spin as if driven by a breeze, building to a blizzard. Ivanov's grand *pas de deux* is also marvellous; in many productions, it is the only part of his choreography still danced.

The Nutcracker was also criticised for being 'a children's ballet'. So it is: as a holiday treat, it has been many people's first experience of ballet. Most productions have put children onstage for the party scene, whether or not they have a child playing Clara; the experience has drawn many young people into dance careers. For all its dramatic unevenness, *The Nutcracker* is full of transformations, from the magical growing tree to the emotional journey of Clara, a child who is starting to grow up. The poignancy of Tchaikovsky's music can express both childlike wonder and the drama of leaving childhood behind.

Other Stagings

*Nutcracker*s vary considerably. The heroine is usually called Clara, as in Petipa's scenario, or Marie, as in the original Hoffmann tale; different divertissement numbers are included or dropped; many attempts have been made to reshape the story. Most productions use children, giving young dance students an early experience of being onstage. There have been literally hundreds of stagings around the world. In 2010, the critic Alastair Macaulay reported on twenty-eight stagings in America alone, only a fraction of the number being danced today.

In 1967, Rudolf Nureyev staged a Freudian *Nutcracker* for the Royal Swedish Ballet. It becomes a coming-of-age story: Clara is danced by an adult ballerina, who then becomes the Sugar Plum Fairy, while Drosselmeyer becomes her prince. Many productions have followed suit: doubling Clara and the Sugar Plum Fairy gives the ballerina a much more substantial role.

In taking a fresh look at the ballet, many choreographers have looked back to the Hoffmann story, which is much creepier than the Dumas-influenced ballet scenario. The difficulty is fitting darker narratives to Tchaikovsky's radiant score.

Swan Lake

Choreography: Marius Petipa and Lev Ivanov
Music: Pyotr Ilyich Tchaikovsky
Premiere: 17 February 1894 (second act only); 15 January 1895 (complete ballet), Mariinsky Theatre, St Petersburg
Original cast: *Odette/Odile* Pierina Legnani; *Siegfried* Pavel Gerdt

Swan Lake is ballet's most iconic work. It combines romantic softness with the formal brilliance of Imperial classicism, a story of enchantment and escape set to a Tchaikovsky score full of passionate melancholy and idealism. The tutu and swan headdress have become the symbol of a ballerina; her thirty-two *fouetté* turns in *Swan Lake* remain ballet's most famous display of virtuosity.

Tchaikovsky wrote that he was keen to try writing ballet music. Authorship of the first *Swan Lake* libretto is disputed, but the ballet's themes must have appealed to the composer. He had already written three works in which a mortal man falls in love with an enchanted woman: the operas *Undine* and *Mandragora*, and his music for the play *The Snow Maiden*. His niece and nephew also remembered Tchaikovsky creating a family entertainment called *The Lake of Swans*, in which the children took part, rocking on wooden toy swans. Tchaikovsky's score is freer than *The Sleeping Beauty* or *The Nutcracker*. In the later ballets he would work to Petipa's detailed scenarios; for *Swan Lake* he wrote much longer stretches of dramatic music. This work comes closer to the simpler storytelling and less elaborate staging of Romantic ballet, with a truly Romantic theme of impossible love.

The grown-up version of the ballet had a rocky start. The first production, staged by Julius Reisinger at Moscow's Bolshoi Theatre in 1877, was a failure, followed by other unsuccessful attempts. In 1894, after

Tchaikovsky's death the previous year, the ballet's second act was chosen as part of a St Petersburg performance dedicated to the composer's memory. It was such a success that the entire ballet was staged in 1895 at the Mariinsky Theatre, with Ivanov choreography for Acts II and IV, while Petipa choreographed Acts I and III. This new version found lasting fame.

Synopsis

Act I. The gardens of the palace. Courtiers and peasants gather to celebrate Prince Siegfried's birthday. Siegfried enters, heralded by trumpets, and greets the guests, including his tutor Wolfgang and his friend Benno. A *pas de trois* is danced by two women and a man. The Princess Mother arrives with her ladies, and the revellers hastily hide their drinking goblets. She gives Siegfried a crossbow, his birthday present, and tells him he must marry. At a grand ball, he will be introduced to potential wives. Siegfried is downcast: he has no wish to marry. His mother leaves. Wolfgang, now tipsy, tries to dance with a peasant girl and collapses. The peasants dance. A flight of swans passes overhead – the first appearance of Tchaikovsky's famous 'swan' theme – and Siegfried decides to go hunting with his companions.

Act II. By the lake. Still melancholy, Siegfried orders his companions away. He sees a swan approach, and is amazed when it turns into a beautiful woman. She is frightened to see Siegfried, who tries to reassure her, promising not to shoot. In a passage of formal mime, omitted in Soviet and some later productions, Odette explains that she is the Queen of the Swans. The lake was made by her mother's tears, when the magician Von Rothbart turned Odette into a swan. She can appear as a woman only between midnight and dawn. The spell will be broken if a man promises to love her and be faithful. Siegfried vows to do so.

Von Rothbart appears in the form of an owl. Siegfried prepares to shoot him, but Odette prevents him. Odette and Siegfried leave. The *corps de ballet* of swans runs in, as if flying in a zigzag line. Seeing them, the returning huntsmen take aim. Siegfried runs on, ordering them not to shoot. Odette follows, pleading for the safety of her flock, standing in front of them to protect them. After a waltz for the swans Odette returns. Siegfried searches for her among the swans.

The *pas de deux* that follows is framed by the *corps* of swans, who form soft groupings as a background to the dance. Odette keeps moving to and from Siegfried, stepping away and returning to him. At last she leans back against him, and he rocks her in his arms. At the end of the duet, Siegfried turns Odette slowly as she beats one foot in tiny, trembling *petits batte-ments*; she balances and falls to the side, caught in his arms.

The *pas de deux* is followed by the famous 'dance of the little swans', four cygnets who link arms and spring through a perky unison dance, and a joyful dance for two big swans. Odette's variation follows, stretching into big 'swan' *arabesques* and ending with a diagonal of pirouettes. As dawn approaches, all the swans dance, with Odette cutting through the *corps*. Siegfried begs her to stay, but Odette tears herself away, her arms rippling as she turns back into a swan.

Act III. The palace ballroom. The guests assemble for the ball, with a grand entrance for Siegfried and the Princess Mother. Six princesses, all prospec-tive fiancées, dance with Siegfried. He dutifully partners them, but he is thinking of Odette: at the end of the dance, he explains that he cannot marry any of them. Trumpets sound, and two new guests arrive: Von Rothbart and his daughter Odile, who is disguised to look exactly like Odette. Siegfried is enchanted, and leads Odile away from the ballroom. The Princess Mother, Von Rothbart and the courtiers watch a divertisse-ment of national dances: a Spanish dance, a Hungarian *czárdás*, a Neapolitan dance and a Polish mazurka. Siegfried returns with Odile. In their dance together, the famous 'Black Swan' *pas de deux*, Von Rothbart directs Odile as she entices Siegfried. The true Odette appears at the window. Von Rothbart casts a spell so that Siegfried and the other guests will not see her. To stop Siegfried's doubts, Odile then imitates Odette's movements, echoing the Swan Queen's poses. In the coda, Odile dances thirty-two *fouettés*, dazzling Siegfried with her whirling turns. Entranced, Siegfried declares that he will marry her. At Von Rothbart's insistence, he swears to be true to her – breaking his promise to the real Odette. With mocking laughter, Von Rothbart and Odile reveal the deception and vanish from the ballroom. Siegfried rushes out in search of Odette.

Act IV. The lake. Left alone by their queen, the swans perform a melancholy dance, now joined by a group of black swans. Odette returns in despair: Siegfried has broken his vow. She tries to kill herself, but the swans prevent her. A storm rises. Siegfried enters, finding Odette among the swans, and begs her forgiveness. She grants it, but tells him she must die. Von Rothbart tries to drive Siegfried away, but the lovers decide to defy him by dying together. Odette flings herself into the lake, and Siegfried follows. Von

Rothbart dies, destroyed by their sacrifice. In an apotheosis, Odette and Siegfried are reunited in death, travelling to a land of happiness.

Traditionally danced as a double role, Odette-Odile offers a ballerina the chance to play contrasting characters, the Swan Queen and her wicked double. This is just the start of *Swan Lake*'s dualities. Ivanov's lakeside Acts II and IV are lyrical and soft, whereas Petipa's Acts I and III, set at court, have diamond-sharp clarity. The division of the choreography becomes part of the ballet's story, its drama embodied in the different choreographic styles.

In the lakeside scenes, Ivanov moves away from the grand formal structures and hierarchies established by Petipa. The *corps de ballet* don't just frame the *pas de deux* for Odette and her prince, they participate in it. Their ever-changing patterns emphasise the lines and shapes of the duet, while their steps remind us of their swan nature, echoing Odette's own delicate, birdlike movements. In *arabesque*, Odette will lift her arms like wings; in her first dance, she moves her head and shoulders like a bird preening its feathers. In her repeated *sissonne* jumps, she seems to strive for flight, yearning for freedom.

Whether Odette moves among her flock or dances with Siegfried, Ivanov makes dramatic use of stage space. She constantly moves towards Siegfried and away again. In the mime scene, she takes two steps forward, and then one back: when Margot Fonteyn coached the role, the dancer Donald MacLeary remembered, she said that this showed Odette caught up by her own story, then remembering herself and retreating again. It's a drama of trust, resolved when she lets Siegfried rock her in his arms.

The dual role can be stereotyped as the vampy bad girl Odile against the virginally pure Odette, but in fact it's Odette who seeks physical closeness and reassurance. Odile's dances say 'look, don't touch', as she displays her power and beauty while slipping out of Siegfried's grasp. And though her glittering steps are a hard-edged contrast to Odette's lyricism, she must also evoke her rival, showing us why Siegfried is fooled.

Like most nineteenth-century ballets, *Swan Lake* has been changed over time. Originally, the lyrical scene for Odette and Siegfried included Siegfried's friend Benno who did quite a lot of the partnering, but he is edited out of most post-war productions. Diaghilev's Ballets Russes danced a shortened, two-act version of the ballet; other companies followed with one-act versions, focused on material from Act II. These included George Balanchine's 1951 version, which kept Ivanov material but re-choreographed the group sections.

Soviet productions cut the formal mime passages and gave the ballet a happy ending, in which Siegfried fights and defeats Von Rothbart, with the apotheosis music becoming an expression of triumph. They also follow Alexander Gorsky in adding a perky jester for the court acts, increasing the amount of male bravura dancing and horrifying western critics. While most productions include the Act I *pas de trois*, Act II and the Black Swan *pas de deux*, Act IV has been frequently re-choreographed to fit different conclusions.

Petipa's ballets focused on female roles, with much more dancing for ballerinas than for their partners. From the 1960s on, and particularly with the influence of Rudolf Nureyev, the male roles have been expanded, often to the point of distortion. As the choreographer Mark Morris put it, 'It's like, "Odette, I know you're very upset right now, but would you mind standing over there while I do these seventeen meaningless pirouettes?" '[25] In Yuri Grigorovich's 1969 production, Von Rothbart becomes Siegfried's Evil Genius, constantly undermining him.

Other Stagings

While 'traditional' stagings have tweaked and re-choreographed the ballet, other choreographers have set out to create new versions of *Swan Lake*. John Neumeier's *Illusions – Like Swan Lake*, created for Hamburg Ballet in 1976, tells the story of King Ludwig of Bavaria, a fragile monarch who supported the composer Richard Wagner, built extravagant fantasy castles and went insane. Neumeier makes Ludwig's life a parallel to Siegfried's story, also drawing connections between Ludwig and Tchaikovsky's homosexuality. In Act II, Ludwig watches a court performance of *Swan Lake* and steps into it, taking the place of the ballet's Siegfried – who then becomes the staging's Benno. Although the framework is different, Neuemeier's Act II stays very close to the text danced by The Royal Ballet in the 1950s, complete with Benno. In Act III the homosexual Ludwig sees his sympathetic wife Natalia as the Black Swan; in the last act, Ludwig dies, carried away by the figure in black who has dogged his steps throughout the ballet.

In 1987, Mats Ek created his own *Swan Lake* for the Cullberg Ballet, a surreal narrative with androgynous, bald-headed swans, dressed in tutus and danced by both men and women. Matthew Bourne's 1995 contem-porary-dance staging, set in modern Britain, has a repressed Prince falling in love with a male Swan. The production has become a global hit, with long runs on Broadway and in the West End. Its great strength is in creating a Swan that is a new image of beauty and freedom.

Raymonda

Choreography: Marius Petipa
Music: Alexander Glazunov
Libretto: Lydia Pashkova
Premiere: 17 January 1898, Mariinsky Theatre, St Petersburg
Original cast: *Raymonda* Pierina Legnani; *Jean de Brienne* Sergei Legat; *Abdérâme* Pavel Gerdt

Raymonda has a luscious score, marvellous dances and a foolish plot by Lydia Pashkova, a society novelist and columnist. In the words of the Russian balletomane Prince Lieven, 'it has everything but meaning'. Set in medieval France, with crusaders and Saracens passing through, the ballet is a meandering tale filled with prophetic dreams and last-minute rescues. It was Petipa's last success, packed with dances, and particularly female solos: the role of Raymonda was created for Pierina Legnani, the first Odette-Odile of *Swan Lake*. As Alexandra Danilova wrote in her memoirs, 'For a ballerina, it's a wonderful opportunity to show every facet of your talent, with several variations in widely different styles.'[26]

Act I. Scene 1. The castle of Countess Sybille, Provence. It is the birthday of Raymonda, the niece of the Countess Sybille, and celebrations are planned. The Countess tells the story of the White Lady, whose statue stands in the courtyard: she is an ancestor who protects the family traditions. Jean de Brienne, Raymonda's fiancé, sends her a portrait of himself: he will soon return from the Crusades, where he is fighting alongside King Andrew II of Hungary. A Saracen lord, Abdérâme, arrives to court Raymonda, offering her valuable presents. She rejects him.

Scene 2. Left alone on the terrace, Raymonda falls asleep. The White Lady leads her into an enchanted garden, where she meets Jean de Brienne and dances with him. Then he vanishes, and Abdérâme appears, declaring his love for Raymonda. She appeals to the White Lady to save her, and the stage is filled with elves and goblins. Frightened, Raymonda swoons. Her companions carry her into the castle.

Act II. Festivities are held at the castle. Abdérâme is among the guests, bringing a troupe of Moorish and Spanish entertainers. As they dance, he tries to abduct Raymonda. Suddenly Jean de Brienne and his knights return from the Crusades, just in time to rescue Raymonda. King Andrew orders

Abdérâme and Jean de Brienne to settle their dispute in single combat. Jean de Brienne is victorious, and the lovers are united.

Act III. The castle courtyard. Everyone celebrates the wedding of Raymonda and Jean de Brienne. In honour of King Andrew, the dances are Hungarian in style, from a character dance for the booted *corps de ballet* to the gorgeous variations for Raymonda and her friends.

Plenty of ballets have silly plots. *Raymonda*'s trouble is that the story affects both pacing and characterisation, despite various attempts to revise and reshape the full-length version. Later stagings tend to put Jean de Brienne into the first act, and to build up the conflict between Raymonda's two suitors, her fiancé and Abdérâme. (Audiences may end up preferring Abdérâme, the Orientalist fantasy, to the virtuous Jean de Brienne.)

The ballet has had most success when staged as a suite of dancing. *Raymonda* is packed with divertissements to lovely music: classical dancing in Act I, character dances in Act II and a mixture of the two in the fabulous 'Hungarian' Act III. In this act Petipa colours classical steps with character detail – a hand placed behind the head, arms folded across the chest while feet skip through quick steps. Raymonda's own Act III variation is particularly fine, with imperious handclaps followed by gliding bourrées to a piano melody: she seems to command the music, then to fall under its dreamy spell.

Other Stagings

Several full-length productions have tried to make more sense of *Raymonda*'s story, with mixed results. In 1964, when Rudolf Nureyev staged the three-act work for the touring section of The Royal Ballet, he expanded Raymonda's dream: Abdérâme haunts Raymonda's fantasies until he is defeated by her fiancé. The complete work fell out of repertory, but Nureyev revived Act III as a divertissement, in magnificent cream-and-gold Byzantine designs by Barry Kay. Nureyev went on to restage the three-act version for several other companies, including the Paris Opéra Ballet. Similarly, Yuri Grigorovich's 1984 production for the Bolshoi Ballet focused on Raymonda's choice between her two suitors.

George Balanchine returned many times to *Raymonda*. In 1946 he and Alexandra Danilova, who had fond memories of the Mariinsky production, staged it in New York for the Ballet Russe de Monte Carlo, with designs by Alexander Benois. The production was soon cut down to a *divertissement*.

Balanchine later created several divertissement ballets to Glazunov's music, drawing on Petipa's original and creating new dances. His 1955 *Pas de dix* was made for Maria Tallchief, André Eglevsky and four supporting couples; most of the music comes from the 'Hungarian' last act. Balanchine's 1961 *Raymonda Variations* has a garden setting and a different mood, with a principal couple, soloists and a *corps de ballet*. In 1973, Balanchine created still another *Raymonda* suite, *Cortège hongrois*, as a farewell for the retiring ballerina Melissa Hayden. It featured a leading 'classical' couple, a 'character' pair and sixteen supporting couples.

In 1983, Twyla Tharp used dances from *Raymonda* and Glazunov's *Scènes de ballet* for *The Little Ballet*, danced by Mikhail Baryshnikov and four female soloists. He wears a modern shirt and trousers, while the women's costumes suggest the ballet student uniforms of nineteenth-century Russia. Tharp shows Baryshnikov, a dancer now in the West, with the echoes of his and ballet's past.

4

THE BALLETS RUSSES
AND AFTER

THE BALLETS RUSSES of Serge Diaghilev brought ballet to the forefront of the arts, as if with a thunderclap. From its first sensational season in Paris in 1909, this was the most exciting dance company in the world – but Diaghilev went far beyond that, creating a meeting place for all the arts. Dance-lovers were bowled over by such stars as Vaslav Nijinsky, Anna Pavlova, Tamara Karsavina and Alicia Markova, and choreographers such as Mikhail Fokine, Bronislava Nijinska, Léonide Massine and George Balanchine. Diaghilev also helped to launch musical careers from Stravinsky to Prokofiev, commissioned ballet scores from established names such as Ravel, Debussy, Richard Strauss and Satie, with designs by Bakst, Benois, Picasso, Matisse, and costumes by Chanel – the list is dazzling. Where Romantic ballet had been part of a wider cultural movement, the Ballets Russes *led* cultural fashion, driving innovation in dance, music and design. Diaghilev's Ballets Russes was a whirlwind of creativity, innovation, scandal and wonder. It lasted for twenty years, and planted the seeds of future ballet companies wherever it went.

Yet the company was created, not by a dancer or choreographer, but by an impresario. There have been many bright and influential managers in ballet's history – Louis-Désiré Véron at the Paris Opéra, Ivan Vsevolozhsky at the Imperial Theatres – who encouraged and supported revolutions in art. But Diaghilev caused them. He was not a choreographer, musician or painter, though he was knowledgeable in all three fields. His great gift was in bringing artists together, fostering collaboration and talent, then creating a blaze of publicity to launch it into the world.

Diaghilev was born in 1872 in Novgorod, into a provincial gentry family. In 1890 he came to St Petersburg to study law, quickly joining artistic circles. He wasn't immediately interested in ballet, but his new friends included the artists and eager balletomanes Alexandre Benois and Léon Bakst. The young Diaghilev summed up his own personality in a letter of 1895, written to his stepmother:

> I am firstly a great charlatan, though with *brio*; secondly a great *charmeur*; thirdly, I have any amount of cheek; fourthly, I am a man with a great quantity of logic, but with very few principles; fifthly, I think I have no real gifts. All the same, I think I have just found my true vocation – being a Maecenas. I have all that is necessary save the money – *mais ça viendra* [but that will come].[1]

Maecenas, the Roman nobleman and patron of poets, was an unusual role model for a twenty-three year old, but Diaghilev's first four points reveal the swagger and daring with which he would remake the role of patron and impresario.

The friends launched a new journal, *Mir Iskustva (The World of Art)*, in 1899. As editor, Diaghilev commissioned and discovered new artists, researching art of the past and bringing the two together with a new gloss. By 1899, he also had a foothold at the Imperial Theatres, appointed to edit the *Annual* of the Theatres. Characteristically, he produced an intelligent, artistic volume that went way over budget. He also planned a new production of the ballet *Sylvia*, designed by artists from the *Mir Iskustva* group. He was making a name for himself in St Petersburg, but his autocratic personality was also making him enemies. Mariinsky officials complained that the young Diaghilev should not be given such authority over a major new production. In the row that followed, Diaghilev refused to resign, but he was dismissed by the tsar – which amounted to a permanent ban from working in the Imperial Theatres. With his best Russian career option stopped, he began to look further afield.

Putting a brave face on his dismissal, Diaghilev arranged more exhibitions, including a superb show of Russian historical portraits: a revelation of Russia's past, imaginatively arranged in the romantic setting of St Petersburg's Tauride Palace. At a banquet given in his honour, Diaghilev made an unexpected and characteristic speech:

> Don't you feel that this long gallery of portraits of the big and small people that I brought to live in the beautiful halls of the Palais Tauride is only a grandiose summing-up of a brilliant, but, alas! dead period of our history? . . . We are witnesses of the greatest moment of summing-up in history, in the name of a new and unknown culture, which will be created by us, and which will also sweep us away.[2]

The year was 1905: the exhibition opened at a time of protest, food shortages and violence. Weeks before, the Imperial Guard had fired on protesters
marching towards the Winter Palace to petition the tsar. At least a thousand
people died, shot or trampled in the panic. In the aftermath, strikes and
protests erupted across Russia in the revolution of 1905. There was a strike
by dancers at the Mariinsky Theatre, who called for greater artistic
autonomy in their own art: Fokine, Pavlova and Karsavina were among the
leaders. In response, the management demanded that all dancers and
choreographers sign an oath of loyalty. The dancer Sergei Legat, who
signed, committed suicide shortly afterwards. At the funeral, Anna Pavlova
laid a wreath with the inscription: 'To the first victim at the dawn of freedom
of art from the newly united ballet company.'[3] The strike was peacefully
resolved, but the dancers' attitude had changed; they no longer felt their old
bond with the Russian court.

The Mariinsky rebellion was political, but it was also a protest against the
torpor of the Imperial Theatres. Russian schooling, with its blend of French,
Italian and Danish influences, was producing outstanding dancers, but with
Petipa and Ivanov gone, there was no leading choreographer. The existing
repertory included beautiful choreography, but much of it was in long,
formulaic ballets with mediocre music. Productions had become frames for
star dancers, who felt free to interpolate favourite solos from other ballets,
and to wear their own costumes and jewellery, whether or not they fitted the
ballet. Casting was arranged by hierarchy. *The Sleeping Beauty* had shone as
a complete production, a total work of art, converting Bakst and Benois to
ballet – but other ballets in the repertory had no such unity.

Fokine's wish to reform ballet gained momentum in 1904, when the
American modern dancer Isadora Duncan visited St Petersburg. 'How
strange it must have been to those dilettantes of the gorgeous ballet, with
its lavish decorations and scenery, to watch a young girl, clothed in a tunic
of cobweb, appear and dance before a simple blue curtain to the music of
Chopin!' Duncan wrote. 'Yet even for the first dance there was a storm
of applause.'[4]

Duncan's performances were groundbreaking in several vital ways. She
claimed 'serious' concert music for dance, interpreting the music in fluid,
atmospheric dances. She danced barefoot, and her 'tunic of cobweb'
revealed much more of her body than the conventional ballet tutu, with its
corsets and stiffened skirts. Fokine was hugely impressed: 'Duncan
reminded us of the beauty of simple movements,' he wrote. She proved that
'all the primitive, plain, natural movements – a simple step, run, turn on
both feet, small jump on one foot – are far better than all the enrichments

of ballet technique, if to this technique must be sacrificed grace, expressiveness and beauty.'[5] In 1910, with the Ballets Russes fully launched, Diaghilev would say, 'We do not deny that Duncan is a kindred spirit. Indeed, we carry the torch that she lit.'[6]

Proposing a Mariinsky ballet on the story of *Daphnis and Chloë* to the Mariinsky authorities, Fokine argued for general reforms in the art form:

> The ballet should be staged in conformity with the epoch represented.
>
> The dance pantomime and gestures should not be of the conventional style established in the old ballet . . . but should be of a kind that best fits the style of the period. The costumes also should not be of the established ballet style (short tarlatan tutus) but be consistent with the plot . . . The footwear should match the costumes in authenticity.
>
> In the interests of retaining the scenic illusion, the action must not be interrupted with applause and its acknowledgement by the artists.
>
> The music should not consist of waltzes, polkas and final gallops – indispensable in the old ballet – but must express the story of the ballet and, primarily, its emotional content.[7]

The proposal went unanswered, but Fokine pursued these principles in his later career. Although he kept the *pointe* shoe, he used it sparingly, for the supernatural being or the specialist: sylphs, firebirds and acrobats go on *pointe*. In *The Pharaoh's Daughter*, Petipa ballerinas had worn tutus with Egyptian motifs on the overskirt. Dancers in Fokine's Egyptian ballets wore period wigs, eye make-up and costumes. He also shifted ballet's gender balance; whereas Petipa had focused on dances for women, Fokine created strong roles for both sexes. On the Ballets Russes' triumphant first night in 1909 the biggest success went to Adolph Bolm, who danced the virile Polovtsian Chief in the Polovtsian Dances (from Borodin's opera *Prince Igor*). Nijinsky, with his soaring leap and uncanny ability to mould himself into different personalities and physicalities, would prove to be the major star of the company's early years.

As Fokine worked on reforming ballet, Diaghilev was ready to bring Russian art to the West. In 1906 he arranged an exhibition of Russian art in Paris, accompanied by concerts of Russian music. All the while, he was building up contacts in the Parisian art and social worlds, making connections and finding patrons. These would be essential to his future company, which created vastly expensive productions without state support. Setting the fashionable world agog would be an essential survival strategy for the Ballets Russes.

Meanwhile, Diaghilev's Paris seasons were increasingly ambitious. For his Russian opera season in 1908, he presented Feodor Chaliapin in the Western premiere of Mussorgsky's *Boris Godunov*. Chaliapin's bass voice and his intense, naturalistic acting were framed by a magnificent new production, gorgeously designed and dressed. Diaghilev had sent the painter Ivan Bilibin, an expert on old Russia, to northern villages, 'buying up from the peasants a mass of beautiful hand-woven sarafans, head-dresses and embroidery, which had been hoarded in chests for centuries', wrote Diaghilev.[8] The *Boris Godunov* production shows Diaghilev the impresario already formed. His eye for combining artists was unmatched, while his readiness to search peasant Russia for costumes shows the love of historical research that would inform many future productions.

For the 1909 season Diaghilev planned to add Russian ballet to Russian opera. He knew that Paris had nothing to rival the dancers of the Imperial Ballet, and he was already close to ballet circles – in 1908 he met the rising star Vaslav Nijinsky and fell in love with him. Fokine's ballets were the obvious choice for repertory, though Diaghilev was quick to suggest amend-ments to some of the them, adjusting titles, designs and music. Since the Paris Opéra was not available, the season was to be held at the less fashion-able Théâtre du Châtelet. Knowing the need for a 'society' audience, and well aware of its tastes, Diaghilev had the whole theatre refurbished: the boxes were hung with velvet, the orchestra pit was expanded, and the foyer decorated with banks of fresh flowers. The first night of the Ballets Russes, 19 May 1909, was a sensation. The repertory was dominated by Fokine: *Le Pavillon d'Armide*, featuring Karsavina and Nijinsky, the new Polovtsian Dances from *Prince Igor*. Later in the season, *Les Sylphides* and *Cléopâtre* were presented, and Anna Pavlova arrived, to be hailed as a great artist.

Pavlova did not stay long with the Ballets Russes. Her taste was conserv-ative and sometimes questionable; she disliked Stravinsky's music for *The Firebird*. After dancing in the early Diaghilev seasons in Paris and London, she set off on her own, tireless world tours. Where the Ballets Russes focused its activities on Europe, with a few visits to the Americas, Pavlova travelled the globe. Her dancing and her personal magnetism brought ballet to the widest possible audience. Theodore Stier calculated that, in sixteen years as her music director, he had travelled 300,000 miles and conducted 3,650 performances. Wherever she went, Pavlova inspired young people to take up dancing: Robert Helpmann in Australia and Frederick Ashton in Peru, both to be leading lights of British ballet, were converted by Pavlova. 'She was a spirit, a flame', remembered Ashton, who saw her when he was thirteen. 'Seeing her at that stage was the end of me.

She injected me with her poison and from the end of that evening I wanted to dance.'[9]

While Pavlova took ballet to every audience she could find, Diaghilev pushed for more daring experiments in dance. New ballets were created, with new scores and new designs, pushing for greater unity of the arts within ballet productions. He also presented some classics of the past, such as *Giselle*, but though the dancers were admired, it was the new productions that caught the western public's attention. Fokine's *Schéhérazade*, with its opulent designs by Bakst and lurid sex-and-violence storyline, had a sensational impact, changing fashion and interior design styles almost overnight.

For all Fokine's insistence on research, many of his most successful works were exotic fantasies. In the absence of surviving information, he made up dances for his Polovtsian warriors; the Oriental luxury of *Schéhérazade* is how the West wanted to see the East. For European audiences, both works added to the general sense that Russian ballet meant passion, scale, bright colour and 'primitive' emotion. Russian dancers had been evoking the exotic for decades; now they themselves were seen as exotic, a quality that gave them extra glamour.

So far, Diaghilev had presented his Russian seasons with borrowed dancers, who appeared during their time off from the Imperial Theatres. In 1911 he was ready to create his own ballet company, a year-round troupe, with Nijinsky as its principal star. Enrico Cecchetti became the new company's ballet master, with Fokine as its choreographer – though not for long. Diaghilev was eager to develop Nijinsky as a choreographer. The notoriously touchy Fokine resented what he saw as Diaghilev's favouritism, and resigned in 1912. In promoting his lover, Diaghilev took a gamble, with remarkable consequences. Nijinsky's four ballets were controversial, and only one has survived. Yet with *L'Après-midi d'un faune* and *The Rite of Spring*, he made conceptual leaps forward, experimenting with the separation of music and dance, developing new movement idioms and risky subject matter. Both ballets also caused huge and exciting scandals, doing the company's image no harm at all.

It did not last. In 1913 the Ballets Russes set sail for South America – without Diaghilev, who hated and feared sea travel. In Buenos Aires, Nijinsky suddenly married Romola de Pulszky, a well-born Hungarian dancer. Diaghilev was devastated, and dismissed him. In the aftermath of this break-up, it became clear that Nijinsky was suffering from mental illness, which overcame him completely by 1919.

Diaghilev took Fokine back for his 1914 season, but he was already looking for a new star, a replacement for Nijinsky both as dancer and choreographer. He found him in Léonide Massine, a Moscow-born and trained dancer with huge dark eyes and a vivid character style. While Diaghilev had leading roles created for Massine, he also educated him to be a choreographer, showing him paintings and sculptures, encouraging him to listen to music, introducing him to possible collaborators. It worked: Massine was to become one of the most admired choreographers of his day. In 1921 he married and – like Nijinsky before him, though less drastically – lost Diaghilev's favour. He would make returns to the Ballets Russes for the rest of the company's existence.

The company made it through the war years, with periods of creativity and of privation. In 1917 the Russian Revolution broke out; it would cut the Ballets Russes off from its roots. Diaghilev never returned home. In 1921, finding himself without a choreographer, he decided to revive *The Sleeping Beauty* in London. Renamed *The Sleeping Princess*, it was staged by Nicolai Sergeyev, a former *régisseur* at the Mariinsky Theatre, who had brought his notebooks of Stepanov notation when he fled the revolution. A galaxy of Mariinsky-trained ballerinas danced the leading roles, while Bakst designed a production of great magnificence. The ballet ran for three months in London, but was so expensive that it lost money and closed with debts. The production had a great impact on a generation of British dancers, choreographers and dancegoers, creating a respect for Petipa and the classical past. This production is also the inspiration for American Ballet Theatre's seventy-fifth anniversary production, staged in 2015 by Alexei Ratmansky.

After the financial failure of *The Sleeping Princess*, Diaghilev returned to France, where he found a new base in Monte Carlo, and to one-act ballets. Aware of the need to keep the interest of his audiences, he launched into a period of frequent experiment, from *Le Train bleu*, with costumes by Coco Chanel, to *Ode*, which used film projections. Some observers, particularly in Britain, saw all this innovation as a brittle attempt to stay ahead of fashion. Yet the 1920s also witnessed the creation of major works, and a renewal of classicism in dance.

Diaghilev's last two choreographers, Bronislava Nijinska and George Balanchine, both came to him from post-revolutionary Russia, which was creating its own radical extensions of classicism. Born in 1891, Nijinsky's sister Bronislava was the only female choreographer to work for the Ballets Russes. After dancing with the company in its early years, she spent the war years in Russia, where she worked closely with avant-garde artists, particularly the constructivist painter Alexandra Exter. Bronislava's choreography in early Soviet Russia seems to have been both modernist and neo-classical: she returned to traditional technique to extend and transform it. Reuniting with Diaghilev in 1921, her first work was to create some new dances for *The Sleeping Princess*. She went on to create *Les Noces*, her fiercely austere image of a Russian peasant wedding, and *Les Biches*, a vividly sophisticated portrait of a new social milieu.

Diaghilev's last new choreographer was to be the most influential of all. Georgi Balanchivadze was born in St Petersburg in 1904, the son of a Georgian composer; his brother Andrei would also become a composer. The young Balanchine was placed in the Imperial Ballet School, but it wasn't until his second year, when he was cast as a cupid in Petipa's *The Sleeping Beauty*, that he fell in love with ballet. He also learned the piano and, from 1919, trained at the Conservatory of Music; Stravinsky would later say that Balanchine could have been a concert pianist – but there are plenty of good pianists, while 'a choreographer such as Balanchine is, after all, the rarest of beings'.[10] He began to choreograph in Russia, forming a group called the Young Ballet, and in 1924 left the country with a small group of dancers that included his first wife, Tamara Geva, and Alexandra Danilova, who would be known as his second. They made their way to the Ballets Russes, where Balanchine followed Nijinska as resident choreographer. His early works included *La Chatte*, for which the ballerina Olga Spessivtseva wore a tutu and cat-ears designed by the sculptor Naum Gabo in mica, a new form of plastic. *Apollo*, which Balanchine created in 1928, was a landmark in twentieth-century ballet, looking forward to the new classicism that the choreographer would forge in America.

Diaghilev died in Venice in 1929. Without him, his company collapsed. For the ballet audience, the death of Diaghilev and then of Pavlova in 1931 left, as Arnold Haskell put it, 'a terrifying silence'.[11] For dancers and choreographers, the most prestigious platform for their art had gone: they needed to find new work.

Throughout the Diaghilev era his dancers had worked outside the company, dancing at the Imperial Theatres, at European society parties and at music halls, organising their own tours and companies. The choreographers he dismissed went on to create ballets elsewhere. The Ballets Russes also inspired rival troupes. In 1920 a wealthy Swedish Francophile, Rolf de Maré, launched the Ballets Suédois, which starred the dancer and choreographer Jean Börlin, a student of Fokine. Like Diaghilev, the Ballets Suédois hired leading artists. Scores written for the company included Darius Milhaud's *La Création du monde* and Arthur Honegger's *Skating Rink*, both with designs by Fernand Léger. The 1924 work *Relâche* was an exercise in Dadaism by Francis Picabia, featuring an *entr'acte* in which the artists Man Ray and Marcel Duchamp played chess and what may have been the first use of film in a ballet. None of these works survived: the dance seems to have been overwhelmed by the other elements.

In 1928, Ida Rubinstein, a charismatic mime who had appeared in several Diaghilev ballets, launched her own company – Les Ballets Ida Rubinstein. Like de Maré, she had a lavish budget, and infuriated Diaghilev by luring away his regular collaborators, including Stravinsky, Bronislava Nijinska and Maurice Ravel. Again, the ballets did not survive, but the scores she commissioned were restaged by other companies.

When Diaghilev died, the obvious course was to put his troupe, or something like it, together again. René Blum, director of the theatre at Monte Carlo, created a company called the Ballet Russe de Monte Carlo, with Balanchine as choreographer. Balanchine also brought into the group three 'baby ballerinas', Irina Baronova, Tatiana Riabouchinska and Tamara Toumanova. All were in their early teens, and all were discovered in the studios of former Mariinsky stars Olga Preobrazhenska and Mathilde Kschessinska, now teaching in Paris after fleeing revolutionary Russia. The émigré teachers were a vital link with the old Imperial tradition, both for the second generation of Ballet Russe companies and for the new national companies that developed in the wake of Diaghilev: Margot Fonteyn would study with Preobrazhenska.

The multiple Ballet Russe companies have a complicated, intertwined history, with dancers and choreographers moving from one to another, and troupes being taken over, relaunched, reworked. They shared a flamboyant performance style, with big personalities and colourful ballets, something their audience hoped for and came to expect. Blum was soon joined by Colonel W. de Basil (born Vasiliy Grigorievich Voskresensky), a former Cossack colonel, dance-lover and showman who began to dominate the new company. Balanchine left, joining the short-lived Les Ballets 1933 before heading for America. At the Blum-de Basil Ballet Russe de Monte Carlo, audiences welcomed the new 'baby ballerinas' and some of the new ballets, which included works by Balanchine and also Massine's latest development, the 'symphonic ballet', danced to concert music. In 1936, Blum left to form his own company, and he was soon joined by Massine. From 1939, de Basil's company was known as the Original Ballet Russe. (The other troupe, taken over by the Russian-American banker Sergei Denham, would soon be billing itself as 'the one and only'.)

In various forms, the Ballet Russe model lasted until the 1960s, helping to develop the global ballet audience. The de Basil company spent the war years in Australia and in North and South America, before folding in the late 1940s. In Australia, the Ballet Russe dancer Edouard Borovansky would found a school in Melbourne and, in 1944, a company, helping to establish a native Australian ballet. The Denham Ballet Russe toured successfully until the late 1950s. By then, the soaring cost of travel meant that touring was hard to sustain. The itinerant, cosmopolitan companies were outpaced and sometimes absorbed by new companies. Although some artists continued to tour with Diaghilev-inspired companies, others had put down roots, developing schools and companies that would grow to national status.

The Dying Swan (Le Cygne)

Choreography: Mikhail Fokine
Music: Camille Saint-Saëns, 'Le Cygne' from *Le Carnaval des animaux*
Designs: Léon Bakst
Premiere: 22 December 1907, Hall of Nobles, St Petersburg
Original cast: Anna Pavlova

Quickly created as a concert number for Anna Pavlova, *The Dying Swan* became one of the most famous dances in the world. The construction is simple: the ballerina circles the stage in a long *pas de bourrée*, fluttering and trembling as the swan tries to take her last flight. At last the swan sinks to the floor and dies. The whole dance lasts a couple of minutes.

When Pavlova asked Fokine to create a solo for a charity performance, they were both fresh from early triumphs: she had achieved the rank of prima ballerina a year earlier, while he had just created *Le Pavillon d'Armide*, his first major success. Fokine had recently learned to play Saint-Saëns' 'Swan' on the mandolin, so the music came quickly to mind – and he immediately realised that the slender, fragile Pavlova would make a perfect swan. The dance was created quickly: 'It was almost an improvisation,' he remembered. 'I danced in front of her, she directly behind me. Then she danced and I walked alongside her, curving her arms and correcting details of poses.'[12]

Simple as it was, *The Dying Swan* reflected Fokine's balletic reforms, his wish to make ballet's academic language more expressive and less showy. 'I make use of the technique of the old dance and the traditional costume,' he told the critic Arnold Haskell:

> and a highly developed technique is necessary, but the purpose of the dance is not to display technique but to create the symbol of the ever-lasting struggle in this life of all that is mortal. It is a dance of the whole body and not of the limbs only; it appeals not merely to the eye but to the emotions and the imagination.[13]

The Dying Swan and *Swan Lake* are unrelated, but together they fixed the public image of the ballerina as swan. Above all, the solo was associated with Pavlova, who asked for her Swan dress as she died. Two days after her death, she was remembered in a performance given by the Camargo Society, which was set up to nurture British ballet. As Philip J. S. Richardson described it, the music of Saint-Saëns was conducted by Constant Lambert, and the curtain went up on an empty stage, 'with the spotlight playing on someone who was not there. The large audience rose to its feet and stood in silence while the tune which will forever be associated with Anna Pavlova was played.'[14]

Other Stagings

The fame of *The Dying Swan* made later ballerinas eager to dance it – though without shaking off Pavlova's image. Robert Helpmann, one of the many dancers who chose a ballet career after seeing Pavlova dance, said that other ballerinas danced *The Dying Swan* – but Pavlova was a swan dying. The solo has also been referenced in alternative performances; it's a famous set piece for the drag company Les Ballets Trockadero de Monte Carlo, whose swan is moulting, while Charles 'Lil Buck' Riley has danced to this music in the Memphis jookin style of hip hop dance, with intricate footwork that includes going on *pointe* in sneakers.

Les Sylphides (Chopiniana)

Choreography: Mikhail Fokine
Music: Frédéric Chopin, Prelude op. 28 no. 7; Nocturne op. 32 no. 2; Valse op. 70 no. 1; Mazurka op. 33 no. 2; Mazurka op. 67 no. 3; Prelude op. 28, no. 7; Valse op. 64, no. 2; Valse op. 18
Designs: Alexandre Benois
Premiere: As *Chopiniana*, 8 March 1908, Mariinsky Theatre, St Petersburg. First performance as *Les Sylphides*, 2 June 1909, Diaghilev's Ballets Russes, Théâtre du Châtelet, Paris
Original cast (1908): Olga Preobrazhenska, Anna Pavlova, Tamara Karsavina, Vaslav Nijinsky

Sylphs dance in a moonlit glade, floating in soft tulle dresses, watched by a dreaming poet. Fokine's *Les Sylphides* looks back to the Romantic era, but it was also a groundbreaking work: a ballet that set a mood rather than telling a story.

The first version of *Les Sylphides* was created in 1907 for a charity perform-ance, under the name *Chopiniana*. The dancers performed different scenes to music by Chopin, mostly in national dress – a polonaise in Polish costume, a tarantella, a scene in which Chopin was inspired by a muse figure. The exception was the Waltz in C sharp minor, danced by Mikhail Obukhov with Anna Pavlova, who wore a Romantic tutu which evoked the era of Marie Taglioni. The next year, this number became the basis of a revised *Chopin-iana*, a series of Chopin dances for women in 'sylphide' dresses and a single male soloist. It was this version, renamed *Les Sylphides*, that Diaghilev pres-ented in his first Paris season. In Russia, the ballet is still known as *Chopin-iana*, and is often danced with the Polonaise op. 40 no. 1 as an overture.

Synopsis

The curtain rises on a tableau of sylphs, grouped symmetrically around the figure of a male poet. The setting is a forest, lit by moonlight, with a ruined monastery seen through the trees. The first dance, a nocturne, is an ensemble; the sylphs softly group and regroup, forming straight or winding lines, with brief sequences for the poet, the ballerina and two female solo-ists. A series of variations follows: an airy waltz for the first soloist, a mazurka with soaring jumps for the ballerina, another mazurka for the poet, and the Prelude, danced with 'listening' gestures, for the last female soloist. The *corps de ballet* creates a changing frame for the soloists. Onstage throughout, the *corps* moves to new patterns, from formal lines to much softer curving chains, linked in a range of gentle poses. Neighbouring sylphs hold hands, sometimes across the body or overhead, creating repeated arching lines; they sink to one knee in clouds of tulle.

The ballerina and the poet dance another waltz, in which she floats between his hands (at one point, he draws her back with a caressing gesture to the sylphide wings on her costume). The ballet ends with an ensemble waltz. The dancers return to the opening pose, but as the curtain falls, two groups of the *corps de ballet* move forward, opening out the scene.

With its Taglioni setting and costumes, *Les Sylphides* looks nostalgic, but this was a ballet that pushed for change, part of Fokine's fight against what he saw as the empty virtuosity and spectacle of the Imperial Theatre. *Les Sylphides* echoes Taglioni, and Ivanov's lakeside scenes for *Swan Lake*, but it also draws on the dancing of Isadora Duncan, with her 'natural' movement and use of music written for the concert hall: at her 1904 debut in St Petersburg, she had danced to at least two of the Chopin pieces that Fokine would use in *Les Sylphides*. The steps of *Les Sylphides* are still those of classical ballet, with *pointe*work and jumps, but it avoids all flashiness in favour of musicality and purity of style. Fokine wrote of that first waltz:

> The choreography different from all other pas de deux in its total absence of spectacular feats. There was not a single entrechat, turn in the air, or pirouette . . . One might surmise that the execution of this number was simple and easy. In reality, however, tricks which enthuse the public, and especially the balletomanes, are much more easily performed by the ballerina than this waltz, which looks like such a simple dance . . . Right then I conceived the idea of creating a ballet . . . of maidens floating around a solitary youth infatuated with beauty.[15]

Vision scenes were a familiar part of nineteenth-century ballet, whose heroes regularly dream elaborate *corps de ballet* numbers. But *Les Sylphides* is self-contained, its hero part of the ballet's world, not a link to some outside reality. This was essentially a new genre: *Les Sylphides* is about its music, about its mood, about dancing. The dancers are listed in the programme by their own names; they have no character but movement. Plotless ballet, the pure dance works of Balanchine and others, starts here. The ballet was an influence on Balanchine in other ways: 'Fokine invented curved lines in ballet,' he told the interviewer Solomon Volkov. Where Petipa had 'everything figured out in straight lines: the soloists in front, the *corps de ballet* in back', Fokine 'invented the ensemble in ballet. Fokine took a small ensemble and made up interesting, strange things for it.'[16]

Les Sylphides was one of the most popular ballets in the Diaghilev repertory, danced throughout the company's history and quickly acquired by other troupes. In 2011 rare film footage of Diaghilev's Ballets Russes was discovered in the British Pathé collection by Susan Eastwood and Jane Pritchard. It shows a performance of *Les Sylphides* at the 'Fête de Narcisses' in Montreux, Switzerland, in June 1928.

Polovtsian Dances from *Prince Igor*

Choreography: Mikhail Fokine
Music: Alexander Borodin
Designs: Nicholas Roerich
Premiere: 18 May 1909, Diaghilev's Ballets Russes, Théâtre du Châtelet, Paris
Original cast: *Polovtsian girl* Sophia Fedorova; *Polovtsian woman* Helen Smirnova; *Polovtsian chief* Adolph Bolm

In *Les Sylphides*, Fokine reimagined ballet's ethereal, feminine side; with the Polovtsian Dances, he created a smashing celebration of virile masculinity. On the first night of the Ballets Russes' first Paris season, *Prince Igor* brought the house down. It went on to become the most performed ballet of the entire Diaghilev era.

For that first season, Diaghilev relied on existing works, most of them by Fokine. He decided to include a scene from Borodin's opera *Prince Igor* – which had been a huge hit for Chaliapin in Diaghilev's earlier series of Russian concerts – and asked Fokine to create new dances. In later seasons, it was performed without singers.

Synopsis

The scene is a warrior camp at dawn. Warriors wake and greet each other. A group of women dance with veils to Borodin's lamenting chant. At the thundering change in the music, the chief leaps forward in an exultant solo full of leaps and spins. His men follow, brandishing their bows as if firing arrows. Fokine brings his groups of male and female dancers on in swift alternation, contrasting softer with more explosive dancing, building to a speedy finale.

Several of the most important qualities of the early Ballets Russes – the reassertion of male dancing, Fokine's reforms, a glamorous 'exotic' Russianness – were united in *Prince Igor*. The choreographer considered it one of his most important works, demonstrating the power of group dances. Fokine had been reluctant to take the last-minute commission. He preferred to start by researching ethnographical material for his ballets, but he knew nothing about the Polovtsi, Borodin's ancient and now extinct Tatar tribe. At last, setting to work, he decided that 'if the Polovtsi did not actually dance this way to the music of Borodin, that is exactly how they should have danced'.[17] In Fokine's ballet they danced with fierce abandon. During performances, according to dance historian Cyril Beaumont, bows were often smashed to pieces as the male dancers pounded them on the floor.

Schéhérazade

Choreography: Mikhail Fokine
Music: Nikolai Rimsky-Korsakov (parts I, II and IV of his symphonic poem *Schéhérazade*)
Libretto: Léon Bakst, Alexandre Benois, Mikhail Fokine
Designs: Léon Bakst

Premiere: 4 June 1910, Diaghilev's Ballets Russes, Paris Opéra
Original cast: *Zobeide* Ida Rubinstein; *Golden Slave* Vaslav Nijinsky;
Chief Eunuch Enrico Cecchetti; *Shah* Alexis Bulgakov

When the curtain went up on *Schéhérazade* in 1910, it revealed a staggering richness of colour. Bakst's design for a harem was draped in swags of deep green and blue, with dashes of coral and rose pink, piled high with cushions and lit with many lamps. The Shah and his brother wore royal blue and crimson, the odalisques green and pink, in soft fabrics that slid and billowed around their bodies. It's a spectacular show of excess, framing an Orientalist fantasy of sex and violence.

Although the ballet is named for the heroine of the *One Thousand and One Nights*, she does not appear. Fokine's ballet tells the prologue to that story, in which the Shah acquires his violent distrust of women. The choice of Rimsky-Korsakov's music was controversial, both because one movement was cut and because a different story was imposed on a symphonic work: the composer had different episodes from the *One Thousand and One Nights* in mind. In his letters, Rimsky-Korsakov had expressed shock at Isadora Duncan's appropriation of concert music, saying that he would not want her to dance his own *Schéhérazade*.

Synopsis

The Shah sits in his harem, with his favourite wife, Zobeide, his brother and his other wives. His brother has hinted that the Shah's wives have been unfaithful, so he decides to test them, leaving as if to go hunting.

As soon as the Shah is gone, the women bribe the Chief Eunuch to open the locked doors to the male slaves' quarters. Two doors are opened, and the men rush in to embrace the women. Zobeide insists that the third door should be open, despite the Chief Eunuch's reluctance. He opens the door and lets in the Golden Slave, who leads an orgiastic dance with Zobeide.

Suddenly the Shah returns, with his brother and his guards. The orgy becomes a massacre, with the Shah himself killing the Golden Slave. Zobeide confronts the Shah, who is tempted to pardon her, but she snatches a dagger and kills herself.

Harem fantasies were a staple of nineteenth-century painting and story-telling, and had already established themselves in ballet with works such as *Le Corsaire*. The Ballets Russes *Schéhérazade* tapped into an established appetite, given extra punch by the lavishness of the staging, the charisma of the leading performers, and Fokine's gift for pacing. The Ballets Russes ballerina Lydia Sokolova remembered his 'wonderful feeling of working things up to an orgy . . . a lot of excitement that gradually built. It didn't just go straight into the finales, the thing built and built and built, and, of course, that is what held the public so.'[18]

The public were certainly held, swooning over the sexual presence of Nijinsky's Golden Slave and entranced by the designs. Inspired by Bakst's greens and blues, the jeweller Cartier set emeralds and sapphires together for the first time since the Mughal emperors. The ballet had an immediate influence on dress fashions and a lasting impact on interior design. By the 1920s, though audiences still clamoured for it, Diaghilev thought the ballet needed refreshing: he hoped that Henri Matisse would redesign it, but this project was never completed.

A century on, *Schéhérazade*'s seductions and death scenes are camp rather than daring. The appealing score and still-effective promise of *Arabian Nights* fantasy keep it in the repertory. When the Kirov (now Mariinsky) Ballet began to stage Diaghilev works in the 1990s, *Schéhérazade* was one of the most popular.

The Firebird (L'Oiseau de feu)

Choreography and libretto: Mikhail Fokine
Music: Igor Stravinsky
Designs: Alexander Golovin, with additional costumes by Léon Bakst
Premiere: 25 June 1910, Diaghilev's Ballets Russes, Paris Opéra, Paris
Original cast: *Firebird* Tamara Karsavina; *Ivan Tsarevich* Mikhail Fokine;
The Beautiful Tsarevna Vera Fokina; *Koschei* Alexis Bulgakov

The Firebird was the first completely new ballet created for Diaghilev's Paris seasons: new choreography, a story created from Russian folklore and new music by the twenty-eight-year-old Igor Stravinsky, making his Western European debut. Diaghilev had originally commissioned a score from Anatoly Liadov, writing, 'I want a ballet and a *Russian* one; there has never been such a ballet before. . . .'[19] Liadov proved a slow worker – when asked how work was going, he is said to have replied that he had bought music paper – so the job went to the young Stravinsky. This early work shows Stravinsky still under the influence of his teacher, Rimsky-Korsakov, though it was still too 'modern' for Anna Pavlova, for whom the title role was originally planned.

The plot was worked out by Fokine, Alexander Golovine and others in the Diaghilev circle. Fokine worked closely with Stravinsky on the score, but not in the old Petipa fashion of strict minutage given to the composer. In his memoirs, Fokine describes collaborative sessions in which he acted out the story for Stravinsky. The resulting ballet has a brilliant ballerina role for the imperious Firebird, elements of Russian folk dance for the other characters, and a thrilling final coronation scene, suggested by Stravinsky in place of the usual celebratory dances.

In Golovin's original designs, Fokine remembered, the magic garden was like 'a Persian carpet interwoven with the most fantastic vegetation'.[20] Bakst designed the costumes for Ivan Tsarevich and for the Firebird, whose elaborate costume included tunic, undertrousers, trousers, feathers, ropes of pearls and long plaits. Golovin's designs were destroyed by damp, and in 1926 the ballet was redesigned by Natalia Gontcharova. She created a marvellous vista of onion domes for the final coronation scene, a fairy-tale Russian city. The Firebird was later dressed in a more traditional tutu. As an acknowledged Diaghilev classic, *The Firebird* joined the repertory of the later Ballet Russe companies. In 1954, The Royal Ballet in London staged an important revival, staged by Diaghilev *répétiteurs* Serge Grigoriev and Lubov Tchernicheva, with coaching from Tamara Karsavina. It was filmed in 1959, with Margot Fonteyn as a fierce, sensual Firebird.

Synopsis

Scene 1. A mysterious garden, with a tree of golden fruit in the centre of the stage. The Firebird darts and leaps across the garden and is gone. Ivan Tsarevitch climbs over the garden wall – he is out hunting. The Firebird reappears, and plucks an apple from the tree. Ivan Tsarevich catches her. She struggles to free herself, without success. At last she offers him one of her feathers as a ransom: if he is in trouble, he must wave the feather, and she will come to his aid. He accepts, and lets her fly away.

A group of young women enter the garden: the Beautiful Tsarevna and her eleven attendants. They dance and play with golden apples, which the Beautiful Tsarevna shakes down from the tree. Ivan steps forward and bows to the Beautiful Tsarevna. They are strongly attracted to each other, but a sudden noise disturbs them. The women leave, warning Ivan that he is in danger: the garden belongs to the magician Kashchei. Ivan runs to the gates at the side of the stage and shakes them. They fly open, and hordes of monsters rush out, seizing Ivan as he tries to flee. More monsters, guards, captives and Kashchei's wives rush into the garden, followed by

Kashchei himself and the Beautiful Tsarevna and her attendants. He attempts to cast a spell on Ivan, who remembers the feather and summons the Firebird.

The Firebird leads Kashchei's subjects in a wild dance. When they collapse in exhaustion, she casts a spell of sleep, leaving just Kashchei and Ivan awake. She tells Ivan to fetch Kashchei's soul, which is kept in a large egg. Ivan finds and smashes the egg, and darkness falls.

Scene 2. Kashchei is vanquished, and his captives have been freed. Against a backdrop of a city of spires and domes, Ivan and his Beautiful Tsarevna are crowned.

The Firebird shows the Ballets Russes' revolution in staging, with music, design and dance closely linked. It also shows Fokine's reforms in action. Only the Firebird dances on *pointe*, setting her apart from the other characters as a supernatural creature. In their low-heeled slippers, the Beautiful Tsarevna and her companions are gentler, while the monsters of Kashchei's kingdom have weighted character dances.

When Karsavina coached Fonteyn, she remembered what Fokine had told her: 'Forget your graces. The Firebird is powerful, hard to manage, rebellious. Here is no human emotion.'[21] Karsavina added that the Firebird 'is proud, arrogant. She gives the feather only to buy her freedom, not to help the Prince.' Fonteyn later passed on Karsavina's advice to the ballerina Monica Mason:

> On the very first entrance in *Firebird*, she said, 'This is your territory, your domain, and you don't fly over it, you soar ... Even a sparrow notices if another sparrow comes to perch on his tree, his branch. So imagine what it must be like for the Firebird to have a man invade her territory and actually *capture* her.'[22]

At the same time, there are erotic elements in the Firebird's *pas de deux* with Ivan tsarevich, as both struggle for dominance, their bodies braced together.

The 'Danse infernale', in which Kashchei's creatures are forced to dance, is another example of how Fokine's choreography 'built and built and built', with driving steps fitted relentlessly to Stravinsky's beats. There is no dancing in the final scene of Fokine's version: the dancers process into a coronation tableau, as Stravinsky's music builds from a simple folk tune to a thrilling, clangorous finale.

Other Stagings

George Balanchine staged several versions of *The Firebird*, using one of Stravinsky's suites rather than the complete score. Balanchine's 1949 production used designs by Marc Chagall, originally created for a Ballet Theatre production in 1945, and simplified the story. It was the newly founded New York City Ballet's first box office hit, and helped to establish Maria Tallchief as the first American-born, American-trained ballerina, dancing a commanding Firebird with speedy, off-balance steps. In 1970 the ballet was revised by Balanchine and Jerome Robbins (who choreographed the material for Kashchei and his subjects), with Gelsey Kirkland as a lighter, sparkling Firebird. The ballet was revised again in 1980 for the statuesque Karin von Aroldingen in a gown with a long train. In 1985, New York City Ballet reverted to the Tallchief version of the choreography for the title character, while keeping the Robbins dances.

In Maurice Béjart's politicised version of *The Firebird*, created in 1970, a male Firebird represents the spirit of revolution. The *corps de ballet* consists of partisan figures in dungarees, blue tunics and trousers, suggesting the uniform of Chinese communists. Becoming their leader, the Firebird wears a red leotard. He dies in battle, but is reborn in triumph, like a phoenix rising from the ashes. This version was created for the Paris Opéra Ballet and was later performed by Béjart's own Ballet du XXᵉ Siècle and the Alvin Ailey American Dance Theater.

In 2012, Alexei Ratmansky created a new version for American Ballet Theatre, with Natalia Osipova as the Firebird. Ivan Tsarevich's journey became psychological, starting with a prologue in which he dances his frustrations. The Firebird is one of a flock (an idea Ratmansky also used in his version of *The Little Humpbacked Horse*), while the maidens are spiky young women with green hair, although, disappointingly, they all turn conventionally blonde for the finale. Kashchei, the evil sorcerer who controls the maidens, becomes a dancing role. This production was a co-commission with Dutch National Ballet.

Le Spectre de la rose

Choreography: Mikhail Fokine
Music: Carl Maria von Weber, 'L'Invitation à la valse', orchestrated by Hector Berlioz
Libretto: Jean-Louis Vaudoyer, after a poem by Théophile Gautier
Designs: Léon Bakst

Premiere: 19 April 1911, Diaghilev's Ballets Russes, Théâtre de Monte Carlo, Monte Carlo

Original cast: *the Rose* Vaslav Nijinsky; *the Girl* Tamara Karsavina

Je suis le spectre d'une rose
  Que tu portais hier au bal.
  (I am the ghost of a rose
  That you wore at the ball last night.)

Théophile Gautier, Le Spectre de la rose

Le Spectre de la rose was inspired by poets and roses. Reviewing the Ballets Russes work *Carnaval*, in which the character Chiarina throws a rose to her admirer, the poet Jean-Louis Vaudoyer thought of Gautier's 'Le Spectre de la rose', connected the poem to Weber's 'L'Invitation à la valse', and suggested to Bakst that it might make a ballet. Fokine created it quickly, in just two or three rehearsals. Built around Nijinsky's soaring leap and Karsavina's delicate dramatic presence, the ballet's success took even Diaghilev by surprise.

Synopsis

A young woman's bedroom of the 1830s, with high windows, an armchair and a table, decorated in Biedermeier style. To the quiet orchestral opening, a young girl comes home from a ball, carrying a rose. She takes off her cloak and sinks into the chair, falling asleep as the rose slips from her hand.

As the music quickens, the spirit of the Rose soars through the open window, dancing about the room like a petal blown on the breeze. He touches the Girl's hand, and she dances with him, still apparently asleep. As the waltz melody fades, she sinks back into the chair, and the Rose leaps out of the window. She wakes, picks up the rose and presses it to her heart.

Le Spectre de la rose is an intimate ballet. After the riotous colours of his Orientalist ballets, Bakst designed what might have been the set for a play, small scale and romantic. And into this small world soared Nijinsky, with a jump that awed a generation of balletgoers. 'There was no flurry, no strained features, no thud as the feet came to the ground; it was just as though a rose-petal had been caught up by a night breeze . . .'[23] remembered Cyril Beaumont. Bakst's bedroom design included a birdcage hung in the window, which had to be removed to allow for the height of Nijinsky's jump.

When he leapt, Nijinsky seemed to hover in the air, while his whole personality seemed both perfumed and androgynous. 'People who never knew Nijinsky but revered his legend asked me what was the height of his jump, as if that was the most important,' remembered Karsavina. 'But what he really did was the way that he used it. In *Le Spectre de la rose* you couldn't say that he jumped, he just floated over the stage, he was incorporeal. He had a wonderful quality of feline grace . . .'[24] Fokine's choreography used traditional classical steps, but, according to Bronislava Nijinska, it was Nijinsky who transformed them. He adjusted the traditional *ports de bras* into art nouveau lines, curling his arms around his face with soft wrists and fingers.

His costume was a deep pink bodystocking, sewn with silk petals in pinks, reds and purples that merged into each other. That year, 1911, Nijinsky had broken with the Imperial Theatres in a row over his costume for *Giselle*. Benois had designed a short tunic, which Nijinsky wore without the modesty trunks that were required by the Imperial Theatres. This outfit had caused a scandal; Nijinsky had resigned rather than apologise.

Like *The Dying Swan* for Pavlova, *Le Spectre de la rose* remains identified with Nijinsky, but its legendary quality has made later dancers keen to dance it.

Other Stagings

In 1993, Angelin Preljocaj created a new version of *Le Spectre de la rose* for his own Ballet Preljocaj, as part of a Ballets Russes tribute evening. The Weber music was interrupted by a contemporary soundscape, while the stage was divided into two halves: on the left, two men in bullfighter costumes dance with women in soft skirts, while on the right, the Rose and the Girl struggle with each other, slapping their chests together.

Petrushka

Choreography: Mikhail Fokine
Music: Igor Stravinsky
Libretto: Alexandre Benois and Igor Stravinsky
Designs: Alexandre Benois
Premiere: 13 June 1911, Diaghilev's Ballets Russes, Théâtre du Châtelet, Paris
Original cast: *Petrushka* Vaslav Nijinsky; *Ballerina doll* Tamara Karsavina; *Moor* Alexander Orlov; *Charlatan* Enrico Cecchetti

In the autumn of 1910, Stravinsky began work on a piano concerto, a deliberately discordant work that he began to associate with Petrushka, the Russian fairground puppet – a figure like the English Mr Punch. When Diaghilev heard the piece, alongside a Russian dance Stravinsky was composing, he suggested putting them together in a new ballet about the Russian carnival.

Alexandre Benois, who had loved fairground performances as a child, was chosen to design the ballet and create the libretto. 'I was still more tempted by the idea of depicting the Butter Week Fair ... the dear *balagani* [fairground booths] which were the delight of my childhood ...'. The original Petrushka was an active and often brutal character; Benois made him a tragic, introspective figure, stuck in a triangle with the beautiful but dim-witted Ballerina doll and the Moor, 'the embodiment of everything senselessly attractive, powerfully masculine and undeservedly triumphant'.[25]

Stravinsky's music was a bold step forward from *The Firebird*: it was so discordant that the orchestral players burst out laughing when they saw it. The conductor Pierre Monteux had to persuade them that it wasn't a joke, while Fokine struggled to comprehend some of the music too. The ballet also took a risk in casting Nijinsky – the soaring virtuoso of *Le Spectre de la rose*, the sensuous Golden Slave of *Schéhérazade* – in a character role with no dance steps, his hands muffled with mittens. 'I was surprised at the courage Vaslav showed, after all his *jeune premier* success, in appearing as a horrible half-doll, half-human grotesque,' wrote Benois. Audiences and critics were entranced by their hero's latest metamorphosis: *Petrushka* was one of the most acclaimed works of the Ballets Russes.

Synopsis

Scene 1. Admiralty Square, St Petersburg, 1830. The Butter Week Fair is in progress, with showmen, dancers, booths and fairground attractions drawing crowds of people. Two rival street-dancers compete for the crowd's attention. A drum roll quietens the crowd, and the Charlatan pokes his head through the curtains of the central booth. He draws the curtains to reveal three puppets, propped up on stands: a pretty Ballerina doll, the sad-faced traditional clown Petrushka, and the foolish, swaggering Moor. The Charlatan brings them to life: they spring out of the booth to dance across the square. The puppets act out a short drama: Petrushka declares his love for the Ballerina, but is defeated by the Moor.

Scene 2. Petrushka's cell. Petrushka laments his fate, and his fear and resentment of the Charlatan, whose portrait is painted on the wall. The Ballerina is pushed into his cell. Petrushka's hysterical greeting frightens her, and she runs away. Beating the wall, Petrushka dives halfway through it.

Scene 3. The Moor's cell. This is decorated with bright patterns of leaves. The Moor plays with a coconut, trying to break it open with his scimitar and, when he fails, worshipping it instead. The Ballerina enters playing a trumpet. They dance together, but are interrupted by Petrushka. The Moor attacks him and kicks him out.

Scene 4. The fair. As evening falls, the fair is at its height. Coachmen perform a stamping dance. Nursemaids dance with gliding steps. Carnival figures move through the crowd as snow begins to fall. Suddenly Petrushka bursts out of the Charlatan's booth, followed by the Moor and the Ballerina. The Moor kills Petrushka, who falls dead in the snow. Horrified, the crowd turns on the Charlatan, who picks up the body: it is only a puppet. The crowd disperse, and the Charlatan heads back to his booth, dragging the puppet. Then he hears a cry overhead: the ghost of Petrushka appears above the booth, screaming his defiance of the Charlatan. Terrified, the Charlatan flees. Petrushka's ghost collapses as the ballet ends.

Petrushka was hailed as a supreme work of the Ballets Russes, exemplifying the company's way of uniting music, dance and design into a single work. Nijinsky, celebrated for his extraordinary jump, danced no virtuoso steps in this ballet, which instead used his gift for creating an expressive physicality for each of his roles. Petrushka was as much his signature role as the Rose in *Le Spectre de la rose*; after Nijinsky's tragic illness, and his description of himself as the 'clown of God', the clown puppet has since become identified with him. Yet *Petrushka* was successfully revived, by Diaghilev and by other Ballet Russe companies, with other dancers taking the title role.

Cyril Beaumont remembered the individuality of the crowd scenes. The 'people jostle and push each other, struggle to obtain the best view of the peep-show, compare opinions of the merits of the rival street-dancers, banter the proprietors of the stalls – one may see this ballet a score of times and yet find some new by-play which . . . had hitherto passed unnoticed.'[26] Creating these scenes, Fokine could draw on his first cast's shared understanding and nostalgia for the Russia of their childhoods. The music, Karsavina remembered, 'gave me a terrific nostalgia after I left Russia, particularly in the last act with that dance with the Coachmen, which they used to do in real life to keep warm as they waited, and the snow falling. All that reminded me of my country. . . .'[27]

With its focus on mime and historical understanding, *Petrushka* has proved much harder to revive than more dance-based works such as *The Firebird* or *Les Noces*. 'Like *Schéhérazade*, *Petrushka* should have been pickled for posterity in its splendid music, but has failed to retain its vitality on stage,' complained the critic Richard Buckle in 1979. Petrushka, the star role, is often played by star dancers, though it requires expressive mimed movement rather than technical strength. Fokine mocked the old-style virtuosity in *Petrushka*: as one of the street-dancers, Nijinska deliberately parodied the Mariinsky's Mathilde Kschessinska.

The character of the Moor was also drawn from the old Petrushka plays. In recent years, some companies have painted the dancer playing the Moor blue rather than black, to reduce the role's blackface stereotypes. Oakland Ballet pioneered this option in 1991, soon followed by San Francisco Ballet.

L'Après-midi d'un faune

Choreography: Vaslav Nijinsky
Music: Claude Debussy, *Prélude à l'après-midi d'un faune*
Designs: Léon Bakst
Premiere: 29 May 1912, Diaghilev's Ballets Russes, Théâtre du Châtelet, Paris
Original cast: *Faun* Vaslav Nijinsky; *Nymph* Lydia Nelidova

L'Après-midi d'un faune was Nijinsky's first ballet, a breakthrough in choreographic form, and the biggest scandal that the Ballets Russes had yet seen. Encouraged by Diaghilev, and after planning sessions with the impresario and Léon Bakst, Nijinsky started work in 1910. By the time he began developing the choreography with his sister Bronislava Nijinska, the music, the theme and the ancient Greek setting had all been chosen. Debussy's score, with its shimmering afternoon heat, had been written in 1894, in response to Stéphane Mallarmé's symbolist poem about a faun's encounter with nymphs. From the first, according to Nijinska, 'any sweetly sentimental line in the form or in the movement will be excluded'.[28] And though Nijinsky used Debussy's music, his ballet was not set to it: the dancers move across the music, rather than to its beats, with angular poses to fluid musical lines.

All this was radical, but what caused outrage was the faun's final masturbatory gesture. Audience reaction was mixed; the editor of *Le Figaro* was outraged, writing: 'We are shown a lecherous faun, whose movements are filthy and bestial in their eroticism, and whose gestures are as crude as they are indecent.'[29] The sculptor Auguste Rodin and the painter Odilon Redon wrote in support of Nijinsky; the police attended the second performance to see whether Nijinsky's gestures really were obscene, and approved the ballet for further performances. *Le Figaro* shifted its ground to attack Rodin, and all of Paris rushed to see the outrageous new ballet.

Synopsis

A faun basks on a rock in the heat of the day, playing a flute and then eating grapes. A group of nymphs arrive to bathe in a pool. The leading nymph takes off three layers of veils. When the faun approaches the nymphs, they are frightened and run away. One returns to dance with the faun, then takes fright and runs, leaving her scarf behind. The faun takes the scarf and returns to his rock, where he lowers himself onto it with a thrust of his pelvis.

Bakst designed a sun-baked landscape of green and brown. As the faun, Nijinsky wore flesh-coloured tights with brown patches, with pointed ears and a metallic gold wig, while the nymphs wore layered draperies with patterns taken from Greek vases. The choreography recreates the two-dimensional effect of vase paintings: the dancers move in profile, their torsos angled to face the audience, with head and feet turned to the side. The faun's one jump is stiff-legged and stylised, crossing the 'stream' that the nymphs have come to bathe in. All the steps were on a single plane, a line parallel to the footlights, each step clearly articulated, the heel put down first. Nijinsky is said to have taken more than a hundred rehearsals to get the effect exactly right.

The dancers' bodies become a formal design; no acting was wanted. The dancer, teacher and director Marie Rambert remembered Nijinsky raging when a new dancer acted frightened as she walked away from the nymph: 'he said that the movement he gave her was all that was required of her, he was not interested in her personal feelings. And how right Nijinsky was for his particular choreography! It acquired an impersonal, remote character, just like the paintings on Greek vases . . . .'[30]

With its stark, impersonal steps and separation of music and dance, *L'Après-midi d'un faune* is a radical and mesmerising work, raising questions that would preoccupy twentieth-century choreographers decades later. It is the only Nijinsky ballet to have remained in regular repertory: the staging by Rambert's own company is particularly satisfying, even though it lacks the full effect of Bakst's rich designs.

Other Stagings

The most famous reworking of *L'Après-midi d'un faune* is Jerome Robbins'
1953 *Afternoon of a Faun*, discussed in Chapter 5. In 2009, Sidi Larbi
Cherkaoui's *Faun* used the Debussy score, with additional music by Nitin
Sawhney, for a sensuous duet in a forest setting.

The Rite of Spring (Le Sacre du printemps)

Choreography: Vaslav Nijinsky
Music: Igor Stravinsky
Libretto: Igor Stravinsky and Nicholas Roerich
Premiere: 29 May 1913, Diaghilev's Ballets Russes, Théâtre des Champs-
Elysées, Paris
Original cast: *Chosen Maiden* Marie Piltz

The Rite of Spring prompted the most famous riot in theatrical history.
Although Nijinsky's revolutionary choreography is lost, the story of that
first night, and Stravinsky's elemental score, have made this production
legendary.

The idea for *The Rite of Spring* came from Stravinsky, as he was
finishing *The Firebird*. 'I had dreamed a scene of a pagan ritual in which
a chosen sacrificial virgin danced herself to death,'[31] he wrote. He
developed the libretto with the artist Nicholas Roerich, the designer
of Fokine's Polovtsian Dances. Roerich had researched early Russian
life and myths, even taking part in archaeological expeditions. Although
Stravinsky denied it, he too drew on folk material, but subsumed and
transformed it to create the score's ferocious rhythms and harsh sound
world.

Stravinsky worried that Fokine, whom he considered 'an exhausted
artist', would create the choreography. 'New forms must be created,' he
insisted, 'and the evil, the gifted, the greedy Fokine has not even dreamed of
them.'[32] In the event, *The Rite of Spring* was entrusted to Nijinsky. Diaghilev
also hired Miriam Ramberg (later Marie Rambert), who was trained in
Dalcroze Eurhythmics, a method of analysing music through movement. It
was Rambert's job to help Nijinsky decipher the fiendishly complex score.
Stravinsky had ruled out all mime, but Nijinsky went further in search of
'new forms': there was no naturalistic movement, no balletic grace. Dressed
in heavy woollen leggings and shifts, the dancers stood with toes turned in,
tilted heads leaning on fists.

At the first night, the Parisian audience was a mix of society fashionables and fans of the avant-garde, students and artists to whom Diaghilev had given free tickets. When the performance began, they reacted to each other, as well as to the music and the production. 'The theatre seemed to be shaken by an earthquake,' remembered the artist Valentine Gross. 'It seemed to shudder. People shouted insults, howled and whistled, drowning the music. There was slapping and even punching. . . .'[33] In the wings, Nijinsky stood on a chair, shouting numbers to the dancers. Afterwards, Stravinsky remembered, 'we were excited, angry, disgusted, and . . . happy . . . Diaghilev's only comment was: "Exactly what I wanted."'[34] The publicity value of the riot was incalculable; Stravinsky wondered if Diaghilev had had this in mind from the first time he had heard the score.

Synopsis

Scene 1. The adoration of the earth. A tribe gathers to celebrate the coming spring. Directed by an aged seer, they dance in worship of the earth. (Stravinsky's own names for these movements are 'Augurs of Spring', 'Ritual of Abduction', 'Spring Rounds', 'Ritual of the Rival Tribes', 'Procession of the Sage: The Sage' and 'Dance of the Earth'.)

Scene 2. The sacrifice. One of the tribe's young women is chosen as the sacrifice, in a series of dances: 'Mystic Circles of the Young Girls', 'Glorification of the Chosen One', 'Evocation of the Ancestors', 'Ritual Action of the Ancestors'. In the final movement, the 'Sacrificial Dance', the chosen maiden dances herself to death.

Other Stagings

Nijinsky's production had just eight performances, five in Paris and three in London. That summer, he married and broke with Diaghilev. Since then, there have been literally hundreds of stagings of *The Rite of Spring*. Massine re-choreographed it for Diaghilev in 1920. In 1940, Walt Disney's animated film *Fantasia* took the ballet's 'primitive' theme in a new direction, using it to show the development of life on Earth, including a highly effective battle between two dinosaurs.

In 1959, Maurice Béjart reworked *The Rite of Spring* as an orgasmic fertility rite. Groups of men and women dance separately: instead of a sacrifice, the ballet ends with sex, with the chosen couple brought together by the massed ranks of the *corps de ballet*. Kenneth MacMillan's version, created for The Royal Ballet in 1962, featured striking designs by the Australian painter Sidney Nolan: shimmering burnt landscapes, the dancers in orange body tights marked with hand prints. Glen Tetley's staging was created for the Munich State Ballet in 1974 and later revived by the Stuttgart Ballet and American Ballet Theatre. His chosen victim is a young man, killed as a scapegoat but reborn with the spring.

In 1975, Pina Bausch created an unforgettably brutal version of the score for her own company. The stage is covered in a layer of real earth; as the dancers drive themselves through Bausch's churning, machine-like rhythms, they become increasingly mud-spattered and desperate. This superb staging has also been danced by the Paris Opéra Ballet.

From the 1970s, the dance historians Millicent Hodson and Kenneth Archer worked on *The Rite of Spring*, attempting to recover the lost Nijinsky original through sketches, photographs, reviews and notes made on the musical score. They staged the result for the Joffrey Ballet in 1987. Controversially, this version is often credited as 'choreography by Nijinsky', despite the very large element of guesswork involved. It has been danced by many more companies, including the Mariinsky Ballet and Birmingham Royal Ballet.

Parade

Choreography: Léonide Massine
Music: Erik Satie
Libretto: Jean Cocteau
Designs: Pablo Picasso
Premiere: 18 May 1917, Théâtre du Châtelet, Paris
Original cast: *Chinese Conjurer* Léonide Massine; *Acrobats* Lydia Lopokova, Nicholas Zverev; *The Little American Girl* Maria Chabelska

Parade brought together a group of avant-garde artists. The idea came from the poet and artist Jean Cocteau, who encouraged Satie and Picasso to work with the Ballets Russes for the first time. Subtitled 'A Realistic Ballet', *Parade* prompted the poet Guillaume Apollinaire, who wrote its programme note, to use the word 'surrealism' for the first time in print. The ballet has a circus theme, something Picasso was already fond of painting. His drop-curtain, painted in a naïve style, shows a winged Pegasus and foal with an acrobat, clowns and other performers; once the curtain went up, the ballet included the first Cubist works created for the theatre. Satie's score features the sound of sirens and typewriters.

Synopsis

In French theatre, a 'parade' is a trailer, a promise of coming attractions. The ballet shows the show advertising the show: we never get to the performance itself. A French and an American manager appear. Their costumes are massive Cubist structures, eleven feet high: a skyscraper, flags and a megaphone for the American, with a pipe, houses and trees for the Frenchman. They introduce variety acts: a Chinese conjurer, who plays tricks with an egg, and a 'little American girl', a child impersonator whose act involves imitating Charlie Chaplin and miming the sinking of the *Titanic*. A pantomime horse appears, followed by a pair of acrobats. The whole cast returns, urging the audience to come to the show – without success. The pantomime horse collapses.

Parade was created during the First World War; its first performance took place in Paris, with the German army only a hundred miles away. With the Russian Revolution of 1917, the Ballets Russes would be an émigré company, increasingly cut off from its Russian roots. Yet *Parade* showed the company's continuing vitality. As before, Diaghilev could gather artists around him, experimenting with and pushing his latest choreographer. The ballet fell out of repertory after 1926, when Diaghilev tried, unsuccessfully, to sell Picasso's front curtain to raise money for new ballets. Massine revived it for the Joffrey Ballet in 1973. Modern interest in the ballet tends to focus on Picasso's designs.

La Boutique fantasque

Choreography: Léonide Massine
Designs: André Derain
Music: Gioachino Rossini, arranged by Ottorino Respighi
Premiere: 5 June 1919, Diaghilev's Ballets Russes, Alhambra Theatre, London
Original cast: *Shopkeeper* Enrico Cecchetti; *Cancan dancers* Léonide Massine, Lydia Lopokova

Diaghilev's wartime visit to Italy resulted in several Italian-themed ballets, including *Les Femmes du bonne humeur* (*The Good-humoured Ladies*), which had been Massine's first big success, and *La Boutique fantasque*, a vivacious comedy set in a toyshop. The theme of dolls coming to life was a familiar one in ballet, but Massine gave it a witty and sophisticated energy. André Derain's bright, post-impressionist designs presented 'an enchanting, totally unrealistic shop,' Massine wrote, 'with large arched windows opening onto a fantastic view – a harbour with exotic plants and an old-fashioned paddle-steamer with white wheels . . .'[35] The ballet was an immediate hit, adored by the London audience at its premiere and championed by the Bloomsbury set: the work was both avant-garde and popular.

Synopsis

The setting is a toyshop overlooking the bay of Naples. The shopkeeper and his assistant open up the shop, chasing out an urchin who is trying to steal money. Customers arrive: two English spinsters, an American couple with two small children, a Russian couple with four daughters and a son. The shopkeeper displays his toys: tarantella dancers, four court cards, a snob and a melon seller, a troupe of six Cossacks led by a young woman, two dancing poodles and, as the grand finale, a pair of cancan dancers. The American family buy the male cancan dancer while the Russians buy his partner. The assistant wraps up the dolls, to be collected later. The customers leave and the shopkeeper closes the shop.

At midnight, the toys come alive and dance again. The cancan dancers are filled with sadness at their impending separation. The other toys help them to escape.

In the morning, the customers come to collect their purchases. They are amazed and angry to find empty packages – until the toys erupt into the shop, harassing the customers and driving everybody out.

Massine's choreography was influenced by the paintings of Georges Seurat and – particularly for the cancan dancers – Henri de Toulouse-Lautrec. The ballet is a comedy of character dancing, demanding vivid movement and personality rather than classical lines. The customers are types, national caricatures, while the toys offer contrasting dances, often with a folk or character edge. Tamara Karsavina praised Massine's way of uniting action and dancing, remembering that even the non-dancing ladies were given their own way of moving, 'a special walk and a sway of crinolines'.[36] Already studying with the Spanish gypsy dancer 'Felix', in preparation for his ballet *Le Tricorne*, Massine gave the Neapolitan dance Spanish-style footbeats; the poodles were inspired by frisky fox-terriers he had seen on an Italian beach. His own cancan doll was rakish and dapper, inspired by a figure in Seurat's painting *Le Cirque*, while Lopokova's doll had an innocent, pouting quality.

'Perhaps it was the contrast between the fluttering, pink-petticoated, mischievous Lopokova, taunting and being taunted, and her greasy and sinister-looking partner, which caused the cancan to be so well received,' Massine wrote.[37] The cancan dancers became signature roles for Lopokova and Massine: they exploded into twisting, spinning, swooping dances, ending with Lopokova in the splits.

The Three-Cornered Hat (Le Tricorne)

Choreography: Léonide Massine
Music: Manuel de Falla
Designs: Pablo Picasso
Premiere: 22 July 1919, Diaghilev's Ballets Russes, Alhambra Theatre, London
Original cast: *the Miller* Léonide Massine; *the Miller's Wife* Tamara Karsavina; *the Corregidor* Léon Woizikowski; *the Dandy* Stanislas Idzikowski

While the Ballets Russes was on tour in America, Diaghilev travelled through Spain with Massine and the composer Manuel de Falla, meeting the gypsy dancer Felix on the way. While de Falla took note of popular and folk music as source material for the new ballet, Felix taught Massine Spanish dance.

Picasso's set design has a concentrated simplicity: a red and white bridge arching over a Spanish town, against a dark blue sky with stars. The costumes are a marvellous mixture of the stylised and the naturalistic: the Miller's Wife has real lace on her dress, while other characters have the frills drawn onto their costumes, in free, curling lines. Karsavina remembered that Picasso designed her dress at a rehearsal, to be sure that the costume would move with the dancing. The story is based on the novel *El sombrero de tres picos* by Pedro Antonio de Alarcón.

Synopsis

Picasso's drop-curtain shows a group of spectators at a bullfight, a small picture framed by an expanse of grey. As the music starts, there are cries of 'olé' from behind the curtain, the stamp of feet and clatter of castanets. The curtain rises to show a village scene, with a bridge and the Miller's house. The Miller stands outside, trying to teach his caged songbird to sing. His wife comes out and teases him; they flirt and dance together.

As they go to the well to draw water, a dandy passes by on the bridge, and blows kisses to the Miller's wife. A procession passes by: the governor of the province, the Corregidor, with his guards and his wife, who is carried in a sedan chair. Elderly and vicious, the Corregidor wears a three-cornered hat, the symbol of his office. He admires the Miller's Wife, and the procession moves on. The Miller flirts with a village girl. His wife is indignant; they quarrel and make up.

When the Miller's Wife is alone, the Corregidor returns, and watches her dancing. He invites her to dance. She teases him, making him dance faster, and he collapses. The Miller returns, and he and his wife laugh at the Corregidor. When the Corregidor vows revenge, they ignore him, and launch themselves into a triumphant fandango. Other villagers arrive, and dance a group dance, with castanets. The Miller's Wife dances a solo with a shawl, followed by the Miller's *farruca* (a dramatic flamenco solo traditionally performed by men). This was one of the most spectacular set pieces Massine ever created for himself, a fiery solo full of snapped fingers and stamping steps.

As the dancing ends, the Corregidor's henchmen arrive to arrest the Miller, surrounding him with their striped cloaks. Left alone, the Miller's wife laments until the Corregidor arrives and declares his love for her. She rejects him angrily, but he chases her onto the bridge. She pushes him into the water and, when he continues to chase her, holds him off with a musket.

Left alone, the Corregidor takes off his wet hat and coat, puts on the Miller's dry clothes, and goes to sleep. The Miller arrives, having escaped from the guards. He spots the Corregidor's clothes and takes them away. When the guards arrive, they find the Corregidor dressed in the Miller's hooded coat. Mistaking him for the Miller, they arrest him. The Miller, his wife and the villagers celebrate with a final *jota*.

Renewing a Ballets Russes tradition, *Le Tricorne* was a synthesis of the arts, with a vivid score, sunbaked designs and Massine's vigorous storytelling. It was to be the choreographer's favourite of his own works. '*Le Tricorne* had begun as an attempt to synthesise Spanish folk dances with classical techniques,' he wrote, 'but in the process of evolution it emerged as a choreographic interpretation of the Spanish temperament and way of life.'[38]

De Falla brought real and invented folk tunes into his rousing score, which crackles with rhythmic clapping, castanets, lyrical and lively melodies. Massine borrowed Spanish dance steps but shaped and adapted them for the ballet stage, adding some classical steps and his own 'twisted and broken gestures'. With heeled shoes, stamped footwork and character dance colouring, *Le Tricorne* was miles away from the traditional 'ballet Spanish' of *Don Quixote*. When the work was first danced by Ballet Theatre (now American Ballet Theatre) in 1943, Massine cast the Spanish dancer 'La Argentinita' as the Miller's Wife.

Les Noces (The Wedding)

Choreography: Bronislava Nijinska
Music and text: Igor Stravinsky
Designs: Natalia Gontcharova
Premiere: 13 June 1923, Diaghilev's Ballets Russes, Théâtre Gaîté-Lyrique, Paris
Original cast: *Bride* Felia Dubrovska; *Bridegroom* Léon Woizikowski

When Diaghilev invited Nijinska to choreograph Stravinsky's *Les Noces*, he had a clear image of the ballet in mind. 'You remember the first scene,' he told her. 'We are in the house of the bride. She sits in a big Russian armchair to one side of the stage, while her friends comb and plait her hair.' Nijinska was having none of it:

> 'No, Sergei Pavlovitch,' I interrupted, 'There must be no armchair, no comb and no hair!' I took a sheet of paper and sketched the bride with plaits three metres long. Her friends holding her tresses formed a group around her. Diaghilev burst out laughing – which with him was often a sign of pleasure. 'What happens next? How can the girls comb such long plaits of hair?' he asked. 'They won't comb them,' I said. 'Their dance on *pointe* and hers will express the rhythm of plaiting.'[39]

Diaghilev questioned the *pointe*work, too: since Fokine's reforms, ballet's peasant characters didn't go on *pointe*. *Pointe*work, Nijinska replied, 'will elongate the dancers' silhouettes and make them resemble the saints in Byzantine mosaics'.[40] Diaghilev was convinced.

Stravinsky started work on the score in 1914. When he heard the first sketches, Diaghilev wept and said that this would be 'the most beautiful and the most purely Russian'[41] creation of his company. Scored for four pianists, percussion and singers, it is a stark and driven score, ending with the chiming of bell and piano in unison. The singers chant Stravinsky's own text, a collection of wedding sayings, comments and clichés by the bride, the groom, the family and the guests. Stravinsky compared the text to scenes in James Joyce's *Ulysses*, 'in which the reader seems to be overhearing scraps of conversation without the connecting thread of discourse. But *The Wedding* might also be compared to *Ulysses* in the larger sense that both works are trying to *present* rather than *describe*.'[42]

Staging the work, Nijinska insisted on stripped-down designs. Natalia Gontcharova's sumptuous first draft was full of bright patterns and colours; in the final version, the men wear plain shirts and leggings, while the women have dark, plain dresses. There is nothing to distract from the bold shapes and churning rhythms of Nijinska's unstoppable ballet.

Synopsis

Scene 1. The blessing of the bride. The bride is surrounded by her friends, who braid her long hair. Holding the very long plaits, they cross and recross their feet on *pointe*. Standing in groups, they bend sideways from the waist, creating a fan of torsos. In one of the ballet's most famous images, the bride and her friends create a pyramidal group, a pile of faces with the bride looking out over the top of the pyramid.

Scene 2. The blessing of the groom. The groom stands in a semicircle of his friends. They bow and move through stamping dances, with more geometric pile-ups and crouching, frieze-like lines. The groom's parents bless him.

Scene 3. The departure of the bride. With her long plaits looped around her neck, the bride prepares to leave. Her parents mourn her departure.

Scene 4. The wedding feast. The two families sit on a raised inner stage. Below them, a massed *corps de ballet* of men and women dance in celebration. Bells chime and the bride and groom retire to bed.

Nijinska saw 'a dramatic quality' in:

> the fate of the bride and groom, since the choice is made by parents to whom they owe complete obedience . . . The young girl knows nothing at all about her future family nor what lies in store for her. Not only will she be subject to her husband, but also to his parents. It is possible that after being loved and cherished by her own kin, she may be nothing more in her new, rough family than a useful extra worker, just another pair of hands . . .[43]

Stravinsky's text for the bride is full of laments, remembering when the 'cruel' matchmaker came to part and 'tear' her hair for the wedding. The plaiting is both traditional and symbolic, showing the uniting of the two families, but also suggesting the loss of virginity. The *pointe*work is stabbing, going down into the floor with hard force. Yet *Les Noces* does not make the bride a tragic heroine. The ballet is rooted in human experience but remains powerfully objective, dominated by the collective power of the ensemble.

Nijinska turns her dancers into a machine of movement, piling them up in geometric formations, stamping and crouching. Although she brought back *pointe*work, she doesn't use it to separate the sexes, who often dance the same steps; there is no supported *adagio*. All the dancers work like peasants, driving through patterns or building weighted shapes, showing the collective will of an entire society. The momentum and energy of Nijinska's choreography make *Les Noces* both harsh and exhilarating, a fierce masterpiece.

Les Noces was a divisive ballet at its premiere, both championed and attacked. Nijinska revived it for de Basil's Ballet Russe in 1936, when the ballerina Irina Baronova asked to dance in the *corps de ballet*, for the experience of working with the choreographer. (In the end, she danced one of the leading wedding guests.) The musical forces made the ballet expensive to perform, and it was in danger of falling from the repertory after the Second World War. In 1966, Frederick Ashton, who had danced for Nijinska in Ida Rubinstein's company, invited her to restage *Les Noces* for The Royal Ballet. The staging was a triumph, confirming the ballet's status as a twentieth-century classic. It has since been revived by other companies, including the Paris Opéra Ballet and the Mariinsky Ballet.

Other Stagings

In 1965, Jerome Robbins choreographed *Les Noces* for American Ballet Theatre, with set designs by Oliver Smith and costumes by Patricia Zipprodt. Where his *Afternoon of a Faun* from 1953 had updated the action to the present day, Robbins' *Les Noces* remains a peasant wedding. He had not seen Nijinska's version in 1965 (and admitted after The Royal Ballet revival that if he had, he would have been disheartened about creating his own), but he was influenced by photographs of Diaghilev's company rehearsing. Robbins' bride has six long strands of hair, which her friends dance around her braiding before she is carried offstage, wrapped up in her own plaits. Robbins gives his bride and bridegroom more personal emotion, and does not use *pointe*work. He revived the work for New York City Ballet in 1998; it was to be his last work.

In 1982, Jiří Kylián staged the ballet for Nederlands Dans Theater, under the title *Svadebka*. John F. Macfarlane's set is a wooden cabin, while the costumes are stylised nineteenth-century clothes, with buttoned bodices for the women. Kylián uses a running, skipping vocabulary, opening with the groom kissing the bride's cheek, and including a *pas de deux* for the couple. In Angelin Preljocaj's 1989 staging, the dancers throw around life-sized bride dolls, which wear white wedding dresses and veils.

Les Biches

Choreography: Bronislava Nijinska
Music: Francis Poulenc
Designs: Marie Laurencin
Premiere: 6 January 1924, Diaghilev's Ballets Russes, Théâtre de Monte Carlo, Monte Carlo
Original cast: *The Hostess* Bronislava Nijinska; *The Girl in Blue* Vera Nemtchinova; *Athletes* Leon Woizikowksi, Anatole Vilzak, Nicholas Zverev; *Girls in Grey* Lydia Sokolova, Lubov Tchernicheva

When the Ballets Russes became a permanent company in 1911, Diaghilev had made Monte Carlo his headquarters. The company would return to the Riviera regularly thereafter. In the mid-1920s, Diaghilev increasingly staged premieres there. This was a 'French' period for the Ballets Russes, featuring French composers and artists; many of the ballets reflected chic Riviera life. Nijinska created several of them, including *Le Train bleu*, whose athletic, leisured characters wore costumes by Coco Chanel, and *Les Biches*, which has proved the most enduring of this group of ballets.

The title can be translated as 'The Does' (female deer); it was sometimes used as a term of endearment. The scene is a house party, full of bright young things: male athletes who seem to have stepped straight off the beach, a *corps de ballet* in pink with feathers in the dancers' hair, a hostess in lace with strings and strings of pearls. It was one of the earliest ballets to present its dancers in modern dress (Nijinsky's *Jeux*, created in 1913, was the first).

The designs were by the painter Marie Laurencin, who created a drop-curtain, in her signature soft colours, of a woman surrounded by leaping animals. Poulenc was just twenty-three when he wrote the playful, brilliant score, which wittily combines influences from Chopin to jazz.

Synopsis

The setting is an airy drawing room with a big window and a blue couch. Twelve young women enter, fashionable and frivolous in pink dresses and ostrich plumes. Their dance is full of chattering beaten steps. Sometimes they pause and 'laugh' together, shaking their shoulders.

Three young athletes enter, fresh from the beach in their bathing costumes. Their trio includes muscular poses, showing off their chests and biceps, as well as turns and jumps. When the pink women return, they are fascinated, circling and framing the dancing men.

The girl in blue enters, dressed in a short, androgynous velvet coat with tights, *pointe* shoes and white gloves. She glides across the stage on *pointe*, holding up her gloved hand, ignoring the guests. All these characters come and go, flirting and watching each other. When one of the athletes dances with the velvet-coated figure, the pink women peep at them from over the back of the sofa.

The hostess appears, waving a cigarette holder and playing with her strings of pearls. Her sophisticated solo is full of changes of pace: very fast beaten steps contrast with long strides with sumptuous backbends, or pauses to glance archly over her solo. She dances with two of the athletes in a flirtatious trio; when she leaves, they hurry after her.

The blue-coated figure and the third athlete dance a duet full of tilting angles. It's followed by a duet for two women in grey. They dance side by side, one with her arm across the other's shoulder; at the end they embrace, then check that nobody is watching. The whole cast return for the stylish, speedy finale.

'*Les Biches* has no real plot,' wrote Poulenc, 'for the good reason that if it had it might well have caused a scandal. In this ballet, as in certain of Watteau's pictures, there is an atmosphere of wantonness which you sense if you are corrupted, but which an innocent-minded girl would not be conscious of. . . .'[44] Poulenc is talking himself up, enjoying the knowing atmosphere. The naughtiness of *Les Biches* is also airy and athletic, a very different world from the heavy, perfumed fantasy of *Schéhérazade* or the sleepy heat of *L'Après-midi d'un faune*.

In *Les Biches*, Nijinska used classical language to create a very up-to-the-minute picture of a leisured society at play. The footwork of the Hostess' solo is as fast as any 1920s Charleston, her upper body as free. *Les Biches* plays with satire and sexuality; the athletes' virtuosity is comic, and the hinted flirtations are gay as well as straight.

The 'page boy' costume of the girl in blue went through several versions before the premiere. Vera Nemtchinova started out with a much longer frock coat, like a porter's uniform. Seeing it, Diaghilev called for the scissors, cutting a wide V-neck and shortening the skirts of the coat until it just covered the dancer's buttocks. 'I feel naked!' exclaimed Nemtchinova. 'Then go and buy yourself some white gloves,'[45] Diaghilev replied. The gloves became a famous part of the role, highlighting the flat hand poses in Nijinska's choreography. Nijinska worked out her own role, the Hostess, on one of the *corps* women, a young Irish dancer called Ninette de Valois, who went on to found The Royal Ballet.

With its fizzing score and frivolous atmosphere, *Les Biches* was very popular, revived by the de Basil company and by the Markova-Dolin company (which renamed it *The House Party*.) In 1964, Nijinska revived it for The Royal Ballet – at Frederick Ashton's request, rather than that of de Valois; Ashton had danced for Nijinska in Ida Rubinstein's company, and had been deeply influenced by her. *Les Biches* has since been revived by many other companies.

Apollo (originally Apollon Musagète)

Choreography: George Balanchine
Music: Igor Stravinsky
Designs: André Bauchant
Premiere: 12 June 1928, Diaghilev's Ballets Russes, Théâtre Sarah-Bernhardt, Paris
Original cast: *Apollo* Serge Lifar; *Terpsichore* Alice Nikitina; *Polyhymnia* Lubov Tchernicheva; *Calliope* Felia Dubrovska

Apollo is iconic. Some works are clear turning points, moments where you can see a new approach take shape. This ballet is a starting point for Balanchine's vision of dance, a way forward for classicism in the twentieth century. It's a statement of intent.

Originally called *Apollon musagète*, Stravinsky's score was commissioned by Elizabeth Sprague Coolidge for a festival of contemporary music in the United States. Adolph Bolm staged a version in Washington DC in 1928. Balanchine's staging, created for the Ballets Russes and starring Serge Lifar, proved to be definitive. The first staging had scenery and costumes by André Bauchant: short, stiff skirts for the muses, with caps that covered their hair. (In 1929, Chanel designed new costumes.) The designs were much simplified in revivals, and the ballet is danced today with muses in plain white tunics, Apollo in white tights and sometimes with a one-shouldered tunic. Bauchant's naturalistic mountain set has become a simple staircase.

The theme is the birth and youth of the god Apollo, who instructs Calliope, Polyhymnia and Terpsichore – the muses of poetry, mime and dance – before leaving to join the other gods on Olympus. Balanchine and Francis Mason called him 'a wild, half-human youth who acquires nobility through art'.[46]

Synopsis

The ballet opens with the birth of Apollo, his mother Leto stretching in stylised childbirth on a raised platform. On the stage below, Apollo jumps forward, limbs bound tight by swaddling bandages. Two handmaidens unwrap him, and he spins off the last wrappings, whirling so that the fabric flies off. He dances a solo, steadying himself as he learns to control his limbs. Two handmaidens bring him a lute – moving in a 'wheelbarrow' pose, where one moves forward in a deep crouch on *pointe*, the other supporting her, like someone pushing the wheelbarrow. They put Apollo's hands to the strings of the lute.

After a blackout, we see a more mature Apollo, playing with confidence, circling his arms. Three muses join him from different corners of the stage and bowing into *arabesques penchées* around the lute. Apollo dances with them, then gives each a symbol of her art: a tablet for Calliope, muse of poetry, a mask for Polyhymnia, muse of mime, a lyre for Terpsichore, muse of dance.

Calliope's solo is to an Alexandrine rhythm (the one most commonly used in French poetry). Her dance has a writing gesture; at the end, she writes on her hand. Polyhymnia dances with one finger to her lips, but finally opens her mouth as if in a shout. Apollo is displeased with the ends of both solos. Terpsichore starts her dance by plucking at the ground with pointed feet, her footwork suggesting the playing of the lyre. Apollo approves.

He dances a solo that ends with him sitting on the ground, one hand outstretched. Terpsichore joins him, touching her pointed finger to his, like Michelangelo's image of God and Adam on the Sistine Chapel ceiling. The *pas de deux* is full of innovative partnering, including the 'swimming lesson', where Apollo bends his head and Terpsichore lies balanced on the nape of his neck.

Calliope and Polyhymnia rush in to join them in a joyful coda, which includes Apollo 'driving' the three muses as if they were the horses in his chariot. Stravinsky's score suggests Zeus, king of the gods, calling his son Apollo home. Apollo blesses the muses and leads them to Olympus. Originally, the ballet ended with Apollo at the top of the rock, the muses in a line behind him, with Leto bidding him farewell from the ground.

The early years of Diaghilev's Ballets Russes had been characterised by brightly coloured ballets, full of fierce exoticism. After the fairy-tale qualities of *The Firebird* and the fury of *The Rite of Spring*, Stravinsky had moved into stripped-down neo-classicism with his taut score for *Apollo*. Choreographing the ballet, Balanchine was to make a comparable shift, returning to the nineteenth-century roots of classical ballet and bringing them into a modern age. 'I look back upon the ballet as the turning point in my life,' the choreographer wrote:

> In its discipline and restraint, in its sustained oneness of tone and feeling, the score was a revelation. It seemed to me that I could, for the first time, dare not use all my ideas; that I, too, could eliminate. I began to see how I could clarify, by limiting, by reducing what seemed to be myriad possibilities to the one possibility that is inevitable.[47]

Yet Balanchine's 'inevitability' is also sharp-edged and unexpected. His young god anticipates Pete Townshend's swinging guitar arm by decades, or walks on his heels in a quick toddling gait. A moment where he makes his hands 'flash', closing them into fists and opening them sharply, was inspired by a flashing advertisement for Bovril that Balanchine had seen in Piccadilly Circus. This is classicism that could take freely from the modern world. The dancing is full of daring, off-balance moves; it has slow, radiant steps, but the effect is streamlined, speedy and exact.

In 1978, Balanchine revised *Apollo*, cutting the opening scene with Leto and removing the set. Instead of climbing to Olympus, Apollo and the muses end the ballet in a striking group taken from the final dance. Apollo takes a braced position while the muses group themselves behind him, each with an outstretched leg at a different angle, suggesting the rays of the sun.

The Prodigal Son (Le Fils Prodigue)

Choreography: George Balanchine
Music: Sergei Prokofiev
Libretto: Boris Kochno

Designs: Georges Rouault
Premiere: 21 May 1929, Diaghilev's Ballets Russes, Théâtre Sarah-Bernhardt, Paris
Original cast: *the Prodigal* Serge Lifar; *the Siren* Felia Dubrovska

The Prodigal Son was the last ballet created by Diaghilev's Ballets Russes, and Prokofiev wrote the music. Where *Apollo* looked forward to Balanchine's later classicism, *The Prodigal Son* is dramatic and expressionist. Serge Grigoriev, the company's *régisseur*, remembered that Diaghilev took a particular interest in this ballet – perhaps partly because such a dramatic theme would be new for Balanchine, who was known for the cool restraint of his choreography.

The idea and the libretto came from Diaghilev's secretary Boris Kochno, who was thinking both of the Biblical parable and its appearance in Alexander Pushkin's story 'The Station Master'. Pushkin describes a series of pictures on the station master's wall, showing three images from the parable – which in turn became the three scenes of the ballet. For designs, Diaghilev turned to Georges Rouault, who had never created for the theatre before, but whose work drew on both religious themes and Byzantine imagery. He took so long over his designs that the desperate Diaghilev eventually got a key from the concierge of Rouault's hotel and made off with several sketches, which became the basis for the set, designed in great swipes of muddy colour.

When Prokofiev arrived to see rehearsals, he was appalled: he had imagined a naturalistic approach, with real glasses of wine and real cushions in the orgy scene, and was shocked by the stylised acrobatics of Balanchine's choreography, which drew on circus techniques, especially in the *pas de deux*. 'I could talk to Prokofiev, but he wouldn't talk to me,' Balanchine remembered, while Rouault didn't speak, and even balanced a chair on his nose during rehearsals. 'Still,' Balanchine added, 'I finally got it through my stupid head what art and music were, especially new art and music.'[48] Like the title role of *Apollo*, the Prodigal was created for Serge Lifar. It's an ardent, athletic role, moving from adolescent rebellion through sexual experience to broken need. The Siren's dances have an icy power, with a dominatrix edge.

Synopsis

Scene 1. The Prodigal's home. Two servants prepare wine jars. The Prodigal enters, full of energy. His father appears with the Prodigal's two sisters and leads them all in prayer, pushing the Prodigal's head down in worship. The Prodigal rebels, leaving with his servants, leaping over the low fence in an explosive jump.

Scene 2. A group of bald-headed revellers gather together, dancing with strange, staggering movements. They greet the Prodigal and his companions, and urge him to drink. The Siren enters, dressed in a tall hat and trailing a long red cloak. As she dances, she winds the cloak around her thighs, ending on the floor hidden by her train. The Prodigal uncovers her and they dance a cruelly erotic *pas de deux*, in which she dominates him completely. There is more revelry; the Prodigal collapses on the table, as the bald-headed companions lift the Siren over him in a long swoop. The table is lifted upright, becoming a pillar, which the Prodigal collapses against. The revellers and the Siren strip him and leave. He crawls away.

The table then becomes a boat for the thieves to sail away. Standing arched at the prow, the Siren becomes the boat's figurehead and her long train a sail.

Scene 3. Left alone, the ragged Prodigal drags himself homewards, leaning on a staff. He is exhausted and despairing. He reaches the gate but collapses. His sisters bring him into the family home, to their father. The Prodigal falls at his feet, then crawls slowly up his father's body. The father takes his son in his arms, and wraps his cloak around him.

Balanchine's earliest dances in Russia had been noted for sexiness and acrobatics, and for expressionist drama that was much less characteristic of his later work. All these qualities appear in *The Prodigal Son*. The dances for the revellers are grotesque: their bald-headed wigs and toddling steps make them look strangely misshapen. In her solo, the Siren arches back, supporting herself on her hands and *pointes*, kicking high as she crab-crawls across the stage. In the *pas de deux*, the awed Prodigal lifts her by thrusting his head and shoulders between her legs; she later arches herself around him, hands gripping ankles, and slides slowly down his body to the floor.

In rehearsals, Dubrovska began by being coquettish, until Balanchine and Diaghilev told her to think more seriously about the role. 'And then Balanchine said just the right thing, just the perfect word to make me understand,' Dubrovska told the critic Barbara Newman. ' "You have to be a snake. A snake. You hypnotize him. You don't kill him, but . . ." Everything was in my eyes and in showing myself. Not one smile. You have to conquer him and bring him to his knees.'[49]

The Green Table

Choreography: Kurt Jooss
Music: Fritz Cohen
Libretto: Kurt Jooss
Designs: Hein Heckroth
Premiere: 3 July 1932, Ballet Jooss, Théâtre des Champs-Elysées, Paris
Original cast: *Death* Kurt Jooss

Subtitled 'A Dance of Death', *The Green Table* was created when the First World War was still a fresh memory, while fears of a new conflict increased. Politicians and profiteers push the world into war, before Death claims the victims.

The choreographer Kurt Jooss emerged from Germany's *Ausdruckstanz* ('dance of feeling') movement rather than from ballet, but unlike others in the movement, he aimed to combine ballet with modern dance, to create an expressive dance with a moral message. In 1927 his company became the resident troupe at the Essen Opera, where he choreographed new versions of several of Diaghilev scores, including *Petrushka* and *The Prodigal Son*. In 1932 Jooss created *The Green Table* for a competition sponsored by the Archives Internationales de la Danse in Paris. It won first prize, and became the signature work of the Ballet Jooss.

Synopsis

A group of diplomats, wearing morning suits and grotesque face masks, gather on both sides of a foreshortened green baize table. They argue spitefully to Cohen's insinuating tango rhythms, played on two pianos. As the debate gets stormier, we hear a snatch of the soldiers' marching theme. Both sides pull out pistols and shoot.

After a blackout, the figure of Death appears, a helmeted skeleton dancing a relentless marching solo. He moves to the back of the stage as a soldier with a flag summons up an army. In brief scenes, Jooss shows the battle, the fleeing refugees, the soldiers' brothel and the homecoming of the few survivors. Death is a recurring figure, claiming soldiers, an old mother, a young woman in the brothel, a female partisan. Death leads his line of victims across the stage.

The ballet ends with a return to the green table, where the diplomats agree peace – for now – and return to their discussions.

Jooss drew on the medieval tradition of the Dance of Death, in which artists depicted Death coming to people of all kinds. Jooss' Death figure is inescapable but not cruel. Dancing with each victim, he draws them away from life; in some cases, particularly for the young prostitute, death comes as a release. In contrast to the masked and mincing diplomats, Death and the people move with broad, powerful movements.

Originally danced by Jooss' own company, *The Green Table* later entered the repertory of ballet companies, including Dutch National Ballet, the Joffrey Ballet and Birmingham Royal Ballet.

Les Présages (The Portents)

Choreography: Léonide Massine
Music: Pyotr Ilych Tchaikovsky, Fifth Symphony
Designs: André Masson
Premiere: 13 April 1933, De Basil's Ballet Russe de Monte Carlo, Théâtre de Monte Carlo, Monte Carlo
Original cast: *Action* Nina Verchinina; *Passion* Irina Baronova, David Lichine; *Frivolity* Tatiana Riabouchinska; *Fate* Léon Woizikowski

In the 1930s, Massine continued to make character ballets, but he also experimented with a new style of 'symphonic ballet'. Ballet had been using concert music since *Les Sylphides*, but choreographers had usually chosen scores with a dance form, such as Chopin's waltzes and mazurkas, or a definite programme – symphonic poems rather than straight symphonies. Massine's choice in *Les Présages* of Tchaikovsky's Fifth Symphony and, then, for the 1933 ballet *Choreartium*, Brahms' Fourth Symphony, caused outrage among music purists: how could choreographers co-opt such music? The debate faded as audiences flocked to see the ballets; dancing to concert music is now commonplace.

Nevertheless, there is a clear difference between the later, plotless works of Balanchine and others and the Massine-style symphonic ballet. Massine's works were insistently thematic, with symbolic content and allegorical characters.

Les Présages, the first and perhaps the most popular of Massine's symphonic works, has bold symbolic designs by André Masson, a surrealist painter who later turned to abstract expressionism. His backdrop is full of signs and symbols, with a stylised mask, flames and shooting stars. As the ballet proceeds, lighting brings out its different colours: darkness for the 'passions' in the second movement, threatening red for the warlike fourth movement.

Synopsis

First movement. Action is represented by a statuesque woman in a red classical Greek dress. She leads the *corps de ballet* – as a massed group, or in pairs or single dancers. A *pas de trois* of two women and one man, danced with sensual movements, symbolises temptation.

Second movement. A pair of young lovers representing Passion enter down a line of light across the darkened stage. Their duet is interrupted by the monstrous green Fate, who tries to lure the woman away. In one of the ballet's most famous moments, she runs back to her partner, who lifts her high over his head: for decades, dancers would call this kind of lift a 'Présages lift'. The bat-like Fate exits walking backwards on his heels.

Third movement. Frivolity is represented by a virtuoso ballerina in a short, pale blue tunic, surrounded by a carefree female *corps de ballet*. The dancing is fast and full of intricate footwork.

Fourth movement. The figure of Fate leads men to battle, with massed ranks of male dancers. The Hero (the male Passion of the second movement) joins them, though Passion, Action and Frivolity urge him to avoid the conflict. In the finale, men lift women into the air and run carrying them, the women's chiffon costumes billowing out behind them as Tchaikovsky's trumpets ring out. The Hero triumphs over Fate.

The choreography blends classical technique with a more expressionist, modern dance style; in 1930, reviving his production of *The Rite of Spring* in New York, Massine had cast Martha Graham as his Chosen Maiden, while Nina Verchinina studied for a year with the German modern dancer Mary Wigman. Massine's Fate was often compared to the dancing Death of Kurt Jooss' *The Green Table*, created in 1932.

The symphonic ballet fell out of fashion after the Second World War, overtaken by Balanchine's pure dance aesthetic. However, in the twenty-first century, Alexei Ratmansky has returned to experiment with this style.

Gaîté Parisienne

Choreography: Léonide Massine
Music: Jacques Offenbach, orchestrated by Manuel Rosenthal with the collaboration of Jacques Brindejonc-Offenbach
Libretto and designs: Étienne de Beaumont

Premiere: 5 April 1938, Ballet Russe de Monte Carlo, Théâtre de Monte Carlo, Monte Carlo
Original cast: *The Glove Seller* Nina Tarakanova; *The Flower Girl* Eugénie Delarova; *Peruvian* Léonide Massine; *Baron* Frederic Franklin; *Officer* Igor Youskevitch

Gaîté parisienne is an operetta ballet, a frothy affair that helped to launch the Ballet Russe de Monte Carlo, the successor to the Ballets Russes companies of Diaghilev, René Blum and Colonel W. de Basil. *Gaîté Parisienne* was in the style of Massine's successful *Le Beau Danube*, with a nineteenth-century European setting and a cheerful story of meetings and love affairs. It's set in Paris during the Second Empire, when Offenbach's career was at its height. The music is selected from a range of his operettas, and includes the 'Infernal Galop' from *Orphée aux enfers*, the tune most associated with the cancan. Doubtful about Manuel Rosenthal's arrangement of Offenbach music, Massine consulted Stravinsky, who replied 'Léonide, if you reject this score you are an idiot; you will be rejecting what must be the greatest success of your career.'[50] The ballet became the new company's signature work.

Synopsis

The setting is Tortoni's, a fashionable café in Paris. Four waiters and four cleaning women prepare for the evening's entertainment, dancing and swinging white cloths. With a swish of skirts, a Flower Girl enters, dancing with the waiters and giving each of them a nosegay. Six *cocodettes* – women of easy virtue – are the next to arrive, dancing a mazurka with their three partners.

When the Glove Seller enters, with her basket on her arm, the men rush to admire her. The Peruvian rushes in as her dance finishes, carrying two carpet-bags. The *cocodettes* flirt with him, while the Flower Girl puts a flower in his lapel. He wriggles with pleasure at all this female attention, then spots the Glove Seller – but goes on dancing and wriggling even as she tries to put a glove on his hand.

A handsome Baron enters. The Flower Girl is interested, but he turns to the Glove Seller. They dance a flowing waltz together, ending with the Glove Seller poised on the Baron's shoulder.

A group of soldiers strut in, led by their Officer. The women greet them, in a dance full of saluting and marching, ending with an apparent farewell: the women pretend to weep and hang about the soldiers' necks, as if sending them off to war. The next arrival is La Lionne, a fashionable beauty, with her admirer the Duke and one of her friends. Men rush to greet and admire La Lionne, circling, partnering and lifting her in a waltz. The Officer flirts with the Glove Seller.

The Peruvian returns, douses himself in perfume and approaches the Glove Seller. She dances with him, flirting in order to tease the Baron. The Baron is furious with her, while the Duke is furious with La Lionne. The Glove Seller dances on, as quarrels break out among the men. When a fight starts, the guests take sides, and the café is cleared. The Peruvian hides under a table, and is the last to be ejected from the café.

The Baron and the Glove Seller return. Their quarrel reconciled, they dance harmoniously together. Other guests return, followed by a troupe of cancan dancers with their dancing master, for a riotous cancan. The other guests return and join the dance, concluding with the 'Infernal Galop'. At its end, the guests prepare to depart. The Glove Seller leaves with the Baron, the Flower Girl with the Duke, La Lionne with the Officer. The Peruvian is left alone.

Gaîté parisienne is full of bustle, with dancers coming and going between their short numbers. They're often onstage in the background, watching the dancing or pursuing their own plotline; they even dance between numbers, waltzing in and out.

The role of the Glove Seller was strongly associated with Alexandra Danilova, but it was actually created by Nina Tarakanova. Tarakanova's heroine was a naïve young woman, in contrast to the more flirtatious Flower Girl. When Danilova took over the role, a year later, her Glove Seller was much more sophisticated. On the first night of the company's 1941 New York season, the ovation that greeted Danilova in *Gaîté parisienne* actually stopped the show; it became an opening-night tradition for the company. In 1988, American Ballet Theatre staged a new production of the ballet, with costumes by the fashion designer Christian Lacroix.

5

NATIONAL BALLETS

'BUT FIRST A SCHOOL,' said George Balanchine, when Lincoln Kirstein invited him to form a ballet company in America.[1] In Britain, Ninette de Valois was putting the same principle into practice. Both had worked with Diaghilev – indeed, Balanchine would go on working with the later Ballet Russe companies into the 1940s – but when it came to setting up permanent companies, they didn't follow the international model. Instead, they looked back to the roots that had originally nourished it: a national company, fed by its own school.

Balanchine and de Valois were not alone: between the diaspora of former Diaghilev artists, and the dancers and audiences they had inspired, a wave of new companies sprang up in the West. Many were short lived, or went through various names on their way to long-term success. The companies that are now New York City Ballet, American Ballet Theatre, The Royal Ballet, and more, had to find ways of naturalising ballet, making an art that was associated with Russia adjust to new and very different circumstances. There were also the existing ballet companies, neglected after the decline of Romantic ballet but ripe for revival. The 1930s were to be a time of energy and experiment, often on a shoestring budget.

In fact, de Valois was ahead of the diaspora. Born Edris Stannus in Ireland in 1898, she had joined Diaghilev's Ballets Russes in 1923. A quick, intelligent dancer, she soaked up all the influences she could find: 'I saw the whole of the theatre in relation to the ballet,' she remembered in a radio interview. '. . . I just had everything on a plate. What could I do but stand and sort it out like a jigsaw puzzle, and realise that we had absolutely *nothing* in England and all I wanted to do was to get back and start something.'[2] She left the Ballets Russes after two years, determined to do just that.

She started by founding her own school, the Academy of Choreographic Art, which opened in London in 1926. Her aim was to make her group of pupils the resident dance company of an existing theatre: they could gain stage experience by performing in dramatic productions, while the company grew and developed. The company found a home at the Old Vic and Sadler's Wells theatres, run by the formidable Lilian Baylis, who presented Shakespeare and opera to loyal local audiences. The new Vic–Wells Ballet graduated from dancing in opera and theatre to its own small productions, launching its first complete evening of ballet in 1931.

At this point, Britain had no surviving native ballet tradition, but it had a clear love of ballet, with a loyal audience for the Ballets Russes. Many ex-Diaghilev artists settled in London, where they helped to encourage the fledgling British Ballet. In 1920, Marie Rambert had opened her own studio in London. In 1924, Massine sent her a new student, the young Frederick Ashton, who had been smitten with ballet after seeing Anna Pavlova as a child in Peru. When a ballet for a charity performance was discussed in Rambert's studio in 1926, Ashton made suggestions – and was promptly asked to choreograph the whole thing. A *Tragedy of Fashion*, his first work, was chic and fun; Diaghilev went to see it more than once. It was also the first Ashton work to be designed by Sophie Fedorovitch, a young artist who became his close friend and collaborator. Ashton went on working for Rambert, but also made ballets for the new Vic–Wells and elsewhere. By 1935 de Valois could afford a resident choreographer, and invited Ashton to join her as an architect of the future Royal Ballet.

Rambert lacked de Valois' ambition and eye for long-term planning, but she had a gift for spotting choreographers. Antony Tudor (born William Cook in 1908) began studying with her in 1920, while still working as an accountant at Smithfield meat market. To give some idea of Tudor's dedication, he would come to class after a ten-hour shift that had started at 5 a.m. Rambert later hired him as secretary and stage manager, allowing him to give up accountancy. He was a fine mime, and became an intelligent teacher: the choreographer Agnes de Mille said he was the first to help her to understand 'the principles behind the technique'.[3] Tudor made his first ballets for Rambert, including two of his most important works, *Lilac Garden* and *Dark Elegies*. He also danced for the Vic–Wells Ballet, but was given little opportunity by de Valois, who also suggested that he spend time with the de Basil Ballet Russe, to gain experience. Instead Tudor left to form his own company, and in 1939 went to America to join the newly formed Ballet Theatre.

Although de Valois let Tudor go, her Vic–Wells Ballet was becoming the pre-eminent British company. An early milestone was the staging of *Giselle* and the full-length *Swan Lake* for Alicia Markova, the British-born ballerina discovered by Diaghilev. Staged by Nicolai Sergeyev, using the notation he had brought with him from the Mariinsky Ballet, the classical revivals gave Markova a chance to dance the great roles, while setting a superb classical example for the young company. They also built the nineteenth-century classics into the heart of British ballet.

From the start, de Valois believed that the repertory should have the classics as its bedrock, alongside major modern works and new ballets on British themes. This idea of balanced repertory has been so influential that it no longer looks radical. In 1934 the full-length *Swan Lake* was not an obvious choice: even Diaghilev had revived a shortened version. The dance historian Beth Genné points out that *Giselle, Coppélia, The Sleeping Beauty* and *Swan Lake* became the full-length 'classics' of the Western ballet repertory mostly because de Valois promoted them as such.[4] As her company grew to international fame, with Margot Fonteyn as the company's first home-grown ballerina, its classics became familiar and admired around the world. De Valois used Petipa as well as Ashton to develop a native British style of ballet.

The balance of Ashton, de Valois and music director Constant Lambert produced a distinctive company. De Valois trained quick, strong dancers, with a focus on clean execution and good footwork – qualities she had herself as a dancer. Ashton added a three-dimensional richness to this cut-and-dried foundation. While dancing for Nijinska, he had learned a lavish use of the torso. He would always urge his dancers to bend, to move on a bigger, more sensuous scale, to develop their own personal glamour. Ashton would describe great ballerinas he had seen, even giving imitations of Pavlova, Olga Spessivtseva, Tamara Karsavina and others. 'He used to talk in visions,' remembered the ballerina Lynn Seymour, who created several roles for Ashton, '... always trying to get you to live up to these images.'[5] Fonteyn, de Valois' discovery, was to be Ashton's greatest muse; from the sophisticated, witty ballets of his Rambert period, he began to show a new tenderness and lyricism. 'Had I not been able to work with Margot I might never have developed the lyrical side of my work,' Ashton told the photographer Keith Money. 'As it was, it evolved into a personal idiom.'[6]

The fortunes of British ballet were transformed by the Second World War, which saw a surge of public interest in the arts. Kathleen Ferrier sang in factories, Myra Hess gave piano recitals in the National Gallery, Margot Fonteyn danced through the Blitz: all three became national heroines. The theatre director Tyrone Guthrie, no fan of ballet, remembered that 'The Ballet was a sellout always and everywhere ... what everybody wanted almost as much as food or drink during those years was to see youthful and beautiful creatures beautifully moving through ordered evolutions to a predestined and satisfactory close.'[7] In 1940, London's Arts Theatre club put on daytime ballet performances, aimed at an audience of working civilians and servicemen on leave. Despite the Blitz, 'Lunchtime Ballet' was so successful that it was followed by After Lunch Ballet, Teatime Ballet and an early-evening Sherry Ballet. Mona Inglesby founded a new and very successful company, the International Ballet, in 1941, and toured tirelessly. At one point the Vic–Wells Ballet, by now renamed the Sadler's Wells Ballet, gave three performances a day, until the exhausted, underfed *corps de ballet* started fainting onstage.

It was not simply that audiences needed some escape from the war, or that widespread touring was bringing ballet to a new public. As the dancers performed on stages literally shaking from bomb blasts, to an audience that had ignored air-raid warnings for the sake of seeing them, ballet built a new bond with its public. For the first time, it came to be seen as a native art form. The Sadler's Wells Ballet profited most from the change: at the end of the war, it was invited to become the resident company at the Royal Opera House, an acknowledgement of its national status. Growing into its new, larger home, the company could flex its dance muscles. Ashton, back from the war, was choreographing with new authority and depth. When the Sadler's Wells Ballet toured America in 1949, a sensational performance of *The Sleeping Beauty* made Fonteyn a world star and gave the company an international reputation overnight.

* * *

By then, New York was already an established ballet city. Balanchine's new School of American Ballet had opened in New York on 1 January 1934. The name reflected his determination to create a school of and for his adopted country. His biographer Bernard Taper suggests that Balanchine chafed at the self-conscious Russianism of the Ballet Russe de Monte Carlo, with its nostalgic, old-school glamour. Since Diaghilev's day, European dancers had been rechristening themselves with Russian names; Balanchine's new ballet would be openly and honestly American. The training would be rigorous and classical, drawing from imperial tradition – at his suggestion, the walls of the first premises were painted a grey-blue he remembered from the Imperial School. But he had no wish to turn Americans into fake Russians.

Kirstein, Balanchine's new associate, eagerly supported this new direction. The son of a Boston department store owner, he had fallen in love with ballet at a young age. As a student, Kirstein helped to found the

Harvard Society for Contemporary Art, a forerunner of New York's Museum of Modern Art, and had co-founded a literary magazine that published poems by Ezra Pound and T. S. Eliot. He was to work tirelessly in the service of American ballet, and of Balanchine's vision for it. 'America was the newest-found land, a vast continent of infinite resource and possibility, with no built-in or hereditary prejudices . . .' wrote Kirstein:

> Its young girls were not sylphides; they were basketball champions and queens of the tennis court, whose proper domain was athletics. They were long-legged, long-necked, slim-hipped, and capable of endless acrobatic virtuosity. The drum majorette, the cheerleader of the high-school football team of the thirties filled his eye . . . Balanchine did not wish to impose an exhausted if correct 'classicism' as an academy on top of their own strong stylisation; he was to give their type a new turn which would transform their peculiar Americanism into a new classicism. . . . The pathos and suavity of the dying swan, the purity and regal hauteur of the elder ballerina, were to be replaced by a raciness, an alert celerity which claimed as its own the gaiety of sport and the skill of the champion athlete.[8]

In March 1934, Balanchine began work on *Serenade*, his first American ballet, designed to teach the senior class the difference between classwork and performance. At the start of the finished ballet, seventeen women stand in diagonal lines, toes pointing forwards, all with one arm outstretched. Each woman moves her hand to her brow, curves it across her breast, then drops both arms into a simple first position. As Tchaikovsky's opening motif comes to a close, they turn their feet out. *Serenade* shows women becoming ballet dancers.

Balanchine would later put the slanting lines of that first grouping down to chance. 'I had seventeen dancers, and I placed them [so that they] almost looked like orange groves in California,' he said later. 'If I only had sixteen, an even number, there would be two lines.'[9] The 'orange grove' comparison is poetic and very American, even as Balanchine downplays the choice. The orange grove had another effect: as Ruthanna Boris, one of the first cast, remembered, these were 'lines where everyone could be seen'.[10] It's an unusually democratic design. *Serenade* is an ensemble ballet. The *corps* doesn't stand about: the dancers run, flowing in and out of patterns, lines forming and breaking. The look of speed isn't simply a matter of tempo. Balanchine asked his dancers to step off balance: instead of holding steady on the standing foot, they shift their weight onto the other leg, often when it's still in the air. It gives the dancing a sense of risk and expansiveness: they step out of their own space. These were the qualities that would inform Balanchine's American ballet.

Admittedly, there were interruptions. Their first company, the American Ballet, folded in 1938, after a stint at the Metropolitan Opera, where Balanchine's aesthetic clashed with the management's expectations. While the choreographer went on to Broadway and Hollywood, Kirstein founded another company, Ballet Caravan, whose repertory was greatly influenced by American folklore. The two came together again for a wartime goodwill tour of South America in 1941, for which Balanchine choreographed two major works, *Concerto Barocco* and *Ballet Imperial*. In 1946 they founded Ballet Society, whose first performance included the premiere of *The Four Temperaments*; two years later, this last company became New York City Ballet.

In the meantime, other companies had developed. In 1940, Ballet Theatre – soon to be renamed American Ballet Theatre – was launched on a grand scale. Where Balanchine's and Kirstein's companies grew from modest beginnings, ABT was a substantial, and substantially well-funded, enterprise from the start. It was supported and led by Lucia Chase, an heiress who had studied dance and performed with a company led by Mikhail Mordkin, a partner of Anna Pavlova. ABT started out with a substantial budget, former Ballet Russe stars and an eclectic repertory. It presented new works and revivals from Fokine, Massine, Nijinska and Balanchine, plus new and recent works by British and American choreographers. The Russian dancers were joined by a new generation of Americans, including Nora Kaye, who established herself as the dramatic dancer of her generation in Antony Tudor's 1942 *Pillar of Fire*. Agnes de Mille, who had worked with Tudor in London, created *Rodeo*, a hugely popular Americana ballet for the Ballet Russe de Monte Carlo, and soon came to work for American Ballet Theatre. From within its own ranks, the company discovered Jerome Robbins.

Born Jerome Rabinowitz in New York in 1918, he studied music and a range of dance styles, including ballet, modern dance, Spanish, oriental and what was known as 'interpretative dance'. In 1940, after dancing in musicals, he joined Ballet Theatre, where he worked with Mikhail Fokine and was cast as Petrushka. Still dancing, he was given the chance to make *Fancy Free*, a ballet about sailors on shore leave that he began working out on tour, snatching rehearsals where he could. It was an instant smash hit, with twenty-two curtain calls on opening night and immediate acclaim at home and on Ballet Theatre's first British tour. It was expanded into the musical *On the Town*, then a movie. For the rest of his career, Robbins would move between Broadway, ballet and films, working as director and choreographer.

For all Robbins' fame and eclectic schedule, ballet kept a large claim on him. In 1948 he saw the first performance by the newly formed New York City Ballet, including a 'rapturously' danced performance of Balanchine's *Symphony in C*. Smitten, Robbins wrote at once to the company, asking, 'Do you need someone . . . Is there any way you need me?'[11] Within months, he was dancing and choreographing for the company. Although he would leave to found his own company, and to work in other forms, the association with New York City Ballet would last for the rest of his life.

* * *

Britain and America were essentially building their ballet companies from scratch. France had a long-established tradition that had stagnated. At the Paris Opéra, most of the leading dancers were imported stars; male dancing had faded in the face of the *travesti* tradition, in which women played male roles. Diaghilev's Ballets Russes, with its powerful dancers, male stars and new choreography, offered a searing contrast. Jacques Rouché, appointed to the Opéra in 1914, brought in Ballets Russes stars and worked to develop French repertory, but it was a Diaghilev star, Serge Lifar, who was to shake the Paris Opéra awake. Rouché commissioned Balanchine to create a new ballet and suggested that he might become the company's ballet master. Balanchine fell seriously ill, and Lifar, who was starring in the new ballet, stepped in to complete it. By the end of the project, he had become director of the company.

Lifar's stardom, his personal glamour and his outsize personality were important weapons in his campaign at the Paris Opéra. In the face of the theatre's bureaucracy, he forced through reforms, driving out old customs, such as the tradition of leaving the auditorium chandeliers on during the performances. He immediately raised the profile of male dancing, increased discipline among the dancers and created a great many ballets. His approach to classicism was idiosyncratic: he added two new positions of the feet to the traditional five, for instance, and tried to create new relationships between dance and music. He also revived nineteenth-century classics, particularly *Giselle*, encouraging a generation of new French stars.

Lifar remained in charge during the Nazi occupation of France, taking the company on tours as ordered by Joseph Goebbels. At the end of the war Lifar was dismissed from his position and charged with collaboration. He was cleared of all charges and reinstated, at the wish of the dancers. Lasting until 1959, his reign at the Paris Opéra was autocratic, and could be stifling: there were limited opportunities for other choreographers, though Balanchine did create *Symphony in C* for the company in this period.

Given few chances at the Paris Opéra, young French choreographers began to experiment in smaller companies. The most spectacular was Les Ballets des Champs-Elysées, led by former Diaghilev librettists Boris Kochno and Jean Cocteau. Following the Diaghilev tradition of ballet as a stylish meeting place for the arts, the productions of this company were strikingly designed and produced. Roland Petit, a Paris Opéra dancer, made his name as a choreographer here, creating distinctive, highly theatrical works. From the existentialist crisis of *Le Jeune Homme et la Mort* to the gamine sexiness of his *Carmen*, Petit had a gift for catching the moods and fashions of his time.

Façade

Choreography: Frederick Ashton
Music: William Walton
Scenery: John Armstrong
Premiere: 26 April 1931, Cambridge Theatre, London
Original cast: *Yodelling Song* Lydia Lopokova; *Polka* Alicia Markova; *Popular Song* William Chappell, Walter Gore; *Tango Pasodoble* Lydia Lopokova, Frederick Ashton

Façade, one of Ashton's earliest surviving ballets, shows the chic and charm of his early work for Marie Rambert. The first performance was for the Camargo Society, which supported and encouraged the development of British ballet through performances for a subscription audience in London's West End. *Façade's* original cast included two Diaghilev ballerinas, Lopokova and Markova, in jaunty and unexpected roles.

William Walton's music was written to accompany poems by Edith Sitwell. At first, Ashton had hoped to use Walton's original version, with recitation; when Sitwell refused, he used Walton's orchestral suite. The ballet is a divertissement, almost a revue, satirising different dance styles. Over the years, Ashton added several new numbers. The 'Country Song' and 'Nocturne Peruvienne' aren't always included, but the 1941 'Foxtrot' is firmly established as part of the ballet.

Synopsis

Façade opens with a 'Scotch Rhapsody' for a man and two women in Highland dress. In 'Yodelling Song' a milkmaid enters with a stool, partnered by three mountaineers, who turn her on her stool and also form the cow, its udder made by the hands of one man, with another man's arm for the tail. In the 'Polka', a dancer appears in a straw boater hat, and patterned dress, taking off her skirt to dance a lively solo.

In the 'Foxtrot' two couples dance a fond pastiche of 1920s social dances, drawing on the Charleston, the Black Bottom and other popular dances. The 'Popular Song' is a soft-shoe number for two men in boaters and blazers: the dance is quick and witty, but they dance it with deadpan boredom, as if this were their hundredth performance. The 'Country Dance' features a country girl, a yokel and a squire.

In the 'Tango Pasodoble', a Latin gigolo dances with a naïve debutante. He is bent on seduction, running his hands up and down her back. He dips her and even flips her right over; she is not quite sure what is going on, but goes along with it anyway. (The 'Noche espagnola', added in 1941, was an extra solo for the gigolo character.) The ballet ends with a spirited finale.

Les Rendezvous

Choreography: Frederick Ashton
Music: Daniel François Auber, arranged by Constant Lambert
Designs: William Chappell
Premiere: 5 December 1933, Vic–Wells Ballet, Sadler's Wells Theatre, London
Original cast: Alicia Markova, Stanislas Idzikowski, Ninette de Valois, Stanley Judson, Robert Helpmann

Light-hearted and joyful, *Les Rendezvous* was also Ashton's first substantial classical work, a celebration of dancing. The ballet 'has no serious portent at all,' Ashton said, 'it is simply a vehicle for the exquisite dancing of Idzikowski and Markova.'[12] Showing dancers meeting and flirting, it demonstrated Ashton's mastery of solo and *corps* dances. William Chappell's designs, revised several times, suggested the Romantic era, with ribbons and tulle for the women.

Using pure and demanding classical steps, Ashton adds wit and social warmth in the meetings and greetings. The lyrical arms and twisting, turning upper bodies give the dancers individual personality – they change their minds, go this way and that, come to a stop and swoop onwards.

Constant Lambert, the music director at Sadler's Wells, chose and orchestrated the music, drawn from Auber's opera *L'Enfant prodigue*. Lambert, who had a long affair with the young Fonteyn, was an important influence on the company and on Ashton, suggesting themes and music, helping to develop and strengthen its productions.

Les Rendezvous opens with an ensemble in which dancers greet and acknowledge each other. The best known of Chappell's designs set the ballet in a park, a place for young people to meet and amuse themselves – and so they do. Women break off bounding jumps to exchange air kisses, men bow, everyone whirls into airy partner dances. The ensembles are full of patterns, circles and lines.

A female quartet forms a square formation; the dancers then run to change places within the pattern, their dances full of flicked wrists and gesture from the shoulder. The dances for these four women were one of Ashton's revisions. 'A year after the premiere of *Les Rendezvous*, he added the four "little girls" who are customarily danced by young company members,' wrote the critic Alastair Macaulay:

> It is very hard to imagine *Les Rendezvous* without them. And this addition changed the meaning of the ballet. These four are only semiparticipants in the main action. They are innocent voyeurs, junior relatives of the *corps* in *Les Biches*. The fragrance they add to the ballet is a suggestion of excited prenubile or, at any rate, predebutant observation of adult mores.[13]

The social mood continues in the virtuoso dances Ashton created for his leading dancers. The man's display jumps, and pirouettes are coloured by more 'thrown' gestures. When he partners the ballerina, they are framed by the *corps de ballet*: pairs of men lift the women, swinging them back and forth, as the female quartet weaves in and out. The *adagio* ends with the ballerina lifted high by four men, the women framing her and her partner admiring her from a distance. There's also a prancing *pas de trois*, in which the woman moves back and forth between her male partners.

The ballerina's solo, created for Markova, shows Ashton remembering Pavlova's use of her eyes and hands. The ballerina crosses her wrists and opens her arms, with a last little flutter of her hands, her torso bending and swaying. She exits with a flourish – 'well pleased', the critic David Vaughan points out, 'with her own virtuosity'.[14]

A male *pas de six* is full of strutting and poses on one knee, with handclaps offstage. The finale brings the whole cast on in more encounters, even sneaking in a quick game of blind man's buff before they bid each other farewell. As the curtain falls, the four women of the *pas de quatre* shrug lightly – another throwaway gesture that would become an Ashton trademark.

Serenade

Choreography: George Balanchine
Music: Peter Ilyich Tchaikovsky, Serenade in C for String Orchestra, op. 48
Premiere: 9 June 1934 at the estate of Felix M. Warburg, White Plains,
New York
Costumes: William B. Okie Jr; since 1952, Karinska

Balanchine created *Serenade* to teach the young dancers of his new School
of American Ballet the difference between classwork and performance. He
made steps for whatever pupils showed up: seventeen on the first night,
nine on the second, six on the third. One dancer arrived late; another fell
and started to cry. Balanchine put both incidents into the dance. When
male students joined the class, partnering became possible.

Once he had decided to turn *Serenade* into a stage work, Balanchine
revised the ballet, keeping and sometimes emphasising the steps prompted
by accidents. In the first production, soloist moments were shared between
nine dancers. Balanchine revised and reshaped the leading roles several
times, but *Serenade* is now danced by three leading women. It remains
an unusually democratic ballet: the corps de ballet is in constant motion,
flowing in and out of patterns. Karinska's costumes have become standard
wih long blue tulle skirts for the women, deeper blue tights and tunics for
the men.

Originally, Balanchine used the first three of Tchaikovsky's four movements, the Sonatina, Waltz and Elegy. In 1941 he added the fourth movement, the Russian Dance, but placed it third, before the Elegy. The ballet's
mood is romantic but fresh: the dancers run with youthful energy, expan-
sive and bright.

First movement. This opens with seventeen women arranged in slanting
lines, each with one arm raised. Moving their arms to first position and
turning their feet out, their pose becomes explicitly classical. Dancing, they
break into smaller groups. One woman emerges in a whirling, jumping
solo. Others respond, until they are all spinning in a large circle, before
swiftly returning to the ballet's opening tableau. Another woman arrives
late, finding her place in the group. A man enters at the back of the stage,
walking towards the latecomer. The others exit.

Second movement. This is a waltz, and the couple dances together. The
other women return, and the latecomer dances among them. As another

soloist spins forwards, two lilting lines of dancers advance and cross behind her. When the waltz ends, all but five women leave.

Third movement. The five women sink to the floor in the splits, turning towards each other to take hands. Rising, they wind through intricate chains, breaking apart and speeding up as the 'Russian' melody sounds. A man rushes in and partners one of the women. As the music finishes, and the dancers run off, she falls, her head buried in her arms.

Fourth movement. A woman enters leading a man, guiding him towards the fallen dancer. The man helps her up, and partners both women, singly or together. At last, he leaves with the woman who led him in (sometimes nicknamed 'the Dark Angel'). Left alone, the other woman sinks to the floor. Six women enter, reaching to her. She gets up, runs through them to embrace another woman, and sinks to her knees. Three men lift her high and carry her across the stage, the other dancers following in a procession.

It's easy to read hints of a story in *Serenade*'s whirling dances: love and rejection, or a suggestion of death and transcendence in the final procession, with a woman carried high. One beautiful grouping, in which the ballerina lies looking up at her partner, who stands framed by the arms of the 'Dark Angel', echoes Canova's statue of Psyche and a winged Cupid. But these are only suggestions, echoes rather than a narrative. The ballet's dramas are implicit, not to be pinned down, and Balanchine meant to keep them that way. In conversation with his biographer Bernard Taper, Balanchine described one of *Serenade*'s incidents in terms of fate. Would he tell his dancers that, Taper wondered? 'Balanchine drew back in mock horror. "God forbid!"'[15] The point to the ballet is not a story but the rush of Tchaikovsky's music, the dancers swirling and eddying to its melody.

The dancer and critic Nancy Reynolds points out that *Serenade* is a favourite among dancers. 'In contrast, perhaps, to some of Balanchine's more technically difficult ballets, in which the performer may feel inadequate, *Serenade* makes dancers feel beautiful.'[16] It is Balanchine's most widely performed ballet.

Lilac Garden (Jardin aux lilas)

Choreography: Antony Tudor
Music: Ernest Chausson, *Poème* for violin and orchestra, op. 25
Designs: Hugh Stevenson

Premiere: 26 January 1936, Ballet Rambert, Mercury Theatre, London
Original cast: *Caroline* Maude Lloyd; *her Lover* Hugh Laing; *the Man she Must Marry* Antony Tudor; *an Episode in his Past* Peggy van Praagh

Antony Tudor's *Lilac Garden* is a ballet of intense, repressed emotion. Caroline, its heroine, is about to make a marriage of convenience to a man she does not love. Before the wedding, at a party in a garden full of lilac trees, she sees the man she loves among the guests, without quite having the chance to say goodbye to him.

Tudor set *Lilac Garden* in what was then the recent past, urging his dancers to read Edwardian novels to get a sense of the period's social codes. Atmosphere is a vital part of the ballet: the dancer Hugh Laing remembered that, for the premiere at the tiny Mercury Theatre, Tudor had lilac water sprayed in the auditorium. 'It was Antony Tudor who first put his women in long dresses, the Edwardian dresses his mother wore,' Agnes de Mille explained:

> The effect was startling and a real shock to the imagination. The audience was called upon to accept the balletic gesture as a form of simple dramatic communication. It was also asked to watch women who looked like their mothers and aunts kicking over their heads, or wrapping their legs around men's bodies.[17]

Synopsis

The ballet opens with Caroline and her fiancé standing side by side, not touching, both looking away to the sides. She grips her own elbow, sliding her hand down her arm to her wrist. It's a tiny movement, showing her tension and unhappiness without breaking decorum. From this stiff pose, she moves eagerly when she catches sight of her lover, a young man in uniform – but she gestures to him to keep away. The rest of the ballet is a series of meetings and partings, characters trying to reach out to each other without making their emotions public.

Caroline's brief dance with her lover is interrupted by her fiancé's ex-mistress, then by other guests: the lovers don't have a chance to be alone. Looking for her lover in the garden, Caroline turns this way and that, her stiff changes of direction showing her frustration.

Her fiancé has his own encounter with his ex-mistress, who hurls herself at him, risking discovery with her abandon – but they too are interrupted. A female guest sees Caroline's snatched meeting with her lover, but is sympathetic. She warns another guest to say nothing, and helps Caroline upright when she buries her face in her hands.

As the music reaches its climax, with the whole orchestra picking up the violin theme, the dancers freeze for several bars, formally grouped with Caroline in a swooning backbend. For a moment, Caroline steps out of the frozen tableau, reaching to her lover. Then she withdraws, returning to her swooning pose in her fiancé's arms. The other dancers come to life, make formal farewells and prepare to leave. At the last moment, Caroline's lover presses a bunch of lilac into her hand. She bids goodbye to her guests. As she gestures to her lover, her fiancé draws her hand back. She takes his arm and walks away, leaving her lover alone in the garden, his back to the audience, in a sorrowful pose.

The most powerful moment in *Lilac Garden*, the frozen tableau, is both huge and still: emotion expressed in an absence of movement, and in tiny details and changes of movement. This is characteristic of a ballet in which feeling is choked down for the sake of the conventions, while Chausson's lush music pours out what the characters are not admitting. Caroline chooses to go on with her loveless marriage, to accept the role society has in mind for her.

Tudor's choreography sets flowing motion against stiff, tight movements. He asks his dancers to suppress the muscular effort of the choreography: it has classical steps, but frames them in unfamiliar ways, covering up preparations. Women in flowing dresses move stiffly on straight legs, shifting from *pointe* to *pointe*, their arms held by their sides.

Lilac Garden was staged for American Ballet Theatre in 1940, where it has remained in regular performance. 'We perform Tudor because we must,' said Mikhail Baryshnikov, who directed the company in the 1980s. 'Tudor is our conscience.'[18] Tudor thought the designs of the 1952 New York City Ballet production were too lavish:

> They were divinely beautiful costumes, but the people wearing the costumes could not have had the thoughts my people had. The ambience of the family was in the wrong place. It became a rich family. My ladies aren't rich. Caroline's family is falling on worse days, trying to keep up a respectable picture – otherwise, why is she going to marry that other man?[19]

For Tudor, social milieu and psychology were closely bound together; he had a very clear image of the world that his heroine submits to.

Les Patineurs

Choreography: Frederick Ashton
Music: Giacomo Meyerbeer (arr. Constant Lambert)
Scenery: William Chappell
Premiere: 16 February 1937, Vic–Wells Ballet, Sadler's Wells Theatre, London
Original cast: *Blue Skater* Harold Turner; *Couple in White* Margot Fonteyn, Robert Helpmann; *Girls in Blue* Mary Honer, Elizabeth Miller; *Girls in Red* June Brae, Pamela May

Ashton's enchanting skating ballet uses the virtuosity of classical ballet to suggest the dazzle – and the occasional bumps – of skaters. William Chappell's park setting frames the stage with trellis archways, hung with Chinese lanterns. He dressed the dancers in Victorian winter clothes: cosy fur-trimmed jackets, little caps and ballet slippers that look like boots.

As with Ashton's earlier *Les Rendezvous*, Constant Lambert chose the music, the 'skating ballet' from Meyerbeer's opera *Le Prophète*, plus numbers from the same composer's *L'Étoile du nord*. Lambert's arrangement was originally intended for a new ballet by Ninette de Valois – until Ashton heard it, and begged to use it instead. He had seen very little skating when he started work on the ballet. Elizabeth Miller, one of the first cast, knew how to skate and helped with advice. Ashton used gliding *chassés*, little bouncing steps on *pointe* that evoke skates chipping into the ice, all manner of skaterly jumps and spins. This was, Ashton remembered, the first time he had done 'something that was simply for virtuosity, just to show dancers off',[20] reflecting the growing strength of the young Vic–Wells Ballet.

At the start of *Les Patineurs*, the *corps de ballet* glides in, skating in pairs. Soloists weave in and out. A virtuoso skater in blue throws off dazzling leaps and spins with a light-hearted shrug. There is a slower, more romantic *pas de deux* for a couple in white. Two women in blue whirl through pirouettes and *fouettés*, while two red girls, less experienced, come down to earth with a thud, before picking themselves up and skating on.

For the finale, all the different characters whirl in and out; a group glides past behind the arches, carrying the white girl aloft. The *corps* skates on in winding single file, brought up short when the woman in front slips over. As she gets up, the dancers notice that snow has started to fall, just as the music changes tempo. Responding to the falling flakes and the building excitement of the music, they leap into new dances and whirl away home, leaving the blue boy spinning ever faster as the curtain falls.

Dark Elegies

Choreography: Antony Tudor
Music: Gustav Mahler, *Kindertotenlieder*
Designs: Nadia Benois
Premiere: 19 February 1937, Ballet Rambert, Duchess Theatre, London
Original cast: *First Song* Peggy van Praagh; *Second Song* Maude Lloyd, Antony Tudor; *Third Song* Walter Gore; *Fourth Song* Agnes de Mille; *Fifth Song* Hugh Laing

Dark Elegies is a portrait of bereavement. To Mahler's *Kindertotenlieder* (*Songs on the Death of Children*), a community shares its grief after the death of their children. Nadia Benois' backcloth shows a stormy landscape of rocks, sea and trees blown by the wind. The four men and eight women are dressed in simple peasant costumes; the singer is usually onstage with them, wearing similar clothes.

Tudor's dance style is spare and simple, drawing on folk dances and the expressionist modern dance of the 1930s. His gestures are understated: dancers contract their torsos as if sobbing, rock or sway, or make a cradling gesture for a child who is not there. The stark movement forms a contrast to Mahler's highly emotional music.

The first five songs are a scene of bereavement, dances for the ensemble with solos for two women and one men. As one woman dances her grief, the *corps de ballet* dancers kneel with their backs to her, sharing her sorrow but still separate. In another, they watch with sympathy. The second scene suggests a new day, and a sense of resignation. At the end, the dancers quietly walk off in pairs.

Checkmate

Choreography: Ninette de Valois
Music: Arthur Bliss
Designs: Edward McKnight Kauffer
Premiere: 15 June 1937, Vic–Wells Ballet, Théâtre des Champs-Elysées, Paris
Original cast: *Black Queen* June Brae; *Red Knight* Harold Turner; *Red King* Robert Helpmann

Ninette de Valois, founder of The Royal Ballet, was also its first choreographer, though as time went on she increasingly stepped back from this role.

Her most lasting works were created in the 1930s, dramatic ballets that combined precise technique with closely researched themes, often with deliberately British topics and designs: the biblical *Job* (1931) drew on William Blake's illustrations, while *The Rake's Progress* (1935) was inspired by a series of paintings by William Hogarth. Annabel Farjeon, who danced a pawn in the first cast of *Checkmate*, loved dancing Ninette de Valois' work. 'Technically the steps were not difficult,' she wrote, 'but to get the style correct – that balance between restraint and display, that sense of period and character – was a problem that these ballets always posed.'[21]

Checkmate is a symbolic ballet, a game of chess played by Love and Death. Like *The Green Table* or *Les Présages*, two other ballets of the 1930s, it shows stylised characters driven by fate. Looking back, it's easy to read the threat of the impending Second World War into de Valois' ominous theme, though this was not commented on at the time. De Valois herself told her dancers to 'move as if "moved" by fate – to imagine being "lifted or pushed along the board"'.[22]

The theme was suggested by the composer Arthur Bliss: the dramatic score was his first for ballet. The bold designs are by Edward McKnight Kauffer, an American artist best known for his graphic work. Influenced by the Italian Futurists, he was a leading figure in London Underground's superb pre-war poster campaigns. His sets and costumes blend stark geometric angles and sharp colour, with chess-inspired headdresses to identify the figures.

Synopsis

Before the frontcloth, figures of Love and Death are seen at a chess table. Death takes off his glove to play, revealing a skeletal hand. Fighting for the lives of their subjects, they begin to play.

The curtain rises, and the Red Pawns and Knights assemble. The Red Knights are confronted by the two Black Knights. The Black Queen appears, to a shimmering, menacing fanfare – a glamorous, feminine figure who bewitches one of the Red Knights. The Red pieces parade in, led by ceremonious Bishops and stomping Castles. They prepare the way for the frail, elderly Red King, who is led in by his devoted, younger wife.

The Black Queen leads the attack on the Red pieces, sword in hand. The Red Queen pleads for mercy, but is taken by the Black Knights. The Red Knight challenges the Black Queen, but is weakened by his fascination for her: when he hesitates to kill her, she takes his sword as well as her own and stabs him. Love and Death step onto the board to see this turning point in the game.

The Black Queen dances in triumph, brandishing her two swords. The Red King retreats, but he cannot escape: Black pieces drive him across the board, using their staffs to trap and harry him. The Black Queen closes in to kill him: checkmate.

Billy the Kid

Choreography: Eugene Loring
Music: Aaron Copland
Libretto: Lincoln Kirstein
Designs: Jared French
Premiere: 16 October 1938, Ballet Caravan, Chicago Opera House, Chicago
Original cast: *Billy* Eugene Loring; *Mother and Sweetheart* Marie Jeanne; *Pat Garrett* Lew Christensen; *Alias* Todd Bolender

Eager to create an American ballet, Lincoln Kirstein and his collaborators in Ballet Caravan turned to specifically American themes. *Billy the Kid* is a ballet western, the tale of a notorious outlaw set against the westward progress of the pioneers. It was created when the western genre was at a peak of popularity, with hundreds of novels and films set in the American west. Copland would go on to write scores for two more celebrated dances on the theme of cowboys and pioneers, Agnes de Mille's *Rodeo* and Martha Graham's *Appalachian Spring*.

Synopsis

Prologue. The pioneers travel westward. A path of light suggests the setting sun. Pat Garrett crosses the stage, with men and women following after him.

Scene 1. A street in a frontier town, north of the Mexican border. Townsfolk pass: cowboys, Mexicans, saloon women. Billy's mother enters, her son clinging to her skirts. A fight breaks out: a gunfighter misses his target, accidentally killing Billy's mother. Billy stabs him dead, then flees. The townsfolk take away the body of Billy's mother. The dead gunfighter will reappear as 'Alias', who represents all the men Billy has killed.

Scene 2. The desert. Billy has become a notorious outlaw. A solo reveals his speed and violence. A posse of three men arrives, looking for Billy, who hides and shoots the leader. Blackout. Billy plays cards with Pat Garrett by a campfire. Billy cheats, and is caught out by Garrett. When Garrett leaves, Billy feels he should have killed him. Garrett returns with a posse; in the shoot-out, Billy kills Alias. Captured by Garrett, Billy is taken to jail. His sweetheart grieves for him.

Scene 3. In jail. Billy plays cards with his jailer, Alias, then finds a chance to shoot him and escape. Shielded by Mexican women and then Alias, now playing an Indian guide, he is led away. Pat Garrett leads a posse by, without seeing Billy. Billy sleeps, and dreams of his sweetheart – a dream ballet in which she dances on *pointe*. Guided by Alias, Garrett finds Billy. Billy wakes, but does not see Garrett or Alias. Laughing at his own fears, he lights a cigarette – giving Garrett a target to aim at. He shoots Billy. The Mexican women grieve over his body.

Scene 4. The desert. As in the prologue, Garrett leads pioneers forward to the West.

The ballet uses mime gestures, like those of childhood games, to suggest pistols or horseback riding. Characters become 'invisible' – hidden by darkness or scenery – by holding a hand in front of their faces. Billy's dream, which gives him a moment of romantic happiness in contrast to the rest of the story, would become a familiar device in ballets and musicals (it was already an established cinematic technique). The storytelling is stylised and full of duplications: in a Freudian twist, the same dancer plays Billy's mother and his sweetheart, while another plays all the men killed by Billy (twenty-one by the time he was twenty-one years old). Pat Garrett, a friend of Billy's who will become the sheriff who kills him, appears throughout the ballet.

Ballet Imperial (also Tchaikovsky Piano Concerto No. 2)

Choreography: George Balanchine
Music: Pyotr Ilych Tchaikovsky, Piano Concerto No. 2 in G
Designs: Mstislav Doboujinsky
Premiere: 25 June 1941, American Ballet Caravan, Teatro Municipal, Rio de Janeiro
Original cast: Marie-Jeanne, William Dollar, Gisella Caccialanza, Fred Danieli, Nicholas Magallanes

In 1941, led by Balanchine and Lincoln Kirstein, Ballet Caravan set off on a goodwill tour of South America. The tour was sponsored by the Office of

the Coordinator of Inter-American Affairs under the Roosevelt adminis-
tration, which gave Kirstein 'a check which seemed so large that I was as
scared as if I had stolen it'.[23]

Aiming to show that the classical tradition was alive and well in America,
Balanchine created *Ballet Imperial* as a homage to Petipa, a new work in
the Imperial tradition. The women wore tutus, with a crown for the
ballerina; Mstislav Doboujinsky's original scenery showed a view of the
river Neva from the Winter Palace. The choreography is full of courtly
grandeur.

The leading role was created for Marie-Jeanne (originally Marie-Jeanne
Pelus). The first ballerina trained entirely at the School of American Ballet,
she was known for the speed, daring and clarity of her dancing. With its
turns, leaps and beaten steps, her role in *Ballet Imperial* is still considered
one of the toughest in the Balanchine repertory. The ballerina and her cavalier are supported by a leading female and two male soloists.

First movement. This opens with eight couples standing on a diagonal,
facing each other at a slight distance. The men approach their partners,
who bow and join them in quick, formal dances. They are joined by eight
women from the *corps de ballet*. As they make a circular grouping, the
soloist runs in, winding in and out of the circle, preparing the way for the
ballerina, who dances to the piano cadenza. After her solo, she is joined by
her cavalier. The soloist dances a *pas de trois* with two men, before the
leading couple return for a glittering finale.

Second movement. This is slower and more romantic in mood, suggesting
a vision scene. The ballerina and her partner move through a maze of *corps
de ballet* women. In their *pas de deux*, the cavalier pleads with the ballerina
in formal mime.

Third movement. This is dashing and brilliant. The ballerina is carried in
on her partner's shoulder, before dancing a speedy solo. There are brief
dances for the cavalier and the three soloists of the first movement, before
an ensemble finale.

Ballet Imperial is deliberately grand. Kirstein argued that it was 'not an
American ballet. It is a Russian ballet, danced by an American company'.[24]
It is more rooted in the past, in images of aristocracy and formal hierarchy, than other Balanchine tutu works. The dancer Ruthanna Boris once
asked Balanchine why he didn't revive Petipa's *Paquita*, and he replied:

'Because if we do *Paquita*, everybody will see what I stole for *Ballet Imperial*.'[25]

In 1973, Balanchine presented the ballet under the title *Concerto No. 2*, with a plain backdrop and much simpler costumes, with soft chiffon skirts rather than tutus. He also dropped the passage of mime for the cavalier. Some viewers missed the old formal glitter. Both versions are still danced by other companies: The Royal Ballet, which first staged *Ballet Imperial* in 1950, still dances it under that title. The Mariinsky Ballet, the company evoked in this work, first danced it in 2004 with soft skirts and the title *Ballet Imperial*.

Concerto Barocco

Choreography: George Balanchine
Premiere: 27 June 1941, American Ballet Caravan, Teatro Municipal, Rio de Janeiro
Music: Johann Sebastian Bach, Double Violin Concerto in D minor
Scenery and costumes: Eugene Berman
Original cast: Marie-Jeanne, Mary Jane Shea, William Dollar

In *Ballet Imperial*, Balanchine had looked back to St Petersburg classicism. In *Concerto Barocco*, from the same period, he created pure classicism without nostalgia. Danced to the music of J. S. Bach, the ballet responds to the baroque music's formal clarity, playing with its rhythms and architecture. There are touches of jazz in Balanchine's response to Bach, a joyful syncopation.

The violinist Nathan Milstein, who suggested the music, remembered Balanchine saying he was attracted to two aspects of Bach: 'the mathematical precision of his music and, at the same time, its purely emotional and unfeigned straining for God'.[26] His ballet reflects both the clarity and the emotion of the music.

First movement. This opens with eight *corps de ballet* women, who stay onstage throughout the work. Dancing intricate patterns, they also show the bold shifts of weight of Balanchine's style, giving their dance a combination of precision and scale. (Early film of *Concerto Barocco* shows the dance on a small performing space, yet the women still give the impression of covering ground.) Two ballerinas enter with the two solo violins, dancing together or winding in and out of the *corps de ballet*.

Second movement. One of the soloists returns with a male partner. The mood becomes lyrical, the ballerina moving with a new grandeur of scale.

Her partner lifts her through rising arcs, this way and that, higher and higher. At the end of their duet, he slides her in repeated swoops, down to the floor and up into *arabesque*.

Third movement. In this speedy finale all ten women dance with bright speed and rhythm, with crisp swings of the arms and springs from closed to open positions, left and right. As the ballet ends, they all sink onto one knee.

Concerto Barocco was originally performed to designs by Eugene Berman. Since 1951 it has been danced in practice clothes against a blue backdrop, focusing attention on the clean patterns of the dancing. Suki Schorer, who danced a soloist role in the ballet, described Balanchine's care for:

> exactitude in timing – the syncopation. He works for hours to get that right. It's as though an ounce makes all the difference. And for all its refinement, he likes it 'jazzy'. There's one place where the *corps* almost does the Charleston on *pointe*. In some of my most brisk and classical movements, he kept saying, 'Make it jazzy. Lead with the hip.'[27]

Pillar of Fire

Choreography: Antony Tudor
Music: Arnold Schoenberg, *Verklärte Nacht*
Designs: Jo Mielziner
Premiere: 8 April 1942, Ballet Theatre, Metropolitan Opera House, New York
Original cast: *Hagar* Nora Kaye; *Young Man from the House Opposite* Hugh Laing; *the Friend* Antony Tudor; *the Eldest Sister* Lucia Chase; *the Youngest Sister* Annabelle Lyon

In his first work for Ballet Theatre, Tudor developed the style he had created with *Lilac Garden*, exploring the emotions of a repressed and unhappy woman in her desperate search for love.

The ballet's theme comes from its music. Schoenberg's string sextet was inspired by a poem by Richard Dehmel, a tangled tale of love and forgiveness. A couple walks in the moonlight, and the woman admits she is pregnant by another man: afraid that she would never find love, she slept with a stranger, only to meet her true love afterwards. Her new lover reassures her:

their love is so great that her child will be his too. Tudor developed this theme into a psychological drama, showing the other man and the community around his heroine, Hagar.

The ballet's title, like the heroine's name, is Biblical. 'I decided on *Pillar of Fire* because Hagar, like Hagar in the Bible, was a lost soul,' Tudor said. 'She thought she had lost a life of sexuality – and sexuality helps a lot of people out of their problems.'[28]

Synopsis

The ballet is set in the early twentieth century. The set shows two houses facing each other. Hagar sits brooding on the steps of her house. She watches people go by, young lovers and unmarried women: Hagar is afraid that she will be left a spinster.

In love with the Friend, Hagar fears he does not love her. The Eldest Sister torments her by urging their Youngest Sister to flirt with the Friend. In despair, Hagar approaches the young man from the house opposite. In their duet, she pushes against him and turns away, sexually needy but repressed. She lies at his feet, then turns sideways, lifting one knee defensively. At the climax of their *pas de deux*, she jumps straight at him, legs braced around his torso. He takes her into the house opposite.

Hagar returns alone, filled with shame. She is rejected by everyone: her sisters, their neighbours, even the man who seduced her. When the Friend returns, Hagar tries to flee, but he holds and supports her. They dance tenderly together, and walk away to a happy future.

Tudor chose an Edwardian setting for the ballet, since Schoenberg's music was written in 1899. As with *Lilac Garden*, it evokes what was a recent but more uptight past. Hagar's emotional state is explored with sexual frankness. When she leaps at the young man from the house opposite, the critic Edwin Denby wrote in the ballet's first season, 'The audience watches spellbound, shocked and moved at the same time.'[29]

In this role, Nora Kaye made her reputation as a great dramatic ballerina. She remembered Tudor's care in creating the ballet's psychological setting, the identity and relationships of the characters. 'When Tudor started rehearsing with the three sisters and even before he started the actual steps – the choreography – he talked about our characters and the small town in which we lived,' Kaye said. 'He even described the wallpaper of our house. It was so clear in our minds that we couldn't have done a wrong movement if we'd tried.'[30]

Rodeo (The Courting at Burnt Ranch)

Choreography: Agnes de Mille
Music: Aaron Copland
Scenery: Oliver Smith
Costumes: Kermit Love
Premiere: 16 October 1942, Ballet Russe de Monte Carlo, Metropolitan Opera House, New York
Original cast: *Cowgirl* Agnes de Mille; *Champion Roper* Frederic Franklin; *Head Wrangler* Casimir Kokich

Agnes de Mille was a choreographer of Americana, bringing ballet into Broadway musicals and popular American dance into ballet. Like Jerome Robbins, she moved between musicals, film and ballet companies, but her particular focus was on storytelling, with an emphasis on American folk style.

She was born in 1905 into a rich, artistic family. Her father, William Churchill de Mille, was a successful playwright; her uncle was Cecil B. de Mille, the film director famous for the sweep and spectacle of his Hollywood movies. After seeing performances by Anna Pavlova and modern dance pioneer Ruth St Denis, de Mille decided to become a dancer, creating her own recital programmes. She moved to London in 1932, where she danced in and choreographed musicals. She also danced with Marie Rambert's company, where she appeared in the premiere of Antony Tudor's *Dark Elegies*. Back in America, she created dances for Broadway musicals and Hollywood films, and worked with Ballet Theatre (now American Ballet Theatre) from its first season.

Rodeo was her first big popular success. Having moved to the US during the Second World War, the Ballet Russe de Monte Carlo asked de Mille to create a ballet on American themes – a growing genre among American dance companies, but a departure for the glamorous touring ballet troupe. A Cinderella story with a tomboy heroine, de Mille's ballet celebrates the already mythic American West, a land of cowboys, champion ropers and big open spaces. Images of riding and lariat-twirling are built into her dances, but so are American dance styles, from tap dancing to square dancing. 'I'm contemporary, I'm American, I come from my own background, I have to speak from my own background, and that would be American vernacular,'[31] de Mille said in a 1973 television interview.

Aaron Copland had already composed a Wild West ballet in *Billy the Kid*. For *Rodeo*, he created a bright, optimistic score with textures as open and bright as a prairie. There's a thrilling energy to his theme for *Rodeo*'s evening social dance. In music, as in dancing, *Rodeo* makes a European traditional form thoroughly American.

Synopsis

Scene 1. The corral. Cowboys prepare for the Saturday night rodeo. The men's dances evoke the moves of the horses and of lassoing. The Cowgirl heroine, dressed in trousers, tries to join in, but the men cold-shoulder her. They're much more interested in the prettily dressed, feminine city girls visiting the rancher's daughter. The Champion Roper, the Head Wrangler and the other men show off their skills. When the Cowgirl tries to ride a bucking bronco, she is thrown and humiliated. Everyone else leaves for the evening dance, leaving the Cowgirl behind.

Frontcloth scene. In the blackout, the audience hears clapping and stamping feet. The lights go up on a traditional square dance for four couples and a caller.

Scene 2. Everybody is dressed up for the dance, ready to show off. The Cowgirl arrives, still in her working clothes. The Champion Roper tries to tidy her up, cleaning her face and dusting her down, and urges her to dance. The Cowgirl is infatuated with the Head Wrangler, and is jealous when he dances with another girl. The Champion Roper tries to cheer her up. She runs away, returning in a bright red dress. Suddenly, both the Wrangler and the Roper want to dance with her – but the Roper appeals to her with a tap dance and a kiss. She realises that she loves him, and the ballet ends with celebration dance.

The outsider heroine trying to deal with conventional romance from the outside would become a de Mille theme. Told that she wasn't pretty enough to act in Hollywood, forging a career in ballet choreography – which was, and is, a male-dominated field – de Mille clearly identified with her Cowgirl. The traditional romantic comedy ending, with the Cowgirl remaking herself to get her man, has been criticised by some feminist critics; on the other hand, the heroine and the tap-dancing Roper remain an unconventional pair. In de Mille's first scenario, the Head Wrangler outdanced the Cowgirl until she fell into his arms. In the final ballet, she remains independent and individual. It's a vivid theatrical role for a dancer, mixing assertive dancing, wistfulness and cocky bravado.

Rodeo was an immediate hit, greeted with standing ovations and twenty-two curtain calls. As a result, de Mille was commissioned to create the dances for the musical *Oklahoma!*, and *Rodeo* was taken into the repertory of American Ballet Theatre and other companies. In 2015, Justin Peck staged a new version at New York City Ballet, using Copland's orchestral suite. With the curious title of *Rōdēʾo: Four Dance Episodes*, Peck's plotless work, for fifteen men and one woman, is an athletic one.

Suite en Blanc (Noir et Blanc)

Choreography: Serge Lifar
Music: Edouard Lalo (music from the ballet *Namouna*)
Premiere: 19 June 1943, Paris Opéra Ballet, Paris Opéra, Paris
Original cast: Solange Schwartz, Yvette Chauviré, Lycette Darsonval, Serge Lifar

Suite en blanc, sometimes called *Noir et blanc*, is a set piece for a classical company. Since taking over the reins in 1929, Lifar had revitalised the Paris Opéra, demanding more respect for dance, overhauling the dancing and the repertory, and producing a new generation of home-grown stars. In *Suite en blanc* he showed off his dancers, from ballerinas to *corps de ballet*, in the still-new plotless genre. It also reflects Lifar's own theories of ballet, with parallel as well as turned-out positions and slanting, off-balance poses.

The music was from Edouard Lalo's *Namouna*, a perfumed score that had divided audiences at its 1882 premiere. (It has since been used by Alexei Ratmansky in *Namouna – a Grand Divertissement*.) The ballet is danced against a black backdrop, with platforms at the back of the stage. The women wear white, while the men wear black tights with white blouses.

It opens with the full company posed in a tableau. They exit, leaving three women in long Romantic tutus to dance a trio known as the Siesta. After they exit, two men leap on to dance the *pas de trois* with a ballerina in a high tutu. They take turns partnering her and displaying their own jumps. The Serenade is danced by another ballerina with a *corps de ballet* of eight women, followed by a *pas de cinq* for a woman with four men. La Cigarette, perhaps the ballet's most famous solo, is danced by the chief ballerina, who winds her arms in curling lines, backed by a *corps de ballet* of women.

The principal male solo is a virtuoso mazurka, followed by a *pas de deux* for another ballerina and her partner. After one last ballerina solo, known as La Flûte, the whole company returns for the finale. Lifar uses the *corps de ballet* to link the different soloist numbers; it acts as a frame for the leading dancers or provides linking movements from one dance to the next.

Fancy Free

Choreography: Jerome Robbins
Music: Leonard Bernstein

Scenery: Oliver Smith
Costumes: Kermit Love
Premiere: 18 April 1944, Ballet Theatre, Metropolitan Opera House, New York
Original cast: Harold Lang, John Kriza, Jerome Robbins, Muriel Bentley, Janet Reed, Shirley Eckl

Fancy Free was Jerome Robbins' first ballet. With a jazzy score and a story of sailors on shore leave, it was an immediate smash hit, making the names of Robbins and his composer, Leonard Bernstein. 'This is Robbins' first go at choreography,' wrote the critic John Martin, 'and the only thing he has to worry about is how in the world he is going to make his second one any better.'[32] The ballet was developed into the musical *On the Town*, later filmed with Gene Kelly. Robbins' subject was less unusual in musical theatre, which was well supplied with sailors; for ballet, the theme of everyday, contemporary life was unusual.

Synopsis

Manhattan on a summer night, a street scene with a bar and a street lamp. Inside, the bartender polishes glasses and reads his newspaper. Three sailors on shore leave arrive, swinging round the street lamp, dancing and strutting and teasing each other. One enters the bar, his companions follow – and one is tricked into paying for the drinks. They look out for company, sharing chewing gum. A young woman passes, very aware of the sailors. Watching her, they lean so far forwards they almost fall over, then try to attract her attention. One catches her bag, imitating her, and throwing it between his friends. The sailors compete for her attention, and two race after her when she leaves. The last, knocked down in the scuffle, picks himself up and is delighted to meet a second girl. He buys her a drink and dances with her, until his friends return with the first girl. The sailors agree to a dance contest: the women will judge it, and the loser will leave the other pairs alone.

The first sailor shows off with spectacular steps, jumping onto the bar and drinking a beer while miming more turns with his free hand. The second number, by the sailor who danced with the second girl, is softer and more sentimental: the girls sigh approval, while the sailors hold their noses. The third solo is a sinuous Latin dance.

The women can't decide, while the sailors start to fight among themselves. They don't even notice when the women slip away. At last the sailors pick themselves up, dust themselves down and realise they've been left alone. They have another drink, trick the sentimental sailor into paying again, and head out into the evening. Just as they resolve to avoid girls, a third woman walks down the street. The sailors idle away in the opposite direction – then turn around and chase after her.

Robbins described *Fancy Free* as 'a jazz ballet, light in mood', asking Bernstein for a score that would be 'bang-away, hot boogie-woogie, dreamy, torchy . . . not sentimental or romantic at all'.[33] The choreography moves easily between styles: the first sailor's solo includes multiple pirouettes and double air turns, while the third – first danced by Robbins himself – is full of Latin moves. Robbins chose a young cast, all American-born, at home in anything he threw at them.

Fancy Free was hailed around the world as a distinctively American ballet. It's full of observed behaviour, things Robbins had seen in his own New York. 'In addition to plundering his recollections of sailors parading their jaunty personas (more often a bluff) through Times Square and studying the popular dances of the day, Robbins also kept his eyes primed for the telling gesture, the interesting pattern,' writes his biographer Deborah Jowitt. ' "If we were on a train and we looked out a window and saw planes flying in formation, Jerry used it in the ballet," said [Janet] Reed. "Everything he saw that he could use, he did." '[34] The first cast saw their own personalities reflected in their roles.

Decades on, Robbins' up-to-the-minute New York now evokes a bygone era. The aggression of the bag-snatching scene now seems more threatening than it did in 1944: despite the woman's high-heeled strut and no-nonsense air, there's tension in Bernstein's insistent piano rhythms. Robbins gives his different characters distinct danced personalities, not just in the sailors' solos but also in their overflowing energy and camaraderie. The three women have smaller roles, but are similarly distinct in personality and style.

Symphonic Variations

Choreography: Frederick Ashton
Music: César Franck, *Symphonic Variations*
Designs: Sophie Fedorovitch
Premiere: 24 April 1946, Sadler's Wells Ballet, Royal Opera House, London
Original cast: Margot Fonteyn, Pamela May, Moira Shearer, Michael Somes, Henry Danton, Brian Shaw

Symphonic Variations, Ashton's first post-war ballet, was a distillation of experience and thought, created for a new beginning. After the war, the Sadler's Wells Ballet moved to the much larger stage of the Royal Opera House. Symbolically, the company opened with *The Sleeping Beauty*, reawakening a theatre that had been closed in the war years. It also discovered that much of its existing repertory was dwarfed by its big new home. The mime and facial expressions of ballets created for small theatres could not reach the depths of the opera house auditorium. In *Symphonic Variations*, Ashton's solution was to fill the large stage with just six dancers.

As the company learned to make *The Sleeping Beauty* radiate throughout the house, *Symphonic Variations* – which had the first three Auroras in its cast – would project into the theatre in the same way. It was a turning point in Ashton's career: the culmination of his work so far, the start of a new, mature phase. As Balanchine had with *Apollo*, Ashton in *Symphonic Variations* found the courage to eliminate all inessentials, putting his faith in pure dance.

Ashton remembered the war as 'a period of enormous frustration to me because I felt I hadn't said nearly enough to be ready to die on it.' While serving in the Royal Air Force, Ashton had time to read and think: 'because I was rather unhappy, I went in for mysticism,' he told the writer John Selwyn Gilbert. 'I read St Theresa of Avila and St John of the Cross and lots of books about mystics and mysticism. After all, one was told that it was the end of the world.'[35] He also listened to César Franck's *Symphonic Variations*.

Ashton's initial plan for the ballet was very elaborate and literary, with ideas of turning seasons, fertility, spiritual marriage and divine love. Working on the ballet, he stripped these ideas back, refining and clarifying until he had a pure dance work. He reduced the number of dancers, removing the *corps de ballet*, and further refined and revised his choreography into a new simplicity.

Similarly, his collaborator Sophie Fedorovitch pared back her designs. She and Ashton had spent time cycling together in the Norfolk countryside: on one journey, they found themselves in 'the most marvellous glade, filled with sunshine, and this had the most terrific effect on us; I said, This is the colour it's got to be, a sort of greenish-yellow.'[36] Fedorovitch's first drafts for the scenery include stylised leaves; her final version is a glowing expanse of spring green, with black lines flowing across it. 'It is easy to feel how *Symphonics* takes its place in the line of English lyric poetry,' wrote the critic Alastair Macaulay. 'Its dances, to use Milton's (and Mark Morris') terms, are both allegro and penseroso, active and contemplative. The ballet's pastoral spirit is like Marvell's garden: "Annihilating all that's made To a green thought in a green shade." And its quiet mysteries are those of Keats' Grecian urn.'[37]

Symphonic Variations opens with three women in a line, standing with one foot gently crossed over the other – a pose that will echo through the ballet. The women move on the piano line, dancing in unison in cool, clean, sculptural lines. The dance warms and opens up as the men join them. All six dancers stay onstage throughout the ballet, dancing alone or in combinations. They will stop and stand, still and harmonious, as others dance on around them.

The classical steps have a distinctively Ashtonian tenderness. When a woman is lifted in low, skimming lifts, she curves one arm around her partner's head. The three women form a circle around a single man, bending into a loop of *attitudes*. For some transitions, the dancers simply join hands and run around the stage. *Symphonic Variations* is known as an exhausting ballet to dance, but it creates a feeling of serenity, of release and renewal.

Le Jeune Homme et la Mort

Choreography: Roland Petit
Music: Johann Sebastian Bach
Scenario: Jean Cocteau
Designs: Georges Wakhevitch
Premiere: 25 June 1946, Ballets des Champs-Elysées, Théâtre des Champs-Elysées, Paris
Original cast: Jean Babilée, Nathalie Philippart

The Ballets des Champs-Elysées was a chic, intimate troupe, creating new works with charismatic young dancers and a distinctive sensibility. Its founders included Boris Kochno and Jean Cocteau, both veterans of Diaghilev's company who saw ballet as a meeting-place of the arts, the home of artistic collaboration. The company's productions were smallscale but accomplished. Roland Petit made his name with *Les Forains*, an appealing 1945 work about a troupe of circus artists, with music by Henri Sauguet.

Le Jeune Homme et la Mort caught a mood of post-war Parisian disillusionment. This was the period that produced the existentialism of Jean-Paul Sartre, the alienation of Albert Camus. The ballet's hero, a suicidal artist in paint-spattered overalls, is both vulnerable and brutal. It was a sensational showcase for Jean Babilée, a dancer of explosive technique and presence. He was partnered by Nathalie Philippart, his wife, a dancer of

Left Bank looks, with a tousled fringe that recalls the singer and bohemian Juliette Gréco. At Cocteau's suggestion, Petit created the ballet to a jazz score, then switched to the grandeur of J. S. Bach at the dress rehearsal.

Synopsis

A young artist sprawls on his bed in a Parisian garret, smoking, looking at his watch. He wears paint-spattered jeans (sometimes dungarees), his chest bare. At last a young woman appears at the door: dark bob, black gloves and a bright yellow dress. He runs to her, she ducks away and he follows her around the room. She's cool and taut, he's twisting and agonised, pleading as she slaps him down, falling at her feet. At last she pulls a stool to the garret's central pillar, pulling out a noose that hangs from the rafters. Returning to the young man, she puts her gloved hands around his neck, then leaves. Driven to a passion, he throws a chair against the wall, twists over the table, then finally goes to the noose and hangs himself, one leg kicking as he dies.

Around him, the walls of the garret lift up out of sight, revealing the Paris skyline, lurid with flashing neon signs. Now dressed in a long robe, with a skull mask and towering platform shoes, the woman returns. At her command, the young man comes down from the noose to stand beside her. She places the skull mask on his face, and leads him away over the rooftops.

With a small cast, big theatrical gestures and a gymnastic male role, *Le Jeune Homme et la Mort* has been revived by many companies, for a range of stars including Rudolf Nureyev, Mikhail Baryshnikov, Nicolas Le Riche, Roberto Bolle and Ivan Vasiliev.

The Four Temperaments

Choreography: George Balanchine
Music: Paul Hindemith, *Theme with Four Variations (According to the Four Temperaments)*
Original decor: Kurt Seligmann; practice dress since 1951
Premiere: 20 November 1946, Ballet Society, Central High School of Needle Trades, New York
Original cast: *Melancholic* William Dollar; *Sanguinic* Mary Ellen Moylan, Fred Danieli; *Phlegmatic* Todd Bolender; *Choleric* Tanaquil LeClercq

Ballet Society reunited Balanchine and Kirstein in a new, subscription-only company that, in two years' time, would become New York City Ballet. It launched at the unlikely venue of the Central High School of Needle Trades, on a stage without an orchestra pit – and that performance included *The Four Temperaments*, a milestone in modern choreography.

Balanchine had commissioned the score some years earlier, when he had some extra money, made from his work on Broadway. 'I asked Hindemith if he could do something with piano and a few strings, something I could play at home.'[38] What Hindemith delivered was a set of variations on a three-part theme. The four variations are named for the four humours, or 'temperaments', of Hippocratic and medieval physiology. The idea was that the body and mind were governed by the balance of physical elements: black bile (melancholic), blood (sanguinic), phlegm (phlegmatic) and yellow bile (choleric). The long influence of this system lingers in the English language, which retains these four terms to describe states of mind.

At first, the ballet was performed in elaborate and much criticised costumes by the surrealist painter Kurt Seligmann. Since 1951 the ballet has been danced in practice dress.

Synopsis

Hindemith opens his score by stating the three-part theme, which is danced by three different couples. Even within the theme itself, Balanchine builds, develops and echoes motifs, before launching into the variations. The first woman spins from foot to foot, flexing and pointing her free foot as she goes. The second woman develops that spin into a full spin on *pointe*, while the third takes those turns in a deep *plié*, her free foot crossed over her knee. 'The image created by the third girl as she is spun is blithe, even comical,' wrote the critic Arlene Croce; 'could Balanchine have been thinking of the bass fiddle the forties jazz player spins after a chorus of hot licks?'[39]

In each of the main variations, the first part of the theme is danced by a soloist or soloists, who is then joined by more dancers for the second and third parts.

Melancholic. A male soloist dances the first part of the theme in huge, curving shapes, bending forward and arching back. Two women join him, circling him. To the third part of the theme, a *corps* of four women strides in, with a high kick on each step. The Melancholic soloist collapses, but pulls himself up for an extraordinary exit, backing out while in a deep backbend.

Sanguinic. The first part of the theme is danced by a ballerina and her partner, who move sunnily this way and that; her dances are full of hip-thrusting, off-balance moves, but remain courtly. Another four *corps* women join them, scampering and bending in lines. The variation ends with the ballerina carried through skimming lifts.

Phlegmatic. The male soloist extends an arm, then crumples, folding at wrist, elbow, shoulder and right through his body. He is easily mesmerised by his own moves, taking hold of his own foot and lifting it to gaze at it. A *corps* of four joins him, forming lines and mazes that he climbs over and through, or opening out into a syncopated chorus line.

Choleric. The Choleric ballerina enters with explosive steps, legs kicking high. When a partner joins her, she erupts out of his hands in a series of jumps. She is joined first by four men, then four women. Emerging from their midst, she puts her hands to the raised feet of two women standing in *arabesque*, who swivel out of her way. It's as if she were an angry showgirl bursting through saloon doors.

The ballet's whole cast assembles for the finale, forming geometric patterns, resolving into couples and *corps de ballet* lines. As the ballet closes, the men raise their partners into soaring lifts, arcs of movement set against the turning, thrusting lines of the *corps*.

With its angular lines and explosive force, Balanchine's choreography for *The Four Temperaments* was radically modern, yet is rooted in academic classicism, all the way back to French courtliness. Confronted by the high-kicking quartet, the Melancholic soloist greets the four with a deep bow; the Phlegmatic soloist is full of elegant gestures, though he goes bonelessly floppy while pursuing them. The dances are full of contrasts in scale, in shape, in stage space, brilliantly assembled. Balanchine loved the theme and variations format; in *The Four Temperaments* he develops it with breathtaking intricacy and clarity.

Symphony in C (Le Palais de cristal)

Choreography: George Balanchine
Music: Georges Bizet, Symphony No. 1 in C major
Designs: Léonor Fini.
Premiere: 28 July 1947, Paris Opéra Ballet, Paris Opéra, Paris

Original cast: *First movement* Lycette Darsonval, Alexandre Kalioujny; *Second movement* Tamara Toumanova, Roger Ritz; *Third movement* Micheline Bardin, Michel Renault; *Fourth movement* Madeleine Lafon, Max Bozzoni

In 1947, Balanchine was invited to work as guest choreographer at the Paris Opéra, where he revived *Apollo, Le Baiser de la fée* and *Serenade* before creating a work for the company. In compliment to his hosts, Balanchine chose a little-known work by a French composer, a symphony Bizet wrote when he was just seventeen. In France, the ballet was titled *Le Palais de cristal*, and the dancers of each movement were dressed in different jewel tones. When he restaged it in New York, it was renamed *Symphony in C*, danced by women in white tutus and men in dark costumes, against a blue cyclorama. This has become the standard version, though the Paris Opéra Ballet uses the original title and coloured costumes.

Each of the four movements has its own ballerina, supported by her partner, two soloist couples and a small *corps de ballet*. The choreography is classical and radiantly fresh. It demands technical strength from the whole company, and contrasting qualities from its four ballerinas.

First movement. Bright and sparkling, this is led by a speedy ballerina.

Second movement. This *adagio* lies at the heart of the work. Framed by her *corps*, the ballerina of this movement dances to the wistful oboe melody, her partner lifting her in soaring arcs. At the end of the movement, she falls back into his arms. Although *Symphony in C* has four ballerinas, the second-movement ballerina stands out from the others: the part was originally danced by Tamara Toumanova, a major star, and remains a cherished role. It was the sight of Tanaquil LeClercq dancing this part that made Jerome Robbins beg to join Balanchine's New York City Ballet; when the ballerina Suzanne Farrell returned to the company after an absence of five years, she made her return as the second-movement ballerina of *Symphony in C*.

Third movement. This has a lively folk-dance flavour, which Balanchine echoes in his steps. This ballerina's role is full of jumps, in which she is matched by her partner.

Fourth movement. The fourth ballerina whirls on. She is joined by the dancers from the previous three movements. While the principals and soloists dance in the centre, the *corps* lines the back and sides of the stage, performing *battement tendu*, a classroom step in which the foot slides smoothly across the floor until it is fully pointed, then smoothly back. *Tendus* were very important to Balanchine, who used them to establish fundamentals of ballet technique, insisting on maximum turnout and tightly crossed fifth positions. In *Symphony in C* members of the *corps* look like dancers at the *barre*, while the principals show the dazzling feats that practice will lead to. For the last minutes, the entire cast dances the same beaten jumping steps, moving in exhilarating unison before proceeding with a flourish to the final pose.

Theme and Variations

Choreography: George Balanchine
Music: Pyotr Ilych Tchaikovsky, Theme and Variations from Orchestral Suite No. 3
Designs: Woodman Thompson
Premiere: 26 November 1947, Ballet Theatre, New York City Center, New York
Original cast: Alicia Alonso, Igor Youskevitch

Theme and Variations evokes nineteenth-century Russian ballet, celebrating its courtliness and its dreamy visions in a suite overflowing with virtuoso dancing. This is a masterpiece that feels longer than it is: the ballet is so rich, with such a range of mood, that it's hard to believe Balanchine could conjure up so much dance invention in little more than twenty minutes.

In 1947 full-length performances of ballets such as *The Sleeping Beauty* were still rare in the West: the ballet would not have its American premiere until the Sadler's Wells Ballet danced it in New York two years later. American audiences knew *The Sleeping Beauty* through excerpts and suites, such as American Ballet Theatre's *Princess Aurora*. Max Goberman, the company's music director, suggested that Balanchine might make a companion work to the Theme and Variations from Tchaikovsky's third orchestral suite – something like *Princess Aurora*, with a virtuoso male role for Igor Youskevitch. Having looked at the score, Balanchine replied, 'But of course.'

Balanchine had a particular affection for Tchaikovsky's orchestral suites. He choreographed the fourth suite twice, under the title *Mozartiana*. And he loved variations on a theme, a device that lies at the heart of many of his ballets. A year earlier, he had made radical use of this format in *The Four Temperaments*; now he used it to look back, remembering his own St Petersburg training.

The curtain goes up on an assembled ballet court, with a ballroom setting and assembled ranks of women in tutus, led by the ballerina and her partner. The leading couple dances the theme – pointing one foot in *battement tendu*, a position that will echo through the complex variations that follow – before bowing to each other and leaving. The *corps* of twelve women takes over, picking up the theme motifs. Balanchine weaves in specific echoes of *The Sleeping Beauty*: the critic Arlene Croce summed up the ballerina's fast solos as 'Aurora rewritten in lightning',[40] full of references to the Petipa ballet.

Although the ballerina recalls Aurora, her partner's dances are infinitely tougher than those of Petipa's Prince. Ballet Theatre had asked for a work that would show off Youskevitch, and they certainly got it. His demanding second solo starts with eight *ronds de jambes sautés* (a jump in which the lifted front leg draws circles in the air before landing), alternating with balances in which the dancer steps straight onto high tiptoe. It's followed by a series of eight double *tours en l'air* – in which the dancer spins twice in the air before landing – with a pirouette between each jump. Famously strong technicians admit to nervousness over *Theme and Variations*; Mikhail Baryshnikov called it the most difficult ballet he ever danced.

Balanchine also remembers the nineteenth century's dreams and visions. In the seventh variation, the ballerina dances an *adagio*, surrounded by *corps* women. Holding hands in a line, they support her as she moves from pose to pose, shifting and changing within her held balance. Her dancing has the quality of Aurora's vision scene: soft, ethereal, still regal.

The finale is a grand polonaise. For the first time, Balanchine brings on male partners for the *corps* women, sweeping the whole company into a regal procession. *Corps* patterns bloom out of nowhere: one bold diagonal grouping springs into sight with almost no warning, before the leading couple reappears to lead the last of the dancing. The ending is one of what Lincoln Kirstein called 'Balanchine's applause-machines', when the dancers direct waves of brilliant dancing straight out at the audience, a rush of dancing as the orchestra builds to a climax.

In 1970, Balanchine choreographed the other movements of Tchaikovsky's orchestral suite. The new material was very different in mood, featuring women in flowing ball gowns, with loose hair and sometimes bare feet. The new material was not well received: some critics even wondered whether this was a parody of romanticism. New York City Ballet still dances the full *Tchaikovsky Suite No. 3*, but other companies stick firmly with the original *Theme and Variations*.

Etudes

Choreography: Harald Lander
Music: Carl Czerny, arranged by Knudåge Riisager
Premiere: 15 January 1948 (as *Etude*), Royal Danish Ballet, Copenhagen, with Margot Lander, Hans Brenaa, Svend Erik Jensen. Revised version 18 February 1951; final version for the Paris Opéra Ballet, Paris, 19 February 1952

Etudes is a classroom ballet. It puts the dancer's daily class on stage, building into a spectacular display of technique. Long preparation leads to theatrical dazzle.

The ballet moves from *barre* work to centre practice and *pas de deux, pas de quatre, pas de six* and ensemble work. Along the way, the ballet moves from sylph-like Romantic ballet, with a ballerina in a long tutu, to later classicism, with short, high tutus. The staging is simple, with white costumes and dramatic lighting. Dancers are shown in silhouette, picked out by spotlights – at the *barre* section, we see spotlit legs working, with the rest of the body in shadow – or they whirl along paths of light. Ensemble and soloists all join in the show-stopping finale.

The idea for *Etudes* came from composer Knudåge Riisager. On an autumn day in Copenhagen, he heard a child playing piano exercises through an open window. Listening to the music, and seeing leaves blown and spun by the wind, Riisager realised that this could be a ballet. Riisager's orchestration is emphatic and brightly coloured, using plenty of percussion. (The English National Ballet staging traditionally adds a rock drum kit to give it extra wallop.)

Etudes is a company showcase, with glitzy leading roles and work for *corps* and soloist dancers. It has become a staple of the international repertory, danced all over the world, from Copenhagen and Paris to American Ballet Theatre and the Australian Ballet.

Scènes de ballet

Choreography: Frederick Ashton
Music: Igor Stravinsky

Designs: André Beaurepaire
Premiere: 11 February 1948, Sadler's Wells Ballet, Royal Opera House,
London
Original cast: Margot Fonteyn, Michael Somes, Alexander Grant,
Donald Britton, John Field, Philip Chatfield

If *Symphonic Variations* was Ashton's personal statement of classicism,
Scènes de ballet was the first time he set out to pay homage to Petipa.
Looking back to the grand divertissements of the nineteenth century,
Ashton has both a sure sense of classicism and a touch of irony, following
the spiky elegance of Stravinsky's score.

Ashton first heard the Stravinsky music on the radio, while he was
taking a bath. Fascinated by what he heard, particularly by Stravinsky's
complex, changing rhythms, he rang the BBC to find out what it had been.
Since no recordings of the music were available in Britain, the BBC arranged
for it to be played privately for the choreographer. The score was written in
1944, when Stravinsky was offered a huge fee to create a ballet number for
a Broadway show that would feature Alicia Markova and Anton Dolin. The
composer called the music 'featherlight and sugared', but was proud of its
construction. 'The "Apotheosis" was composed on the day of the liberation
of Paris,' he remembered. 'I interrupted my work every few moments to
listen to the radio reports. I think my jubilation is in the music.'[41]

Having chosen his music, Ashton found new levels of rigour in
constructing the ballet. The dazzling *corps de ballet* patterns were inspired
by geometry, with Ashton bringing a volume of Euclid to rehearsals. 'I, who
at school could never get on with algebra or geometry, suddenly got fascinated with geometrical figures, and I used a lot of theorems as ground
patterns for *Scènes de ballet*,' he said:

> I used to drive the girls mad trying to solve these theorems, moving
> them from one position to another. I also wanted to do a ballet that
> could be seen from any angle – anywhere could be front, so to speak. So
> I did these geometric figures that are not always facing front – if you saw
> *Scènes de ballet* from the wings you'd get a very different, but equally
> good picture. We would get into terrible tangles, but when it finally
> came out I used to say, QED![42]

The ballerina role was created for Margot Fonteyn, who was at that time
planning to work in Paris with the choreographer Roland Petit. Ashton was
feeling possessive about his muse, worried that she would pick up too much

Parisian sophistication. *Scènes de ballet* has a kind of pre-emptive chic. The tutus – designed by André Beaurepaire, but with a lot of input from Ashton – have geometric patterns on the bodices. The colours are slightly acid, yellow and grey-blue. The dancers of the *corps de ballet* wear hats and pearls with their tutus, suggesting women of the 1940s rather than members of a fairy-tale court. Ashton's classicism is still social, but compared to the youthful softness of *Les Rendezvous*, it's grander and more sophisticated.

Scènes de ballet opens with its men, the leading dancer performing *entrechats six* in the centre while the others are paired in heroic poses. The female *corps de ballet* enters in two lines, then breaks into more intricate groupings. Movements are passed from one line of women to the next, travelling through the whole group in little ripples. Heads shake or nod, bobbing on the rhythm. Ashton can set his cast dancing to several different rhythms at once, while moving through their geometric patterns.

The ballerina's first solo is quick and diamond-hard. The *pas de deux* has distinctive, Ashtonian lifts, the ballerina floating just off the ground as she runs on *pointe*. Her role has echoes of Aurora in the fast first entrance, and when she is partnered in turn by the ballet's men it recalls the Rose Adagio from *The Sleeping Beauty*. Her second solo is sensuous, danced with her partner lying at her feet, her arms curling and drifting like smoke. For the apotheosis, first the ballerina and then supporting women are raised in arcing lifts from side to side.

Ashton was proud of *Scènes de ballet*, a favourite among his own works, saying: 'It has a distant, uncompromising beauty which says, I am here, beautiful, but I will make no effort to charm you.'[43]

Fall River Legend

Choreography: Agnes de Mille
Music: Morton Gould
Scenery: Oliver Smith
Costumes: Miles White
Premiere: 22 April 1948, Ballet Theatre, Metropolitan Opera House, New York
Original cast: *the Accused* Alicia Alonso

'Lizzie Borden took an axe, and gave her mother forty whacks. When she found what she had done, she gave her father forty-one.' *Fall River Legend* draws on one of the most famous murder cases in American history. The deaths of Lizzie Borden's father and stepmother, in the Massachusetts town of Fall River in 1892, were covered in newspapers and even in a skipping rhyme. De Mille takes a free, stylised approach to the story, and changes the ending: where Borden was acquitted, de Mille's Accused is hanged for the crime.

The ballet was created very quickly in 1948, with composer Morton Gould and de Mille rushing to complete the work in time. Nora Kaye, for whom the role of the Accused was created, fell ill at the last minute, and the first performance was danced by Alicia Alonso.

Synopsis

Prologue. A woman is accused of murdering her father and stepmother: a speaker reads out the charge. The gallows stands ready to hang her. The scene changes to a stylised skeleton version of a Victorian house, with the interior and staircase visible.

Scene 1. The Accused watches herself as a child with her parents and the people of Fall River, the town where they live. A spinster figure, dressed in black, becomes friendly with the parents. The mother dies and the spinster becomes the Accused's stepmother.

Scene 2. Inside the house. The Accused, now grown up and playing her own role in the story, lives unhappily with her father and stepmother. She meets the Pastor, a handsome and sympathetic man, to whom she is attracted. Her father puts an end to the meeting. Inside the house, the step-mother is frightened when the Accused picks up an axe – but the Accused simply goes outside to chop wood.

Scene 3. The Accused watches the Fall River people enjoying themselves, feeling isolated. She becomes obsessed with the axe. When the Pastor invites her to a dance, her stepmother intervenes, suggesting that the Accused is unbalanced. Frantic, the Accused calms herself and leaves with the Pastor.

Scene 4. A prayer meeting. The Accused is greeted by the congregation and the Pastor. She dances happily with the Pastor until her stepmother appears. She suggests that the Accused is mad, and leads her away.

Scene 5. The Accused watches happy couples pass by. She looks at her father and stepmother, and picks up the axe. There is a blackout.

Scene 6. The crime has been committed. A drop-curtain shows the parlour dripping with blood. The Accused appears in a dream, dancing in her white petticoat. She sees her mother, who embraces and dances with her – but is shocked to see bloodstains on her petticoat. She scolds and comforts her daughter.

Scene 7. The drop-curtain rises to show the house, now silhouetted against a blood-red sky. In a long, silent sequence, neighbours run in to watch the house, suspicious that something terrible has happened. The Accused walks through the parlour. When she opens the front door, the orchestra crashes in, as she rushes into the street. The townspeople enter the house, finding the bloody axe and the mother's white shawl. They confront the Accused, who collapses at the Pastor's feet.

Scene 8. The house set is cleared away, leaving only the gallows. The Accused waits for her own execution, the Pastor at her side. Dancers rush through, as if in the Accused's memories. Passers-by stand to watch her. At last she is left alone, and turns to face the gallows. She stands rigid, then twitches, letting her head fall as if her neck has been broken.

In *Fall River Legend*, Agnes de Mille combines the Americana of earlier works such as *Rodeo* with the ideas of repression and psychological drama explored by Antony Tudor, together with the 1940s interest in Freudian psychology. Like the Cowgirl of *Rodeo*, the Accused is an outsider who feels excluded from love and romance. This time, her exclusion leads her into frustration and murder. While the modern dance choreographer Martha Graham explored Greek myth, de Mille treats an American story as stylised legend, with a sense of fate in the Accused's crime.

De Mille's choreography builds in big reactions and sidelong glances, with physical mannerisms, such as the stepmother stroking her face with her fourth finger. The critic Luke Jennings points out that the flashback structure and bleak humour reflect early film noir.

Cinderella

Choreography: Frederick Ashton
Music: Sergei Prokofiev
Designs: Jean-Denis Malclès
Premiere: 23 December 1948, Sadler's Wells Ballet, Royal Opera House, London

Original cast: *Cinderella* Moira Shearer; *The Prince* Michael Somes; *Cinderella's Stepsisters* Frederick Ashton, Robert Helpmann; *The Fairy Godmother* Pamela May; *Spring* Nadia Nerina; *Summer* Violetta Elvin; *Autumn* Pauline Clayden; *Winter* Beryl Grey

Prokofiev's music for *Cinderella* is a fairy-tale ballet, but not a nineteenth-century one. Instead of Tchaikovsky's radiant certainty, the music has surprisingly sharp edges, from scenes of dreamy magic to hectic energy and touches of sourness. Frederick Ashton's production adds its own division. It responds to the spiky mystery of the score with distinctive, Petipa-inspired classical dances, and adds a broad stripe of British pantomime comedy.

Written during the war, the score was first staged by Rostislav Zakharov at the Bolshoi Ballet in 1945, with a production by Konstantin Sergeyev following in 1946. Ashton, increasingly interested in recent classical music, created his version in 1948. This was the first three-act ballet by a British choreographer, and an immediate success.

Synopsis

Act I. The house of Cinderella's father. While Cinderella sits by the fire, her stepsisters embroider a shawl to wear to the court ball. They quarrel among themselves, and leave. Left alone, Cinderella remembers her dead mother. Her father tries to comfort her, until the stepsisters return and scold him for it. When a mysterious beggar-woman appears, Cinderella gives her bread, but the sisters drive her away.

The sisters prepare for the ball, with the help of dressmakers, a hair-dresser and a dancing master. The sisters try to copy his steps in a gavotte. At last they set out for the ball, leaving Cinderella behind. She tries to cheer herself up by dancing with a broom – first imitating her stepsisters' clumsy gavotte, then drawn into a dreaming solo in which she imagines herself at the ball.

The beggar-woman returns, and casts off her disguise: she is Cinderella's fairy godmother. She summons fairies of the four seasons, who dance for Cinderella and help to dress her for the ball, with a *corps de ballet* of stars. When Cinderella is ready, she is warned that she must leave the ball before the clock strikes twelve, when the magic will fade and Cinderella will be a scullery maid again. Cinderella sets off for the ball in a glittering coach.

Act II. A ball at the Palace. Courtiers take part in a formal dance. The jester appears, and Cinderella's father and stepsisters arrive. Each dances a solo.

Two gentlemen ask them to dance – one very tall, one very short. The bossy older sister starts with the short partner, but manages to swap. A fanfare announces the arrival of the Prince. As the court dances, mysterious music is heard, and Cinderella appears. She is so beautiful that the court stops to watch her in wonder, as she walks slowly down the steps. Even her stepsisters fail to recognise her.

The Prince is enchanted and makes her a present of an orange, the rarest fruit in his land (to the march from Prokofiev's earlier opera, *The Love for Three Oranges*). More oranges are handed out to the stepsisters, who quarrel over who gets the largest. Their dance ends with a jaunty trot in circles around the stage – Ashton quoted the 'oompah trot' that Fred Astaire and his sister Adele used to dance onstage in the 1920s. Cinderella dances a sparkling solo, including a moment when, with her back to the audience, she rises on *pointe* and arches into a backbend. The Prince joins her for a duet. Other guests return for a waltz; caught up in the dance, Cinderella forgets the fairy's warning. Twelve o'clock strikes. Courtiers, seasons and stars close up in a fierce, mechanistic formation, marking out the clock rhythms and barring Cinderella's exit. Her clothes change back to rags, and she flees the Palace, leaving a slipper behind.

Act III. The house of Cinderella's father. Cinderella wakes by her own fireside – the position she was in just before the fairy godmother arrived. Was it all a dream? She finds the second slipper in her apron pocket, and realises that she really did go to the ball and dance with the Prince. The sisters arrive, telling Cinderella about the ball and showing off their oranges. Messengers rush in, explaining that the Prince is looking everywhere for the woman who lost her slipper at the ball. When he arrives, the sisters try on the slipper, which is much too small. Cinderella kneels to help, and the second slipper falls out of her apron pocket. The Prince recognises her, and asks her to marry him. Cinderella forgives her stepsisters. The scene changes to an enchanted garden, where the Prince and Cinderella dance together, surrounded by stars.

Prokofiev wrote that 'What I wanted to express above all in the music for *Cinderella* was the poetic love of Cinderella and the Prince . . .',[44] yet his hero and heroine have surprisingly little music. In Ashton's version, this is underlined by the ballet's second strand. The Ugly Sisters were originally danced by Robert Helpmann, one of the Sadler's Wells Ballet's biggest stars, and Ashton himself. Ashton mocked Helpmann and himself in their solos – Helpmann's imperiousness, Ashton forgetting his steps. The Ashton sister, wrote the critic Edwin Denby, 'becomes the charmer of the evening. She is the shyest, the happiest, the most innocent of monsters . . . At the Prince's she is terrified to be making an entrance; a few moments later, poor monster, in the intoxication of being at a party she loses her heart and imagines she can dance fascinatingly . . .'[45] Adored by audiences, the Helpmann-Ashton double act performed the roles for decades, developing extra jokes along the way. It's easy for the roles to become coarse and stale, pushing the ballet off balance.

Yet this *Cinderella* also has ravishing dances. The season variations gave Ashton a chance to explore Petipa-like female variations. The Spring variation is full of bounding jumps – suggesting 'buds bursting', the first-cast Nadia Nerina remembered. Summer is languorous, while Autumn spins through off-balance turns like a leaf caught on a gust of wind. Winter is grandly glamorous, drawing frosty circles on the floor. The sparkling *corps* dances respond brilliantly to the sinister touches in the music: the stealthy undertow of the waltz, the threatening clockwork of midnight. Ashton also provides a marvellous entrance for Cinderella at the ball. Appearing at the top of the stairs, she walks slowly down on *pointe*, gazing out and up. The combination of dreamy gaze and technical difficulty gives her an unearthly beauty.

Other Stagings

The fairy-tale narrative and Prokofiev score have been very popular among companies and choreographers, in both traditional and revised versions. Rudolf Nureyev's 1986 staging for the Paris Opéra moves the story to Hollywood of the 1920s and 1930s. Nureyev himself danced the 'fairy godfather', a movie director who discovers Cinderella. The dance set pieces and designs by Petrika Ionesco evoke different movies and stars of the period, including *King Kong* and Betty Grable. When Cinderella makes her entrance at the ball, now a Hollywood party, she is lit up by the camera flashes of the admiring photographers.

Alexei Ratmansky's production, created for the Mariinsky Ballet in 2002, was his first evening-length work. It's a quirky version, with Cinderella wrapped up in brown woolly jumper and leggings, a glamorous stepmother and a 1920s ball scene, with costumes by Elena Markovskaya. Ratmansky is both satirical and soft-hearted: his shy Cinderella dances goofily at the ball, gaining confidence from the courtiers, who applaud their Prince's favourite. Searching for Cinderella around the world – a sequence dropped by many choreographers, including Frederick Ashton – the Prince rejects seduction attempts by male as well as female dancers. Ratmansky falls down in the classical set pieces, with limited choreography for the male season fairies, who wear strange wigs and painted faces. Ratmansky restaged this production for the Australian Ballet in 2013.

David Bintley, who had danced the 'Ashton' sister with The Royal Ballet, created his own production for Birmingham Royal Ballet in 2010. Danced by women, his Sisters are skinny and dumpy – showing off their dancing, or unduly fond of cake. Superbly designed by John Macfarlane, this staging has fine theatrical touches. Bintley's Cinderella keeps her mother's dancing slippers as a keepsake. When the disguised fairy godmother appears as a barefoot beggar-woman, Cinderella gives her the slippers – but has to push herself to do so, looking at her slippers, at the godmother's feet and back again. Cinderella is a fairy-tale heroine, kind and generous, but it's very touching to see one who has to work at it.

Christopher Wheeldon's 2012 staging, a co-production for Dutch National Ballet and San Francisco Ballet, makes more changes to the story. It opens with a new prologue, showing Cinderella with her parents. When her mother dies, and Cinderella weeps at the grave, a magical tree springs up from her tears. The image of the tree runs through the ballet – and is something Wheeldon would return to in his 2014 ballet *The Winter's Tale*. In other changes, this Cinderella is guided by four male Fates, dancers with gilded faces. As in Rossini's opera on this theme, the Prince decides to swap places with a friend for the ballroom scene – in this case, his friend Benjamin falls in love with Clementine, the nicer of the two sisters. This production has remarkable designs by Julian Crouch and puppeteer Basil Twist, who directed the scene where Cinderella's coach is conjured out of green wheels from under the tree: her billowing cloak turns into a canopy, and masked figures become the horses that gallop her away.

Carmen

Choreography: Roland Petit
Music: Georges Bizet
Designs: Antoni Clavé
Premiere: 21 February 1949, Ballets de Paris, Princes Theatre, London
Original cast: *Carmen* Renée (later Zizi) Jeanmaire; *Don José* Roland Petit; *the Toreador* Serge Perrault

After his success with the Ballets des Champs-Elysées, Petit broke away to found his own Ballets de Paris. *Carmen*, starring Petit and his future wife

Renée (Zizi) Jeanmaire, opened in London, where the audience burst into applause as soon as the curtain went up. Antoni Clavé's designs were sharp in line and colour, framing a bold theatrical experience – the very latest thing. As Carmen, Jeanmaire cropped her hair into a gamine fringe and wore a dress so short it was essentially a corset, revealing her beautiful legs. Like *Le Jeune Homme et la Mort*, Petit's *Carmen* combined modishness with a touch of sexual grit.

Synopsis

Scene 1. A street in Seville. Carmen and another young woman, both workers at the local cigarette factory, chase down an outside staircase and break into a fight. Just as Carmen gets the better of her opponent, Don José arrives. He separates the women, and is about to arrest Carmen – but is instantly smitten by her. Instead of taking her to jail, he makes a rendezvous with her.

Scene 2. Lilas Pastia's tavern, a bar with steps to an upstairs room. Don José arrives at the tavern, and dances a stamping habanera, urged on by the crowd. Carmen arrives and dances seductively. Besotted, José carries her off to her bedroom above the bar.

Scene 3. Carmen's bedroom, the next morning. José opens the curtains to let in the morning light. He washes, drying his hands on the curtains, but is jealous to see Carmen looking into the street. In their explicit *pas de deux*, Carmen lies on top of José as he arches off the ground, or slithers down his body from a high lift. Three of Carmen's brigand friends enter and whisper to her. She nods to José, and they leave together.

Scene 4. A back street in Seville. Carmen and her accomplices, including José, lurk in the darkness. On Carmen's instructions, José stabs a traveller. Carmen and her friends steal his money.

Scene 5. In front of a bullring. Carmen appears in the crowd, superbly dressed. A swaggering toreador makes a triumphant entrance, and is attracted to Carmen. Noticing this, José dashes up to her, as if to strangle her. They confront each other in a duel, until Carmen almost hurls herself onto his knife. Inside the bullring cheers celebrate the toreador's victory, while José stands horrified over Carmen's body.

Other Stagings

Alberto Alonso's *Carmen Suite*, staged in 1967 to a score by Rodion Shchedrin, is a concentrated version of the Carmen story. Shchedrin reworks Bizet's music with very different orchestration. In 1992, Mats Ek staged *Carmen* to Shchedrin's suite – see chapter 8.

Pineapple Poll

Choreography: John Cranko
Music: Arthur Sullivan, selected and orchestrated by Charles Mackerras
Designs: Osbert Lancaster
Premiere: 13 March 1951, Sadler's Wells Theatre Ballet, Sadler's Wells Theatre, London
Original cast: *Poll* Elaine Fifield; *Captain Belaye* David Blair; *Jasper* David Poole; *Blanche* Stella Claire; *Mrs Dimple* Sheilah O'Reilly

Born in South Africa in 1927, John Cranko created his first ballet for the Cape Town Ballet Club at the age of sixteen. By the time he was twenty, he had joined Britain's Sadler's Wells Theatre Ballet, which took some of his short works into its repertory. Cranko immediately connected with his new audience, making a range of ballets for the young company. He hit the jackpot with *Pineapple Poll*, a comic ballet that showed off his heroine's *fouettés* while telling its story with crisp economy.

It's a Gilbert and Sullivan ballet: the plot came from W. S. Gilbert's *Bab Ballads*, while the music is a well-paced selection from Arthur Sullivan's music. Osbert Lancaster's sets designs are immensely detailed cartoons of a nineteenth-century port and ship. His costumes help to establish the ballet's characters as cheerful comic types: Jack Tar sailors in wide-legged trousers, wives and sweethearts in brightly striped dresses, the gallant captain with plenty of nautical braid.

Synopsis

Scene 1. Portsmouth Harbour, outside the Steampacket public house. Sailors and their wives and sweethearts assemble in the square. Jasper, the potboy at the Steampacket, rushes around serving drinks.

Poll bounds into the square, with a basket of trinkets and flowers. Her lively dance is full of fast spins and flex-and-point footwork. The sailors rush up to buy trinkets for their girlfriends. Jasper, who is in love with Poll, searches his pockets for money to buy her something but, though she dances with him, she doesn't take him seriously. Their dance is part comic, part romantic: when he lifts her on his back, she sticks her legs in the air, crossing and uncrossing her feet. She chases Jasper off, but looks at his present as if reconsidering.

When the dashing Captain Belaye enters, every woman onstage swoons over his good looks. He inspects his crew, chucks Poll under the chin and dances a nautical solo, with hornpipe steps and gestures suggesting rope pulling or looking through a telescope. As he dances, the besotted women-folk fan themselves or flutter around him, until their sailor boyfriends pull them away. Smitten, Poll spins herself offstage.

Left alone, Belaye is joined by his fiancée Blanche and her aunt Mrs Dimple, who brandishes an umbrella and keeps interrupting the lovers. As they leave, Poll and the other women return for a listless, lovesick dance.

Scene 2. The quayside, by the ship HMS *Hot Cross Bun*. Sailors go up the gangplank, walking with a curious gait. Poll decides to stow away on Captain Belaye's ship. She finds a sailor's uniform and strides on board. Jasper arrives, looking for Poll. He finds her discarded clothes and believes she has drowned herself.

Scene 3. On board HMS *Hot Cross Bun*. Belaye drills the crew, not noticing that Poll is drilling on *pointe*. When he orders the cannon to be fired, the members of the crew hold their hands to their ears, while Poll faints. Belaye leaves the ship to collect Blanche and Mrs Dimple. The wives and sweethearts tear off their own disguises: like Poll, they have come on board as 'sailors'.

The real crew returns, along with Jasper, and eventually the sailors forgive their girlfriends. Belaye is promoted to the rank of Admiral and gives his captain's uniform to Jasper. Poll, impressed by the change in Jasper, transfers her affections to him. In the grand finale, Mrs Dimple is transformed into a figure of Britannia, holding a trident with her umbrella as the shield.

In this early ballet, Cranko knitted *fouettés* and hornpipe steps together in an affectionate comedy. Although the characters are broadly drawn, they are created with likeable energy, with fun for supporting as well as starring roles. A 1959 recording shows Merle Park as Poll, in a performance conducted by Charles Mackerras, who chose and arranged the music.

Daphnis and Chloë

Choreography: Mikhail Fokine, 1912; Frederick Ashton, 1951
Music: Maurice Ravel
Designs: John Craxton
Premiere: 3 April 1951, Sadler's Wells Ballet, Royal Opera House, London
Original cast: *Chloë, a shepherdess* Margot Fonteyn; *Daphnis, a goatherd* Michael Somes; *Lykanion, a married woman from the town* Violetta Elvin; *Dorkon, a herdsman* John Field; *Bryaxis, a pirate chief* Alexander Grant

Commissioned by Diaghilev, Ravel's score for *Daphnis and Chloë* is a lush, shimmering masterpiece. The first production, staged by Mikhail Fokine in 1912, had limited success, despite designs by Bakst and a cast that included Vaslav Nijinsky and Tamara Karsavina. It was thoroughly upstaged by the scandal of Nijinsky's own *L'Après-midi d'un faune*. Ashton, who loved Ravel's score and wanted 'to rescue it from the concert hall', had been considering the ballet since the 1930s, but it was not until 1951 that he created his own version.

Unlike Fokine, who evoked a carefully researched classical Greece, Ashton set the ballet in a timeless present-day setting. The young lovers of his staging are close to the natural world and its old gods. The painter John Craxton, who lived in Greece, designed contemporary landscapes, sunbaked browns and lush greens. Margot Fonteyn advised him on the costumes, simple shirts and trousers for the male dancers, soft dresses for the women. In 1994, The Royal Ballet had *Daphnis and Chloë* redesigned by Martyn Bainbridge in a stylised 'Greek' style in pale colours, which lacked the timeless quality of the original 'contemporary' designs. Craxton's designs have since been restored.

Synopsis

Scene 1. A sacred grove. Villagers bring garlands, paying tribute to the god Pan and his nymphs. The shepherd Daphnis and his sweetheart Chloë are among the worshippers. Lykanion, a village woman, flirts with Daphnis. Another shepherd, Dorkon, makes advances to Chloë, who rejects him. The villagers suggest a dance contest between the two shepherds. Dorkon's dance is aggressive (the music suggests the villagers' jeering laughter at his clumsiness), while the lyrical Daphnis wins. Left alone, Daphnis is joined by Lykanion, who seduces him, then goes on her way.

Pirates invade the island. Bryaxis, the pirate leader, carries Chloë off. In despair, Daphnis prays to Pan. To hushed music, which includes Ravel's innovative use of a wind machine, nymphs appear, followed by Pan himself.

Scene 2. The pirates' cave. Women wait for the pirates' return. The pirates arrive, celebrating their victory. Bryaxis rushes in, carrying Chloë, and dances in triumph. Chloë is forced to dance for them, her hands bound. A mysterious storm rises, and the god Pan appears. The pirates flee, and Chloë is rescued.

Scene 3. Near the sacred grove. The sun rises, and Chloë returns, miraculously saved by the god. The lovers dance together, and all celebrate.

Chloë was to be one of the finest roles Ashton made for Fonteyn. It captured her child-of-nature quality, which could be both innocently sensuous and virginal; she seemed at one with Craxton's warm landscape. When Fonteyn confronted the pirates, the critic Arlene Croce wrote, 'I had the impression that the crime was as much or more against nature, and she couldn't understand how it could be happening.'[46]

In contrast to Chloë, Lykanion is frankly sexual. Seducing Daphnis, she repeatedly whips her leg around his waist and back again, her upper body writhing; when he lifts her, her beating foot suggests the moment of orgasm. Daphnis is a lyrical, rather passive role, full of flowing lines.

Ashton's choreography for the *corps de ballet* has a radiant simplicity, matching the glow of its score. The dancers wind through lines and chain dances, forming friezes about the central couple, with a luxurious ripple to their shoulders, as if they felt the Mediterranean sun on their skin. The finale builds in waves, with lines of dancers who suddenly leave the stage for the music's climax, when Chloë joyfully circles the spinning Daphnis, before the *corps* rushes back for the ending.

Other Stagings

John Neumeier's version, created for Frankfurt Ballet in 1972, evokes the period when Ravel wrote the score. Jürgen Rose's designs give the ballet an Edwardian setting with art nouveau flourishes. The leading characters are students studying archaeological remains. Neumeier sticks fairly closely to Ravel's plot outline: Chloë is still abducted by pirates, but it is Daphnis who rescues her. In 2014 Benjamin Millepied created a new staging for the Paris Opéra Ballet – see chapter 8.

Afternoon of a Faun

Choreography: Jerome Robbins
Music: Claude Debussy, *Prélude à l'après-midi d'un faune*
Costumes: Irene Sharaff
Decor, lighting: Jean Rosenthal
Premiere: 14 May 1953, New York City Ballet, New York
Original cast: Francisco Moncion, Tanaquil LeClercq

Restaging the Debussy music associated with Nijinsky's *L'Après-midi d'un faune*, Robbins moved the action from ancient Greece to a present-day ballet studio. He remembered seeing a teenage dancer (the young Edward Villella) at the *barre*, stretching 'his body in a very odd way, almost like he was trying to get something out of it. And I thought how animalistic it was . . . that sort of stuck in my head.'[47]

The dancers wear practice dress, the young man bare-chested. Jean Rosenthal's set is a floating, insubstantial ballet studio, its walls and ceiling made of translucent white silk that trembles in the breeze. The fourth wall of the stage becomes the 'mirror' into which the dancers gaze, watching themselves and each other.

Synopsis

The ballet opens with a young man asleep on the floor. He wakes, rolls over and stretches, watching himself in the mirror, and tries out positions and moves. A woman approaches the studio, visible through the silk wall. She pauses at the door, tests her *pointe* shoes, catching her reflection. As she warms up at the *barre*, the man wakes up and steps in to partner her. Dancing together, they look at their reflections rather than each other, observing their own bodies as he lifts her or as they both sink to the ground. As they kneel close together he looks away from the mirror to kiss her on the cheek. She lifts her hand to her cheek, stands and backs out of the room, still watching her reflection. Left alone, the man goes back to sleep.

Afternoon of a Faun was based on Robbins' own observation of dancers. He remembered seeing a couple rehearsing the *Swan Lake adagio*, 'watching themselves in the mirror, and I was struck by the way they were watching that couple over there doing a love dance and totally unaware of the prox- imity and possible sexuality of their physical encounters'. He changed his mind about where the ballet's 'mirror' should be, trying it at the side as well as at the front, but found that 'when it's straight front, I think something much more arresting happens'.[48]

Rehearsing the dancer Antoinette Sibley, he told her about her character's frame of mind: 'It's a very hot day, you've just washed your hair, you've got your prettiest, cleanest practice clothes on, you feel wonderful, you're just going to look at yourself in the mirror and have fun'.[49]

Robbins had also read the Mallarmé poem that inspired Debussy: Francisco Moncion, who danced in the first cast, remembered that 'the gestures he used were evocative of Mallarmé's faun – such as pushing through the reeds on a hot, humid afternoon'.[50]

Sylvia

Choreography: Frederick Ashton
Music: Léo Delibes
Designs: Robin and Christopher Ironside
Premiere: 3 September 1952, Sadler's Wells Ballet, Royal Opera House, London
Original cast: *Sylvia* Margot Fonteyn; *Aminta* Michael Somes; *Orion* John Hart; *Eros* Alexander Grant; *Diana* Julia Farron

Sylvia was the first ballet performed at the new Opéra Garnier in Paris in 1876, with choreography by Louis Mérante. It's a mythological ballet, a story of gods and mortals loosely inspired by *Aminta*, an entertainment that the poet Torquato Tasso wrote for the court of Ferrara in 1573. The Mérante production had a mixed reception: its greatest appeal lay in Delibes' sweet, fresh score. When Tchaikovsky saw the ballet in 1877, a year after completing his own *Swan Lake*, he was enchanted. 'It is the first ballet in which the music constitutes not just the main but the only interest,' he wrote. 'What charm and elegance, what riches in the melody, the rhythm, the harmony. I was ashamed. If I had known this music before, I would not have written *Swan Lake*.'[51]

The ballet has been frequently restaged. Diaghilev planned a lavish revival for the Imperial Theatres in 1900, and resigned when the project was cancelled. The next year, Lev Ivanov and Pavel Gerdt choreographed a version for the Mariinsky Ballet; Ivanov died before the production was completed. It was also staged by Léo Staats in Milan and at London's Empire Theatre.

Sylvia was Frederick Ashton's second evening-length ballet. His first, *Cinderella*, had responded to a modern score with classical dance and very English comedy. For *Sylvia*, he was in more nostalgic mood, evoking the Paris Opéra's nineteenth-century spectacles, with lots of classical dancing and some touches of comedy, particularly for Eros. Robin and Christopher Ironside's sets are influenced by the classical landscapes of Claude Lorrain, while the costumes mix tutus with Greek draperies and motifs.

Synopsis

Act I. A sacred wood. Woodland creatures dance in the moonlight before the shrine of Eros, the god of love. The shepherd Aminta arrives, and hides when he sees Sylvia approaching. The ballerina crosses the bridge at the back of the stage, and makes her first entrance to a dance full of horn calls: she is a huntress, one of Diana's nymphs, and has sworn to reject love. She and her attendants mock Eros, brandishing their hunting-bows at his statue. Catching sight of Aminta's cloak, they pull him from his hiding place. Sylvia is outraged: blaming Eros, she aims an arrow at the statue. Aminta shields the statue, stepping in front of it, and is shot by the arrow. In revenge, the statue comes to life, firing one of his own arrows at Sylvia. Shaken, she plucks the arrow from her heart, and leaves.

Dawn breaks. On their way to the fields, peasants dance in honour of Eros. The hunter Orion appears, and takes cover to spy on Sylvia. She returns and dances in mourning for Aminta: struck by Eros' arrow, she has fallen in love. Orion emerges from his hiding place and abducts her. A young shepherd finds Aminta's body, and summons his friends, who weep over the body. When a cloaked hermit passes by, they beg him to help. He brings Aminta back to life by plucking a flower, magically changing its colour and pressing it to Aminta's lips. He then reveals himself to be Eros, and tells the restored Aminta to go in search of Sylvia.

Act II. Orion's island cave. Orion tries to woo Sylvia, offering her jewels and fine clothes. She refuses, holding on to Eros' arrow, which reminds her of her love for Aminta – but Orion takes it from her. She encourages him to drink, and dances for him until he falls asleep. She retrieves the arrow and prays to Eros for help. The god appears, showing Sylvia a vision of Aminta, and takes her back to him.

Act III. The sea coast near the temple of Diana. A festival is in progress, honouring the god Bacchus. Aminta arrives, seeking Sylvia. A boat arrives with Eros, Sylvia and her attendants. The lovers are reunited.

Orion arrives in pursuit of Sylvia. She takes refuge in the temple of Diana. After fighting Aminta, Orion tries to break into the temple. Furious, Diana appears and kills him. She then turns angrily on the lovers – until Eros reminds Diana that she herself had fallen in love with the shepherd Endymion. She relents and gives the lovers her blessing.

Ashton's *Sylvia* was created for Margot Fonteyn, a world-renowned ballerina at the height of her technical powers, to show off her range and variety. In the first act alone, she goes from Amazonian huntress to love-stricken woman, from bounding jumps to trembling bourrées. In the second act, she's a seductress, tempting and tricking Orion. The last act displays her as a classical ballerina, with a solo full of intricate footwork and changes of direction to Delibes' pizzicato score, and a *pas de deux* with Aminta that blends tenderness and bravura.

'The part has everything for Fonteyn,' wrote the critic Clive Barnes:

> . . . It gives us Fonteyn triumphant, Fonteyn bewildered, Fonteyn exotic, Fonteyn pathetic, Fonteyn in excelsis. The range of her dancing is unequalled, the heart-splitting significance she can give to a simple movement unsurpassed. The whole ballet is like a garland presented to the ballerina by her choreographer.[52]

This was both a strength and a weakness. *Sylvia* needs a ballerina with the authority to pull the whole performance together, to give momentum to its meandering plot. She has the best of its choreography; many of the *corps* dances are pretty but conventional. The ballet's comedy, from the mischievous Eros to a dance for a pair of sacrificial goats, can be sugary.

Created to show off Fonteyn, *Sylvia* lost popularity without her. Ashton revised it as a two-act and then a one-act version, before it fell from the repertory. In 2004, Christopher Newton reconstructed it for The Royal Ballet, in a co-production with American Ballet Theatre. In this revival, *Sylvia* has become popular around the world, also entering the repertory of the Staatsballett Berlin and the Mariinsky Ballet.

Other Stagings

Delibes' score has been a draw for other choreographers. In 1950, George Balanchine created his *Sylvia pas de deux*, a showcase for Maria Tallchief and Nicholas Magallanes. Tallchief pointed out that Balanchine had given her French-style *ports de bras*, 'rather than the grand Russian manner one might expect in a virtuoso pas de deux'.[53]

In 1997, John Neumeier created an updated version of the ballet for the Paris Opéra in 1997, subtitled 'Three Choreographic Poems on a Mythical Theme'. Neumeier has said that he wanted to get rid of *Sylvia*'s 'operetta' qualities, focusing instead on 'an Amazon at that fragile moment between adolescence and womanhood. Torn between strength and vulnerability, she has difficulty in finding a balance between aggressiveness and tenderness, between denial and self abandon, and only succeeds in discovering true love with the awakening of her own sensuality'.[54]

The painter Yannis Kokkos designed spare, stylised settings for Neumeier's *Sylvia*: a blue tree against a green wall, a crescent moon on a plain backdrop, a broken classical statue. The men wear variations on modern clothing, sweaters and dungarees, while the nymphs wear leather shorts and bodices. Neumeier's choreography blends classical steps with quirkier moves: circled arms, flexed feet, waggled knees.

When Mark Morris staged *Sylvia* for San Francisco Ballet in 2004, it was received warmly and with some surprise. Morris has a reputation for irony and irreverence, as in *The Hard Nut*, his sharp, if tender-hearted, reworking of *The Nutcracker*. But he played *Sylvia*'s nymphs-and-shepherds love story straight, staying close to the libretto of Louis Mérante's 1876 production (the plot is essentially the same as in Ashton's version). Allen Moyer's set designs were based on French nineteenth-century panoramic wallpaper, while Martin Pakledinaz's costumes were gently Greek. Morris' works for ballet companies often keep aspects of his contemporary dance choreography – the weighted physicality, the democratic group dances. In *Sylvia* he made a more purely balletic work, while keeping his own distinctive voice. Morris' Sylvia is athletic; he's praised the character as feminist. The critic Paul Parish points out this Sylvia's distinctive run, 'with a circular gait like a horse's, the feet reach out in front like hooves, toe pointed, and kick up to the back'.[55] The grand *pas de deux* for Sylvia and Aminta becomes a dance with a veil, with echoes of *La Bayadère* or Ashton's *Thaïs*.

Scotch Symphony

Choreography: George Balanchine
Music: Felix Mendelssohn, Symphony No. 3 in A minor, op. 56, 'Scotch' (second, third and fourth movements)
Women's costumes: Karinska
Men's costumes: David Ffolkes

Premiere: 11 November 1952, New York City Ballet, New York City Center, New York

Original cast: Maria Tallchief, André Eglevsky, Patricia Wilde

Both Mendelssohn and Balanchine came to this work after visits to Scotland. Mendelssohn, who visited in 1829, was succumbing to the Romantic fashion for all things Scottish, which would also produce the ballet *La Sylphide*. When New York City Ballet appeared at the Edinburgh International Festival in 1952, Balanchine enjoyed seeing the landscape and the military tattoo – which would later influence his choreography for *Union Jack* – and made *Scotch Symphony* soon afterwards.

The ballet is a celebration of romantic and indeed Romantic Scottishness: 'Part *La Sylphide*, part *Brigadoon*,'[56] wrote the critic Alexandra Tomalonis. The ballet establishes dramatic moods without turning them into a plot. This is not a story ballet, but an evocation of Romantic themes, with ethereal dances for the ballerina and lively material for the second ballerina and the ensemble.

First movement. It opens with eight couples, dressed in kilts or tulle, in dances that have a Scottish flavour, with echoes of Highland dancing in the raised arms and prancing steps. A virtuoso woman, dressed in tartan, shows off her speedy, steely footwork. Her beaten steps are as strong as a male dancer's – something underlined by her *pas de trois* with two male Highlanders. At the end of the first movement, another man appears; the *corps de ballet* greets him, and then leaves.

Second movement. In this *adagio* the man meets a mysterious, sylph-like ballerina, and they dance a long *pas de deux*. Following Mendelssohn, rather than any narrative logic, Balanchine brings on a troop of Highlanders at a solemn strain in the music. They group protectively around the ballerina, barring her partner's way to her – then lift and throw her into his arms, before leaving again on another change in the music.

The ballet ends with an ensemble, including another *pas de deux* for the ballerina and her partner.

Western Symphony

Choreography: George Balanchine

Music: Hershy Kay

Costumes: Karinska

Sets: John Boyt
Lighting: Jean Rosenthal
Premiere: 7 September 1954, New York City Ballet, New York City Center, New York
Original cast: *Allegro* Diana Adams, Herbert Bliss; *Adagio* Janet Reed, Nicholas Magallanes; *Rondo* Tanaquil LeClercq, Jacques d'Amboise

With *Western Symphony*, Balanchine created his own version of the Americana genre – although he came at it from a new angle. Where Agnes de Mille and Eugene Loring used western themes as a way of creating a new, American vocabulary for ballet, Balanchine created a suite of formal dances with a cowboy backdrop.

This would be the first of several ballets in which Balanchine used classical dance to celebrate aspects of American popular culture, and his love of his adopted country. He adored movie westerns (though he was less keen on later, 'psychological' additions to the genre), liked to wear western-style clothes such as string ties and plaid shirts, and loved the West itself: he commissioned the score after a visit to Wyoming. Hershy Kay's first attempt was rejected as 'too much like Copland'; Balanchine was not aiming for another *Rodeo* or *Appalachian Spring*. Instead, Kay created a classical symphony based on popular western songs, including 'Red River Valley', 'Good Night, Ladies' and 'The Girl I Left Behind Me'. The male dancers wear cowboy hats and western shirts; the women, on *pointe*, are dressed as stylised saloon girls. John Boyt's backdrop, added a year after the premiere, is a classic western street of storefronts. The choreography is full of classical steps, woven into hoedown patterns.

First movement. A leading couple dances a *pas de deux* to bar-room piano, the man flapping his cowboy hat in admiration at her speedy footwork.

Second movement. A cowboy drives in a team of horses – two lines of women who ripple their arms like reins – and dances a vision scene with a ballerina before driving out of town.

Third movement. This is an exuberant rondo with a 'Diamond Lil' heroine in an outrageous hat, who shakes out her ruffles before showing off her footwork, while her partner soars through jumps. (The ballet originally had a scherzo movement, which was soon dropped.)

Balanchine was to return to this brand of Americana in later works, with existing music orchestrated by Hershy Kay. This group includes *Stars and Stripes*, in which regiments of dancers strut to marches by John Philip Sousa, the Gershwin ballet *Who Cares?* and *Union Jack*, which celebrated two hundred years of American independence by staging Balanchine's twist on traditional British dances.

The Concert or, The Perils of Everybody

Choreography: Jerome Robbins
Music: Frédéric Chopin, Berceuse, op. 57; Prelude, op. 28, no. 18; Prelude, op. 28, no. 16; Waltz in E Minor; Prelude, op. 28, no. 7; Waltz, op. 64, no. 1; Prelude, op. 28, no. 7; Waltz, op. 64, no. 1; Mazurka in G major; Mazurka, op. 24, no. 4; Ballade, op. 27, no. 3
Costumes: Irene Sharaff
Lighting, decor: Jean Rosenthal
Premiere: 6 March 1956, New York City Center, New York
Original cast: Tanaquil LeClercq, Todd Bolender, Yvonne Mounsey, Robert Barnett, Wilma Curley, John Mandia, Shaun O'Brien, Patricia Savoia, Richard Thomas

In *The Concert*, Robbins spins farce, vaudeville jokes and unexpected fantasy out of Chopin piano music. It was Robbins' first ballet to Chopin, a composer who would become an essential element of his ballet career. The jokes of *The Concert* sing because, however improbably, they are rooted in the music.

The ballet shows the daydreams of an audience at a concert recital. The piano is onstage, the pianist arriving with pompous gravity. His audience follows in ones and twos, bringing their own chairs. They are stock comic types: arty culture-lovers, a henpecked misogynist dragged along by his battleaxe wife, a ditzy heroine in a big hat, a timid, bespectacled young man. Irene Sharaff dresses the dancers in blue leotards with comic accessories, hats and socks and waistcoats: the husband, with his cigar, moustache and glasses, is a Groucho Marx clone. Getting settled, they offend each other by sitting in the wrong chairs, rustling sweet papers, getting ostentatiously carried away by the music.

The different piano pieces prompt different fantasies. The husband imagines carrying off the woman in the hat and murdering his wife, who brings him back to earth with a laser glance. Other sections become jokes about ballet. The gorgeous 'mistake waltz' is so nearly a pretty group number, if only the women didn't keep getting out of step (and sidling back to the right place, hoping nobody notices).

Robbins also teased the music's ballet associations. The ditzy woman tries on more hats to the famous *Sylphides* prelude (op. 28, no. 7), while the husband plots murder to its repeat. He also plays tricks with the audience's musical expectations. Having said that he wanted to 'denude certain pieces of their banal titles – "Butterflies", "Raindrop" etc.',[57] he included both butterfly and umbrella dances, but set them to quite different pieces of music. That's a clever in-joke, but the raindrop dance, set to a melancholy prelude in E minor (op. 28, no. 4), gives *The Concert* a curious, wistful sequence. Dancers put out their hands to test for rain, shrug and put up umbrellas, walking to and fro. By the end, everyone is huddled under a single umbrella, looking up at the sky.

The rollicking mood returns with the final dance, in which the dancers turn into butterflies for a triumphant finale – until the pianist, exasperated beyond endurance, chases them away with a butterfly net.

Robbins made some cuts and revisions to *The Concert* after the premiere (originally, the wife also fantasised about murdering her husband). He revised it further for his own Ballets U.S.A. in 1958, adding a comic drop-curtain by Saul Steinberg. The Royal Ballet production of 1975 had a curtain designed by Edward Gorey, but it has since reverted to the Steinberg design.

Agon

Choreography: George Balanchine
Music: Igor Stravinsky
Lighting: Nananne Porcher
Premiere: 1 December 1957, New York City Ballet, New York City Center, New York
Original cast: Diana Adams, Arthur Mitchell, Todd Bolender, Barbara Milberg, Barbara Walczak, Roy Tobias, Jonathan Watts, Melissa Hayden

Agon, Stravinsky's last ballet score, takes the names of its movements from a seventeenth-century dance manual. The music itself is stringently modern, based on the twelve-tone system, in twelve sections, to be performed by twelve dancers. Balanchine's choreography combines rigorous mathematical logic with searing energy. He called it his 'IBM ballet', 'more tight and precise than usual, as if it were controlled by an electronic brain'.[58] But it's a brain of wit and – particularly in the *pas de deux* – great sexual presence.

Lincoln Kirstein was eager to have a third Stravinsky score for New York City Ballet, to go with *Apollo* and the 1948 *Orpheus*. Stravinsky rejected suggestions for another mythic ballet. It was the composer who suggested a ballet based on a manual of French court dances: sarabandes, galliards, *branles*.

The dancers wear plain practice costumes on a bare, brightly lit stage: everything is stripped down, revealing the workings of the ballet's machinery. Before Stravinsky started writing, he and Balanchine worked out what combinations of dancers should be used for each movement, and how long each section should be. When Balanchine received the score, 'only the actual sound was a surprise to me.'[59]

The ballet is organised in three sections. The curtain rises on four men, their backs to the audience (as directed by Stravinsky in the score). As they turn, and start to dance, the music begins with a fanfare. Their dance is followed by a double *pas de quatre* for eight women and a triple *pas de quatre* for all twelve dancers.

This opening section is followed by the first *pas de trois*. Two women and a man dance the brief opening, moving quickly to the fanfare before winding into angular chain dances. The man's solo is based on a sarabande, his feet flexed and pointed. The two women dance a galliard in unison. As in *The Four Temperaments*, Balanchine's steps have courtly echoes and angular elegance, with playful touches. The man rejoins them for a coda, the dancers moving in and out of canon to spikily twelve-tone music.

The second *pas de trois*, for a woman and two men, opens with another fanfare. The men partner the woman, turning her as she poses on *pointe*. The two men dance a *branle simple* in canon form. In Stravinsky's dance manual, an engraving showed two trumpeters accompanying the *branle simple*, and he orchestrated this number accordingly. Each of the men takes the part of one of the trumpets.

The *branle gai* is a solo for the woman, who dances to two rhythms at once, following both the orchestra and a set of castanets. The two men join her for a *branle double*, ending the second section.

The fanfare introduces the *pas de deux*, one of Balanchine's most extraordinary inventions. The man supports and manipulates the woman as she bends and unfolds herself into bold, extreme shapes. She ends a partnered turn bending into *attitude penchée*, her raised leg hooked around his neck; lifted into the air, she opens her legs wide. In perhaps the ballet's most famous moment, the man leads her through a promenade turn – but she is holding her foot behind her head, while he partners her as he lies on the floor, scuttling along at her feet.

The *pas de deux* dancers are joined by three more couples in the *danse de quatre duos*, and then by the other four women for the *danse de quatre trios*. The ballet ends as it began, with the four men posed with their backs to the audience.

In his original programme note, a cautious Balanchine called Stravinsky's score 'a new piece of diabolical craftsmanship; sounds like this have not been heard before; it may take rather developed ears to hear them.'[60] In the event, *Agon* was an immediate hit with audiences and critics. Its intricacies are stark but also exhilarating; in its ruthless precision, the choreography also encompasses moments of humour and swagger, and the cool intensity of its *pas de deux*. It was instantly recognised as a masterpiece.

6

SOVIET BALLET

W HEN THE RUSSIAN Revolution broke out in 1917, Diaghilev's Ballets
Russes were dancing *The Firebird* in Paris. In the final scene, Ivan
Tsarevich and his Imperial sceptre were replaced by a Russian peasant
wearing a cap of liberty and waving a red flag. It was a gesture, a blatant
attempt to reframe the ballet to appeal to a new political system. For
Diaghilev, it turned out to be a dead end: he and his company became
emigrés. Back in Russia, ballet had to adapt in order to survive. It faced
drastic political change, from civil war to Stalin's terror. Yet it reframed
itself so successfully that ballet became Russia's flagship cultural art, a
source of pride at home and wonder abroad, the favoured entertainment
for state occasions. 'If I think about having to see *Swan Lake* in the evening,
I start to get sick to my stomach,' the Russian premier Nikita Khrushchev
admitted to ballerina Maya Plisetskaya. 'The ballet is marvellous, but how
much can a person take? Then at night I dream of white tutus and tanks all
mixed up together . . .'[1]

As a favoured art form of the royal family, ballet was in a vulnerable
position after the revolution. When the Bolsheviks took power, they swiftly
commandeered the townhouse of Mathilde Kschessinska, the ballerina
who had been the mistress of a tsar and two grand dukes. Performances
stopped. Artists of the Bolshoi issued a statement condemning the violence
of the Bolshevik rise to power, and many dancers left Russia, including such
stars as Kschessinska, Tamara Karsavina and Mikhail Fokine.

Yet the theatres reopened – faster in Moscow, which now became the
capital of Russia, than in Petrograd, where some artists rejected the
authority of the new People's Commissariat for Enlightenment (known as
Narkompros). Once open, the Bolshoi and the Mariinsky stayed open,
despite civil war, food and fuel shortages, inflation and bitter cold. They

welcomed a new audience of workers and peasants. After caution on both sides, this new public quickly became enthusiastic, flocking to see the old nineteenth-century repertory. Asaf Messerer, who went on to become a celebrated Bolshoi dancer and teacher, remembered going to the ballet in the winter of 1919:

> It is cold in the theatre, the audience sits in felt boots, in fur coats, under the cupola hangs a cloud of frost from the breathing of the spectators. The winter of 1919 was in general unprecedentedly fierce and hungry. Moscow was drowned deeply in snow, stiff dead horses were lying on the street, no one removed them ... And suddenly – the Bolshoi Theatre! The red velvet of the stalls and the boxes, gold, the radiance of the light in the crystal pendants. All of this seemed almost unreal, and yet it was reality. The joyful luxury of the décor, the sound of the instruments being tuned in the orchestra, darkness slowly descending upon the auditorium after the chandelier had faded, the curtain flying up, and, finally, the bright stage, on which, not privy to the severe frost, stood a graceful ballerina in a short tutu and friskily gay.[2]

As the dance historian Christina Ezrahi points out, ballet's appeal was escapism, a glimpse of extravagance and spectacle in dark and hungry times. In 1919, Anatoly Lunacharsky, head of Narkompros, replied to a colleague's argument that the bourgeois theatre must be rejected and torn down. 'Comrade Bukharin would wonder at the fact that not once have the workers demanded of me that I increase their accessibility to the revolutionary theatre, but they ceaselessly demand opera and ballet. Perhaps Comrade Bukharin would be distressed at that. It distresses me a little.'[3] Given the choice, the proletariat wanted Imperial ballet. By the end of the year, the Mariinsky and the Bolshoi theatres acquired official status and state subsidy.

At the same time, the revolution had unleashed a rush of experimentation in art. The new Bolshevik government took the arts very seriously, seeing them as a vital part of the transformation of Russia's culture, identity and social structure. The artists who responded to the call of Narkompros tended to be young and radical. This generation developed new forms and movements, exploring futurism, constructivism, industrial forms and atypical combinations. They soaked up Western artistic influences from jazz and foxtrots to Hollywood movies. This burst of innovation covered many different art forms: film, painting, theatre, typography. Sergei Eisenstein discovered and developed new film techniques, the painters Kasimir

Malevich and Wassily Kandinsky worked with Narkompros on art education and reform. The spirit of experiment also extended to dance. Fokine was asked to direct the Mariinsky, though negotiations broke down over his salary demands. Isadora Duncan was invited to form a Russian school, and danced by torchlight in freezing theatres while the audience sang revolutionary songs to accompany her. While the Mariinsky and the Bolshoi were performing their pre-revolutionary repertory, young choreographers were using classical training to radical effect.

Bronislava Nijinska, who had returned to Russia during the First World War, worked closely with constructivist artists. In Moscow, the Bolshoi-trained Kasian Goleizovsky created his own 'Chamber Ballet' for experimental work. He used classically trained dancers in erotic, acrobatic dances, performed in cabarets and small theatres. Ballerinas would dance traditional *arabesques* or *attitudes* from unexpected angles: on the floor or tilted in a partner's arms, rather than standing upright. Fedor Lopukhov, brother of the ballerina Lydia Lopokova, also used classical technique as the basis for experiment. In 1923 he staged his *Dance Symphony*, also called *The Greatness of the Universe*, to Beethoven's Fourth Symphony. Although it was performed only once, the *Dance Symphony* is a landmark work: a non-narrative ballet that explored the structure of its music through classical steps. The final scene linked all the dancers – who included Georgi Balanchivadze, Alexandra Danilova and Leonid Lavrovsky – in a cosmic spiral.

Balanchivadze, soon to be renamed Balanchine, admired Lopukhov and Goleizovsky. Their work, which featured winding chain dances and acrobatic movements, was a powerful influence on him. 'Seeing Goleizovsky was what first gave me the courage to try something different on my own,'[4] he told his biographer, Bernard Taper. He arranged his own evenings of 'Young Ballet', with a group that included Lavrovsky and Vasily Vainonen, who would become two of the most important Soviet choreographers. When Nijinska and Balanchine choreographed for Diaghilev, both reasserted the importance of classical technique, while responding to popular Western idioms, such as jazz. This free combination of the old and the new seems to have been characteristic of a generation of Russian dance artists.

All the arts were up for redefinition and debate: should the pre-revolutionary heritage be reformed according to Soviet principles, or swept away altogether? Proletkult, an independent rival to Lunacharsky's state department, pushed for a new proletarian art, which would owe nothing to the pre-revolutionary past. Its adherents dismissed ballet as a hopelessly tainted, Tsarist art. Between financial shortages and political debate, the Bolshoi and the Mariinsky were repeatedly under threat of closure. Lunacharsky, a supporter of the avant-garde, also defended tradition – including traditional ballet: 'To lose this thread, to allow it to break before being used as the foundation of a new artistic culture – belonging to the people – this would be a great calamity ... Can ballet be abolished in Russia? No, this will never happen.'[5]

Vladimir Lenin, the Bolshevik premier, came down on the side of tradition in art, arguing in 1922 that the new proletarian culture should develop from existing knowledge, rather than starting again from scratch. That year, Lopukhov staged a very popular new production of *The Sleeping Beauty*, in which he aimed for both fidelity to the tradition of Marius Petipa and new development. Where he thought errors had crept in, he corrected them, restoring passages of music that Petipa had cut, choreographing his own version of the Lilac Fairy's solo and cutting mime passages. In his staging and in his writings on ballet, Lopukhov presented *The Sleeping Beauty* as a work of 'symphonic' dance beauty. He saw the old ballet's dance architecture as a model for the future: as he would say, 'Forward to Petipa!'[6] 'Although rabidly supporting advanced and at times weird ideas,' the Soviet dance historian Natalia Roslavleva wrote in summary of Lopukhov, who directed the former Mariinsky from 1922 to 1931, 'he was a serious connoisseur of the classical ballet.'[7] In 1927, he united advanced and classical material in *The Ice Maiden*, a successful ballet that combined fairy-tale storytelling, classical steps and new acrobatic techniques, particularly for the title character. He called it 'a classical ballet in a 1927 interpretation.'[8]

The explosion of new ideas was to be snuffed out. Lunacharsky lost influence after Lenin's death in 1924. In 1928, Joseph Stalin came to power, pushing for greater state control in all areas of life, including culture. More conservative attitudes began to dominate the arts. The change was crystallised when the first Soviet Writers' Congress, held in 1934, rejected modernist experiment in favour of 'socialist realism', an unadventurous, naturalistic style that would be used to glorify the state. Pushkin and Tolstoy were approved exemplars for writers, Rimsky-Korsakov and Tchaikovsky for composers. For ballet, the nineteenth century was a more problematic model. While Lopukhov cut Petipa's mime scenes, Soviet intellectuals were questioning the pure-dance content of ballet.

In the late 1920s, the critics Alexei Gvozdev and Ivan Sollertinsky argued that ballet should focus on telling modern Soviet stories. It should ditch the supposedly empty virtuosity of dance set pieces in favour of plot-based mime. (Gvozdev was particularly offended by the thirty-two *fouettés* made famous by *Swan Lake*: 'No matter into what topic one inserts 32 fouettés . . . they still don't acquire topical expressiveness, they still don't become intelligent expressions of the dramatic order.')[9] Leading dance professionals – including Lopukhov and future Mariinsky director Agrippina Vaganova – were asked their opinions. They supported ballets on contemporary themes, but they also insisted on the importance of classical dancing over mime.

The Red Poppy, created at the Bolshoi Ballet in 1927, showed that mimed dance-drama on Soviet themes could be popular. Set in a Chinese port, it showed Soviet sailors coming to the aid of oppressed Chinese workers, with mimed action and folk-flavoured dances. Simpler and less daring than *The Ice Maiden*, it offered a template for *fouetté*-free choreography. The new emphasis on dramatic ballets led to the appointment of theatre director Sergei Radlov as head of the State Theatre of Opera and Ballet, which the Mariinsky was now called. He worked on a number of influential productions, including *The Flames of Paris*, *The Fountain of Bakhchisarai* and the libretto for Prokofiev's *Romeo and Juliet*.

While debate raged over repertory, the training of dancers continued under one of the most influential teachers in ballet's history, Agrippina Vaganova. Born in 1879, she danced at the Mariinsky from 1897 until 1916. Not considered pretty, and without influential protectors, she nevertheless moved slowly up the ranks. Her strong technique earned her the nickname 'The Queen of the Variations', and she shone in soloist rather than ballerina roles. She began to teach after the revolution, realising that teachers were in short supply. By 1921, she was teaching at the Leningrad Choreographic Technikum (the Mariinsky school had been renamed to suit the new political climate, like St Petersburg itself). She urged her pupils to analyse which muscles created which danced effect, and to 'dance out of the body', moving from a strong and expressive back. The result was a powerfully expansive classical style. She wasn't keen on the experimental works of the 1920s, but when her early pupils danced in them, she helped them meet choreographers' new demands.

When Soviet ballet turned towards dramatic ballets, Vaganova's students were ready. Roslavleva points out that 'Soviet choreographers started taking advantage of Vaganova-trained pupils (they expressed not only the Vaganova system, but the *age* they lived in, with its soaring spirit). Vaganova, in turn, was also influenced by the style of Soviet choreography and this did not fail to be reflected in her work.'[10] Marina Semyonova, the first great Soviet ballerina, wrote that Vaganova 'demanded that the image, emotions and content of the dance be conveyed by the *entire body*. The body was our instrument.'[11] This expressive quality would light up the mime sequences and limited steps of the new Soviet style, known as the *dramballet*, or dramatic ballet. Galina Ulanova, another Vaganova-trained ballerina, would make an extraordinary impact in dramballet's mimed moments. Around the world, audiences cheered her headlong run to Friar Laurence in *Romeo and Juliet*, while the statuesque death of Maria in *The Fountain of Bakhchisarai* was a cherished moment in Soviet culture.

The dramballet was gaining ground. After 1936, it became the only safe option. The storm centred around *The Bright Stream*, a ballet Lopukhov had created for the Maly Theatre of St Petersburg in 1935. Lopukhov had been dismissed from the former Mariinsky when his ballet *The Bolt* was condemned for apparently mocking the Soviet ideal. Nevertheless, the Leningrad regional committee of the Communist Party invited him to create a new ballet. Like *The Bolt, The Bright Stream* had a score by Dmitri Shostakovich, and a modern-day Soviet setting, this time a collective farm. It was a romantic comedy, with disguises and assignations, ending with a celebration of the farm's production success. Lopukhov and his co-librettist, Adrian Piotrovsky, declared:

> We strove for our ballet to be a danced ballet, that dance was the basic and most important artistic-expressive means of the production. Such a demand by no means contradicts searches for a realistic style. But the fact of the matter is that realism in ballet has to be realised with its specific means, that is, above all with the means of dance and, in partic- ular, of classical dance.[12]

After the ballet's success in Leningrad, Lopukhov was invited to become artistic director of the Bolshoi, and to stage *The Bright Stream* there. This time, factory workers were invited to give their opinion on the work in rehearsal. Reactions were overwhelmingly positive. The premiere was a success, and the ballet was even chosen for the special performance on Stalin's birthday. Then disaster struck: an editorial in *Pravda*, the state newspaper, attacked the ballet on account of its 'formalism'. It accused the production of presenting ballet 'dolls', artificial peasants based on pre-revolutionary ballet. A realistic folk ballet should take folk dances as its model; Lopukhov's work was dismissed as 'an unnatural mixture of false-folk dances with numbers of dancers in tutus'.[13] Shostakovich was already under a cloud due to Stalin's dislike of his opera *Lady Macbeth of the Mtsensk District* but, as Christina Ezrahi has shown, this was more than guilt by association: the whole basis of Lopukhov's work was under threat.

The attack on *The Bright Stream* came two years after the murder of the rising politician Sergei Kirov, whose death served as a pretext for Stalin's great purge of the late 1930s. It was an era of terror and show trials. In a panic, ballet artists rushed to distance themselves. Vaganova published an analysis of the 'falsitudes' of Lopukhov's work. *The Bright Stream* was to be his last important dance. Vaganova arrived at work to find a notice announcing her 'resignation'. Piotrovsky was arrested in 1938, and died in prison. The former Mariinsky was one of many Soviet institutions and places to be renamed in Kirov's honour.

Although there was no explicit ban on classical dance, *The Bright Stream* remained as an awful warning against classicism and light-heartedness. Seeking safe subjects, choreographers turned to approved classic literature: Shakespeare, Pushkin, Lope de Vega. The greatest success, and the most important of the dramballets, was Leonid Lavrovsky's *Romeo and Juliet*, staged at the Kirov in 1940. With Ulanova as Juliet, this would become Soviet ballet's flagship work, staged in Moscow in 1946 and filmed in 1954. When the Bolshoi Ballet made its first Western appearance, in London in 1956, *Romeo and Juliet* with Ulanova was a revelation to a new audience. As a student, the British ballerina Antoinette Sibley saw a rehearsal. She took Ulanova, then forty-six, for a ballet mistress, until 'she took off her woollies and in front of our eyes, no makeup, no costume, no help from theatrical aids whatsoever, she became fourteen years old. I've never seen any magic like that in my entire life. It was the sort of miracle that it is to have a baby . . .'[14] The limitations of Soviet choreography were noted, but the power of the dancers was overwhelming.

The Bolshoi's tours were one result of a change in government. After Stalin's death in 1953, and the rise of Nikita Khrushchev as Soviet premier, the terror and the purges of the 1930s were acknowledged. The new era sought to 'de-Stalinize' Russian society, to restore and revitalise the Soviet project. High culture, particularly ballet, was increasingly promoted as a sign of Soviet civilisation. At the same time, it was acknowledged that culture had stagnated under Stalinist repression. The dramballet had run its course: ballets on Soviet themes were still being created, but few could match the popularity of *Laurencia* or *The Fountain of Bakhchisarai*, let alone *Swan Lake*. The 1953 ballet *Native Fields*, whose heroine dreams that her fiancé will return from Moscow to build an electric power station, became synonymous with dramballet's failings. 'We had bugles and flags, like good Young Communists,' dancer Nikola Ostaltsov told documentary-maker Angus Macqueen. 'At the back, they would drag a painted tractor with lights on . . . Sadly, it had a short stage life. We loved it – we got real lemonade on stage. Realism is realism.'[15]

Igor Moiseyev pointed out that the turn away from dancing had stifled the development of Soviet ballet: 'our latest productions suffer from a common fault, the poverty of dance form . . . We have justly criticised many old ballets because they did not combine the dance with healthy thought, but we cannot permit new ballets to have healthy thought uncombined with dance.'[16] In the climate of Khrushchev's 'thaw', new artists moved away from mime, putting more dancing into their ballets.

Yuri Grigorovich, born in 1927 and trained at the Leningrad school, made his name with a 1957 production of *The Stone Flower*, three years after Leonid Lavrovsky had staged a mime-heavy version. Grigorovich put much more dancing into the Soviet-themed fairy-tale, giving the supernatural Mistress of the Copper Mountain virtuoso steps and using the *corps de ballet* to reflect the leading characters' state of mind. The work was poorly received on Western tours, where its increased dance content was nothing new, but it identified Grigorovich as the new force in Soviet dance. *The Stone Flower* was quickly restaged in Moscow, where prima ballerina Maya Plisetskaya made a commanding Mistress of the Copper Mountain. The young lovers were danced by Vladimir Vasiliev and Ekaterina Maximova, two strong and immensely charismatic dancers who were just out of school. Vasiliev's virile presence contrasted beautifully with Maximova's mischievous femininity; marrying in 1961, they became Soviet ballet's golden couple, acclaimed around the world.

The Legend of Love, created in 1961, built on the success of *The Stone Flower*, telling its story in dance sequences. After this, Grigorovich moved to Moscow to become director of the Bolshoi Ballet, which he would direct until 1995 and continue to influence afterwards. He made *Spartacus*, his most famous work, in 1968, with Vasiliev a magnificent Spartacus, devouring the stage in vast jumps. This perfected the model of Grigorovich choreography: characters expressing their emotions in extremely athletic steps, backed by a *corps de ballet* that echoed and amplified the stars' themes.

Grigorovich's move to Moscow was part of a pattern of Soviet ballet: Leningrad had tended to produce more choreographers, and more stars, who were then called to Moscow. Until Grigorovich took over, the Bolshoi was a showcase for Russian ballet, but had lagged behind in creativity. Just as Moscow had become the Soviet capital, in preference to the Westernised St Petersburg (renamed Petrograd in the First World War, and then Leningrad), the Moscow ballet company received greater state prestige. It was the Bolshoi that made the first Western tours. When the Kirov was not permitted to venture west, in 1961 its rising star Rudolf Nureyev defected.

In the aftermath of Nureyev's defection, the Kirov was under even more state scrutiny. At the same time, the 'thaw' began to freeze again; after Khrushchev's disgust at an exhibition of abstract paintings, there was another push towards socialist realism in art. *The Legend of Love* and *The Bedbug* (an experimental work by Leonid Yakobson whose cast included the young Natalia Makarova) were singled out for criticism, accused of Western influence and undue eroticism. Makarova and Mikhail Baryshnikov also defected from the Kirov's increasingly sterile atmosphere. Yuri Soloviev, who did not defect, was found shot dead in 1977, apparently by his own hand.

There was stagnation at the Bolshoi, too. By the 1970s, star dancers such as Vasiliev, Maximova and Plisetskaya were accusing Grigorovich of favouritism – his wife, the lyrical ballerina Natalia Bessmertnova, danced most opening nights – and of stifling talent. Isolated from the West, riven by politics and official scrutiny, Soviet ballet was still lavishly supported by the state, but facing artistic dead ends.

The Flames of Paris

Choreography: Vasily Vainonen
Libretto: Nikolai Volkov, Vladimir Dmitriev
Advising director: Sergei Radlov
Music: Boris Asafiev
Designs: Vladimir Dmitriev
Premiere: 7 November 1932, Kirov Theatre, Leningrad. Restaged 7 June 1933, Bolshoi Theatre, Moscow
Original cast: *Jeanne* Feya Balabina; *Jerome* Alexei Yermolayev; *Thérèse* Nina Anisimova

In *The Flames of Paris*, Soviet ballet celebrated the Russian Revolution by looking back to the French Revolution. The ballet was originally created in four acts: an uprising in Marseilles; a ball at the palace of Versailles, where the actress Mireille rejects the corrupt court to join the revolution; the storming of the Tuileries; and a final act of celebrations. The storming of the Tuileries, a spectacular scene, was performed on 6 November 1932 to mark the fifteenth anniversary of Russia's own revolution of 1917. The next night, the complete ballet had its first performance in Leningrad, while Moscow dancers performed the third act. *The Flames of Paris* joined the Bolshoi repertory in 1933, with a cast that included Vakhtang Chabukiani as Jerome.

Vasily Vainonen had worked with Balanchine's 'Young Ballet' group, where he created his spectacular, acrobatic 'Moskovski Waltz'. In *The Flames of Paris* he created several leading roles, but the ballet's main hero was the revolutionary crowd itself. Boris Asafiev's score drew on French songs of the period, particularly the Marseillaise, and 'Ça ira' which was sung during the storming of the Tuileries: the huge cast closed ranks and slowly advanced on the footlights, muskets in hand, to the song's menacing drumbeat. In the twenty-first century, Alexei Ratmansky called this 'a mise-en-scène of genius . . . You know, the accent is on count two, it's very syncopated, which is very common for Vainonen's style. That makes it very, very exciting.'[17]

In celebrating the revolutionaries, Vainonen used folk dances from the period, both for the *corps de ballet* and for individual soloists. The large-scale carmagnole and the fierce Basque dances were particularly admired. The character dancer Nina Anisimova, who danced Thérèse, worked closely with Vainonen on her role; colleagues from the first production observed that she created many of her own steps. She went on to become one of Soviet ballet's first female choreographers, creating the evening-length ballet *Gayaneh*, famous for its *pas de deux* and its sabre dance, to music by Aram Khachaturian.

Descriptions of the first production vary, particularly in the details of the first act. This synopsis focuses on the action common to all accounts.

Synopsis

Act I. Near the castle of the Marquis of Beauregard, 1792. The high-handed Marquis mistreats the old peasant Gaspard and his children, Jeanne and Jacques. A group of Marseillais, including Philippe and Jerome, pass through on their way to Paris to support the revolution. Finding Gaspard and his family in distress, they help them against the Marquis, storming his castle. The Marquis flees to Versailles, while the family join the revolutionaries as they set off for Paris.

Act II. A ball at the palace of Versailles. The actress Diana Mireille and her partner Antoine Mistral lead an entertainment for the court. The performance is interrupted by the Marquis, who warns the aristocrats about the uprising. Suggesting counter-revolutionary action, he writes a letter to the Prussians, asking for assistance. The French king signs the letter. While the court is at supper, Antoine finds a scroll describing the Prussian plan. Seeing the actor with the document, the Marquis kills Antoine, fearing he may give away the secret. Mireille finds the scroll in her dead partner's hands, and decides to warn the revolutionaries. The Marseillaise, the song of the revolution, is heard in the distance. Mireille flees the palace.

Act III. A square in Paris, where the revolutionaries have gathered. The Parisians welcome detachments from the provinces, including the Marseillais, the Basques – including the brave Basque woman Thérèse – and groups from the Auvergne. Diana Mireille arrives and warns them of the counter-revolutionary plot. Philippe calls on the people to storm the Palace of the Tuileries. They dance a carmagnole, and prepare to storm the Tuileries, singing the revolutionary song 'Ça ira'.

Act IV. Scene 1. The Tuileries Palace. Crowds of people storm the palace. In the fighting, the Marquis tries to kill Jeanne, but Philippe fights him. The people take possession of the palace.

Scene 2. A Paris square. The people celebrate the capture of the Tuileries. Diana Mireille performs a dance of victory, personifying the goddess of reason. Jeanne and Philippe, who are getting married, dance a virtuoso *pas de deux* (often performed as a gala number). The carmagnole is sung and danced.

Iris Morley, a British critic living in Moscow, described the impact of *The Flames of Paris* in the Bolshoi performance. In her account, the actress Mireille sounds like the embodiment of ballet itself, transformed from a courtly art into one eager to serve the revolution:

> From being the petted servant of the aristocrats, she revolts from her slavery. During the banquet which follows, her lover and partner is killed for inadvertently discovering a political secret, and Diane, left alone in the now phantasmagoric ballroom, runs out to join in the Revolution. The visual climax of the huge dark stage, lit only by the sinister glow of the chandeliers, is very effective. The solitary lament of the actress in her scarlet dress has the quality of a flame flickering in an abandoned world.[18]

Morley describes Marina Semyonova's performance in the last act, in which Diane is transformed 'into a Goddess of Reason' in a *pas de deux*:

> in which the dawning passion for neo-classicism is glimpsed. This dance is composed entirely of lifts in which the marble figure of the dancer soars into the air, a symbol of the age. . . . [Semyonova] alone, unique

among living ballerinas, has that divine harmony of form and movement which has power to remind us of some great statue living in the
flesh; of a Victory unfolding into the air before our astonished eyes. In
the body of Semyonova, the pupil of Vaganova, there shines that flawless
purity of style which Russians say is the essence of their school at
its best.[19]

In Morley's rapturous description, Semyonova is as much a symbol of
1932 as of 1792: as Mireille becomes the spirit of revolution, the dancer
playing her becomes the embodiment of Russian ballet, almost of Russia
itself.

Other Stagings

The Flames of Paris stayed in repertory until the 1950s: sections of it were
filmed in 1954, alongside *The Fountain of Bakhchisarai* and *Swan Lake*. In
2008, as director of the Bolshoi Ballet, Alexei Ratmansky restaged it, going
back to the Bolshoi's past as a way of redefining the company's future. 'I
thought it would be a reconstruction, but I soon figured out that very little
of the choreography really could be reconstructed,' he said. 'Ideologically,
it's so dated. So we thought that, if we are to revive the ballet, give it new life,
we need to change the story somehow.'[20]

Ratmansky put more emphasis on the ballet's leading characters. The
revolutionary Jerome falls in love with the new character Adeline, the
virtuous daughter of the wicked Marquis, who takes her with him when he
flees to Paris. In the court scene, Ratmansky drops the subplot of the
counter-revolutionary plan and Antoine's death, while there is a darker
edge to the revolutionary scenes, including a puppet-show in which
puppets of the king and queen are torn to pieces. In the last act, the wicked
Marquis is discovered and guillotined. When Adeline's horrified reaction
shows that she is his daughter, the revolutionary mob turns on her, sending
her to the guillotine. Ratmansky's ballet ends with Vainonen's implacable
'Ça ira' scene, with the advancing revolutionaries overtaking the grieving
Jerome.

Ratmansky's production reflects his own fascination with ballet's
history, and his wish to acknowledge both the past and present-day perspective. At its best, the production holds both in balance. Ilya Utkin and
Evgeny Monakhov's designs evoke period engravings with a threatening
edge: one backcloth shows the Place des Vosges in Paris, drawn in sharp
perspective, with one side of the square coloured red: that red angle

suggests the bloodstained blade of the guillotine. The mix of new and old material is sometimes clumsy, while Ratmansky's new duets are thinly characterised.

As well as 'Ça ira', Ratmansky included or adapted several of Vainonen's best-known scenes. In the court ballet, the *adagio*, male variation, gavotte and coda are by Vainonen, as is the bravura classical *pas de deux*. Vainonen's Basque dance is now performed by Jeanne (in heeled shoes) and Philippe, rather than by character dancers. Ratmansky has adapted the farandole, the carmagnole and 'Ça ira', which are now credited 'after Vainonen'.

This new production revived interest in the original ballet. Mikhail Messerer strongly disagreed with Ratmansky's view that much of Vainonen's version was too dated for reconstruction. In 2013, Messerer staged *The Flames of Paris* for the Mikhailovsky Ballet. This was created as a faithful recreation of the Vainonen production, changing as little as possible. Messerer's biggest alteration came in the first act, which omitted the storming of the Marquis' castle.

The Fountain of Bakhchisarai

Choreography: Rostislav Zakharov
Music: Boris Asafiev
Libretto: Nikolai Volkov after Alexander Pushkin
Direction: Sergei Radlov
Designs: Valentina Khodasevich
Premiere: 28 September 1934, Mariinsky Theatre, Leningrad
Original cast: *Maria* Galina Ulanova; *Zarema* Olga Jordan; *Khan Ghirei* Mikhail Dudko; *Vaslav* Konstantin Sergeyev

When the Soviet Writers' Congress of 1934 promoted socialist realism, it also produced a canon of acceptable artists. Writers such as Pushkin and Shakespeare offered politically safe subject matter in dangerous times. In dance, one of the first results was *The Fountain of Bakhchisarai*, which has been seen as the true start of dramballet.

Pushkin's poem was inspired by the 'fountain of tears' in the Palace of Bakhchisarai in the Crimea. The warlike Khan Ghirei fell in love with a Polish woman, and wept when she died, to the surprise of everyone who knew him. He commissioned the fountain to weep forever in her memory. Pushkin, moved by the story, retold it in verse. Several ballets were inspired by this poem (including one, planned but never created, by Filippo Taglioni), but Zakharov's was by far the most successful. The librettist

Nikolai Volkov expanded the poem, providing linking scenes and inventing the character of Vaslav, Maria's devoted lover.

Born in 1907, Rostislav Zakharov trained as a dancer but soon decided on a choreographic career. To prepare himself, he studied dramatic production at the Leningrad Institute of Choreographic Art, with Radlov as his professor. The two worked closely on *The Fountain of Bakhchisarai*. Where *The Flames of Paris* featured folk dance and a classical set piece, the new work set out to ground ballet in the acting 'Method' of Konstantin Stanislavsky, director of the Moscow Art Theatre and one of Stalin's favourite artists. Zakharov made his dancers do 'table work', reading Pushkin and developing backstories for their characters.

The choreography uses simple steps, focusing on mimed storytelling at the expense of dancing. Zakharov also studied collections of Persian art in the Hermitage Museum and other Leningrad collections, seeking imagery for the harem act. The ballet also launched the career of Galina Ulanova, the first Maria. In 1953 the ballet was filmed, with Ulanova as Maria and Maya Plisetskaya as Zarema.

Synopsis

Prologue. In Bakhchisarai, Khan Ghirei laments by the 'Fountain of tears'.

Act I. The park of a castle in Poland. A ball is in progress for Maria, the daughter of a Polish lord. Maria and her fiancé Vaslav dance in the park. A Tatar spy moves stealthily through the garden. The castle doors open, and the guests dance a polonaise in the garden, led by Maria and her father. The polonaise is followed by more traditional Polish dances, a mazurka and a cracovienne. The dancers are interrupted by the Captain of the Guards, who is wounded and brings news of a Tatar attack.

The Polish men defend the castle, but are defeated by the Tatars. The castle is destroyed by fire. Maria, carrying her harp, tries to escape with Vaslav. They are stopped by Khan Ghirei. Vaslav attacks Ghirei, who stabs him to death. Ghirei pulls off Maria's veil, and is amazed by her beauty.

Act II. Khan Ghirei's harem in the palace of Bakhchisarai. The concubines dance, led by Zarema, Ghirei's favourite wife. Ghirei returns from war with his plunder, including the captive Maria. Zarema dances for him, but he is preoccupied. Zarema realises that he has lost interest in her, fascinated by Maria. She tries to regain his interest, but fails.

Act III. Maria's bedroom in the harem, guarded by an older servant. Maria plays her harp – a reminder of her former life. Ghirei enters, and asks her to accept his love. She refuses him. When he leaves, she dances a melancholy dance, remembering her past.

Later that night, Zarema enters the room. She tells Maria how much she loves Ghirei, and how she has lost his favour. She begs Maria to give Ghirei back to her. Maria is bewildered and frightened by Zarema's speech. Zarema sees Ghirei's cap on the floor. Overcome with jealousy, she seizes her dagger.

Ghirei enters, and sees Maria threatened. He tries to stop Zarema, who evades him and stabs her rival. Dying, Maria presses her hand to her wound, falls back against the pillar and slides slowly to the floor, crumpling from a position on *pointe* to a mournful final pose.

Act IV. The courtyard of Ghirei's palace. He has had a fountain built in Maria's memory, the 'Fountain of tears'. His troops bring in trophies, treasure and new concubines, but Ghirei shows no interest. Executioners lead Zarema to her death: she is to be thrown from a cliff.

The Tatar warriors dance, trying to divert Ghirei from his grief. He remains sombre, and orders everyone to leave. In an epilogue, he sits by the 'Fountain of tears', remembering Maria.

The Fountain of Bakhchisarai was one of the few dramballets to survive in repertory past the 1950s, cherished for its association with Ulanova, its Pushkin subject matter and the big emotions it gave to the two leading women. Maria's low *arabesques* and soft lines suggest her modesty and simplicity, while Zarema stands in proud poses or expresses her feelings in wild leaps.

Although the theme and the ballet went unchallenged in the harshest years of Stalinism, some viewers found an alternative reading of the storyline. 'The ballet is about destruction,' the critic Vadim Gayevsky told Angus Macqueen. 'The end of aristocratic culture, the destruction of a harmonious world. This culture is destroyed by a terrifying alien force . . . In those days, people were always afraid but no one talked about it. And the ballet offered a defence against that fear.'[21]

Laurencia

Choreography: Vakhtang Chabukiani
Music: Alexander Krein

Libretto: Evgeny Mendelberg after Lope de Vega's *Fuenteovejuna*
Scenery: Simon Virsaladze
Premiere: 22 March 1939, Kirov Ballet, Kirov Theatre, Leningrad
Original cast: *Laurencia* Natalia Dudinskaya; *Frondozo* Vakhtang
Chabukiani; *Pascuala* Tatiana Vecheslova; *Jacinta* Elena Chikvaidze

Born in Tbilisi, Georgia, in 1910, Vakhtang Chabukiani came from a poor
family, and started his training late. A dashing, charismatic dancer, he was a
strong influence on Soviet male dancing, setting a standard for bravura leaps
and turns. He was particularly acclaimed in the new Soviet works, such as
The Flames of Paris and *The Fountain of Bakhchisarai*. He offered a new
model for ballet heroes, an exuberant warrior rather than a noble cavalier.

As a choreographer, Chabukiani was eager to increase the dance content
of the mimed dramballet. He achieved this by drawing on folk dances. *The
Heart of the Hills*, danced to music by Andrei Balanchivadze, George
Balanchine's brother, was his first big success, particularly the 'Horumi', a
Caucasian war dance. The next year, he turned to Lope de Vega's play
Fuenteovejuna for the subject of *Laurencia*.

Written in Spain in 1614, *Fuenteovejuna* was already associated with
Russian hopes of revolution. The Maly Theatre had staged the play in the
1870s, when Maria Yermolova's Laurencia became a heroine to progres-
sives. In 1938, moreover, the Spanish Civil War gave topical interest to the
story of Spanish peasants fighting against landowners. Chabukiani's staging
followed several other attempts to turn the Soviet-friendly story into a
ballet. Villagers revolt against the commander of their region, who has
raped several young women. The ballet's scenes includes the storming of a
castle, while the Spanish-flavoured dancing varies from folk styles to ballet-
Spanish reminiscent of *Don Quixote*.

Synopsis

Act I. Scene 1. The village of Fuenteovejuna. Young people gather in the
square, dancing and enjoying themselves. Laurencia teases Frondoso, who
is in love with her. Laurencia's friend Pascuala asks Mengo, the violinist, to
play for the dancers.

Military music strikes up, and the Commander of the region appears
with his soldiers. The villagers greet him respectfully, but he ignores them,
struck by the sight of Laurencia. He orders everyone else to leave – though
Pascuala stays with her. When Laurencia rejects the Commander, he orders
his soldiers to bring both women to his castle, but they manage to escape.

Scene 2. By a stream in the forest. Laurencia arrives with a basket of clothes, ready to do her washing. Frondoso declares his love for her, but she can't make her mind up to marry him. When he lifts her high above his head, she wriggles, ready to come down and get on with her laundry. Hunting horns sound in the distance, and the Commander arrives, out hunting. He tries to kiss Laurencia, but Frondoso defends her, pushing him away. Humiliated, the Commander swears revenge.

Pascuala and the village women come to the stream with their washing, though they spend plenty of time teasing Mengo and dancing to his music. Jacinta rushes in, pursued by the Commander's men. Mengo tries to protect her, but the soldiers knock him down. When the Commander returns, Jacinta begs for protection, but he hands her over to the soldiers, who take her away.

The villagers come back to the stream, looking for Jacinta. She returns dishevelled, having been raped. Everyone is horrified by her plight. Laurencia, who has been impressed by Frondoso's courage and devotion, agrees to marry him.

Act II. Scene 1. The village celebrates the wedding of Laurencia and Frondoso, with character dances, a *pas de six* and virtuoso variations for the bride and groom. The festivities stop when the Commander appears. He has Frondoso arrested, and orders that Laurencia should be taken to his castle.

Scene 2. The forest at night. The men gather and plot, cursing and clenching their fists, but lack the courage to fight the tyrant Commander. Laurencia enters, with wild hair and torn dress, having been raped and thrown out of the castle. Full of fury against the Commander, she reproaches the men for their inaction, and calls on the whole village to fight. Led by Laurencia, the men and women of Fuenteovejuna decide to storm the castle.

Scene 3. Inside the castle. Waves of villagers pour into the castle, brandishing knives, scythes and sticks as weapons. They free Frondoso and look for the Commander. When they find him, he tries to buy his way out, but they reject his gold. He is dragged off for execution, and his helmet is set upon a pole. The ballet ends with the villagers dancing in triumph.

Laurencia was an immediate hit, lifted by the performances of Chabukiani and Natalia Dudinskaya, a Vaganova-trained dancer of virtuoso strength. Alongside dramballet mime and folk dances, Chabukiani also used traditional academic steps and forms. The wedding scene includes a formal *grand pas* in the old style, though the storyline and context protected it from accusations of formalism. There is a jarring shift from scenes of rape to *Don Quixote*-style danced fireworks, but Chabukiani does not reduce his heroine to passive victimhood. Although contemporary synopses skirt around the rapes and sexual assaults of the plot, the stage action is clear – and Laurencia responds by grabbing her pitchfork and leading a revolution.

As the dramballet mode fell out of fashion in the 1950s, *Laurencia* was one of the works that lasted longer, due to its virtuoso content. It was revived for Maya Plisetskaya in 1956, while the wedding *pas de six*, and some of the solo dances for Laurencia and Frondoso, have stayed in the repertory as gala numbers. Rudolf Nureyev staged the *pas de six* for The Royal Ballet in 1965. In 2010 the complete ballet was revived for the Mikhailovsky Ballet, in a revised staging by Mikhail Messerer.

Romeo and Juliet

Choreography: Leonid Lavrovsky
Music: Sergei Prokofiev
Libretto: Sergei Radlov and Adrian Pyotrovsky
Designs: Pyotr Williams
Premiere: 11 January 1940, Kirov Ballet, Kirov Theatre, Leningrad
Original cast: *Juliet* Galina Ulanova; *Romeo* Konstantin Sergeyev; *Mercutio* Andrei Lopukhov; *Tybalt* Robert Gerbek

Romeo and Juliet, particularly with Prokofiev's score, is one of ballet's major hits. With star-crossed lovers and feuding families, Shakespeare's play offers the basis for romantic *pas de deux*, family clashes and active fight scenes. There have been many productions, but Leonid Lavrovsky's was the first to achieve international success, setting the template for many of the later stagings.

Prokofiev wrote his score to a libretto by Sergei Radlov (a theatre director and Shakespeare authority who had already worked with the composer) and his colleague Adrian Pyotrovsky. Although he had aimed at a more melodic style since his return to Russia in 1929, Prokofiev used fierce dissonances to depict the violent clashes of the feuding Capulet and Montague families. The ballet has motifs for different characters and situations, such as the scampering theme for the childlike Juliet we first meet, a soaring love theme and more comic themes for Juliet's nurse and Romeo's friend Mercutio.

Initially commissioned by the Kirov Ballet, the project moved to the Bolshoi, which planned to stage the ballet in 1935. The project foundered. In his autobiography, Prokofiev claimed that the score had been dismissed as undanceable. It may have been rejected for other reasons: Prokofiev was out of favour politically, while his proposed happy ending outraged Shakespeare scholars. Instead, the ballet was first produced in Brno, Czechoslovakia, in 1938, with choreography by Vania Psota. Lavrovsky's version followed in 1940, not without more strife. The dancers found the music difficult: they even threatened to boycott the premiere, afraid they would make fools of themselves trying to dance to it. After the first performance, Galina Ulanova, the production's Juliet, toasted the composer in a parody of Shakespeare: 'Never was a tale of greater woe than Prokofiev's music for *Romeo*.'[22] The ballet provided her with the defining role of her career.

Synopsis

Act 1. Scene 1. Verona, early morning. Romeo, a member of the Montague family, dreams of love. Townspeople get up and start work, gradually filling the square.

Tybalt, a member of the Capulet family, arrives. Drunk and spoiling for a fight, he attacks Romeo's friend Benvolio. General fighting breaks out between Montagues and Capulets. The alarm bell is rung. Lord Capulet and Lord Montague arrive to join the fighting. The Duke of Verona arrives, commanding both families to drop their weapons, and decrees that anyone fighting in the town's streets will be sentenced to death. Neither family takes the decree seriously.

Scene 2. After a frontcloth scene of servants preparing for the Capulet ball, we see Juliet, Lord Capulet's daughter, playing with her nurse. Her mother arrives and scolds her daughter: it's time for her to grow up.

Scene 3. Guests head for the Capulet ball. Romeo's friends, Mercutio and Benvolio, persuade him to come to the ball with them, wearing masks to hide their Montague identities.

Scene 4. The Capulet ball. Guests feast at long tables. Juliet is introduced to Paris, whom her parents wish her to marry. The tables are cleared away for the 'Cushion' dance, performed to the music also known as the 'Dance of the Knights'. Carrying cushions, the Capulet men parade and stamp, aggressively masculine. Women join the men, using the cushions to kneel by their partners.

Juliet and Romeo meet and fall in love. As they dance together in private, he carelessly loses his mask: she is enchanted to see his face. Romeo lifts her high, her knees braced against his chest as she looks down at him. Tybalt enters, and they hastily separate. Romeo and his friends leave the ball. As they go, Juliet asks her nurse who Romeo is – she is horrified to hear that he is a Montague.

Scene 5. The Capulet balcony. Juliet dreams of seeing Romeo again. He joins her in the garden, and they declare their love.

Act 2. Scene 1. The square in Verona. The square is busy with townsfolk and entertainers, including a dance for jesters. Mercutio and Benvolio dance with waitresses at the inn. Juliet's nurse arrives with a letter for Romeo: she will marry him.

Scene 2. Friar Laurence's cell. The friar is deep in contemplation, considering a lily and a skull. Romeo rushes in and asks the friar to perform a secret marriage. Waiting for Juliet, he lays the lilies on the floor, strewing her path with flowers. Romeo and Juliet are married.

Scene 3. The square in Verona. Revels continue. Tybalt arrives with a group of courtesans and challenges Mercutio to a duel. Romeo tries to prevent the fight, but Mercutio is killed. The body is carried out. Overcome with grief and anger, Romeo fights Tybalt and kills him. He flees. The Capulets emerge from their palace and mourn Tybalt's death. Filled with grief and rage, letting her hair hang loose, Lady Capulet climbs onto Tybalt's bier and is carried out with the body, calling for revenge. Romeo is exiled.

Act 3. Scene 1. Juliet's bedroom. Romeo opens the curtain, showing the sunrise: he must leave Verona. Juliet draws the curtain back, begging him to stay a little longer. They dance a passionate farewell, and Romeo leaves. Her parents enter, bringing Paris: they have chosen him as her husband. Juliet rejects Paris, who leaves. Her parents reproach her. Left alone, Juliet decides to ask Friar Laurence for help.

Scene 2. Friar Laurence's cell. She prays for help. Seeing a dagger on Friar Laurence's table, she snatches it up. The Friar takes it away, giving her a phial of sleeping potion which will send her into a deathlike sleep. Her parents will place her in the family tomb, and when she awakes she can join Romeo in secret.

Scene 3. Juliet's bedroom. Juliet pretends to accept Paris as a bridegroom. Once she is alone, she agonises over taking the potion, before drinking it and falling back on her bed. Her friends come to celebrate the engagement, dancing around the room, then draw the curtain to find Juliet apparently dead.

Scene 4. In Mantua. Romeo has fled from Verona, and is tormented by thoughts of Juliet. Benvolio arrives, bringing news of Juliet's death. Romeo, who has not heard from Friar Laurence, believes the news, and hurries back to Verona.

Scene 5. The Capulet tomb. Mourners pay their last farewell to Juliet and leave. Romeo enters, in despair. When he lifts Juliet, her body remains stiff, as if dead. He takes poison and dies, falling down the steps of the tomb. Juliet wakes, and finds him dead. She takes his dagger and stabs herself.

Epilogue: The Capulet and Montague families return to the tomb. Finding the bodies of their children, Lord Capulet and Lord Montague take each other's hands, swearing to end their feud.

Lavrovsky's staging was quickly reproduced at Moscow's Bolshoi Ballet, and caused a sensation when the Bolshoi made its first large-scale Western tour to London in 1956, and again in New York in 1959. The impact came from the power and scale of Soviet dancing, with strong backs and spectacular partnering, but also from the huge sincerity of the dancers. In 1959 the critic Edwin Denby reported on Ulanova's performance:

> Faced with marriage to County Paris, Juliet, her mantle flung round her, desperately rushes along the apron [of the stage] to Friar Laurence; armed by him with the sleeping potion, she flings the mantle round her again, and rushes desperately along the apron back home. The fling, the rush, the exact repeat are pure *Perils of Pauline*. But Ulanova's art at that moment is so brilliant the audience breaks into delighted applause.[23]

Lavrovsky wrote that his Shakespearean subject demanded 'the fusion of dance with mime . . . Mime should never descend to trivial, commonplace, imitative gestures, but become a genuine theatrical performance in which characters, emotion and passion are expressed by the movements of the body, instead of by the varied intonations of the voice.'[24] His own favourite scenes were the marriage, the fight between Tybalt and Mercutio, and Tybalt's death: none of them features much in the way of dancing.

This style, with its big, 'silent movie' acting, can easily look naïve and dated, particularly when performed by dancers who are used to more naturalistic or pure-dance approaches. The excitement of Ulanova's run has proved elusive for later generations. Lavrovsky's production reflects its era in other ways: there's a socialist realist approach to the feuding families. In marketplace scenes, the sympathetic Benvolio and Mercutio dance with the tavern's hard-working waitresses, while the unlikeable Tybalt shows lordly arrogance, jostling fruit sellers as he dances with courtesans.

Other Stagings

The impact of Lavrovsky's production was immense. Its blend of 'realism' and operatic scale was a clear influence on the versions of John Cranko and Kenneth MacMillan, discussed in Chapter 7: later *Romeo*s tend to feature big, three-dimensional sets, large casts, plenty of gestural acting. Rudolf Nureyev created a similarly large-scale version for London Festival Ballet in 1977, which he later revised for the ballet of La Scala, Milan, in 1980 and the Paris Opéra Ballet in 1984. It has very busy, intricate choreography, particularly for Romeo, the role Nureyev danced himself. Nureyev researched the period and the play in great detail, bringing his research into the production. His ballet opens with a cart of corpses being taken to burial. Struck by Juliet's lines, 'I'll to my wedding bed/And death, not Romeo, take my maidenhead', Nureyev has a dancer in a skeleton mask lie on top of her.

There have been other approaches. In 1955, a year before the Bolshoi Ballet's London visit, Frederick Ashton choreographed Prokofiev's score for the Royal Danish Ballet. This was a much lighter, more intimate, more classical production. It was a success in Denmark, but Ashton was nervous of reviving it elsewhere once Lavrovsky's staging had been seen in the West: he resisted all the Royal Ballet's requests to stage it, recommending the company acquire the stagings of Lavrovsky or Cranko instead. (Eventually, as director, he agreed that MacMillan should choreograph the ballet.)

Alexei Ratmansky's 2011 staging for the National Ballet of Canada also takes a lighter approach. Richard Hudson's set showed a scarlet fortress looming over Verona: detailed Renaissance architecture in cut-out form, exact but very stylised. The same could be said of Ratmansky's choreography, which is full of dancing, pays attention to supporting characters, but is less passionate when it comes to the story's big duets and final tragedy.

The Legend of Love

Choreography: Yuri Grigorovich
Music: Arif Melikoff
Libretto: Nâzım Hikmet and Yuri Grigorovich
Designs: Simon Virsaladze
Premiere: 23 March 1961, Kirov Ballet, Kirov Theatre, Leningrad
Original cast: *Shirin* Irina Kolpakova; *Ferkhad* Alexander Gribov; *Queen Mekhmene Banu* Inna Zubkovskaya

The Legend of Love was based on a play by the Turkish poet Nâzım Hikmet, *Ferkhad and Shirin*, which was itself based on a Persian legend. A story of love, jealousy and self-sacrifice, the ballet emphasises the importance of duty and of working for the good of the majority.

Grigorovich had been praised for the increased dance content of his first large-scale ballet, *The Stone Flower*. He followed the same approach for *The Legend of Love*, avoiding mime. Like Zakharov for *The Fountain of Bakhchisarai*, Grigorovich studied Persian miniatures for his choreography, but used it to flavour acrobatic dance steps, with tilted hands for the heroine Shirin. He also gave each of the main characters their own *corps de ballet*, who reflect their emotions, and created trios in which Ferkhad, Shirin and Shirin's sister, Queen Mekhmene Banu, reflect on their situation, each picked out in a spotlight. It looks forward to the 'monologue' technique that Grigorovich would employ in *Spartacus*.

Synopsis

Act I. Scene 1. A room in the palace. Queen Mekhmene Banu is in despair: her younger sister, Shirin, is dying. The vizier and the courtiers are distressed. A stranger appears, claiming that he can cure the princess. When he refuses gold, the queen offers him the crown as a reward for curing Shirin. He tells her that she must sacrifice her beauty to save her sister's life. She agrees, and the stranger brings Shirin back to health. When she rises from her sickbed, Shirin cannot recognise her sister, whose face has become disfigured.

Scene 2. The garden of a palace. A group of artists, including Ferkhad, are decorating an arch of a newly built palace. Mekhmene Banu and Shirin enter the garden, with their attendants. Both sisters admire Ferkhad. When the rest of the procession has moved on, Shirin approaches Ferkhad. They fall in love, but when Ferkhad realises she is a princess, he draws back: how could a humble painter hope to marry her?

Act II. Scene 1. A crowd gathers around a spring that has run dry. Only the palace is supplied with water, brought from far away. The only way to bring water to the valley is by carving a channel through a high mountain, a superhuman task.

Scene 2. Sitting veiled in her palace, the queen is tormented by her love for Ferkhad. Jesters try to amuse her, without success. She realises the sacrifice she has made by losing her beauty, and dances in despair.

Scene 3. Ferkhad visits Shirin in her rooms. They dance ecstatically together. In order to be with Ferkhad, Shirin decides to leave the palace with him. Learning of the lovers' flight, the vizier tells the queen. In a rage, she orders that Ferkhad and Shirin be seized and brought back to the palace. Shirin begs her sister not to separate them, but in vain. Mekhmene Banu sets Ferkhad an impossible task: to win Shirin, he must cut through the iron mountain, bringing water to the valley.

Act III. Scene 1. The mountains. Exhausted by his labours, Ferkhad dreams that he has already cut through the rock, and that water flows from the mountain. He imagines that he sees Shirin in the water.

Scene 2. Mekhmene Banu is tormented by her love for Ferkhad. She dreams that she has regained her beauty, that Ferkhad loves her and that they are happy together. Shirin runs into her sister's room, destroying the fantasy. She begs Mekhmene Banu to come with her to the mountains to see Ferkhad.

Scene 3. The people are hopeful: if Ferkhad succeeds, their suffering will end. Mekhmene Banu and Shirin arrive. Ferkhad is overjoyed to see Shirin, but the queen tells him that the lovers can be together only if he gives up his work on the mountain. Ferkhad knows he cannot betray the people. Shirin understands and accepts his decision, and bids him farewell. Ferkhad returns to work, and all admire his self-sacrifice.

Grigorovich originally planned the role of Ferkhad for the young Rudolf Nureyev. Nureyev was eager to suggest ideas and even steps for the role, telling Grigorovich about Balanchine's *Apollo*, which he had seen when

New York City Ballet brought it on tour to Moscow. However, the two fell out later in the rehearsal process, and Nureyev was replaced by Alexander Gribov. Nureyev still hoped to dance *The Legend of Love*. After his defection in 1961, his luggage was sent back to the Soviet Union. It contained a bolt of blue fabric, bought to be used for his Ferkhad costume.

Spartacus

Choreography: Yuri Grigorovich
Music: Aram Khachaturian
Designs: Simon Virsaladze
Premiere: 9 April 1968, Bolshoi Ballet, Bolshoi Theatre, Moscow
Original cast: *Spartacus* Vladimir Vasiliev; *Phrygia* Ekaterina Maximova; *Crassus* Maris Liepa; *Aegina* Nina Timofeyeva

Spartacus tells the story of the slave rebellion against the might of ancient Rome, based on events that took place in AD 71. Initially planned to celebrate the fiftieth anniversary of the Russian Revolution, Yuri Grigorovich's *Spartacus* was a risky production, the fourth major attempt to stage Khachaturian's score in little more than a decade, the third at the Bolshoi itself.

Earlier versions had struggled with Nikolai Volkov's libretto, which put the feast of the decadent Crassus at the heart of the ballet and left the character of Spartacus undeveloped. The composer had resisted all attempts to edit his score into more theatrical shape; by the time Grigorovich came to the work, the Bolshoi leadership put its foot down, and insisted that Khachaturian give him a free hand to adapt the libretto.

He responded by building up the role of Crassus, the Roman general, as well as that of Spartacus. Instead of a mimed villain, Crassus became a dancing role, offering a serious challenge to the hero. Aware that the ballet would have to be staged at the vast Kremlin Palace of Congresses, as well as the merely huge Bolshoi Theatre, Grigorovich and his designer Simon Virsaladze gave it a stripped-down, simple production, with near-abstract scenery that allows the story to move swiftly from location to location. Grigorovich ended each scene with a 'monologue' solo for one of his four characters, focusing on their inner feelings, with a drop-curtain separating the dancer from the rest of the crowded stage. He worked closely and happily with his superlative first cast, who brought passionate individuality to their archetypal roles.

Spartacus is a male-dominated work, with battalions of Roman legionaries, gladiators and slaves. Women appear as virtuous wives, such as

Phrygia, or wicked courtesans, such as Aegina. In the Soviet era and beyond, the ballet became one of the Bolshoi's calling cards, showing off its dancers' energy and power.

Synopsis

Act I. Led by Crassus, the Roman legions fight wars of conquest. Spartacus and his wife Phrygia are among the chained prisoners. In the first of the ballet's 'monologue' solos, Spartacus despairs at his captivity, dancing with his hands bound.

The captives are brought to the slave market. Men and women are sold separately, so Spartacus and Phrygia are parted. Phrygia dances her grief at losing her husband, and her fear of future captivity.

Bought by Crassus, Phrygia is brought to his palace, where mimes and courtesans entertain the guests at an orgy. Aegina, Crassus' mistress, jeers at Phrygia's unhappiness. She glories in lust, wine, gold and power. Crassus calls for entertainment, and two masked, blindfolded gladiators are brought in, and set to fight to the death. The victor's helmet is removed: it is Spartacus. In another monologue, he expresses his horror and grief at having killed another slave: against his will, he is a murderer. He moves from anger to resolution: he must regain his freedom.

Back at the gladiators' barracks, Spartacus incites his fellow gladiators to revolt. They swear an oath of loyalty, and break out of the barracks to freedom.

Act II. Emerging onto the Appian Way, the escaped gladiators meet groups of shepherds, and call on them to join the uprising. The massed ranks of rebels hail Spartacus as their leader, giving him a red cloak of office. As he ponders the responsibilities of power, Phrygia rushes in, rescued from Crassus' villa. They are reunited in a duet full of spectacular lifts. At last, Spartacus drapes first the cloak and then Phrygia over his shoulders: with her support, he will accept leadership.

Aegina leads in a procession of patricians. In her monologue, she dreams of power over Crassus and, through him, access to the world of the Roman nobility. Crassus celebrates his victories, while patrician Romans sing his praises. The feast is cut short by the news that Spartacus' men have surrounded the villa. The patricians flee in terror. Spartacus bounds onto the stage, sword in hand, dancing a bravura solo. The backcloth rises to show his army, now equipped with swords and shields, dancing in triumph.

When Crassus is captured, Spartacus offers him the chance to fight for his freedom, and defeats him almost casually, knocking the sword out of his hand. Crassus prepares to die, but Spartacus lets him go with a gesture of contempt.

Act III. Seeing Crassus tormented by his disgrace, Aegina eggs him on to revenge. Crassus summons his legions, and Aegina sees him off to battle. In her monologue solo, she vows vengeance of her own. She heads to Spartacus' camp, seeking to undermine the rebellion.

Phrygia wakes early, fearful for the future. Spartacus joins her, but their happiness is interrupted by the threat of Crassus' attack. Spartacus prepares for battle, but some of his soldiers desert their leader. Aegina infiltrates the rebel camp, bringing wine and prostitutes. Some of Spartacus' men succumb to temptation, so they are helpless when Crassus and his army attack. Crassus rewards Aegina for her help: he is consumed by his need for revenge.

In the final battle, Spartacus' forces are surrounded and outnumbered by the Roman legions. He and his loyal captains fight until the bitter end. At last, Roman soldiers close in on him, hoisting his dying body aloft on a multitude of spears. Phrygia comes to the battlefield, where she mourns her dead husband.

Spartacus is a ballet on a huge scale. The leading characters express themselves in powerful leaps, acrobatic poses and death-defying lifts, while massed ranks of dancers surge and soar behind them. The Roman legionaries goose-step through high kicks, while their women make Roman – or are they fascist? – salutes. (At curtain calls, all the patrician characters acknowledge the applause with Roman salutes, while the slave characters respond by raising a clenched fist.) Aram Khachaturian's music adds to the wide-screen epic quality, with swooning *adagios*, blaring trumpets and jangling percussion.

With its black-and-white morality and often blatant choreography, *Spartacus* has been accused of kitsch and bombast, especially by Western critics. It remains very popular with audiences in Russia and abroad, particularly for the forceful, athletic quality of its dancing. Spartacus and Crassus both show their power in huge repeated jumps, driving themselves on with superhuman effort. In one duet with Phrygia, Spartacus lifts her overhead, one-handed, and runs across the stage still holding her aloft. Irek Mukhamedov, the Bolshoi's reigning Spartacus from 1981 to 1990, joked that the most rewarding thing about the role was still being alive at the end of the ballet. 'When you're young, it's just getting through it . . . As I got older, the most rewarding thing was being a hero on stage. You lead the other dancers, they are behind you, they follow you.'[25]

Other Stagings

Leonid Yakobson created the first production of Khachaturian's *Spartacus* for the Kirov Ballet in 1956. He drew on the imagery of antique sculpture and vases, and avoided conventional ballet technique: the dancers wore Roman-style sandals, with no *pointe*work for the women. Valentina Khodasevich's designs were a detailed, naturalistic evocation of ancient Rome, with elaborate period costumes and scenery. Although the story follows the same outlines as the Grigorovich version, it has many more supporting characters, such as the owner of a gladiatorial school and several named gladiators. Scenes evoke specific Roman festivities, from the fights at the arena to the saturnalia at Crassus' feast. Crassus himself is a mime role.

Despite being a mixed success, Yakobson's ballet lasted in repertory at the Kirov. He restaged it, with revisions, at the Bolshoi (where Igor Moiseyev also created an unsuccessful production). The Mariinsky Ballet revived Yakobson's *Spartacus* in 2010.

In 1968, the same year as the Grigorovich production, Hungarian choreographer László Seregi staged a new *Spartacus* for the Hungarian National Ballet. To Khachaturian's indignation, he reordered the score so that the work began with the crucifixion of Spartacus, continuing the story in flashback. Seregi's production, which mixed heroic Soviet-style choreography with Hungarian folk elements, was taken into the repertory of the Australian Ballet.

In 2008 the Mikhailovsky Ballet staged an extremely lavish new production, with gilded designs and gold costumes by Vyacheslav Okunev and choreography by George Kovtun.

Ivan the Terrible

Choreography: Yuri Grigorovich
Music: Sergei Prokofiev, arranged by Mikhail Chulaki
Designs: Simon Virsaladze
Premiere: 20 February 1975, Bolshoi Ballet, Bolshoi Theatre, Moscow
Original cast: *Ivan the Terrible* Yuri Vladimirov; *Anastasia* Natalia Bessmertnova; *Prince Kurbsky* Boris Akimov

Prokofiev's music for *Ivan the Terrible* was originally written for Sergei Eisenstein's epic two-part film about Ivan IV of Russia, a medieval tsar much admired by Stalin. The first part, covering Ivan's marriage and presenting him as a national hero, was released in 1944 to great acclaim. The second film, covering the Russian nobility's plots against Ivan and his brutal suppression of them, was suppressed by censors, and not released until 1958.

The idea for the ballet came from conductor Abram Stasevich, who had arranged the film score as a cantata and suggested it to Grigorovich as a ballet score. Stasevich died before he could develop a ballet score, so Grigorovich turned to composer Mikhail Chulaki. The finished ballet uses material from other Prokofiev works, including his Russian Overture, his Third Symphony and the cantata *Alexander Nevsky* (another work drawn from music Prokofiev wrote for Eisenstein).

Synopsis

Act I. Six bell-ringers pull on the ropes of the huge bells hanging overhead, proclaiming the accession of young Tsar Ivan IV. Ivan climbs up to a high throne. Below him, the boyars, powerful noblemen, gather resentfully: they feel they are as highly born as Ivan, and have equally good claims to the throne. Ivan knows that he must choose a bride, and summons a procession of young women. They dance for Ivan, who descends from his throne to approach one woman, the beautiful Anastasia. Prince Kurbsky, the leader of the boyars, is in despair: he is in love with Anastasia. He plots with the other boyars against Ivan.

The bell-ringers announce a foreign invasion. Ivan and Kurbsky lead Russian regiments into battle. There is frenzied fighting, with many deaths, but the bell-ringers proclaim a Russian victory. At home, Anastasia waits anxiously for Ivan's safe return. The soldiers return, joyfully greeting their loved ones, and Ivan and Anastasia are reunited. They dance together, and he carries her offstage as the victory celebrations continue.

Ivan becomes sick, writhing in torment on his throne. Anastasia tries to help him, and he leans on her. Taking advantage of his absence, the boyars plot. One of them approaches the throne, but Ivan suddenly appears and throws him down the steps. Back on the throne, he confronts the courtiers, throwing his golden spear into their midst: he is still in control.

Act II. Ivan and Anastasia are happy and in love. The boyars continue to plot, passing around a cup to pledge their new loyalty to each other. They offer the cup to Kurbsky, who is reluctant to take it. At last he succumbs, seizing the cup.

Realising that they can attack Ivan through Anastasia, the boyars give her the poisoned cup. She drinks the poison, dancing limply as her strength fails, before collapsing in Kurbsky's arms. As he lays her body down, she rises, reaching out for vengeance, and dies. The boyars scatter in terror.

The bell-ringers announce Anastasia's death. The people surround them, on the brink of revolt. Alone, Ivan mourns Anastasia. He sees a vision of her, and she blesses him.

Kurbsky flees the country, dreading the tsar's revenge. Ivan attacks the boyars, cracking a long whip. Ivan forms the Oprichniki, the secret police. They drag in the boyars, pulling them by long ropes around their necks. Kurbsky is forced to drink a cup of poison administered by a mocking devil figure, while the boyars are executed. The devil figure pulls of his mask: it is Ivan.

Ivan exults in his victory, but his sceptre of power is also a burden to him. In the finale, the bell-ringers return, leading a mass of people. As the bells ring out, Ivan seizes the ropes, gathering power in his hands.

Where *Spartacus* divided a streamlined narrative between star dancers and battalions of the *corps*, *Ivan the Terrible* surrounds its three leads with symbolic figures, from bell-ringers to masked clown figures. It's another male-dominated ballet, although the duets with Anastasia – first danced by Natalia Bessmertnova, Grigorovich's wife – were seen as a breakthrough for Grigorovich in creating more erotic choreography. In 1976, *Ivan the Terrible* was acquired by the Paris Opéra Ballet, an unusual example of a Western company staging Soviet choreography during the Cold War period.

7

THE BALLET BOOM

O N 16 JUNE 1961, Rudolf Nureyev defected from the Soviet Union. Ordered home from a tour by the Kirov Ballet, aware that he was in trouble for his reckless interest in the West and Western dance, he turned to two French policemen and begged for asylum. The incident made worldwide headlines: a dancer's 'leap to freedom', was an international incident. Nureyev became an instant celebrity, a male dancer with a glamour and an impact not seen since Nijinsky.

Nureyev would be a transforming influence on Western dance: redefining the male role in ballet, galvanising technique, staging unfamiliar Russian repertory, and forming an adored partnership with Margot Fonteyn. His power and influence were spectacular, but comparison with Nijinsky shows how much ballet had changed. Where the Ballets Russes had revived a stagnating art form, Nureyev – and later defectors Natalia Makarova and Mikhail Baryshnikov – raised the profile of one that was already internationally popular.

By 1961, the post-Diaghilev national ballets were rooted and successful, major institutions in their own right. American Ballet Theatre, the Sadler's Wells Ballet and New York City Ballet had international reputations and honours at home. The Sadler's Wells Ballet had acquired a royal charter to become The Royal Ballet; work was underway to build the State Theater at Lincoln Center, a new home for New York City Ballet. At The Royal Ballet, Nureyev would help to clear away an institutional stuffiness that had built up in the 1950s. In his tireless round of touring, staging ballets and creating productions, he would also lend star presence to a generation of new ballet companies, such as the National Ballet of Canada and the Australian Ballet.

This would be a period of expansion for ballet, with troupes founded and revitalised. In America, the Ford Foundation supported a ten-year programme supporting scholarships and regional companies, including the Boston and Houston Ballets. Between 1965 and 1975, the annual American dance audience grew from one million to over fifteen million. In Cuba, the Cuban National Ballet, founded by Alicia Alonso, received state support after the Cuban revolution of 1959; the company's school became an important training centre for dancers. In this period ballet also reached Japan, which welcomed foreign ballet companies and soon trained dancers of its own.

A new generation of choreographers was also coming through. John Cranko had started his career within The Royal Ballet organisation, but left it in frustration. Born in South Africa in 1927, he came to London to study, joining the Sadler's Wells Theatre Ballet, a touring section created when the main company moved to the Royal Opera House. He immediately began staging works, including the smash hit *Pineapple Poll*. A prolific and energetic choreographer, Cranko had a gift for clear storytelling and an eclectic, inventive sense of theatre. His ballets were driven by situations and themes, with less focus on the dance steps themselves; he was part of a British narrative dance tradition, with a new physical daring. From 1956, when the Bolshoi Ballet made its first Western tour, the athletic choreography and broad strokes of Soviet ballet were to be a significant influence on Cranko.

In 1957 he created *The Prince of the Pagodas*, the first entirely new British three-act ballet, to a commissioned score by Benjamin Britten. It was Cranko's first real misstep. The production was hobbled by a meandering storyline and the score's poor theatrical pacing, issues that have dogged later stagings. The fairy-tale format also showed Cranko struggling to create pure dance, falling back on acrobatics and dramatic lifts. Like Antony Tudor before him, Cranko suffered from a lack of opportunity at The Royal Ballet, and sought openings elsewhere. He started his own musical revue *Cranks*, which became a fashionable hit, created for companies including Ballet Rambert, the Paris Opéra and La Scala, where he choreographed a new *Romeo and Juliet* starring the emerging ballerina Carla Fracci. In 1961, Cranko became director of the Stuttgart Ballet.

Germany, with its strong opera-house tradition, had fine facilities and existing ballet troupes generally attached to opera companies. As an independent art form, ballet was overshadowed. Arriving in Stuttgart, Cranko turned his troupe into Germany's leading ballet company, building a friendly, close-knit organisation with a relaxed family atmosphere. He made the company canteen his office, and was ready to talk to any dancer; he tailored roles to his dancers, particularly a leading quartet with strong, individual personalities. Cranko brought in the Brazilian-born Marcia Haydée, the Danish Egon Madsen and the American Richard Cragun, and he discovered the lyrical German ballerina Birgit Keil within the Stuttgart Ballet's own ranks. They became the company's defining stars. Cranko would celebrate them in his 1973 ballet *Initials R.M.B.E.*, a plotless work to Brahms' Second Piano Concerto. But it was Cranko's dramatic ballets, full of surging emotions and soaring lifts, that launched the company and these dancers to international fame. When the company toured to New York in 1969, the box office was besieged, with queues right around the block. Cranko's works helped to bring a new audience to ballet – and to emphasise the evening-length narrative as the art's most popular form.

Cranko died suddenly in 1973. His star dancers stayed loyal to his company, helping to ensure its survival. They also continued to focus on new works. Stuttgart's Noverre Society, an association of ballet lovers founded in 1958, developed a platform for young choreographers. It has helped to launch choreographers such as John Neumeier, Jiří Kylián and William Forsythe. Kylián would go on to direct Netherlands Dans Theater, another of the new companies established in the 1950s and 1960s. Blending ballet and modern dance, it would be a source of ballet choreographers as the disciplines started to cross over.

Back in Britain, Kenneth MacMillan was another major choreographer who started out in the Sadler's Wells Theatre Ballet. Born in 1929 in Dunfermline, Scotland, he auditioned for the Sadler's Wells Ballet School, forging a letter from his disapproving father. A fine classical dancer, he suffered from crippling stage fright, and was encouraged to try choreography. He was influenced by movements in theatre and film: the Angry Young Men of British theatre, *Nouvelle Vague* and 'kitchen sink' films. MacMillan was eager to break away from fairy tales. In 1955 his first professional work, the spiky, pure-dance *Danses concertantes* was a success; he went on to American Ballet Theatre, where he made two works for Nora Kaye.

His real breakthrough came in 1960, when he staged *The Invitation*, starring the Canadian ballerina Lynn Seymour as a teenage girl who is raped by an older man. The ballet closed with the girl alone, crippled by the experience, devastatingly portrayed by Seymour. The ballet caused a stir, launching MacMillan as a choreographer and Seymour as his muse. It also confirmed sex and corrupt societies as central themes in his work. Taking on three-act story ballets, starting with *Romeo and Juliet*, he pushed for rawer, more personal expression. Earlier Juliets had been virginal, from Ulanova's purity to Marcia Haydée's shy heroine in John Cranko's version. MacMillan's Juliet was rebellious, eager for sexual experience.

In later works, MacMillan drove the story ballet into new territory. *Anastasia* explored the psyche of Anna Anderson, who believed herself to be the last tsar's lost daughter. Having created it as a one-act work about identity in 1967, MacMillan opened it out into a sprawling historical ballet. In *Mayerling* he took this approach to extremes, evoking the crumbling, decadent court of the late Hapsburg Empire. Both ballets had structural flaws, but *Mayerling* in particular creates an entire world onstage, with vividly drawn characters negotiating complex, dangerous societies.

In America, another young company was poised to join the ballet boom. Born Abdulla Jaffa Bey Khan in 1930, Robert Joffrey would say that he had always wanted to have a company of his own. After dancing with Roland Petit's Ballets de Paris and other companies, he founded a school in New York with Gerald Arpino, with a touring company following in 1956. The Joffrey Ballet would soon dance ballets by Balanchine, Ashton and Tudor, along with very popular works by Arpino, who tapped into the 1960s counter-culture, danced to rock music and featuring film projections. The Joffrey Ballet launched a series of important revivals of Diaghilev-era works, and was also among the first to commission ballets from contemporary dance choreographers, such as Twyla Tharp and Mark Morris.

Born in 1941, Tharp had a driven childhood in which she learned ballet, tap, acrobatics, baton twirling, drums, piano, violin, flamenco, elocution, French and shorthand – which, with regular schoolwork, made for fifteen-hour days, scheduled in fifteen-minute slots. Her early choreography was contemporary and postmodern. In 1973 she created *Deuce Coupe* for the Joffrey Ballet. Danced to music by The Beach Boys, and featuring six of Tharp's dancers and fourteen of Joffrey's, it was an enormous hit. More ballets followed, including *Push Comes to Shove* for American Ballet Theatre, starring Mikhail Baryshnikov. Tharp's choreography was eclectic and rigorous, melding high and low culture with an eye for both experiment and the audience.

While new choreographers and new companies helped to bring ballet to a peak of popularity, its established figures were finding new muses and challenges. Frederick Ashton took over from Ninette de Valois as director of The Royal Ballet, and though he complained about the burdens of the job, he polished the company into a new harmony of style, his sense of musicality and line evident across the whole repertory. In the 1950s, as the company became part of the establishment, Ashton had created many formal display pieces, sometimes falling into fussiness. In the 1960s he hit a period of lucid warmth and clarity, blending character and classicism in ballets such as *La Fille mal gardée* and *The Dream* or expressing line at its purest in *Monotones*. This golden period was brought short when the opera house took him at his word, and assumed that he was retiring; Ashton's level of creativity dropped, while The Royal Ballet's classicism was to be weakened in the 1970s and 1980s.

In 1965, New York City Ballet moved to the State Theater at Lincoln Center, the first purpose-built arts complex in the United States. Given lavish new facilities, Balanchine began to choreograph larger-scale, more elaborately designed works, while continuing to experiment. He also focused on a new generation of dancers, particularly his muse Suzanne Farrell. Melissa Hayden, a dancer of the previous era, remembered:

> He loved the new crop of dancers, they had beauty, they had 'bigness' – we were going into a new theatre, and he wanted 'bigness'. We were not small fry any more. His classes changed, technically: he wanted large, flowing steps, covering space, where formerly, for instance, he had talked for hours about the articulation of the foot.[1]

Infatuated with Farrell, Balanchine focused his work on her; when she left the company in 1969, overwhelmed by the pressure, he made ballets for a wider range of dancers. In 1969, Jerome Robbins also returned to New York City Ballet after a decade away, and made some of his best-loved ballets. As the new generation flowered, the older one found new blooms.

La Fille mal gardée

Choreography: Frederick Ashton
Music: Ferdinand Hérold, adapted and arranged by John Lanchbery
Designs: Osbert Lancaster
Premiere: 28 January 1960, The Royal Ballet, Royal Opera House, London
Original cast: *Lise* Nadia Nerina; *Colas* David Blair; *Widow Simone* Stanley Holden; *Alain* Alexander Grant

La Fille mal gardée was first staged by Jean Dauberval in Bordeaux in 1789. From the first, it was loved for its well-observed characters, for the way it wove dancing and storytelling together. It was revived repeatedly, with a range of scores and versions, all keeping the theme of a farm girl whose mother hopes for a grand match, but who finally allows her daughter to marry for love.

Ashton was encouraged to stage his version by the ballerina Tamara Karsavina, who told him all about the production staged at the Mariinsky, and then, 'With her blessing,' Ashton wrote, 'she said, "There it is, take it and embroider it." [2] The result was his happiest ballet, an entrancing blend of pastoral dancing and fresh humanity.

Spoiler warning: the following synopsis gives away some of the ballet's surprises.

Synopsis

Act I. Scene 1. The farmyard. As dawn breaks, the cockerel crows, before dancing with his attendant hens. Lise comes out of the farmhouse, hoping to see Colas. Not finding him, she shakes out a long ribbon and ties it in a lovers' knot for him to find. When Colas arrives, he finds the ribbon and ties it around his staff. He's interrupted by Lise's mother, the Widow Simone, who sends him away. The harvesters arrive, arranging to gather in Simone's harvest. Lise tries to sneak off with them, but Simone catches her, and sets her to churning butter. As Lise sits daydreaming, Colas returns. They share the work, then get sidetracked into a dance, using the ribbons they have exchanged: winding and unwinding them by quick turns, playing horses with high prancing steps and ribbon reins, even an intricate cat's cradle.

The farm girls summon Lise to play. Her watchful mother catches her and chastises her – just as Thomas, the rich proprietor of a local vineyard, arrives with his son Alain. Simone sends Lise off to change her dress: she and Thomas hope that their children will marry. When Lise returns, Alain clumsily dances for her: she is amused but not impressed. Thomas brings in his pony-cart – with a real onstage pony – to take Simone and Lise to the harvest.

In a frontcloth scene, all the characters pass along the front of the stage: Lise and Simone in the pony carriage, Alain dancing with his red umbrella and then with the farm girls, who drive him as the 'horse' of a carriage made of ribbons. Colas follows them, with bravura dancing and bottles of wine for the harvest picnic.

Scene 2. The cornfield. The harvesters dance, bending low with their sickles. The work done, they relax and celebrate. Thomas and Simone urge Lise and Alain to dance together, but Colas sneaks between them to steal kisses, to Lise's delight. A flute player entertains the villagers. Alain steals the flute, but cannot play it. The harvesters mock him, and he is rescued by the indignant Thomas.

Left alone, Lise and Colas dance together. Lise's friends act as a *corps de ballet* for their *adagio*, arranging ribbons in Xs and patterns. Lise spins at the centre of a wheel of ribbons, helping herself to balance by holding the many strands. As Colas lifts her onto his shoulder, she lets the ribbons go, her fingers fluttering. Both dance virtuoso variations and an exuberant finale. (The music for this duet was added to an earlier production for Fanny Elssler.) Finding them dancing together, Simone is angry – but Lise wins her round by suggesting she perform a clog dance. A maypole is brought out, and the harvesters dance, winding in and out. Suddenly a storm breaks, with gusts of wind driving the dancers from one side of the stage to another. In a break in the rain, Colas and Lise spot a rainbow, and pause to pray (though she takes this more seriously than he does). Alain wields his red umbrella, but the winds (and a handy wire) whisk him right up into the air as the curtain falls.

Act II. Inside Simone's farmhouse. Soaked by the storm, Simone and Lise return from the harvest, carrying bundles of hay. Simone locks the door and they sit down to spin, Simone hoping that work will keep Lise out of mischief. Tired out, Simone falls asleep. Lise tries to steal the keys, but Simone wakes up, and plays the tambourine for Lise to dance. At last Simone falls asleep again. Colas opens the top half of the farmhouse door and beckons Lise. She runs to him, and they dance through the door, Colas lifting Lise right up for a kiss.

The harvesters arrive for their pay, waking up Simone, and bringing in a great stack of hay. She pays them, then remembers the time, and rushes off on an errand. Left alone, Lise daydreams of her future life with Colas, imagining her wedding and bringing up three children. When Colas jumps out of his hiding place in the hay, Lise is mortified, but he soothes her. They exchange scarves as a love token.

As Simone returns, Lise needs to hide Colas, and hustles him into her bedroom. Simone is suspicious, but cannot find Colas downstairs. She orders Lise to go to her room and put on her wedding dress; at last she pushes her into the bedroom, and locks the door behind her.

Alain and Thomas arrive with a notary to sign the contract. When it has been signed, Simone gives Alain the bedroom key – but he opens the door to reveal Lise and Colas in each other's arms. The lovers beg Simone for her forgiveness and her blessing; even the notary pleads for them. She agrees, and everyone rejoices. In a final dance, the *corps de ballet* whirls in concentric circles, lifting Simone, Colas and then Lise up for the audience's applause, before everyone dances out of the doors, leaving the farmhouse empty. Alain sneaks back in through the window to collect his beloved red umbrella, and takes it away in triumph.

For Ashton, the old ballet had the quality of a new beginning. For the first phase of his career, he had worked with Fonteyn as his muse. For *La Fille mal gardée*, he turned to a younger generation of dancers, and found a new mood. Fonteyn's elegance and virginal quality were a world away from *La Fille mal gardée*, whose heroine's frank desire for Colas shines through her bounding jumps and trembling *bourrées*.

'There exists in my imagination a life in the country of eternally late spring,' Ashton wrote:

> a leafy pastorale of perpetual sunshine and the humming of bees – the suspended stillness of a Constable landscape of my beloved Suffolk, luminous and calm.
>
> At some time or another every artist pays his tribute to nature: my *Fille mal gardée* is my poor man's *Pastoral Symphony* . . .[3]

The French story became a very English ballet. Played by a man, the Widow Simone draws on British pantomime and music hall traditions. At Ninette de Valois' insistence, traditional folk dances were taught at The Royal Ballet School, but they rarely made their way onstage until Ashton wove them into *Fille*, from stick dances to a full-blown maypole.

At the same time, Ashton looked back to the ballet's older tradition. Karsavina taught him Lise's mime scene, in which she imagines raising a family. She also told him about the real tenderness between Lise and her mother: Simone's ambition is driven by love, not greed.

It's amazing just how much dancing there is in *Fille*, how beautifully steps and characterisation flow together. Chickens are characterised by headbobs and scratching, kicking steps; the corn is cut and gathered in dance patterns. In dance and storytelling, *La Fille mal gardée* is a rich harvest.

Boléro

Music: Maurice Ravel
Choreography: Maurice Béjart
Premiere: 10 January 1961, Ballet du XXème Siècle, Théâtre Royal de la Monnaie, Brussels
Original cast: Duška Sifnios

Maurice Béjart was a divisive but staggeringly popular choreographer: his dances filled sports stadiums in Europe, while British and American critics recoiled from his extravagant theatricality. Born in France in 1927, he founded his own company in 1953, and had his first major hit with an orgiastic version of *The Rite of Spring*, created in 1959. Béjart was a showman, creating works with big philosophical themes and sexy presentation. *Boléro* is one of his simplest works, and is still one of the most popular.

Ravel's *Boléro* was written for Ida Rubinstein, the rich and charismatic star of Fokine's *Schéhérazade*. Launching her own company, she asked Ravel to orchestrate some music by Isaac Albéniz for a Spanish ballet. Finding that the rights were not available, Ravel produced his own *Boléro*. In Rubinstein's version, choreographed by Nijinska, Rubinstein danced on top of a table in a Spanish tavern, to the excitement of frenzied onlookers.

In Béjart's version, a spotlight picks out the leading dancer's hand, which curls in the air before sliding down the dancer's own torso. The light gradually spreads to reveal a huge table and lines of dancers sitting at the edge of the stage. As the soloist repeats the same seductive phrase, the dancers are drawn into dancing, duplicating the phrase, surging closer and closer to the table.

The first staging presented a female soloist (named 'La Mélodie') and a male *corps de ballet* ('Le Rythme'). Béjart later changed it to a male soloist with a *corps* of women, and finally to an all-male cast.

The Two Pigeons

Choreography: Frederick Ashton
Music: André Messager, arranged and partly orchestrated by John Lanchbery
Designs: Jacques Dupont
Premiere: 14 February 1961, Royal Ballet touring section, Royal Opera House, London
Original cast: *The Young Man* Christopher Gable; *The Young Girl* Lynn Seymour; *A Gypsy Girl* Elizabeth Anderton

After the success of *La Fille mal gardée*, Ashton created a second work in the same comic, tender vein, again based on an existing ballet. In Louis Mérante's 1886 production, the hero is tempted by a gypsy girl who is actually his girlfriend in disguise – another of ballet's dual heroines. Ashton updated the story to nineteenth-century Paris, making his hero a young artist and the gypsy girl a separate character.

Synopsis

Act I. An artist's studio, with a view across the rooftops of Paris. A young artist is trying to paint his girlfriend's portrait as she sits on a wicker chair.

She won't sit still, fidgeting and getting distracted, trying to distract him. They quarrel. A neighbour looks in, with a group of the girl's friends. They dance with her, to the young man's exasperation.

Looking out of the window, he sees two white pigeons fly past. The *pas de deux* that follows is full of bird imagery, from comic to touching. The girl waggles her elbows and pecks with her head, suggesting a fluffy, strutting pigeon. Hearing a group of gypsies in the street, they invite them in.

The young man is attracted by the leading gypsy girl. Jealous, his girl-friend tries to separate them. She tries to copy the gypsy girl's glamorous solo, but ends up looking foolish. At last she orders the gypsies away, but the young man decides to follow them, taking his sketchpad. Left with her friends, the girl sees one of the white pigeons fly past the window.

Act II. Scene 1. A gypsy camp. The gypsies dance for sightseers, sometimes picking their pockets. When the young artist arrives, the gypsy men are dismissive, but the gypsy girl flirts with him again. The leading gypsy man is her lover, and she dances a competitive *pas de trois* with him and her new admirer. She starts to mock the artist, and urges him to have a wrestling match with her gypsy lover. The artist loses, and is left tied up. A pigeon crosses the stage, as if to lead him home.

Scene 2. Back at the studio. The girl is alone, when her lover returns, with the pigeon on his shoulder. He begs forgiveness in a *pas de deux* that ends with the reunited lovers sitting on either side of the wicker chair, one pigeon perched on its back. At the climax of the music, the second pigeon flies in to join it.

The Two Pigeons is more sentimental than *La Fille mal gardée*: bohemia and gypsies are stage conventions, less grounded in human reality than the farmers of *Fille*. Yet Ashton created appealing dances and touching leading roles, with a tender final *pas de deux*. He responded to the youth of Lynn Seymour and Christopher Gable, giving their roles a casual, contemporary quality. The young man ends the first-act quarrel slumped upside-down on the chair, his knees hooked over the chairback, his back arched, his arms hanging to the floor. Seymour, fresh from playing a rape victim in Kenneth MacMillan's *The Invitation*, worried that her role might be too sugary, and asked MacMillan to advise; she went on to emphasise the role's mischief and sexuality.

The supporting roles are more broadly drawn: the gypsies are very much stage gypsies. The girl's friends pick up the 'bird' motif, surrounding her in mournful *Swan Lake* groupings – though they still stick their elbows out like pigeons.

In the final *pas de deux*, Ashton makes both lovers bruised and vulnerable, gradually moving from forgiveness to new sensuality. The bird imagery becomes intimate: as the girl sits on the ground, bent forward with her arms folded like wings, the artist reaches through the crook of her arm to caress her; she flutters in response to his touch.

A Midsummer Night's Dream

Choreography: George Balanchine
Music: Felix Mendelssohn
Scenery and lighting: David Hayes
Costumes: Karinska
Premiere: 17 January 1962, New York City Center, New York
Original cast: *Titania* Melissa Hayden; *Oberon* Edward Villella; *Puck* Arthur Mitchell; *Hermia* Patricia McBride; *Helena* Jillana; *Hippolyta* Gloria Govrin

As a child in St Petersburg, Balanchine performed in Shakespeare's *A Midsummer Night's Dream*, playing an elf. 'I still know the play better in Russian than a lot of people know it in English,' he said. With its complicated storyline, fantasy sets and costumes, and long running time, *A Midsummer Night's Dream* looked like the opera-house ballets that Balanchine had generally left behind. More than the play, however, he was drawn to Mendelssohn's music for this, the first original full-length ballet to be created in the United States.

To make a full-length score, Mendelssohn's incidental music for the play was expanded with the overtures to his *Athalie, The Fair Melusine* and *Son and Stranger*, plus *The First Walpurgis Night* and three movements from Mendelssohn's ninth string symphony.

Synopsis

Act I. A forest near Duke Theseus' palace, Athens. Oberon, king of the fairies, quarrels with his wife, Titania. He orders the fairy Puck to bring a flower pierced by Cupid's arrow: the juice of the flower will make Titania fall in love with the first person she sees.

Helena, a young Athenian, is wandering in the forest. She is in love with Demetrius, but when she meets him, he rejects her. Oberon tells Puck to use the flower on Demetrius so that he will return Helena's love. A pair of happy lovers, Hermia and Lysander, are also wandering in the forest, but become separated. Puck mistakenly anoints Lysander, who promptly sees and falls in love with Helena.

Hermia returns, and is dismayed to find Lysander paying attention only to Helena. Puck also brings Demetrius under the flower's spell, so that Lysander and Demetrius are now both in love with Helena, and quarrel over her.

Wishing to punish Titania, Oberon orders Puck to separate Bottom, a weaver, from his companions, give him an ass' head and place him at the sleeping Titania's feet. Under the spell of Cupid's flower, Titania wakes and falls in love with Bottom. She leads Bottom through a *pas de deux*, but he is more interested in eating hay than in her. At last Oberon, his anger over, has Bottom sent away, and releases Titania from the spell.

Puck uses his magic to separate Demetrius and Lysander, who are fighting over Helena, and to sort the human lovers into the right couples. The Duke and his consort, Hippolyta, are hunting in the forest. Discovering the lovers asleep, they awaken them and proclaim a triple wedding.

Act II. The Duke's palace. The weddings are celebrated with dancing and divertissements. When night falls, we return to the world of Oberon and Titania, who are now united and at peace. Puck, having put disorder to rights, sweeps up the last of the night's doings, as fireflies twinkle in the night.

If Balanchine remembered performing in the play in Russia, he clearly also remembered Russian ballet spectacles. Sections of *A Midsummer Night's Dream* recall the more inconsequential vision scenes of the nineteenth century, right down to Hippolyta sweeping through as the goddess of the hunt, and spinning multiple *fouettés* (another rarity in Balanchine ballets). Although Shakespeare's story is told, it's not the focus of the evening. The characterisation is slight, while the formal, ceremonial mime is oddly repetitive: acting out their quarrel, Oberon and Titania go through exactly the same gestures twice.

Although love is a theme of *A Midsummer Night's Dream*, it's celebrated most effectively outside the confines of the story. Titania's duet with Bottom is a comic version of the ballerina and her adoring partner, but she also dances with an unnamed cavalier. When the human lovers assemble in the second act, ideal love is represented by an entirely new couple, who dance a ravishing divertissement duet. For all its lavish design, Balanchine's *A Midsummer Night's Dream* has plenty of plotless dancing.

The ballet also involves many children, who play the ballet's insects and junior fairies. Balanchine's dances for them are delightful, encouraging young students to move with the speed and attack of the adult dancers, and to learn confidence onstage.

Other Stagings

Shakespeare's story and Mendelssohn's music have appealed to many choreographers. Petipa and Fokine both staged versions; see *The Dream* (1964) for Frederick Ashton's lovely production. John Neumeier's evening-length staging, created for the Hamburg Ballet in 1977, separates the three strands of character types by using three different kinds of music. The human lovers are accompanied by Mendelssohn's music, but an onstage barrel organ plays for Bottom and the other 'rude mechanicals', while the fairies, space-age creatures in glittering body tights and skull caps, dance to the music of György Ligeti. This allows Neumeier to pay much more attention to events outside the wood, which he imagines in much greater detail than exists in Shakespeare's play. The ballet starts with a prologue, set the night before the wedding of Theseus and Hippolyta, and introducing the lovers and the mechanicals. Lysander is a gardener, which explains why Hermia's father does not wish her to marry him, while Hippolyta is aware of Theseus' flirting with other ladies of the court. She finds Lysander's love letter to Hermia and falls asleep reading it, suggesting that she is the dreamer of the midsummer night's dream.

The first act, showing events in the magical wood, follows Shakespeare's narrative. In the second act, Theseus finds Hippolyta asleep and wakes her for a *pas de deux* in which love grows between them. The pairs of lovers then beg his permission to wed. In the last scene, the weddings are celebrated and the rustics perform the play *Pyramus and Thisbe*. After the wedding guests have left, Oberon and Titania are united in their own love duet.

Pierrot Lunaire

Choreography: Glen Tetley
Music: Arnold Schoenberg, Pierrot Lunaire
Designs: Rouben Ter-Arutunian
Premiere: 5 May 1962, Fashion Institute of Technology, New York
Original cast: *Pierrot* Glen Tetley; *Columbine* Linda Hodes; *Brighella* Robert Powell

Pierrot Lunaire, one of Glen Tetley's first works, was also one of the first works to blend ballet and modern dance. Born in Cleveland, Ohio, in 1926, Tetley was already twenty when he gave up the idea of a career in medicine to pursue dance. Working with modern dance choreographers Hanya Holm and Martha Graham, he also learned ballet, dancing with Jerome Robbins' Ballets: U.S.A. and American Ballet Theatre. In 1962 he presented his first programme of choreography, including *Pierrot Lunaire*.

'In the antiquity of the Roman theatre began the battle of the white clown of innocence with the dark clown of experience,' Tetley wrote. 'Pierrot and Brighella are their lineal descendants and Columbine their eternal feminine pawn.' Pierrot, a clown dressed in white with a distinctive cap, swings from Rouben Ter-Arturian's white scaffolding set, an introverted dreamer. With echoes of Fokine's *Petrushka*, the bullying Brighella and the seductive Columbine tease and manipulate him, finally stripping Pierrot and climbing into his tower. In the final pose, Pierrot, now strong enough to deal with them, clasps Brighella and Columbine to him, their heads on his breast.

Tetley would go on to an international career in ballet and modern dance: he directed the Stuttgart Ballet after Cranko's death, and has worked with many ballet companies internationally, from American Ballet Theatre to the Royal Danish Ballet.

Romeo and Juliet

Choreography: John Cranko
Music: Sergei Prokofiev
Designs: Jürgen Rose
Premiere: 2 December 1962, Stuttgart Ballet, Württemberg State Theatre, Stuttgart
Original cast: *Juliet* Marcia Haydée; *Romeo* Richard Cragun; *Tybalt* Jan Stripling; *Mercutio* Egon Madsen

John Cranko first staged *Romeo and Juliet* for the ballet of La Scala, Milan, in 1958, with the young Carla Fracci as his Juliet. When he took over the Stuttgart Ballet in 1961, he revived and reworked *Romeo and Juliet*, with great success. Jürgen Rose's designs, a permanent set with a bridge that becomes Juliet's balcony, suggests a cramped Renaissance city, the warring families jostled together.

Synopsis

Scene 1. The streets of Verona. Romeo, a member of the Montague family, is up early, hoping to catch a glimpse of Rosaline, with whom he is in love. His friends Benvolio and Mercutio tease him. As the city springs to life, men bring in carts while women set up marketplace stalls. A brawl breaks out between the Capulet and Montague factions, quickly spreading to the townspeople, who throw fruit and vegetables while the nobility draw swords. The fighting is stopped by the Prince of Verona. Laying down their arms, the two families clasp hands and exchange bows, but their hearts aren't in it; glaring at each other, the two factions pick up their swords again.

Scene 2. The garden of the Capulet house. Juliet plays with her nurse, hopping onto her back, mimicking her when she's out of breath but hugging her afterwards. Lady Capulet, a formal noblewoman, brings Juliet the dress she is to wear to the ball that night – though she holds it back until Juliet shows enough dignity to receive it properly. As her mother leaves, Juliet wants to romp again, but the nurse reminds her that it is time to grow up.

Scene 3. Outside the Capulet house. Guests arrive for the ball, joined by the masked figures of Romeo, Mercutio and Benvolio. Rosaline drops her fan, and Romeo eagerly returns it. The three men dance together, masking their faces and showing off their air turns, before sneaking into the ball.

Scene 4. The Capulet ballroom. The guests dance a cushion dance, the men kneeling at their partners' feet. Juliet enters and dances with Paris, who is to marry her. Juliet catches sight of Romeo, and dances a solo that shows her caught between the two men. Mercutio dances an acrobatic solo, distracting the guests and clearing the ballroom. Meeting in the empty room, Romeo and Juliet yearn towards each other. Reaching for her, Romeo presses his cheek to Juliet's hand. Shy, she takes her hand away, then returns it. The lovers are interrupted by Tybalt. Lord Capulet prevents a fight developing, and the guests leave.

Scene 5. The Capulet garden. Dreaming on her balcony, Juliet sees Romeo in the garden. He helps her down to the garden, and they declare their love. Again, Romeo presses his cheek to Juliet's hand, before dancing a solo demonstrating his love. Their duet is full of lifts and throws: Juliet is spun in the air and caught, or dives into Romeo's arms. He is ready to take her away, but she gestures back to her home. He lifts her back onto her balcony, and they bid each other goodnight.

Act 2. Scene 1. A street in Verona. The crowd is swept up in a carnival, joining in the dancing and watching clowns. Juliet's Nurse finds Romeo, and gives him a letter from Juliet: Friar Laurence will marry them.

Scene 2. Friar Laurence's cell. The lovers are married.

Scene 3. A street in Verona. The festivities are at their height, with dancing on all levels of the set. Tybalt enters, ready to pick a fight. In a phallic joke, Mercutio tests his sword – but they are interrupted by Romeo, who refuses to fight. Mercutio takes up his sword instead, but is killed. Avenging his friend, Romeo kills Tybalt. Lady Capulet arrives to throw herself onto the corpse. When the pallbearers arrive, she climbs onto the bier, clinging to Tybalt's body as it is carried out.

Act III. Scene 1. Juliet's bedroom. Waking in Juliet's arms, Romeo plays with a strand of her long hair, curling it between his fingers. It is dawn, and he must leave, but Juliet urges him to stay. In their *pas de deux*, she clings to him in despair, hanging from his neck. He covers her eyes, kisses her hair, and rushes out.

Juliet's parents enter, ready to arrange her marriage to Paris. Juliet rejects him, begging her parents for help. Left alone, she runs to Friar Laurence.

Scene 2. Friar Laurence's cell. The Friar gives her a potion that will put her into a deathlike sleep. Her parents will believe that she is dead, and she can leave for a new life with Romeo.

Scene 3. Juliet's bedroom. She accepts Paris, takes the potion and falls asleep. Juliet's bridesmaids enter, dancing with flowers. Lady Capulet and the Nurse arrive to prepare her for her wedding, and are horrified to find her apparently dead.

Scene 4. The Capulet tomb. A procession carries Juliet's body to the Capulet tomb. She is lowered into the vault. Paris mourns beside her body. Romeo, unaware of Friar Laurence's plan, enters and kills Paris. Picking up Juliet's body, he cradles her in despair. Laying her back on the tomb, he stabs himself. As he dies, he takes Juliet in his arms, and again strokes the curl of her hair.

Juliet wakes and snuggles into Romeo's arms, then realises he is dead. She runs in shock around the tomb, discovering Paris' body. Taking his dagger, she kisses Romeo and stabs herself, rocking Romeo in her arms as she dies.

Like most of his generation, Cranko had been deeply impressed by the Bolshoi Ballet's Lavrovsky production, with its large-scale storytelling and emotional performances. Returning to the same score, he developed a quicker, more naturalistic mime language. He also adopted Soviet overhead lifts: the critics Nancy Reynolds and Malcolm McCormick point out that the 'often-flashy choreography, particularly his fondness for acrobatic lifts, helped camouflage the technical weaknesses of his young, very green company'.[4] Cranko was creating a company as well as a repertory. Tailoring his ballets to his young, committed performers, he focused on dramatic immediacy over danced depth.

Cranko's star-crossed lovers are romantic. As well as the dramatic lifts, he characterises them with repeated motifs: yearning for each other across a distance, Romeo pressing his cheek to Juliet's hand or playing gently with a lock of her hair. Cranko's Juliet is a shy girl, who returns home after her balcony scene and is respectful to her parents.

Cranko fills the long expanses of Prokofiev's crowd scenes with bustle and activity. The Stuttgart Ballet's *corps de ballet* was smaller than Lavrovsky's, but also more irreverent, and more given to vegetable-throwing. The ballet is now danced by larger companies, but remains a production that can show off a lively smaller ensemble.

Marguerite and Armand

Choreography: Frederick Ashton
Music: Franz Liszt, *La lugubre gondola*, no. 1, and Sonata in B minor, orchestrated by Humphrey Searle
Designs: Cecil Beaton
Lighting: William Bundy
Premiere: 12 March 1963, The Royal Ballet, Royal Opera House, London
Original cast: *Marguerite* Margot Fonteyn; *Armand* Rudolf Nureyev; *Armand's father* Michael Somes; *the Duke* Leslie Edwards

In 1963, Margot Fonteyn and Rudolf Nureyev were two of the biggest stars in the world. Their fame went far beyond ballet. Fonteyn had been an international name since 1949, when she had made her debut in America, featuring on the cover of *Time* magazine in an era when entertainers were rarely given such recognition. Nureyev's defection had made him a face of the moment, an icon of the 1960s. Individually, they were dazzling; together, they generated extraordinary excitement and chemistry. It's no surprise that Ashton, who had choreographed so many roles for Fonteyn, should create a ballet to show off her new partnership.

He chose *The Lady of the Camellias* for his story. Written by Alexandre Dumas *fils*, and adapted by Giuseppe Verdi as the opera *La Traviata*, it's a highly romantic tale of love, self-sacrifice and dying young. Ashton decided to make the ballet after hearing Liszt's piano music on the radio, imagining the whole action in the music – even hearing the tubercular Marguerite's cough in a musical motif. He later found out that Marie Duplessis, the real-life courtesan on whom the character of Marguerite is based, had an affair with Liszt.

The ballet tells the story in flashback, focusing on the lovers; other characters were dropped or stylised, leaving Marguerite and Armand dominating the foreground. Cecil Beaton's designs set the action in a stylised framework, with billowing white curtains to cover scene changes. Marguerite wears red, white or black, always with white camellias.

Synopsis

Prologue. As Marguerite lies on her deathbed, she recalls her affair with Armand. Images of him are projected onto the cyclorama at the back of the stage.

The meeting. Marguerite, a glamorous Parisian courtesan, is surrounded by admirers. When Armand enters, they fall in love: both freeze, staring at each other, until he moves slowly towards her, smitten.

The country. Marguerite has left her life in Paris to live with Armand in the country. While Armand is out, his father calls, telling Marguerite that the affair is damaging the family's reputation. He asks her to renounce Armand. Heartbroken, she agrees – but will not tell Armand the reason, afraid that he will persuade her to change her mind.

The insult. Marguerite returns to her admirers in Paris. Jealous and angry, Armand follows her to a party and humiliates her, throwing money in her face. In deep distress, she leaves. As she sobs, shakes run down her body to her trembling feet: her bourréed steps express her devastation.

Death of the Lady of the Camellias. Marguerite lies on her couch, preparing to die. Armand, whose father has told him of her sacrifice, comes rushing back to her. They are reconciled, and she dies in his arms – climbing up his body, her arms reaching out, before she collapses.

There's 'nothing wrong with a vehicle', Ashton said, 'provided it goes.'[5] *Marguerite and Armand* was created for its star couple, and during their lifetimes nobody else danced it. Ashton's compressed version of the story focuses on the lovers together: the chemistry between Fonteyn and Nureyev was as important as what they danced. Without star power, the romantic flurries and swooning duets lack substance. The ballet's finest moment is Marguerite's shaking bourréed exit: dancers used to line up in the wings to watch it.

In 2000, The Royal Ballet revived *Marguerite and Armand* for a new star, Sylvie Guillem – and the ballet's centre of gravity shifted. Guillem danced it first with Nicolas Le Riche, and later with other partners. Instead of being a vehicle for a partnership, it had become the ballerina's ballet. It has since been danced by many different casts, at The Royal Ballet and the Mariinsky Ballet, but works best when its leads are evenly matched.

The Lesson (Danish title Enetime, sometimes called The Private Lesson)

Choreography: Flemming Flindt
Music: Georges Delerue
Designs: Bernard Daydé
Premiere: Television broadcast 16 September 1963; first staged 6 April 1964, Opéra Comique, Paris
Original cast: *the Teacher* Flemming Flindt; *the Pupil* Josette Amiel; *the Pianist* Tsilla Chelton

Based on a play by Eugène Ionesco, *The Lesson* is a creepy, comic drama about a teacher who keeps murdering his pupils. It was Flemming Flindt's first ever ballet, originally created as a television production. It won several awards, and was soon staged by the Royal Danish Ballet. Where Ionesco's Professor taught everything from arithmetic to linguistics, Flindt's is a ballet teacher. The third character, the teacher's maidservant, becomes his stern pianist. Flindt defines his characters with broad, caricature strokes: the lanky stride of the pianist, the perky ballet student and the tense, twitchy teacher gradually overcome by frenzy. The ballet has been staged by many companies, while the male role is a favourite with dramatic dancers; Rudolf Nureyev performed it frequently.

Synopsis

Set in a basement ballet studio, *The Lesson* opens with a scene of disorder, featuring overturned chairs and scattered papers. The pianist is shocked by the sound of the doorbell. Through a skylight in Bernard Daydé's set, we can see the legs and feet of the waiting pupil, practising her steps on the doorstep upstairs. The pianist rushes to set the room straight before letting her in. When the pupil gets out her *pointe* shoes, the pianist makes her put them away.

The teacher enters nervously, adjusting his collar. He primly sketches out exercises for his pupil, nervous of touching her. She eagerly carries them out. He suggests she try *pointe* shoes, to the pianist's horror. As the lesson continues, he becomes increasingly aggressive, driving her harder. (Ionesco's original stage directions suggest that a 'prurient gleam' in his eyes should become a 'lecherous, devouring flame' as he becomes more domineering.) At last he sends the pianist out, and strangles the pupil. The pianist returns and rebukes him, but helps to remove the body, which they carry out with a goose-step walk. The doorbell rings, and we see the day's next pupil practising her steps on the doorstep.

The Dream

Choreography: Frederick Ashton
Music: Felix Mendelssohn, arranged by John Lanchbery
Scenery: Henry Bardon
Costumes: David Walker
Premiere: 2 April 1964, The Royal Ballet, Royal Opera House, London
Original cast: *Titania* Antoinette Sibley; *Oberon* Anthony Dowell; *Puck* Keith Martin; *Bottom* Alexander Grant

Created for the four hundredth anniversary of Shakespeare's birth, Ashton's version of *A Midsummer Night's Dream* taps into British theatrical traditions. It's a very Victorian *Dream*: like many nineteenth-century stagings of the play, it focuses on events in the magic wood. Its fairies, in tulle and flower headdresses, recall Romantic ballet, while the lovers' costumes and mannerisms are early Victorian, from the period when Mendelssohn wrote the music. Ashton's ballet blends the comic and the fantastic, with rapturous dancing and genuinely funny intrigues.

Synopsis

In a wood outside Athens, the fairy king Oberon quarrels with his queen, Titania, because she will not give him a changeling boy to be his page. To avenge himself, Oberon sends Puck to fetch a magic flower. When the flower's juice is placed on the sleeping Titania's eyes, it will make her fall in love with the first person she sees when she wakes. Titania falls asleep in her bower, Oberon anoints her eyes and waits to see what will happen.

Two lovers, Hermia and Lysander, arrive in the forest. They are pursued by Demetrius, to whom Hermia was promised by her father. Demetrius is chased by Helena, who is in love with him. Oberon orders Puck to enchant Demetrius, so that he will love Helena. Puck confuses the two men, and squeezes the flower into Lysander's eyes. Helena stumbles over Lysander, who is immediately besotted with her, abandoning Hermia. All four lovers fall out.

Bottom the Weaver and his friends arrive in the forest to rehearse a play. Puck puts an ass' head on Bottom, and his companions flee in terror. (Bottom also goes on *pointe*, his footwork suggesting the ass' hooves.) Titania wakes and falls in love with Bottom. She orders her attendants to deck him with flowers, and takes him to her bower.

Seeing the quarrelling lovers, Oberon realises Puck's mistake. He conjures a mist in which the four lovers are suitably paired off. There is virtuoso dancing for Oberon, Puck and four fairies to Mendelssohn's scherzo.

Oberon takes the spell off Titania, who pushes Bottom out of her bower. Reconciled with Oberon, she gives him her changeling boy. Puck takes away the ass' head, and Bottom is left wondering at his dream.

Oberon and Titania return for an ecstatic *pas de deux* to Mendelssohn's Nocturne, before the finale. Like the play, the ballet ends with a shrug from Puck.

Ashton cast Antoinette Sibley with Anthony Dowell, then an unknown *corps de ballet* dancer, as Titania and Oberon, launching one of ballet's great partnerships. It also revealed just how far British male dancing had come. Oberon dazzles and spins in the scherzo, whirling out of turns into deep *arabesques penchées*, requiring great control and a sinuous sense of balance. Dowell was also unusually flexible: when he and Sibley mirrored each other's steps, the high line of his leg matched hers.

Their reconciliation duet, something Ashton added to Shakespeare, is both supernatural and erotic. In an echo of their earlier conflict, Titania darts into a regal *arabesque*, then melts out of it, fluttering in sensual abandon. Throughout *The Dream*, characterisation is built into the dancing: the flitting fairies stop dead at the sight of Bottom, or toss their heads indignantly at Oberon. Ashton blends witty echoes of Taglioni – a dancer Mendelssohn admired – with delicate, Petipa-like patterns.

The human lovers are deftly drawn, individual enough for the mix-ups to be clear and speedy enough not to slow down the action. Their comic sequences are in period, as when the men pompously threaten each other;

all four catch the rhythm of the music as they bounce each other out of the way. Even Bottom has real dances on *pointe*, and a touching mime sequence in which he looks back in wonder on the events of the night.

Romeo and Juliet

Choreography: Kenneth MacMillan
Music: Sergei Prokofiev
Designs: Nicholas Georgiadis
Premiere: 9 February 1965
Original cast: *Juliet* Margot Fonteyn; *Romeo* Rudolf Nureyev; *Mercutio* David Blair

Romeo and Juliet was Kenneth MacMillan's first full-length ballet. Working with John Cranko, who had recently staged his own production, gave him the confidence to approach such a large-scale work. Lynn Seymour, his muse, was the obvious choice for Juliet: MacMillan's first work on the ballet was a version of the balcony scene, created for Seymour and Christopher Gable's appearance on Canadian television.

In all their work together, Seymour and MacMillan were eager to explore new developments in theatre and film. They, and the designer Nicholas Georgiadis, had seen Franco Zeffirelli's production of the play at the Old Vic in 1961, and were impressed by the sexual frankness of the young lovers and the violence of the society around them. (The sensuous moves Seymour made, alone on her balcony, were modelled on those of Zeffirelli's Juliet, the young Judi Dench.)

From the start, the production was planned to have multiple casts, in the manner of *Swan Lake* or *The Sleeping Beauty* – but it was a huge shock when The Royal Ballet management insisted that the starrier Margot Fonteyn and Rudolf Nureyev should dance the first night, not Seymour and Gable. MacMillan resented having casting decisions taken out of his hands; Seymour was devastated. A year later, both left for the Deutsche Oper Ballet in Berlin, where MacMillan was director. In 1967, Christopher Gable retired from dancing to pursue an acting career.

Synopsis

Act I. Scene 1. The marketplace, Verona, early morning. Romeo, who is a member of the Montague family, tries to declare his love for Rosaline. His friends, Mercutio and Benvolio, tease him. As day breaks, the marketplace fills up with townspeople. Three harlots pass through the square, prompting fascination and suspicion. A fight breaks out between Capulet and Montague factions. The Prince of Verona orders the families to end their feud.

Scene 2. Juliet's anteroom, the Capulet house. Juliet, playing with her nurse, is interrupted by her parents, Lord and Lady Capulet. They introduce her to Paris, a young nobleman who has asked for her hand in marriage.

Scene 3. Outside the Capulet house. Guests arrive for the Capulet ball. Romeo tries to court Rosaline, to the annoyance of Tybalt, a member of the Capulet family. Romeo, Mercutio and Benvolio dance a lively trio, then put on masks to join the party.

Scene 4. The ballroom. The Capulets dance a powerful, processional dance. Juliet is presented to the company. Suddenly she and Romeo come face to face, and fall in love. When Juliet plays a lute for her friends, Romeo bursts into dance. When Juliet dances a solo, he joins her. Tybalt is angry and suspicious, so Mercutio and Benvolio distract the company. As the guests go in to supper, Juliet pretends faintness and asks to be left alone. She meets Romeo in the deserted ballroom. He removes his mask. Discovered by Tybalt, he is ordered to leave, but Lord Capulet intervenes, determined to keep the truce. Benvolio and Mercutio urge Romeo to leave with them.

Scene 5. Outside the Capulet house. The guests leave. Lord Capulet restrains Tybalt from pursuing Romeo.

Scene 6. Juliet's balcony. Juliet is on her balcony, thinking of Romeo. Seeing him in the garden, she runs down to meet him, placing his hand on her heart. He dances for her, in giddy, swooping steps, before she joins him in a rapturous *pas de deux*.

Act II. Scene 1. The marketplace. Romeo can think only of Juliet, ignoring the harlots who expect him to dance with them. A wedding procession appears, with entertainers who dance and play mandolins. Juliet's nurse enters, seeking Romeo. After some teasing from Romeo, Mercutio and Benvolio, she gives him a letter from Juliet: he is to meet her at Friar Laurence's cell, where they will be married. He rushes joyfully away.

Scene 2. The chapel. The lovers are secretly married by Friar Laurence, who hopes that this union will end the strife between the Montagues and Capulets.

Scene 3. The marketplace. Interrupting the revelry, Tybalt fights with Mercutio. Romeo tries to prevent the duel, but fails, and Mercutio is wounded. He appears to laugh it off; used to his mischief, the crowd believe him, but it becomes clear that he is dying. Romeo avenges the death of his friend, and is exiled. Lady Capulet laments over Tybalt's body.

Act III. Scene 1. The bedroom. The lovers have spent the night together, but Romeo must leave at dawn. After a *pas de deux*, he embraces Juliet and leaves. Her parents enter with Paris, her future bridegroom. Juliet rebels, refusing to marry him, despite her parents' anger. Left alone, Juliet sits on her bed as the music surges around her, trying to find a way out. At last she runs to Friar Laurence.

Scene 2. The chapel. Juliet begs Friar Laurence for help. He offers her a potion, which will make her fall into a deathlike sleep. Her parents, believing her to be dead, will lay her in the family tomb; Romeo will return and take her away from Verona.

Scene 3. The bedroom. Juliet hides the potion under her pillow. When her parents return with Paris, she tries to persuade them to cancel the wedding. At last, under pressure, she agrees to marry Paris. Dancing with him, she is remote and cold, then suddenly resistant when she meets his eye. He and her parents leave her to calm down. Summoning up her courage, Juliet takes the potion. When her parents and friends arrive to prepare her for the wedding, they find her apparently dead.

Scene 4. The Capulet family crypt. Juliet is laid out on a bier. Her family take a last farewell; Paris remains, grieving in the shadows. Romeo, who has not received the Friar's message, believes that Juliet is dead, and comes to her tomb. He stabs Paris and picks up Juliet's body, carrying her through the motions of their earlier love duet, even though she lies stiff and cold in his arms. Laying her on the bier, he takes poison and dies. Juliet stirs and wakes. Frightened by the vault, she is horrified to find Romeo's body. She seizes his dagger and stabs herself, then crawls painfully over the bier to be with Romeo as she dies.

MacMillan puts Juliet at the heart of his ballet, presenting her as a rebellious, hot-headed teenager. His Juliet drives the action – placing Romeo's hand over her heart in the balcony scene, flatly refusing to marry Paris. (When her parents press her, she jumps back into bed and pulls the covers over her head, a moment of rebellion expressed in an adolescent tantrum.) In the duets, MacMillan's young lovers ride waves of passion, rising and falling in sexual abandon.

For MacMillan, as for other choreographers, Prokofiev's long marketplace scenes led to padding: 'We have a bit too much of Verona's three early-rising prostitutes,'[6] wrote Richard Buckle. At his best with individuals, MacMillan's big ensembles become repetitive. Nicholas Georgiadis' fine sets and costumes (frequently revised over time, not always for the best) are starkly monumental. The danced drama, particularly for Juliet, is both large in scale and intimately personal.

At key moments in the story, MacMillan makes blunt choices, aiming for rawness of expression. Where Lavrovsky's Juliet had run passionately to Friar Laurence in search of a solution, MacMillan's sits on her bed and stares into space as the music surges around her, expressing her turmoil. Perhaps the boldest departure came in the tomb scene, where MacMillan wanted death to look ugly. His Romeo dances with Juliet's corpse, hauling her dead body through the soaring poses of the balcony scene. 'A gorilla at London Zoo had just had a baby,' Christopher Gable told the dance writer Barbara Newman:

> . . . and didn't know how to look after it, and it died. But they couldn't take it away from her. She dangled it around and played with it sometimes, and it didn't do anything, and she kept walking around with it . . . Well, that was the image I had in my mind. I used to drag Lynn around the stage, and she'd just let her legs fall apart, all open and exposed and ugly. I think she's the only one who does that; all the other ballerinas make pretty shapes on the floor. And I also used to rock, the way you rock when you go into that bad, grief place.[7]

Dying in her turn, Juliet crawls across the tomb to reach Romeo, not quite making it: these lovers are not united in death.

Monotones

Choreography: Frederick Ashton
Music: Erik Satie, *Trois Gymnopédies* (*Monotones II*), *Prélude d'Eginhard*, *Trois Gnossiennes* (*Monotones I*)

Designs: Frederick Ashton
Premiere: *Monotones II* on 24 March 1965; *Monotones I* on 25 April 1966
Original cast: *Monotones I* Antoinette Sibley, Georgina Parkinson, Brian Shaw; *Monotones II* Vyvyan Lorraine, Anthony Dowell, Robert Mead

In *Symphonic Variations*, Ashton had pared down his choreography to create limpid classicism. In *Monotones*, he created a concentrated image of his own style, two linked trios that present fluid, harmonious line in absolute form.

Monotones started out as a short dance for three dancers dressed in white, made for a 1965 gala and danced to Satie's *Gymnopédies*. The next year, Ashton added another *pas de trois*, for dancers in green, which he named *Monotones I*. The original dance was renamed *Monotones II*; the two are now performed together, green followed by white.

The 'white' *Monotones II* opens with a woman in the splits on the floor, bent forward over her outstretched leg. She holds this position as her two male partners raise her upright and slowly turn her round. The pose is extreme, but the movement must be serene, with no jerks or exaggerations. The three move through sculptural groupings, a chain of movement that stretches wide or closes in until the three stand side by side, arms linked in a rounded fifth position. The 'continuity of his line is like that of a master draftsman whose pen never leaves the paper,'[8] wrote the critic Arlene Croce.

In *Monotones II*, the dancers wear white body tights with belts and caps. In *Monotones I*, two women and a man wear pale green tights with belts and Phrygian caps. Where *Monotones II* has a lunar calm, *Monotones I* is terrestrial, more grounded, while keeping the mood of flowing serenity.

In the 1960s, *Monotones* was an expression of The Royal Ballet's fundamental classical style, developed by de Valois and perfected by Ashton. That continuity of style was broken after Ashton's directorship; *Monotones* remains beautiful, but all companies must work hard to achieve its radiant calm.

Onegin

Choreography: John Cranko
Music: Pyotr Ilych Tchaikovsky, arranged by Kurt-Heinz Stolze
Libretto: John Cranko after Alexander Pushkin
Designs: Jürgen Rose
Premiere: 13 April 1965, The Stuttgart Ballet, Stuttgart

Original cast: *Tatiana* Marcia Haydée; *Onegin* Ray Barra; *Lensky* Egon Madsen; *Olga* Ana Cardus

With his production of *Romeo and Juliet*, Cranko had put the Stuttgart Ballet on the map. With *Onegin*, he created its signature work, a retelling of Pushkin's poem about a disaffected aristocrat and a bookish, idealistic young woman.

Cranko had choreographed the dances for Tchaikovsky's opera *Eugene Onegin* in 1952, and considered creating a ballet version in London for Fonteyn and Nureyev – who had just danced another pair of literary lovers in Ashton's *Marguerite and Armand*. The general director of the Stuttgart Theatre was strongly opposed to the use of Tchaikovsky's opera music for ballet, so Cranko asked Karl-Heinz Stolze to create a 'new' Tchaikovsky score from existing pieces. Stolze's patchwork score drew on Tchaikovsky's piano music, on his opera *The Caprices of Oxana*, the fantasy overture *Romeo and Juliet* and the symphonic poem *Francesca da Rimini*, which provided the music for the third-act *pas de deux*.

Synopsis

Act I. Scene 1. Madame Larina's garden. Tatiana is absorbed in her book, while her sister Olga, their mother Madame Larina and their nurse work on party dresses for Tatiana's upcoming birthday party. A group of local girls arrive, and Olga leads them in a dance. They play an old fortune-telling game with a mirror: whoever looks into the glass will see her beloved.

Lensky, a young poet engaged to Olga, arrives with Onegin, his friend from St Petersburg, who is looking for distraction in the country. He comes up behind Tatiana as she looks the mirror. She is startled, then fascinated by this aloof stranger. Lensky dances a solo, then a duet with Olga. Onegin speaks to Tatiana, but dismisses her as an over-romantic girl.

Scene 2. Tatiana's bedroom. Tatiana has fallen in love with Onegin. We see her dreams of him in the 'mirror' *pas de deux*: as she looks into the frame of the mirror, we see first a reflection of Tatiana, then Onegin, who steps out of the frame to dance with her. Tatiana wakes up to write him a passionate love letter, which she gives to the nurse to deliver.

Act II. Scene 1. Tatiana's birthday party. The provincial gentry celebrate Tatiana's birthday. Onegin is bored, struggling to hide his yawns. He has received Tatiana's letter. In a quiet moment, he tells her that he cannot love her, and tears the letter up, annoyed by her distress. Prince Gremin, a distant relative who is in love with Tatiana, is also a guest at the party. Madame Larina hopes for a brilliant marriage for her daughter, but Tatiana, troubled by Onegin's rejection, hardly notices him.

Onegin decides to provoke Lensky by flirting with Olga. Lensky is furious, and challenges his friend to a duel.

Scene 2. The duel. Tatiana and Olga try to reason with Lensky. Still angry with his friend's betrayal and his fiancée's fickleness, he insists that the duel goes ahead. He is killed by Onegin.

Act III. Scene 1. St Petersburg, the palace of Prince Gremin. Years later, Onegin returns to St Petersburg, having travelled the world. At a ball at the palace of Prince Gremin, he is astonished to meet Tatiana again. Now an elegant, sophisticated woman, she dances a gentle duet with her husband, Gremin. Onegin falls in love with this new Tatiana, and is appalled by his mistake in rejecting her.

Scene 2. Tatiana's boudoir. Onegin has written a love-letter to Tatiana, asking to see her. She does not want to meet him, and clings to her husband, trying to persuade him to stay with her. After he leaves, Onegin arrives and declares his love for her. Tatiana is tempted, but rejects him, tearing up his letter and ordering him to leave.

Cranko's *Onegin* is built around its four main roles, narrowing the focus from his sources in Pushkin and Tchaikovsky. The story includes a party and a ball scene, both of which became dance set pieces in Tchaikovsky's opera, but Cranko rarely looks beyond the central characters, particularly Tatiana. The role was created for his muse Marcia Haydée, who would also be his Kate in *The Taming of the Shrew*. In both ballets, he cast Haydée as an unconventional heroine, at odds with her family and driven by her emotions.

His Tatiana can't help expressing herself, caught up in her book or falling headlong for Onegin. By contrast, the ballet's anti-hero is not so much repressed as repressive, dressed in black with aloof, controlling gestures.

That contrast changes in the two big *pas de deux*, which dominate the ballet. The poem's celebrated 'letter' scene becomes a passionate duet as Tatiana dances with the dream of Onegin she has conjured from her mirror. In the dream Onegin responds to her, but remains remote and unknowable. In the second *pas de deux*, as Tatiana rejects Onegin, he becomes violently demonstrative, hanging onto her wrists as she tries to walk away, or encircling her with his arms, trapping her without touching her. In these acrobatic duets, Tatiana is swung through the air, slid across the floor, flipped and dipped and spun. Cranko matches his lifts to the climaxes of the score, coasting over the music to create a gymnastically breathless style for his impassioned, overwrought characters.

Cranko's focus on Tatiana can push the story off balance. He even puts his heroine and Olga into the duel scene, where their frenzied pleading distracts the dilemma facing Onegin and Lensky. Pushkin's portrait of men trapped in an honour system, with Lensky losing his life in a quarrel he knows to be meaningless, is a key part of the poem; ironically, Pushkin himself would die in a duel.

Song of the Earth (Das Lied von der Erde)

Choreography: Kenneth MacMillan
Music: Gustav Mahler, *Das Lied von der Erde*
Designs: Nicholas Georgiadis
Premiere: 7 November 1965, the Stuttgart Ballet, Stuttgart
Original cast: *the Woman* Marcia Haydée; *the Man* Ray Barra; *the Messenger* Egon Madsen

Mahler wrote *Das Lied von der Erde* in response to a personal crisis: his young daughter had died of scarlet fever and he had been diagnosed with the heart condition that would kill him. Soon after these two crises, he read a translation of Chinese poems from the T'ang dynasty, describing the beauty and transience of life. Setting the poems, he added his own final lines:

The dear Earth blossoms in spring and grows green anew
  Everywhere and forever the luminous blue of distant space!
  Forever . . . forever . . . forever . . . forever . . .

MacMillan's ballet is about death, seen as an inevitable and not unkindly part of life. Wearing a half-mask, the Messenger of Death is present throughout the ballet, sometimes joining in the dances. (In Germany he was called 'der Ewige', the eternal one.) Describing his theme, MacMillan said: 'a man and a woman; death takes the man; they both return to her and at the end of the ballet, we find that in death there is the promise of renewal.'9

MacMillan had hoped to create a ballet to *Das Lied von der Erde* as early as 1959. His proposal was repeatedly turned down by the board of the Royal Opera House, which was nervous of the expense of the musical forces and of using a major concert work for ballet. In 1965, disillusioned by the casting politics that had surrounded his *Romeo and Juliet*, MacMillan staged the work in Stuttgart. A huge success, it was immediately acquired by The Royal Ballet. It is staged in simple practice costumes against a plain cyclorama. The tenor and mezzo-soprano are placed at either side of the stage.

Synopsis

The first song, 'The Drinking Song of Earthly Woe', shows the man dancing with five male companions, leaping and celebrating. At the end, the Messenger claims the Man. In the second song, 'The Lonely One in Autumn', the Woman and three companions dance duets with four men. Left alone, she dances with the Messenger, and is left grieving.

The next three songs show the pleasures of the world. In the third song, 'Of Youth', young people enjoy themselves by a pool and a porcelain pavilion. The ballet has no scenery, but the dancers evoke it, standing on their heads to suggest the reflections in the water. At the end of the song one woman leaps, and is caught by the Messenger.

There are more touches of mime in the fourth song, 'Of Beauty': women pick lotuses by a river bank when a group of young horsemen ride up. The fifth song, 'The Drunkard in Springtime', shows the Man with three companions – but one is the Messenger, and the Man falls into his arms.

The final section, 'Farewell', takes up half the work. The Messenger brings the Man back to the Woman; the three stand together, rocking from side to side. The Man and the Woman dance together before he must leave. Their *pas de deux* is 'like a ritual – impassive, as if they're in the grip of fate', remembered Stuttgart Ballet dancer Reid Anderson. Left alone, the Woman freezes, looking back over her shoulder. She makes a winding journey across the stage, passing through the *corps de ballet* like a woman in a dark forest. Finally, she crosses the stage alone in gliding, rippling bourrées to Mahler's outpouring of sound. The Messenger returns with the Man – who now wears a half-mask, like the Messenger's – come to greet her. Side by side, as the music closes, they walk slowly forwards, reaching into space.

One of MacMillan's most admired ballets, *Song of the Earth* moves between abstract movement and moments of literal imagery. Although MacMillan denied that Martha Graham's style had been a conscious influence, there's a modern dance quality in the ballet's deep *pliés*, flexed feet and grounded movements. In particular, the vocabulary for the Woman is both simple and distinctive, her lines clean but tilted with bends at the waist and knee; the shapes look both unadorned and feminine. Describing the Woman's role, MacMillan told Marcia Haydée, 'Marcia, it's you, as a human being. What you are, that's what I want.'[10]

Notre-Dame de Paris

Choreography: Roland Petit
Music: Maurice Jarre
Sets: René Allio
Costumes: Yves Saint-Laurent
Premiere: 11 December 1966, Paris Opéra Ballet, Paris Opéra, Paris
Original cast: *Quasimodo* Roland Petit; *Esmeralda* Claire Motte; *Frollo* Cyril Atanasov; *Phoebus* Jean-Pierre Bonnefous

Roland Petit had left the Paris Opéra Ballet in 1944, seeking chances to create his own choreography. Returning to the company after more than twenty years, he chose a classic French subject and staged it with cabaret chic.

The costumes are by Yves Saint-Laurent, who was quickly establishing himself as a major fashion designer: he had just shown his famous 'Mondrian' dress on Paris catwalks. There's an echo of that dress, and of the painter Mondrian's geometric paintings, in the colour-blocked costumes for Phoebus and his soldiers. Other costumes have a suggestion of corsets – a Petit trademark – from Esmeralda's bodice to the cut of Quasimodo's jerkin. The large *corps de ballet* is dressed in short tunics in a range of bright colours, giving a pop art quality to Petit's unison choreography. René Allio's set evokes a stylised fifteenth-century Paris, with moving platforms that can whisk the cast into place.

The music was by another man of the moment: Maurice Jarre had recently written Oscar-winning scores for the films *Lawrence of Arabia* (1962) and *Doctor Zhivago* (1965) – both large-scale epics with huge casts. For Petit, he wrote an insistent, percussive score.

Synopsis

Act I. The Fool's Festival. In front of the cathedral of Notre-Dame, peasants gather to celebrate the Fool's Festival, at which the funniest or most grotesque buffoon will be chosen as the 'Fool's Pope'. Quasimodo, the hunchbacked bell-ringer of Notre-Dame, appears. The dancer who plays Quasimodo lifts his right shoulder throughout the ballet, with his right elbow bent, often swinging the other arm and moving with bent legs. Cruelly, the crowd choose him as their pope.

The prayer. Claude Frollo, the archdeacon of Notre-Dame, calls the people to prayer. Quasimodo crouches at his feet.

As the crowd gathers in a tight circle, we see a lifted arm shaking a tambourine over the dancers' heads. The crowd parts to reveal Esmeralda, the beautiful gypsy girl. Frollo, who is obsessed with Esmeralda, orders Quasimodo to abduct her. Quasimodo chases her across Paris, over rooftops and through dens of thieves.

Esmeralda escapes from Quasimodo with the help of handsome Captain Phoebus and his soldiers. She falls in love with the captain. Quasimodo is arrested and sent off to the pillory. Esmeralda pities him and brings him water. Phoebus marches at the head of his soldiers, thinking of Esmeralda.

Phoebus and Esmeralda meet in a tavern, surrounded by soldiers and prostitutes. The lovers' duet is actually a *pas de trois*, with Frollo lurking in the shadows, sometimes partnering Esmeralda, unseen and unacknowledged. He stabs Phoebus and flees, leaving Esmeralda to be arrested for the murder.

Esmeralda is convicted and led towards the gallows. Quasimodo breaks through the guards and carries her away to Notre-Dame. Fugitives have the right to claim sanctuary in the cathedral, so Frollo is forced to stop the crowd from following her.

Act II. In the bell-tower of Notre-Dame, Quasimodo swings from the bell-ropes. Esmeralda appears and thanks him, touching his raised shoulder. They dance together, until Quasimodo rocks her to sleep.

When Quasimodo leaves, Frollo comes in pursuit of Esmeralda. When she rejects him, he hits her.

The cathedral is attacked: the right of sanctuary has been revoked, and crowds pour into Notre-Dame, despite Quasimodo's attempts to hold them off with molten lead. Esmeralda is carried off to the gallows, where she is hanged. In fury, Quasimodo strangles Frollo, and carries Esmeralda's body back to Notre-Dame.

Roland Petit was best known for his sense of theatre, more than for the details of his choreography. *Notre-Dame de Paris* takes this quality to extremes, with fashionable designs, leading roles that make the most of interpreters' personalities, and very little dancing. Where Jules Perrot's *Esmeralda*, the Romantic ballet based on the same novel, evoked teaming crowds of individuals, Petit moves his large *corps de ballet* in blocks, with simple, very repetitive steps and patterns. The roles of Quasimodo (which Petit created for himself) and Esmeralda have proved attractive to star dancers: the ballet is in the repertory of companies including La Scala and the Bolshoi Ballet.

Concerto

Choreography: Kenneth MacMillan
Music: Dmitri Shostakovich, Piano Concerto No. 2
Designs: Jürgen Rose
Premiere: 30 November 1966, Deutsche Oper Ballet, Deutsche Oper, Berlin
Original cast: Didi Carli, Falco Kapuste, Lynn Seymour, Rudolf Holz, Rudolf Kesselheim

MacMillan's *Concerto* is a jazzy pure-dance work, the first he created after taking over as director of the Ballet of the Deutsche Oper. It was designed to challenge and show off a young company, with drilled *corps de ballet* movements and several prominent solo roles.

In the first and last movements, blocks of dancers march in unison, with many quick changes of direction. The costumes are bright and simple, ballet tunics in yellow and orange.

The ballet is dominated by its central movement, a lyrical duet. MacMillan was inspired by the sight of ballerina Lynn Seymour warming up before rehearsal. 'I used to become fascinated by what she was doing rather than what I was supposed to be doing,' he said, 'and I decided to incorporate the idea of the *barre* work into the choreography.'[11] The ballerina's partner supports her, often holding his arms outstretched to form a human version of the *barre* in a rehearsal studio, while she moves in luxurious stretches backwards and forwards. Three other couples move behind them in silhouette.

The last movement opens with a long virtuoso solo for a female dancer. Originally planned as a duet, it became a solo role when a dancer was injured. It's followed by dances for *corps de ballet* and a finale with the whole cast.

Jewels

Choreography: George Balanchine
Music: *Emeralds* Gabriel Fauré, music for *Shylock* and *Pelléas et Mélisande; Rubies* Igor Stravinsky, *Capriccio for Piano and Orchestra;*

Diamonds Pyotr Ilych Tchaikovsky, Symphony No. 3 in D major (last three movements)

Scenery: Peter Harvey

Costumes: Karinska

Premiere: 13 April 1967, New York City Ballet, New York State Theater, New York

Original cast: *Emeralds*: Violette Verdy, Conrad Ludlow, Mimi Paul, Francisco Moncion; *Rubies*: Patricia McBride, Edward Villella; *Diamonds*: Suzanne Farrell, Jacques d'Amboise

Jewels is an evening of three linked ballets: *Emeralds, Rubies, Diamonds*. The idea came to Balanchine after a visit to the showroom of the jeweller Van Cleef and Arpels. 'I like jewels,' Balanchine said. 'I'm an Oriental – from Georgia in the Caucasus, and a Russian. I would cover myself with jewels.' He also added, 'The ballet had nothing to do with jewels. The dancers are just dressed like jewels.'[12] Each ballet has a colour-coded back-drop and costumes; Balanchine did consider a sapphire section, to be danced to music by Arnold Schoenberg, but decided against it: blue shows up less well onstage.

The finished work, 'the first full-length abstract ballet', suggested the scale and confidence of New York City Ballet, now firmly installed in its purpose-built home at Lincoln Center. The company also showed off its youngest generation of ballerinas, particularly the twenty-two-year-old Suzanne Farrell, Balanchine's latest muse.

Emeralds, danced to little-known theatre music by Fauré, is French and romantic in mood. The women wear long tulle skirts, while the men are courtly cavaliers. The first ballerina's solo is full of curling hand and wrist gestures, as if she were admiring her bracelets. the second, danced to the Sicilienne from *Pelléas et Mélisande*, is perfumed and feminine; at one point, the dancer holds her skirts out as she skips through lively footwork. There are also contrasting *pas de deux* and a bright *pas de trois*. An ensemble looks like the end of the ballet, but there is a curious epilogue. The dancers walk slowly to and fro, gradually dispersing, until the three cavaliers are left alone onstage.

Balanchine denied that *Rubies* was about America – the music is by Stravinsky, a fellow Russian – but there's a jazzy, vaudeville quality to the dancing. Like Petipa, Balanchine was more interested in choreographing for women than for men – but there are exceptions, and *Rubies* is one of them. It has a virtuoso male role at its heart, created for Edward Villella, full of jogging runs, corkscrew turns, syncopated leaps and spins. In the *pas de deux*, the man takes the ballerina's weight as she tilts way off balance. The second leading woman has big, 'showgirl' steps, dancing alone or partnered by four men in a high-kicking echo of the Rose Adagio from *The Sleeping Beauty*. The women wear short tunics, the *corps de ballet* prancing and strutting like a chorus line.

Diamonds, danced to music by Tchaikovsky, is an evocation of St Petersburg classicism, with the women in white tutus. It opens with a female ensemble, but the heart of the piece is a *pas de deux* to the second movement of the Tchaikovsky symphony. Meeting from opposite corners, the ballerina and her partner dance with courtly authority. If the balances in *Rubies* have a high-wire quality, those in *Diamonds* create a more intimate drama. The critic Arlene Croce described it as 'a long, supported *adagio* the point of which is to let us see how little support she actually needs'.[13] The ballerina acknowledges her partner, but does not rely on him, remaining remote and elusive. The duet is followed by an airy scherzo, with entries for the ballerina and her partner. In the final movement, the female *corps de ballet* is joined by male partners for a grand polonaise.

Lincoln Kirstein called the *Diamonds* finale:

> one of the best examples of Balanchine's applause-machines ... The audience's empathy and instinctive appetite for block-busting muscular effects devour a big crescendo, gulping at a stage crammed with uniform, symmetrical, head-on movement, and firm primary gesture while the big orchestra builds to a smashing curtain tableau.

Jewels was Balanchine's greatest publicity coup. Promoted with glamorous photo-shoots of ballerinas dripping with precious stones, it was an instant box-office hit. Decades on, at a time when evening-length productions are popular, *Jewels* is a much easier sell than a 'Balanchine triple bill' would be. As Kirstein wrote, 'the very title sounds expensive before a step is seen'.[14] The irresistible name has helped to make *Jewels* one of Balanchine's most widely performed ballets: at the time of writing, thirteen companies have acquired it, including the Bolshoi, the Mariinsky, the Paris Opéra and The Royal Ballet.

Yet it's a fragile work, tailored to the talents of its original cast, less robustly constructed than masterworks such as *Serenade* or *Theme and Variations*. With its misty, remote atmosphere and patchwork of Fauré, *Emeralds* is, as Violette Verdy admitted, 'a difficult way to begin. The audience does not warm up.'[15] For all its high spirits, *Rubies* can tip into coarseness, while the invention in *Diamonds* thins out. It takes an authoritative, stylish performance to give *Jewels* its gemstone glitter.

The Taming of the Shrew (Der Widerspenstigen Zähmung)

Choreography: John Cranko
Music: Kurt-Heinz Stolze after Domenico Scarlatti
Designs: Elizabeth Dalton
Premiere: 16 March 1969, The Stuttgart Ballet, Würtembergische Staatstheater, Stuttgart
Original cast: *Kate* Marcia Haydée; *Petrucchio* Richard Cragun; *Bianca* Susanne Hanke; *Gremio* Egon Madsen; *Lucentio* Heinz Clauss; *Hortensio* John Neumeier

For the twenty-first century, *The Taming of the Shrew* is one of Shakespeare's most problematic plays, a romantic comedy that ends with its heroine declaring women's absolute submission to their husbands. Modern theatre stagings struggle with those aspects of the play, but Cranko's version breezes through them, creating a broad slapstick comedy.

The music is arranged for orchestra and harpsichord, using repeated motifs for characters and moods, such as the 'battling' theme that accompanies Kate's explosions of rage. Elizabeth Dalton's designs place the ballet in an Elizabethan setting.

Synopsis

Act I. Outside Baptista's house. The fop Hortensio, the student Lucentio and the elderly Gremio serenade Bianca, Baptista's pretty daughter. Kate, Bianca's older sister, erupts from the house and chases the suitors away. Baptista explains that Kate, as the elder of the two daughters, must marry first.

A tavern. Petrucchio flirts with two prostitutes, and ends up losing his money (and most of his clothes). Bianca's suitors suggest that he could marry the rich Kate.

Baptista's house. Bianca compares the gifts the three suitors have sent her, trying to decide which man she likes best. She is interrupted by a jealous outburst from Kate. Petrucchio arrives with the three suitors, now disguised as teachers of singing, dancing and music. In the 'lessons', each suitor woos her. Gremio's squeaky 'singing' is voiced by the orchestra, Hortensio is more interested in posing with the mandolin than he is in Bianca; Lucentio, who dances with her, is the most appealing. Kate reacts violently against Petrucchio's declarations of love, assuming he is mocking her, but finally agrees to marry him.

The street. The neighbours joke on the way to Kate's wedding, finding it hard to take the marriage seriously. The three suitors join them, each hopeful that he can soon marry Bianca.

Baptista's house. Kate is dressed for the wedding, but Petrucchio is late. When he arrives, bizarrely dressed, he insults the priest, trips up the wedding guests, and carries off the bride.

Act II. The journey to Petrucchio's house. On the way, riding a horse on wheels, Petrucchio starts 'taming' Kate, refusing to let her drink. When they arrive at his house, he puts out the fire and rejects the food, throwing it away. Kate spends a cold, hungry night alone in the kitchen.

The Carnival. Back in the city, the other characters join in the carnival. A masked stranger greets Hortensio and then Gremio. Believing her to be Bianca, each eagerly agrees to marry her. Too late, they discover they have married the two prostitutes, who were bribed and disguised by Lucentio.

Petrucchio's house. Kate is still cold and hungry, and still being teased by Petrucchio. At last she gives in. In their *pas de deux*, they back towards one another, prickly – she jumps away, and he catches her by her back foot and draws her, hopping, towards him. The dance is still full of lifts and moments of resistance, but it's gentler: when she cries, he rocks her. The quarrel softens to become teasing, ending in a laughing heap on the floor.

The journey to Bianca's wedding. Returning on horseback, Petrucchio teases Kate again, but this time she joins in.

Bianca's wedding. The four new husbands make a bet on whose wife will be most obedient. To everybody's surprise, Kate wins, coming when her husband calls her, an elegant and dutiful wife. Left alone, she and Petrucchio dance lovingly together.

In *The Taming of the Shrew*, Cranko kept the basic narrative of Shakespeare's play, but drops the awkward framing device of Christopher Sly and adds the subplot in which Lucentio tricks Gremio and Hortensio into marrying prostitutes. This new material underlines Cranko's fluency with narrative, turning all his plot twists into easily read action. It also shows his broad approach to the story: you're not supposed to worry about whether these extra marriages will be unhappy.

Two years earlier, Richard Burton and Elizabeth Taylor had starred in Franco Zeffirelli's film version of the play, which may have influenced Cranko: it adds lots of physical comedy for Petrucchio's friends, including disguises, and also introduces Taylor's Kate in a violent, wordless tantrum.

Cranko created Kate for Marcia Haydée, an unconventional ballerina with strong stage presence and a distinctive personality. 'Marcia is so funny because she is so sad,'[16] he said. She gave a vulnerability to the aggressively confrontational Kate, who attacks the suitors without provocation, standing with flat feet and fists on hips. Dancing with Petrucchio, she bicycles the air with flexed feet, or pummels him with her fists. Petrucchio's easy, devil-may-care personality is expressed through big turns and jumps. They are contrasted with Kate's sister Bianca and her suitor Lucentio, who dance a more formal, conventional *pas de deux* that tells us little about them. In this ballet, Cranko has little interest in dancing for dancing's own sake: the steps are there to tell the story, always moving the plot forwards or revealing the characters' reactions.

Dances at a Gathering

Choreography: Jerome Robbins
Music: Frédéric Chopin: Mazurka op. 63, no. 3; Waltz, op. 69, no. 2; Mazurka, op. 33, no. 3; Mazurkas, op. 6, nos 2 and 4; op. 7, no 4 and 5; op. 24, no. 2; Waltz, op. 42; Waltz, op. 34, no. 2; Mazurka, op. 56, no. 2; Etude, op. 25, no. 4; Waltz, op. 34, no. 1; Waltz, op. 70, no. 2; Etude, op. 25, no. 5; Etude, op. 10, no. 2; Scherzo, op. 20, no. 1; Nocturne, op. 15, no. 1.
Designs: Joe Eula
Premiere: 8 May 1969, New York City Ballet, New York State Theater,
Original cast: Allegra Kent, Sara Leland, Kay Mazzo, Patricia McBride, Violette Verdy, Anthony Blum, John Clifford, Robert Maiorano, John Prinz, Edward Villella

Dances at a Gathering started as an idea for a duet. Robbins wanted to make a dance for Patricia McBride and Edward Villella, but as he listened to Chopin, he wanted to add two more couples. In a busy rehearsal schedule, they weren't always available, so he worked with four more dancers – adding more dances, to more Chopin. Worried that the ballet was getting too long, he showed it to Balanchine. 'Make more,' Balanchine said, 'make it like peanuts.'[17] Telling the story, Robbins would mime Balanchine popping nuts into his mouth: just one more, and then another.

The work was Robbins' return to ballet. He had always moved between disciplines, working on musicals and film as well as ballet, but he had spent most of the 1960s concentrating on theatre. He returned with an immense hit: from the first performance, it was loved by audiences and critics alike.

The dances in *Dances at a Gathering* have an improvisatory quality. Reflecting the rehearsal process, there are never more than six dancers onstage until the very end. The women wear chiffon dresses, the men tights, shirts and boots; they sketch steps, move with touches of folk dance, speed up or peel off into different groups. Robbins loved watching dancers at work in the studio, a quality he had dramatised in *Afternoon of a Faun*; in *Dances at a Gathering*, he puts that absorbed quality onstage.

In the first solo, a man dressed in brown puts his hand to the ground. Walking away from the audience, he sketches in steps as if remembering or trying something out. The dancers flow through different groups and combinations: two men in a competitive mazurka, three women grouped together. Halfway through, a woman in green appears for the first time, sketching in glamorous steps without doing them full out. A group pose as if for photographs. Even when the partnering is complex, with women thrown from partner to partner, the mood remains relaxed and airy. In the final piece of music, the whole cast returns to the stage. The man in brown again puts his hand to the floor, and all the dancers seem to watch something moving in the distance. Taking partners, they bow to each other, and stroll away as the curtain falls.

It's so easy to project images and stories onto *Dances at a Gathering*, to compare its steps to moods and situations. Robbins got annoyed by this habit. Writing to the magazine *Ballet Review*, he asked the editor to 'print in large, emphatic and capital letters' the following:

THERE ARE NO STORIES TO ANY OF THE DANCES IN DANCES AT A GATHERING. THERE ARE NO PLOTS AND NO ROLES. THE DANCERS ARE THEMSELVES DANCING WITH EACH OTHER TO THAT MUSIC IN THAT SPACE.

Thank you very much.[18]

In the Night

Choreography: Jerome Robbins
Music: Frédéric Chopin, Nocturnes: op. 27, no. 1; op. 55, nos 1 and 2; op. 9, no. 2
Designs: Joe Eula
Lighting: Thomas Skelton
Premiere: 29 January 1970, New York City Ballet, New York State Theater, New York

Original cast: Kay Mazzo, Anthony Blum, Violette Verdy, Peter Martins, Patricia McBride, Francisco Moncion

Robbins had insisted that the Chopin dances in *Dances at a Gathering* were just dances. When he made a follow-up work, another ballet to Chopin's music, the three contrasting duets created their own thread of drama. After the happy experience of creating *Dances at a Gathering, In the Night* had a much more painful beginning. Recovering from a relationship break-up, Robbins experienced a bad acid trip. Shortly afterwards, he snapped his Achilles tendon. For a choreographer who had always moved and demonstrated when creating, it was a devastating blow. At last, on crutches, he was able to get back to *In the Night*, which proved to be a darker, less carefree approach to Chopin. '*In the Night* is Jerome Robbins' first ballet to deal with mature people,' wrote Arlene Croce.[19]

Although his dancers suggest different kinds of relationships, they also look like established couples; the second and third pair, in particular, have a sense of living with consequences. The Chopin pieces Robbins chose were all Nocturnes, night pieces; the work has a backdrop of a night sky with stars. In the first production, the dancers wore soft coloured dresses and shirts, as they had in *Dances at a Gathering*. When it was staged at The Royal Ballet in 1973, Anthony Dowell designed much grander costumes, with ball gowns for the women, regimental tunics or short jackets for the men. Robbins loved the costumes, and adopted this look for future productions.

The first couple is young and ecstatic: the man turns his parter topsy turvy, as if she were head over heels in love. Yet it's also a courtly dance, with formal bows as well as trusting partnering.

The second pair is sophisticated, autumnal. The dancers walk calmly about the stage, with gentle lifts and mirrored gestures, and a touch of deeper feeling in the trembling beat of the woman's feet when her partner lifts her.

The last couple is probably smashing crockery: the dancers rush on passionately, confront one another or withdraw. 'Jerry definitely said we were having an argument,' remembered Francisco Moncion, who danced the role in the original cast, ' "It's one of those on-again, off-again affairs." '[20] At last the woman returns to the man, gently touching him from his shoulders to his feet, then sinks to the floor in front of him, bowed over. Taking her outstretched hands, he raises her up, lifts her high overhead, and cradles her in his arms. In the last Nocturne, all three couples assemble, acknowledge one another and go their separate ways.

Who Cares?

Choreography: George Balanchine
Music: George Gershwin, orchestrated by Hershy Kay: 'Strike Up the Band'; 'Sweet and Low Down'; 'Somebody Loves Me'; 'Bidin' My Time'; ' 'Swonderful'; 'That Certain Feeling'; 'Do Do Do'; 'Lady Be Good'; 'The Man I Love'; 'I'll Build a Stairway to Paradise'; 'Embraceable You'; 'Fascinatin' Rhythm'; 'Who Cares?'; 'My One and Only'; 'Liza'; 'Clap Yo' Hand's; 'I Got Rhythm'
Costumes: Karinska
Decor: Jo Mielziner
Lighting: Ronald Bates
Premiere: 5 February 1970, New York City Ballet, New York State Theater, New York
Original cast: Karin von Aroldingen, Patricia McBride, Marnee Morris, Jacques d'Amboise

Balanchine and Gershwin had been due to work together on the movie *Goldwyn Follies* when Gershwin died, tragically young. Thirty years later, Balanchine made a ballet out of a selection of Gershwin songs. Although he had worked on Broadway in Gershwin's era, *Who Cares?* evokes 1930s show dances only in passing: like *Western Symphony*, it is a classical dance suite to popular music. Balanchine also commissioned Hershy Kay, the composer of *Western Symphony*, to orchestrate Gershwin's songs, which spreads a thick layer of 1970s light-entertainment glitz over Gershwin's fascinating rhythms.

The first eight songs are staged as a suite of classical dances for an ensemble of fifteen women and five men, with some hoofer steps and showgirl poses (something Balanchine had already evoked in ballets such as *Rubies*).

In the second half, the mood turns late-night and more romantic, with focus on four soloists, a man and three women. 'The Man I Love' is a romantic duet with long 1930s lines. 'I'll build a Stairway to Paradise' is a jazzily athletic solo for a second woman, while a third woman is swift and reckless. The man partners all three, and dances his own solos with throwaway virtuosity.

Symphony in Three Movements

Choreography: George Balanchine
Music: Igor Stravinsky
Lighting: Ronald Bates
Premiere: 18 June 1972, New York City Ballet, New York State Theater, Lincoln Center, New York

Original cast: Sara Leland, Marnee Morris, Lynda Yourth, Helgi Tomasson, Edward Villella, Robert Weiss

Stravinsky died in 1971. A year later, New York City Ballet held the Stravinsky Festival, with an astonishing twenty-two new ballets in a single week, alongside existing Stravinsky ballets. The audience was offered shots of vodka on the way out because, Balanchine said, 'In Russia we don't mourn, we drink the health of the guy who died.'[21] The Stravinsky Festival revealed the power of Balanchine's New York City Ballet, while several of those new works quickly established themselves in international repertory. Given the pressures of the Stravinsky Festival, Balanchine created the ballet – with its complex score, large cast and intricate construction – in a single week.

Stravinsky composed his *Symphony in Three Movements* during the Second World War, for different films. Unusually, he admitted that the music expressed his impressions of the war – but insisted that the symphony itself was not programmatic. Nor is Balanchine's ballet, but it responds to the filmic moods and energy of the symphony.

Symphony in Three Movements opens with the *corps de ballet* of sixteen women standing in a diagonal line – and this simple grouping has such a sense of slicing across space that audiences often applaud at the sight of it. Dressed in leotards, the women wear their hair in ponytails: there's a sharp contrast between the cute youthfulness of the style and the way they move as part of a drastic machine.

It's a large-scale work, with six soloists and five supporting couples. Dancers leap on, followed by small entourages, or spin their way among the jogging *corps*. The second movement is a languorous *pas de deux*, both sensuous and remote. Dancing with cool deliberation, the leading couple move with bent knees and angled palms, folding their hands in and out so that their fingers almost touch. Although there is some partnering, the dancers keep an emotional and sometimes physical distance. Even when they wind their arms around each other, they remain an inch apart.

The *pas de deux* is a moment of calm before the ballet roars onward, the ensemble returning in driving dances, ending with the whole cast assembled in a geometric formation.

Stravinsky Violin Concerto (originally Violin Concerto)

Choreography: George Balanchine
Music: Igor Stravinsky, Violin Concerto in D major

Premiere: 18 June 1972, New York City Ballet, New York State Theater, New York

Original cast: Karin von Aroldingen, Jean-Pierre Bonnefous, Kay Mazzo, Peter Martins

Balanchine had choreographed Stravinsky's Violin Concerto for the Ballet Russe de Monte Carlo in 1941, under the name *Balustrade* – a work that had been harshly reviewed and had few performances. His new version was named for its score, reflecting Balanchine's frustration with fancy titles. 'What's *Balustrade*?' he said to his biographer, Bernard Taper:

> Stravinsky never wrote *Balustrade*; he wrote *Violin Concerto*. The ballet should be announced as what it is. Then musicians can come, the young people who love music and who want to hear the composition – they'll know what they're getting. They don't have to look at the ballet if it bores them. And that's fine with me, that's wonderful.[22]

In choreographing the Violin Concerto, Balanchine used the four movements for two duets, framed by two ensemble movements. The ballet is danced in practice costume: the standard Balanchine uniform of white T-shirt, black tights and white socks for the men, while the women wear leotards with black footless tights and *pointe* shoes.

The opening toccata is bright and exuberant, bringing on the four soloists one at a time, each with a *corps de ballet* of four. One ballerina and four men stand stock still as the music starts, not moving a muscle as Stravinsky launches into the melody. Suddenly the ballerina kicks up her leg and raises her arms, joining hands with the men in a twisting, syncopated line. Making different entries, the soloists switch between male and female ensembles, building different self-contained patterns. One man leads on a prancing chain of women; another hurtles around the stage with a *corps* of men.

The first aria is a duet with a competitive edge. The ballerina and her partner spring into braced positions; she arches back into a crab position and moves around the stage, rearing upright to face her partner. It's angular and full of unexpected contortions.

The mood changes completely for the second aria. This ballerina clings to her partner, wrapping herself around him then standing sheltered in his arms. At the end of the movement, he kneels and she leans against him, his arm curved over her face like a blindfold. This duet was created for Peter Martins and Kay Mazzo, who also danced Balanchine's *Duo Concertant*; the two ballets share linked imagery, with Mazzo as a muse figure manipulated by Martins.

In the final capriccio, dancers arrive in groups to join lively, folk-flavoured steps, skipping on their heels and hopping to Stravinsky's intricate rhythms, Gradually, one group joins another until the whole cast bursts into the finale.

Adagio Hammerklavier

Choreography: Hans van Manen
Music: Ludwig van Beethoven, Adagio from Piano Sonata No. 29, op. 106
Designs: Jean-Paul Vroom
Lighting: David K. H. Elliott
Premiere: 4 October 1973, Dutch National Ballet, Stadsschouwburg, Amsterdam
Original cast: Monique Sand, Sonja Marchiolli, Alexandra Radius, Henny Jurriëns, Francis Sinceretti, Han Ebbelaar

Born in 1932, Hans van Manen trained in ballet and danced in the Netherlands. Escaping the country's 'ballet war' of rival companies, he went to France to join Roland Petit's Ballets de Paris before becoming a founder member of Nederlands Dans Theater, a breakaway group established in 1960. He was the new company's resident choreographer and joint artistic director from 1961 to 1971, first alongside Benjamin Harkarvy and then with Glen Tetley. The company drew on both classical ballet and American modern dance, qualities that would remain central to van Manen's own style. After leaving NDT, he worked as a prolific freelance choreographer, with periods as resident choreographer of Dutch National Ballet and back at NDT. In recent years, van Manen has worked closely with the Mariinsky Ballet.

Like many of van Manen's works, *Adagio Hammerklavier* is a plotless work with a strong edge of sexual drama. He often focuses on relations, and tensions, between the sexes, mixing formal patterns of choreography with eroticised and sometimes fetishised details. His 1972 ballet *Twilight* is a *pas de deux* in which the woman wears stiletto heels that she eventually removes.

One of van Manen's most admired works, *Adagio Hammerklavier* was created for three leading couples, all due to appear in Dutch National Ballet's production of *Swan Lake*. The company's schedule left these six dancers free while the rest of the company worked on the production. Van Manen decided to make a ballet for them, inspired by Christoph Eschenbach's recording of Beethoven's piano sonata, which takes the *adagio* at an exceptionally slow tempo. 'I thought "adagio"', van Manen told the critic Edmund Lee. 'You hardly ever see adagio; you see slow motion, but that's different. That's based on total balance. I always think of adagio as a wheel that you push – and that moment where the wheel is still moving, just before it falls.'[23]

The ballet's designs are both simple and slightly fetishised: the men wear a ballet uniform of white tights and bare chests, but add glittering necklaces. The women wear pale chiffon dresses with *pointe* shoes. White curtains billow at the back of the stage.

Created at a time when choreographers were experimenting with ever-rising lifts, *Adagio Hammerklavier* shows women curling and drooping to the floor. From supported *attitudes*, they'll slip down into the splits, then move forwards on their knees. In other sequences, couples move in unison, striking star poses or turning gently to the rippling piano line. With unexpected assertiveness, walks will turn into stamps. The dancing is understated, gaining drama from small turns of the head or changes of pose, small details that break the line of the choreography.

Manon (also L'Histoire de Manon)

Choreography: Kenneth MacMillan
Music: Jules Massenet, compiled by Leighton Lucas with the collaboration of Hilda Gaunt
Design: Nicholas Georgiadis
Premiere: 7 March 1974, The Royal Ballet, The Royal Opera House, London
Original cast: *Manon* Antoinette Sibley; *Des Grieux* Anthony Dowell; *Lescaut, Manon's Brother* David Wall; *Monsieur G.M.* Derek Rencher; *Lescaut's Mistress* Monica Mason; *Gaoler* David Drew; *Beggar Chief* Wayne Sleep

Manon is set in an eighteenth-century world of riches and poverty, full of characters scrambling to get on. The Nicholas Georgiadis designs of the original production underline that struggle: the sumptuous costumes are rich with lace and brocade, but the scenery frames the characters with rags. Squalor and wealth constantly jostle with each other in a story of sex and money. This is also, rumour has it, a ballet that prompts unusually high interval sales of champagne.

MacMillan took his story from Abbé Prévost's novel *Manon Lescaut*, and from the Puccini and Massenet operas based on it. The music is by Massenet, but not from his opera. As with Cranko's *Onegin* (a clear influence on *Manon*), the ballet takes a selection of the composer's other music – from songs, orchestral suites and other operas – and fashions it into a ballet score. Originally, the music was orchestrated by Leighton Lucas. Since 2011, a new orchestration by Martin Yates has been used in productions around the world. In Europe, the ballet is often called *L'Histoire de Manon*, to distinguish it from the Massenet opera.

The melody of Massenet's song 'Crépuscule' becomes a motif associated with Manon herself, and with her signature step: she lifts one foot and circles it in a small *rond de jambe*. The fluttering step can look tentative, provocative or fragile, as Manon rises to riches as a successful courtesan before coming to grief.

Synopsis

Act I. Scene 1. The courtyard of an inn near Paris. The ballet opens with Lescaut, the heroine's brother, sitting in darkness, wrapped in a cloak. As the lights come up, we see him join a throng of actresses, gentlemen, prostitutes and beggars. They include Madame, who keeps a brothel, and Monsieur G. M., a wealthy client. There are set-piece dances for a group of beggars, and for Lescaut's Mistress. He quarrels with her, and warns that she may end up like one of the cartful of convict women who pass through, waiting to be transported overseas. Manon arrives by coach, and greets her brother Lescaut. She is on her way to enter a convent, but the other characters are fascinated by her beauty, and see her as a prospective courtesan. An old gentleman bargains with Lescaut for her, and they go into the inn to discuss it.

Meanwhile, Manon meets Des Grieux, a young student. They fall in love: Des Grieux dances a lyrical solo, followed by a passionate *pas de deux* with Manon. They run away to Paris together, to the dismay of Lescaut and the old gentleman. When G. M. tells Lescaut that he is also interested in Manon, Lescaut agrees to find her for him.

Scene 2. Des Grieux's lodgings in Paris. Des Grieux writes a letter to his father, but Manon interrupts by declaring her love for him. Des Grieux leaves to post the letter. Lescaut and G. M. arrive, bringing diamonds and furs. They dance a decadent *pas de trois*, in which Lescaut urges Manon into greater intimacy with G. M., helping to wind her around his body. She agrees to become G. M.'s mistress, and leaves with him. When Des Grieux returns, Lescaut urges him to accept the situation, and the money they will gain from it.

Act II. Scene 1. A party at Madame's *hôtel particulier*. Gentlemen formally give Madame their swords at the start of the party, before the prostitutes rush in and dance, hitching up their skirts to show off their legs. Clients choose which girl they want, prostitutes quarrel and compete for attention. Lescaut arrives with Des Grieux, who hopes to catch a glimpse of Manon. Lescaut is already drunk, dancing a lurching, off-balance solo and a comic *pas de deux* with his mistress.

Manon makes a grand entrance with Monsieur G. M. Seeing Des Grieux, she is torn between her new riches and her old love. She dances a seductive solo and a spectacular group dance, in which she is passed from hand to hand, carried overhead by many admirers – as the critic Jann Parry wrote, 'swimming in a sea of lust'.[24] G. M. looks on approvingly, and rewards her with a diamond bracelet. Des Grieux begs her to leave with him. She refuses, then persuades him to take G. M.'s money in a card game. Des Grieux is caught cheating, and flees with Manon.

Scene 2. Des Grieux's lodgings. Manon and Des Grieux declare their love, then quarrel over the jewels G. M. has given her. G. M. and Lescaut arrive with the police, and Manon is arrested as a prostitute. In the struggle, Lescaut is shot and killed.

Act III. Scene 1. The port, New Orleans. The Gaoler of the penal colony awaits the arrival of the convicts deported from France. After a dance for the townspeople, the prostitutes are brought off the ship, and dance mournfully. Manon is one of them, accompanied by Des Grieux, who has claimed to be her husband. The Gaoler shows an interest in Manon.

Scene 2. The Gaoler's room. The Gaoler invites Manon to be his mistress, offering her jewels. When she refuses, he forces her to perform oral sex on him. Des Grieux breaks in and kills him.

Scene 3. The swamp. Manon and Des Grieux have escaped into the swamps of Louisiana. Manon is feverish, and sees visions of her former life. She dances a final *pas de deux* with Des Grieux, and dies in his arms.

Manon is a large-scale company ballet, with bustling crowd scenes, *corps de ballet* dances and many small roles. These are acting as well as dancing roles: the choreography for the *corps* can be thin, but The Royal Ballet in particular is noted for the richness of the characterisation in its Hogarthian crowds of prostitutes and clients. (One of the prostitutes in the big second-act party scene is a girl dressed as a boy. Jennifer Jackson, who danced the role at the premiere, was surprised when she saw her costume, and asked MacMillan to explain. 'You're more expensive,'[24] he told her.[25])

The ballet is best known for its central characters and its passionate *pas de deux*. Des Grieux approaches Manon with a lyrical solo, apparently simple but full of tricky, off-balance turns. When they dance together, he holds her just off the floor, her legs crossing in the air. In the bedroom *pas de deux*, often danced as a gala number, Manon stretches out on the floor before Des Grieux, arms twined sensuously overhead. Antoinette Sibley, MacMillan's first-cast Manon, has described how MacMillan wanted to make erotic use of her inner upper arms, Manon's 'special erogenous zone', showing them off. In the last *pas de deux*, as Manon is dying, she launches herself feverishly into her lover's arms.

MacMillan created the role for Sibley and, when she was injured, for Jennifer Penney. The original Des Grieux was Anthony Dowell, whose flowing line is still visible in the lyrical solos MacMillan created for him, with David Wall as the charismatic, amoral Lescaut. Manon herself is open to interpretation: how much is she naïvely swept along by events? how much does she join her brother in his schemes? Her transition from young love to kept woman can be played in many different ways; in the brothel scene, different dancers might show Manon enjoying her newly discovered sexual power, or being more dependent on her protector G. M.; in the last act, she can be pragmatic as she flees the Gaoler, or furious in her fight for life.

Elite Syncopations

Choreography: Kenneth MacMillan
Music: Scott Joplin, Paul Pratt, James Scott, Joseph F. Lamb, Max Morath, Donald Ashwander, Robert Hampton
Designs: Ian Spurling
Premiere: 7 October 1974, The Royal Ballet, Royal Opera House, London
Original cast: Merle Park, Donald MacLeary, Monica Mason, Michael Coleman, Jennifer Penney, David Wall, Vergie Derman, Wayne Sleep

In the early 1970s, ragtime had a revival. A forerunner of jazz, the syncopated, early twentieth-century style featured in new recordings, for example in the 1973 film *The Sting*, which had an Oscar-winning Scott Joplin soundtrack. MacMillan's *Elite Syncopations* was part of the fashion, a light-hearted ballet showing off The Royal Ballet's stars in relaxed comic dances. MacMillan designed it as an antidote to stress and trouble: 'Something short and light and funny,' he said, describing his next ballet, 'which I can toss off and walk away from.'[26]

Ian Spurling's costumes are wildly decorated body tights, with brightly coloured spots, stars, painted-on buttons and sock suspenders, worn with extravagant hats. The musicians, who play onstage, wear costumes in the same style.

Between their numbers, dancers sit on chairs at the sides of the stage, as if sitting out a number in a dance hall. There are references to 1920s social dances, including the cakewalk and the Charleston, along with more contemporary disco references. In one scene, dancers wear numbers on their backs, as if taking part in a dance marathon.

Although there's no story, the dancers are given characterisations and jokes: shy young lovers, a woman shuffling as she straightens her skirt, the company's shortest man (originally Wayne Sleep) mismatched with its tallest woman, a swaggering virtuoso man. The leading ballerina, glamorous in a red hat and white tights spangled with stars, ends up with a host of admirers.

MacMillan also showed a different side to some of his dancers: Monica Mason, who had danced his Chosen Maiden in *The Rite of Spring*, became a bottom-wiggling vamp. In later revivals, audiences have gone on enjoying the sight of new casts letting their hair down.

Push Comes to Shove

Choreography: Twyla Tharp
Music: Franz Joseph Haydn and Joseph Lamb, arranged by David E. Bourne
Costumes: Santo Loquasto
Lighting: Jennifer Tipton
Premiere: 9 January 1976, American Ballet Theatre, Uris Theatre, New York
Original cast: Mikhail Baryshnikov, Marianna Tcherkassky, Martine van Hamel, Clark Tippet, Christopher Aponte

When Mikhail Baryshnikov defected in 1974, he was hungry to try new kinds of movement. *Push Comes to Shove* brought him together with Twyla Tharp, that most eclectic of choreographers. The result was a joyful mixture of classicism, vaudeville, ragtime and hat tricks, a sensational smash hit.

The switches of *Push Come to Shove* start with its music. Tharp chose Haydn's Eighty-Second Symphony, nicknamed 'The Bear'. Then she added ragtime, the Bohemian Rag by Charles Lamb. Having set Baryshnikov between two musical worlds, she also provided him with two ballerinas and a *corps de ballet*, competing for his attention – which itself reflected Baryshnikov's own reputation as a womaniser. The women wear flapper dresses. Baryshnikov's costume is based on what Tharp herself had worn in her 1975 piece *Sue's Leg*, a satin top, velvet trousers and legwarmers in rich russet colours, worn with jazz shoes and a black derby (bowler) hat.

The ballet opens in ragtime. The male lead sidles into the spotlight, slithering through Tharpian spins, stops and quirks, sometimes moving from a classical base. He's joined by two ballerinas, who circle his spotlight and then sneak closer, playing games with the hat before slinking back into the wings.

As the music shifts to Haydn, Tharp adds intricate ensembles to the mix, with different *corps de ballet* groupings, references to *Swan Lake* and *Giselle*, moments where partners get lost in the ensemble, a second hat and a finale awash with comic false endings.

A Month in the Country

Choreography: Frederick Ashton
Music: Frédéric Chopin, arranged by John Lanchbery
Designs: Julia Trevelyan Oman
Premiere: 12 February 1976, The Royal Ballet, Royal Opera House, London
Original cast: *Natalia Petrovna* Lynn Seymour; *Yslaev, her husband* Alexander Grant; *Kolia, their son* Wayne Sleep; *Beliaev, Kolia's tutor* Anthony Dowell; *Vera, Natalia's ward* Denise Nunn; *Rakitin, Natalia's admirer* Derek Rencher; *Katia, the maid* Marguerite Porter

In 1970, Kenneth MacMillan succeeded Frederick Ashton as director of The Royal Ballet. It was a botched handover: MacMillan had accepted the job in good faith, but Ashton wasn't ready to go. After his golden 1960s period, Ashton had almost stopped making ballets.

Encouraged by the success of a gala dance he had made for Lynn Seymour, evoking Isadora Duncan, Ashton decided to adapt Ivan Turgenev's play *A Month in the Country*, in which a handsome young tutor sets a Russian household at odds. Struggling to find a suitable composer, Ashton consulted Isaiah Berlin, an expert on Russian literature, who suggested

Chopin. Ashton's first thought was, 'Oh no, not again' – Jerome Robbins had recently created three ballets to Chopin music – but he soon came round. The finished work includes Variations on 'Là ci darem la mano', the Fantasy on Polish Airs and the Andante spianato and Grande Polonaise. 'Là ci darem la mano', an aria from Mozart's *Don Giovanni*, underlines one theme of the ballet: the tutor, Beliaev, is a less calculating Don Juan, prompting all the women in the household to fall in love with him.

Synopsis

The Yslaev household. Natalia fans herself, while her admirer Rakitin reads to her, her husband reads, her son works at his lessons and Vera plays the piano. Katia, the maid, tells Yslaev that he is needed on the estate, but he has lost his keys: the whole family search for them, until at last Natalia finds them. Beliaev, the new tutor, enters through the French window, bringing a kite for his pupil Kolya. A handsome young man, he immediately fascinates the ballet's women, from Natalia to Katia.

As the characters come and go, they reveal their feelings in a series of *pas de deux*. Rakitin approaches Natalia, but when he tries to tell her he loves her, she confesses that she loves Beliaev. Yslaev interrupts them, and Natalia runs away, weeping.

Beliaev dances with Vera, in a duet that is brotherly on his side but smitten on hers. Overcome by her feelings, she embraces him, but he does not kiss her. Natalia discovers them, orders Beliaev away, and demands an explanation from Vera. Highly emotional, Vera sobs out a confession. Natalia tries to laugh it off, then becomes angry and slaps Vera's face, instantly regretting it. When Rakitin enters, Vera runs out, and he takes Natalia for a walk in the garden.

Beliaev returns, followed by Katia, who flirts with him and feeds him from her basket of strawberries. When she leaves, he notices Natalia's scarf – and tries to hide it when Natalia herself returns. She puts a rose in his buttonhole, and their hands meet. Admitting their feelings, they dance a passionate *pas de deux*.

Vera discovers them in an embrace, and jealously summons the household. Natalia tries to make light of it; she and her husband follow Vera, trying to calm her down. Rakitin tells Beliaev that he must leave. Beliaev bids goodbye to the bewildered Kolya, who doesn't understand why he is leaving. Natalia enters the empty room, full of despair at the loss of Beliaev. She ends her solo leaning against an armchair, her face buried in her arms. Beliaev returns for a last farewell. Without alerting her to his presence, he kisses the trailing ribbons of her dress, throws the rose at her feet, and leaves. She looks up and sees the flower.

A Month in the Country is balanced between subtlety and melodrama. It's full of delicately shaped solos, intricate footwork or yearning lines revealing its characters' feelings – but there are also grand gestures set to big, crashing piano chords, people bursting through double doors, reacting extravagantly – as when Beliaev makes his first entrance, and all the women respond with a collective flurry of emotion.

This balance is there in its heroine, too. Natalia Petrovna is a self-dramatising woman, bored and susceptible, both caught up in her feelings and indulging them. 'In ballet women are never allowed to grow old,' Seymour wrote:

> We must be perpetually young. We must dance teenage virgins and fairies and childlike courtesans . . . Fred gave me the exceptional oppor-tunity to play a mature woman just a few years younger than myself . . . [Natalia Petrovna's] lassitude heightens her panic – endless hot summers await her and the years hopelessly pass and she verges on becoming a spiteful woman. But Ashton stressed her romantic illusions which fade away, leaving her alone and sad.[27]

With its many characters, precise social setting and detailed, frilly designs by Julia Trevelyan Oman, *A Month in the Country* risks fussiness. Yet the ballet also has wonderful dancing, beautifully characterised. Dancing a solo to Chopin's Fantasy on Polish Airs, Beliaev plants one foot behind him, and turns to face it, flexing the foot as he turns. The texture of the movement is gorgeous, suggesting Polish folk dance but also showing Beliaev's grounded simplicity, in contrast to the fluttering emotions of the women around him. Both Vera and Natalia Petrovna move with quick, conversational feet and fluid upper-body movement, but Vera's is faster, higher, closer to hysteria; even when he shows Natalia's selfishness, Ashton is more interested in her feelings, expressed in broader, richer movement. Dancing with Beliaev, she bourrées forwards in his arms, then lifts both legs in a slow sweep, a move-ment of controlled abandon.

Requiem

Choreography: Kenneth MacMillan
Music: Gabriel Fauré

Designs: Yolanda Sonnabend
Premiere: 28 November 1976, The Stuttgart Ballet, Stuttgart
Original cast: Marcia Haydée, Richard Cragun, Egon Madsen, Birgit
Keil, Reid Anderson

John Cranko died suddenly in 1973, after an allergic reaction on a transatlantic flight. A choreographer who had supported and encouraged many other choreographers, he was remembered in a number of dance tributes, including Glen Tetley's *Voluntaries* and MacMillan's *Requiem*. When MacMillan was suffering from stage fright as a young dancer, Cranko treated him as an assistant, asking him to complete phrases of movement, encouraging him to start making ballets.

In a replay of MacMillan's trouble with the Royal Opera House over the music for *Song of the Earth*, MacMillan created *Requiem* in Stuttgart because his own company's board had rejected the idea of staging Fauré. The ballet was an immediate success, and was restaged at The Royal Ballet in 1983.

Yolanda Sonnabend's designs frame the stage with columns of misted glass. The leading woman wears a white gauzy dress, while one of the leading men wears a loincloth that suggests he is a Christ figure. The other dancers wear body tights marked with patterns that suggest vein systems.

MacMillan's vocabulary for *Requiem* is weighted and muscular, with a strong modern dance influence. In the opening Requiem Aeternum, the cast shuffles on, fists raised in grief and anger. Over the course of the ballet, the mood shifts to hope and transcendence. The man's lament is expressed in positions curled on the floor; the dancers strain and crouch. In the Pie Jesu solo, the ballerina dances a naïve, childlike solo, inspired by the sight of MacMillan's own young daughter at play. For the final In Paradisium, the *corps* processes out, some of the women carried high, leaving the ballerina held high by two men, the central man watching her.

Sinfonietta

Choreography: Jiří Kylián
Music: Leoš Janáček, *Sinfonietta*
Designs: Walter Nobbe
Lighting: Tom Skelton
Premiere: 9 June 1978, Nederlands Dans Theater, Spoleto Festival, Charleston, South Carolina

Original cast: Sabine Kupferberg, Nils Christe, Susan McKee, Roslyn Anderson, Eric Hampton, Eve Walstrum, Alida Chase, Gerald Tibbs, Karen Tims, Leigh Matthews, Eric Newton, Ric McCullough, Arlette van Boven, Michael Sanders

Born in Prague, Czechoslovakia, in 1947, Jiří Kylián studied at the National Ballet School and at London's Royal Ballet School. He joined the Stuttgart Ballet in 1968, just as the company rose to international fame. Encouraged to choreograph, he moved towards modern dance, combining high ballet leg extensions with contracting, Martha Graham-influenced torsos. Many of his early works have hints of folk dance.

Sinfonietta was created for the Charleston Festival, at the suggestion of the festival's director, Joseph Wishy. Kylián had to make the work quickly while on tour, asking the dancers to rehearse overtime to get it ready on time. He believes that the finished work 'reflects the spontaneity and spirit in which it was created, conditioned by the lack of time and the feeling of having to perform an impossible "balancing act"'.[28] At the premiere, the audience were so excited that they stood and cheered, throwing programmes in the air, before the music was even over.

Walter Nobbe's backdrop shows a misty landscape of wide plains. The pastel colours are echoed in the dancers' costumes, dresses and soft slippers for the women, tights and billowing shirts for the men. To Janáček's exultant fanfares, six men run and leap. Two couples dance with slight folk inflections, changing partners. Lying down on the stage, they move their arms in broad sweeps. Although there are duets and a *pas de trois*, Kylián rarely presents his dancers as individuals; they move as a group, expressing shared emotion or ideas. The steps are big and surging, with deep *pliés* and flexed feet. In the finale, the dancers rush in waves, jumping or in soaring lifts. Turning their backs to the audience, they slowly open their arms as they walk towards the landscape.

Mayerling

Choreography: Kenneth MacMillan
Music: Franz Liszt, arranged and orchestrated by John Lanchbery
Scenario: Gillian Freeman
Designs: Nicholas Georgiadis
Premiere: 14 February 1978, The Royal Ballet, Royal Opera House, London
Original cast: *Crown Prince Rudolf* David Wall; *Mary Vetsera, his mistress* Lynn Seymour; *Countess Larisch, his former mistress* Merle Park;

Princess Stephanie Wendy Ellis; *Empress Elisabeth, his mother* Georgina Parkinson; *Emperor Franz Josef, his father* Michael Somes; *Mitzi Caspar, a prostitute, Rudolf's mistress* Laura Connor; *Bratfisch, Rudolf's cab-driver* Graham Fletcher

In 1889, Crown Prince Rudolf, heir to the Austro-Hungarian Empire, died with his teenaged mistress at the hunting lodge at Mayerling. Despite attempts to hush it up, the story leaked out. It has become a subject of fascination and conspiracy theories: was this a suicide pact or a murder-suicide? What were the motives? There have been many fictional accounts of the deaths at Mayerling, often romanticising them as a tragic love story. Kenneth MacMillan's ballet takes a tougher view. It is a dark portrait of its hero's decline, being frank about his affairs, his tense family life, his drug taking, and the stifling world of the Habsburg court.

MacMillan created *Mayerling* in 1978, when he had just stepped down as director of The Royal Ballet. Released from administrative pressure, he launched into a hugely ambitious ballet, with large-scale, glittering court scenes and major roles for many principal dancers. The ballet is full of the athletic, sexually explicit *pas de deux* that had become a MacMillan trademark. It also uses the Royal Ballet tradition of storytelling. The hothouse world of the court, with its hierarchies and intricate relationships, is conveyed in naturalistic gesture and body language, as well as in dance.

Nichola Georgiadis' superb designs help to create the opulent, overstuffed society. His richly patterned costumes suggest the stifling weight of late nineteenth-century dress, while leaving the dancers free to move. The Liszt score is inventively assembled; the music for one of the Empress' scenes was written for the real Empress.

Synopsis

Prologue: The cemetery at Heiligenkreutz before dawn. A coffin is lowered into the grave in a secret burial.

Act 1. Scene 1. The ballroom at the Hofburg (Imperial Palace), Vienna. Crown Prince Rudolf has just married Princess Stephanie of Belgium. The court processes across the stage, moving with dignity but at a hectic pace, before reaching the ballroom and whirling into a waltz. Rudolf offends his parents and his new bride by flirting with her sister, the Princess Louise. Left alone in the ballroom, he meets Countess Larisch, his former mistress, with Baroness Vetsera, who introduces her young daughter Mary. They are interrupted by four Hungarian officers, who wish to involve Rudolf in the Hungarian separatist cause. Larisch tries to renew her intimacy with Rudolf. Rudolf's father, the Emperor Franz Josef, discovers them. Shocked, he orders Rudolf to return to his new wife.

Scene 2. The Empress' apartments at the Hofburg. Returned from the ball, the Empress Elisabeth relaxes with her ladies-in-waiting. Rudolf visits her, seeking sympathy and understanding as he faces his enforced marriage. She remains unresponsive and distant, unable to deal with his hysterical demands.

Scene 3. Rudolf's apartments at the Hofburg. Stephanie is prepared for the wedding night. Rudolf finds her alone, and terrifies her by threatening her with a revolver and showing her a skull. He then sexually assaults her.

Act II. Scene 1. A tavern, some years later. Accompanied by Bratfisch, Rudolf's driver, Rudolf and Stephanie arrive at the tavern in disguise. Seeing Stephanie's unhappiness, Bratfisch tries to distract her. Prostitutes dance, their costumes decorated with military helmets, while Rudolf meets his mistress, the prostitute Mitzi Caspar, and the Hungarian officers. Stephanie leaves in disgust. Police raid the tavern, and Rudolf, Mitzi and the Hungarian officers hide. In despair at the constant surveillance, Rudolf suggests to Mitzi that they should commit suicide together. She indignantly refuses, and reveals his whereabouts to Prime Minister Taafe. She and the Prime Minister leave together.

Scene 2. Outside the tavern. Rudolf meets Countess Larisch, who introduces Mary Vetsera, now a young woman in society. Larisch is chaperoning Mary, and believes she will appeal to Rudolf.

Scene 3. The Vetsera house. Larisch comes to call, finding Mary dreaming over a portrait of Rudolf. Larisch tells Mary's fortune, assuring her that her romantic dreams will come true. Mary gives her a letter for Rudolf.

Scene 4. The Hofburg. A family party is held to celebrate the Emperor's birthday. It's a tense affair, full of surreptitious confrontations. Count Taafe shows Rudolf a political pamphlet that implicates him in the Hungarian cause. The Empress' admirer, Colonel 'Bay' Middleton, offends Taafe and amuses Rudolf by tricking him with a joke cigar. The Empress gives her husband a portrait of his mistress, Katherina Schratt, who then sings to the guests; they listen while lost in their own thoughts. A firework display distracts everyone except the Empress and the Colonel. Bitterly, Rudolf watches them together. The fireworks give Larisch the chance to tease Rudolf with Mary's letter.

Scene 5. Rudolf's apartment at the Hofburg. Mary has been smuggled into the palace, wearing just her nightdress under her coat (a detail based on a real incident). Primed by Larisch, she has moulded herself into Rudolf's fantasy: taking his gun, she aims it at him before firing overhead. Rudolf is mesmerised by her, and they become lovers.

Act III. Scene 1. The countryside in winter, a royal shooting party. Rudolf's gun accidentally fires, narrowly missing the Emperor and killing a member of the court.

Scene 2. Rudolf's apartments. Visiting Rudolf, Larisch is shocked to find him addicted to drugs. The Empress Elisabeth discovers them together, and orders Larisch to leave – not realising that Mary is waiting outside. Mary joins Rudolf, who asks her to die with him.

Scene 3. The hunting lodge at Mayerling. Rudolf drinks with two companions, then dismisses them. Bratfisch arrives with Mary, and tries to entertain them, but withdraws when he realises he has lost their attention. Increasingly desperate, Rudolf makes love to Mary and injects himself with morphine. He takes her behind the screen, and a shot is fired. His companions rush in, and Rudolf reassures them. Left alone, he shoots himself, knocking down the screen to reveal Mary already dead.

Epilogue. The cemetery at Heligenkreutz before dawn. In a scene of weird horror, the body of Mary, fully dressed, is lifted from a cab, laid in a coffin and buried.

Mayerling is an immensely complex ballet. Rather than streamlining events, MacMillan seems eager to pile them up, to cram layers of historical knowledge into a wordless art form. The ballet is overloaded: without a programme note, you wouldn't know that the virtuoso dancers in elaborate uniforms were pressing the Hungarian cause.

Yet it's remarkable how much MacMillan successfully conveys, how powerfully he builds an onstage world. The way his characters sit or stand is dramatically revealing: waiting for her wedding night, Stephanie sits dwarfed in her chair, tense and unhappy. The fortune-telling scene shows different levels of complicity and ambition in the groupie Mary and the manipulative Larisch, all sketched in with deft touches. Every scene moves the characters forward, their different needs and responses helping to push Rudolf further into depravity and despair.

The many athletic, often abandoned *pas de deux* (with Rudolf's wife, his mother, his three mistresses) are precisely contrasted, each one distinct. And though this is Rudolf's story, none of the women are passive: each has her own pressures and choices to face. Larisch may cling to him, but she keeps the last shreds of decorum, hanging on to her position. When Mary fires a gun to seduce Rudolf, she triggers a change in the music: from exciting confrontation, she and Rudolf are suddenly swimming in desire, wrapping around each other with fated intensity. Not all of *Mayerling's* gambles pay off, but the conviction and depth of its storytelling make up for its unwieldiness.

Mayerling has remained in repertory at Covent Garden, and in recent years has joined MacMillan's *Manon* and *Romeo* on international wish lists, with productions at the Moscow Stanislavsky Theatre.

Lady of the Camellias (Die Kameliendamen)

Choreography: John Neumeier
Music: Frédéric Chopin
Designs: Jürgen Rose
Lighting: John Neumeier
Premiere: 4 November 1978, Stuttgart Ballet, Stuttgart
Original cast: *Marguerite Gautier* Marcia Haydée; *Armand Duval* Egon Madsen; *Manon Lescaut* Birgit Keil; *Des Grieux* Richard Cragun; *Monsieur Duval* Reid Anderson

Born in 1942, and trained in America and Britain, John Neumeier danced at the Stuttgart Ballet, where he made his first choreography. He directed the Frankfurt Ballet from 1969, and in 1973 he moved to direct the Hamburg Ballet. He has staged revised versions of classic ballets, such as *Illusions – Like Swan Lake*, and many works inspired by the Diaghilev repertory, and particularly Nijinsky. He has also staged a series of symphonic ballets, particularly to the music of Mahler. He is an important collector of Ballets Russes-related artworks.

Lady of the Camellias is based on the novel by Alexandre Dumas *fils*, which also inspired Verdi's opera *La Traviata* and Ashton's ballet *Marguerite and Armand*. Neumeier follows the novel's plot very closely, even staging its ongoing comparison between Marguerite and another literary courtesan, Manon Lescaut. The ballet uses music by Chopin, without any extra arrangement or orchestration, including the complete Second Piano Concerto, the Romanze from the First Piano Concerto, the Grande Fantaisie sur des airs polonaises, the Grande Polonaise and some original piano pieces.

Synopsis

Prologue. Marguerite Gautier's apartment. After Marguerite's death, the contents of her apartment are to be sold by auction. Nanina, her faithful servant, takes leave of the place for the last time. Curious visitors, buyers and friends of Marguerite come to visit the sale, including the older Monsieur Duval. A young man, Armand Duval, rushes in and collapses. The older Duval supports him, and Armand tells his story. The action returns to this framing narrative at key moments in the story.

Act I. Théâtre des Variétés. A performance of the ballet *Manon Lescaut*, the tale of a courtesan torn between luxury and her love for Des Grieux, is underway. In the audience is the courtesan Marguerite Gautier. She is moved by Manon's plight but disgusted by her infidelity, refusing to accept Manon as her own reflection. Armand is introduced to Marguerite. He fears that his own future may echo that of Des Grieux in the ballet.

After the performance, Marguerite invites Armand to her apartment, using him to annoy the boring Count N. She is overcome by coughing. Armand offers to help and confesses his love. Marguerite is touched but, aware of her fatal illness, keeps him at a distance. Nevertheless, their relationship deepens. As Marguerite hurries from ball to ball, admirer to admirer, Armand is always waiting for her, even when she goes to the country house owned by the Duke.

Act II. In the country. Marguerite is a guest at the home of the Duke. Armand follows her. When the Duke confronts him, Marguerite comes to his defence, choosing her lover over the security of her position. Indignant, the Duke leaves. Left alone, Marguerite and Armand dance ardently together. Marguerite dances this *pas de deux* with her hair loose, suggesting their new intimacy.

In the framing narrative, Armand collapses at the thought of this happier time, now gone. With sorrow, his father remembers the role that he played in the story. Hearing that his son has become involved with a prostitute,

Monsieur Duval visits Marguerite. He tells her that the relationship will damage Armand's reputation, and asks her to end it. She protests, but the image of Manon occurs to her, and she agrees. Armand comes home to find Marguerite gone; Nanina gives him a letter explaining that she has returned to her old life. He rejects it, rushing to Paris, where he finds her with the Duke.

Act III. By chance, Armand meets Marguerite with another courtesan, Olympia. To hurt Marguerite, he flirts with Olympia. Seriously ill, Marguerite visits him, begging him not to humiliate her. Seeing him again, she succumbs to her feelings, and they make love. (Sometimes danced as a gala number, this is known as the 'black' *pas de deux*, for the colour of Marguerite's dress. Armand pulls the dress off her halfway through, and she finishes the dance in her petticoat.) Falling asleep, Marguerite sees another vision of Manon. Waking, she decides to honour her promise, and leaves Armand for the second time.

When they meet again at a grand ball, Armand humiliates Marguerite by handing her an envelope full of money. Already very ill, she collapses.

In the framing narrative, Armand has reached the end of his story. When his father has left, Nanina brings him Marguerite's diary. Reading it, he imagines going with her to the theatre to see *Manon Lescaut* for the last time. In the ballet, Manon dies, poor and exhausted, in the arms of her faithful lover Des Grieux. Deeply affected, Marguerite leaves the theatre, but the ballet's characters haunt her. She longs to see Armand, but dies alone and in poverty. Reading this, Armand closes the diary.

Lady of the Camellias has a clear line of descent from Cranko's story ballets. Made in Stuttgart for Cranko's ballerina Marcia Haydée, it has a theme from literature and opera and a choreographic style filled with complicated lifts, the ballerina manhandled in mid-air. Unusually, Neumeier's Chopin soundtrack features no extra orchestration, while he shows particular fidelity to the novel, making a feature of its comparison between Marguerite and Manon. Both these decisions bring their own problems. The Chopin music floats along beside the ballet: it is not shaped to the story, and the choreography fails to engage with it. The Manon Lescaut theme adds to the ballet's length and meandering quality.

Despite these problems, the appeal of the story, the music and the chance for big emotion has made *Lady of the Camellias* one of Neumeier's most popular works, danced by companies including the Paris Opéra Ballet, American Ballet Theatre, the Bolshoi Ballet and the Royal Danish Ballet, among others.

Gloria

Choreography: Kenneth MacMillan
Music: Francis Poulenc, *Gloria* in G major
Designs: Andy Klunder
Lighting: Bill Besant
Premiere: 13 March 1980, The Royal Ballet, Royal Opera House, London
Original cast: Jennifer Penney, Wendy Ellis, Wayne Eagling, Julian Hosking

Danced to Poulenc's *Gloria*, Kenneth MacMillan's ballet remembers the dead of the First World War. The joyful music sometimes forms a drastic contrast with the agonised action, and sometimes evokes happier times before the war. The ballet is dedicated to MacMillan's father, who had been gassed at the Battle of the Somme in 1916.

The work was prompted by Vera Brittain's autobiography, *Testament of Youth*, which was dramatised by the BBC in 1979. Brittain records the loss of her own generation, a female perspective on the consequences of the war; MacMillan quoted her poem 'The War Generation: Ave' in his programme note.

Andy Klunder's fine set shows no-man's-land, with a skeletal metal framework standing on a sloping hill at the back of the stage. The men wear stylised helmets and tattered, ragged tights, suggesting torn uniforms and torn flesh. The women are ghostly figures in silver grey, wearing caps with knotted plaits at the ears. The Royal Ballet's Edward Watson, who now dances in the ballet, described the impact it made on him as a student: he 'instantly fell in love with it from the moment the curtain went up,' he told critic Jonathan Gray. 'It has that strange silence and that smoky atmosphere, just before the music starts, when it doesn't look like a ballet at all.'[29]

MacMillan returns to the weighted, modern dance-inflected language he had developed in *Requiem*. The ballet is dominated by several soloists. In a more optimistic *pas de quatre*, a woman leaps between her four partners, thrown high in the air. A woman winds herself between two men. A male soloist expresses anger and bitterness, pointing accusingly at the audience. As the ballet ends, he runs in a tearing circle around the stage and up the ramp before falling backwards, out of sight.

Rhapsody

Choreography: Frederick Ashton
Music: Sergei Rachmaninov, *Rhapsody on a Theme of Paganini*

Scenery: Frederick Ashton
Costumes: William Chappell
Premiere: 4 August 1980, The Royal Ballet, Royal Opera House, London
Original cast: Mikhail Baryshnikov, Lesley Collier

Created for Mikhail Baryshnikov, *Rhapsody* has a dazzling virtuoso lead, framed by a lyrical company. The star blazes across the ballet like a visiting comet. When Baryshnikov came to guest star with The Royal Ballet in 1980, he made a new Ashton ballet a condition of his visit, eager to absorb Ashton's style. Instead, the choreographer told him to 'Bring all your steps,' showcasing the visitor's Russian technique.[30] 'I was a bit disappointed,' Baryshnikov admitted to Julie Kavanagh. 'I wanted English ballet and he wanted Russian ballet. I was trying to escape all those steps.'[31]

In insisting on his star's virtuosity, Ashton was following his music, Rachmaninov's Rhapsody on a Theme of Paganini. Niccolò Paganini had been an internationally famous violin virtuoso, a musician whose playing seemed supernatural. Ashton's soloist is the triumphant star – right down to his quick mime of playing the violin. He is both courtly and teasing: the opening solo is full of gestures acknowledging the audience, but he ends the ballet with a shrug – itself a characteristic Ashtonian gesture.

Ashton paired Baryshnikov with Lesley Collier, a distinctive dancer with exceptionally quick feet. The ballerina role is very 'English' in style, full of Ashtonian details and echoes of the classics of Royal Ballet repertory. Her first entrance comes late in the ballet, almost halfway through. Running in across the back of the stage – as Aurora first appears in *The Sleeping Beauty*, one of Collier's best roles – she is lifted by the six men of the ensemble, recalling Ashton's own *Scènes de ballet*.

For much of the ballet, the leading dancers remain in their own orbits. When they do come together, the style often evokes the film musicals of the 1930s, the dancing of Fred Astaire and Ginger Rogers. The male star searches for the ballerina among the six women of the ensemble, who stand half-hiding their faces, like the multiple-masked Rogers in the film *Shall We Dance*. The duet has side-by-side walks, the ballerina ducking behind the man to snuggle under his arm, and back again. Elsewhere, Ashton combines their styles. The man lifts the ballerina in low, skimming lifts, then into a Soviet overhead lift. While the swoop upwards follows the line of the orchestra, she picks out notes of the piano solo with delicate flicks of her wrists.

The two leads remain the main focus of the ballet, but Ashton does give opportunities to the ensemble. The supporting men dance their own assertive steps, as if inspired by the male star's example. He partners the group of six women, who also have their own dance, each woman stepping forward for her moment in the spotlight.

Ashton designed the original backdrop, a pillared classical pavilion. The costumes, by long-time collaborator William Chappell, drenched the cast in gold and glitter, even putting golden dust on Collier's *pointe* shoes and in Baryshnikov's hair. In 1995, The Royal Ballet had the work redesigned by Patrick Caulfield, with brightly coloured geometric patterns on the set and costumes. In 2007 it was redesigned again, with a cloudy, changeable backdrop by Jessica Curtis.

Nine Sinatra Songs

Choreography: Twyla Tharp
Music: Songs sung by Frank Sinatra: 'Softly as I Leave You'; 'Strangers in the Night'; 'One for My Baby (and One More for the Road)'; 'My Way'; 'Somethin' Stupid'; 'All the Way'; 'Forget Domani'; 'That's Life'; 'My Way' reprise
Costumes: Oscar de la Renta
Lighting: Jennifer Tipton
Premiere: 14 October 1982, Twyla Tharp Dance Company, Queen Elizabeth Theatre, Vancouver
Original cast: Shelley Washington and Keith Young, Mary Ann Kellogg and John Malashock, Sara Rudner and John Carrafa, Richard Colton and Christine Uchida, Raymond Kurshals and Amy Spencer, William Whitener and Jennifer Way, Tom Rawe and Shelley Freydont

Twyla Tharp keeps coming back to Frank Sinatra. In 1976 she created *Once More Frank*, a gala duet in which she and Mikhail Baryshnikov danced to 'Somethin' Stupid', 'That's Life' and 'One for My Baby'. There were none of the bravura steps a gala audience expected from Baryshnikov, and the dance was booed. Tharp, who does not give up easily, returned to Sinatra's songs in 1982, to create one of her best-loved hits.

Tharp had been researching ballroom and exhibition dancing (including the partnering of the dance couple Irene and Vernon Castle) for the 1981 movie *Ragtime*. Ballroom partnering is at the heart of *Nine Sinatra Songs*, with a series of duets to songs Sinatra recorded in the 1950s and 1960s. Tharp chose music from this period as a time when, she remembered, 'my parents were still together, when all parents were still together . . . the last time we assumed as a culture that of course men and women lived together and loved for a lifetime'.[32]

By the 1980s, ballroom dancing was falling out of mainstream fashion. Tharp's duets walk a line between evoking the period of the music, without being period pieces. The couples were glamorously dressed by fashion designer Oscar de la Renta, the men in tuxedos, the women in gowns and heeled shoes. A mirrorball hangs over the stage, giving it the look of a ballroom. The ballet has no narrative, but the different couples are vividly characterised through their dances.

The opening duet, to 'Softly as I Leave You', established the ballet's mood with floating, gliding dancing. 'Strangers in the Night' is a tango, showing the connection and the distance between the dancers. The tango head-turns mean that when the man turns to look at the woman, she looks away; a hand to his chest is an intimate touch that keeps him at arm's length.

'One for My Baby (and One More for the Road)' is a late-night duet, the man in a loosened tie and no jacket, the woman sliding around his body. 'My Way' is an ensemble number for these three couples.

The couple in 'Somethin' Stupid' are young, eager and inexperienced: in the first production, the woman wore pink puffed sleeves, suggesting a teenager at a prom. 'All the Way' is polished and romantic, while 'Forget Domani' is a speedy, carefree number with flamenco touches.

The most spectacular duet is 'That's Life', the dancers as battling lovers in an apache number, the woman dragged through steps but fighting back.

In 1983, Tharp revised some of the material to create *Sinatra Suite* for Baryshnikov and Elaine Kudo, who danced versions of 'Strangers in the Night', 'All the Way', 'That's Life' and 'My Way'. 'One for My Baby (and One More for the Road)' becomes a male solo. Even where the steps haven't been altered, giving them to a single couple creates a different kind of drama. In 2010, Tharp returned to Sinatra – and to some of the same songs – again in the Broadway dance musical *Come Fly Away*.

Giselle

Choreography: Mats Ek
Music: Adolphe Adam
Designs: Marie-Louise de Geer Bergenstråhle
Premiere: 6 July 1982, Cullberg Ballet, Norsborg, Stockholm
Original cast: *Giselle* Ana Laguna; *Albrecht* Luc Bouy; *Hilarion* Yvan Auzely; *Myrta, queen of the wilis,* Siu Ander

Born in 1945, Mats Ek is the son of dancer and choreographer Birgit Cullberg, director of the Cullberg Ballet, and the actor Anders Ek, who worked regularly with the filmmaker Ingmar Bergman. After training in dance, Ek switched his attention to theatre, training at Marieborg Folks College and working as a director before deciding to return to dance, joining the Cullberg Ballet in 1972. 'Theatre uses a language close to reality. You can pretend things,' he told the dance writer Lynn Colberg Shapiro. 'Dance is a foreign language [where] there's no space for cheating.'[33]

Ek's choreography uses a sparse vocabulary with several signature steps: deep *pliés* in second position, flexed feet, an undulating move of the spine. The style has its roots in German and American modern dance: Cullberg was a student of both Kurt Jooss and Martha Graham. Many of Ek's works are retellings of existing classics. His breakthrough work was the 1982 *Giselle*. Reworkings of *Swan Lake* (1987), *Carmen* (1992) and *The Sleeping Beauty* (1996) followed.

Ek keeps the Adolphe Adam score and the basic theme of a village girl betrayed by a nobleman, but substitutes ideas of madness for the supernatural theme of the 1841 ballet.

Synopsis

Act I. The village. Giselle is a 'village idiot', naïve and simple, dressed in a skirt and sweater and soft slippers – the ballet has no *pointe*work. She seems to see and hear things that others don't. Hilarion, her fiancé, keeps her tied with a rope. The scenery is a lush green landscape, with rounded hills evoking the female body (there are even trees for nipples). Albrecht, a rich young man in a white suit, is fascinated by Giselle, and she falls in love with him.

Act II. The Institution. Instead of dying and rising from the grave, she is taken to a mental hospital in the second act. The wilis are female patients dressed in white hospital gowns, with a forbidding nurse as the queen of the wilis. The backdrop is decorated with severed female body parts. Hilarion visits Giselle in hospital, but cannot reach her. When Albrecht comes to the hospital, he ends up questioning his own life. Stripped naked, he is sent out to the lush forest of the first act. He is discovered by Hilarion, who covers with him with a blanket.

8

INTERNATIONAL BALLET: CROSSING BOUNDARIES

T HE DANGER OF a boom is that it may be followed by a bust. By the end of the twentieth century, there were fears that the days of ballet as an art form were over. The great expansion of the 1960s and 1970s had faded, while the choreographers who drove it – Balanchine, Ashton, Robbins, Cranko, MacMillan – had died. Every generation complains that the golden age is gone, but in this case there was a real and measurable decline. The number of new ballets finding a place in the repertory plummeted; major companies struggled to find their way forward. Viewers and critics worried; most notoriously, historian Jennifer Homans suggested that ballet was 'a story that may have come to an end . . . there can be little doubt that in the past three decades ballet everywhere has fallen from great heights.[1] It's an extreme position, but she wasn't alone in taking it.

By the time Homans published that, ballet was already rediscovering its confidence. New choreographers emerged, forging careers in ballet rather than abandoning it for contemporary dance. New ballets turned out to be hits again, growing in revival rather than vanishing after a season. Like so many of its own heroines, ballet has a history of coming back from the dead. After a generation of lamenting, the art is showing a new energy.

By the 1970s the dance boom had created an international ballet landscape with major national players. Stars such as Rudolf Nureyev might guest with different companies, but the companies themselves had core local identities. New York City Ballet had been created in Balanchine's image. The Royal Danish Ballet was still shaped by the buoyancy and storytelling of the Bournonville tradition. Behind the Iron Curtain, Russian companies showed a similar distinctive identity, with the aristocratic Kirov Ballet and the gutsy Bolshoi giving *Swan Lake* a different emphasis. Those qualities were literally built into the dancers' bodies, through the preferences of directors and choreographers. Yuri Grigorovich's large-scale choreography at the Bolshoi produced more muscular dancers, whereas those of the Kirov tended to have a leaner silhouette. Although companies would take on ballets from elsewhere, changes in style tended to be developed internally. Ballet had a shared basic technique, but spoke in a range of recognisable accents.

In the 1980s this pattern began to change. For the Soviet Union, where Alexei Ratmansky trained at the Bolshoi Ballet, the thawing of the Cold War meant greater access to other dance cultures. In the West, knowledge of Soviet dance had come when Russian companies toured or their dancers defected, bringing technique and repertory with them. Now the process went the other way, as dancers and information began to move more freely. 'It was so easy for us, the Russian ballet students. Everything was clear,' Alexei Ratmansky, who trained at the Bolshoi school in the 1980s, told the critic Joan Acocella:

We had the Bolshoi Ballet, which was big heroic ballets, story ballets, and that's how ballet should be. And then . . . we got the videos, we got some companies coming to Moscow showing completely different kind of stuff. I was not sure any more that the ballet that I knew, the principles of the ballet that were so hammered in my head during the school years, that they are right. That it's a complete system. I saw the different side of ballet.[2]

Political change brought crisis as well as discovery for ballet companies. The Soviet state had pumped money into ballet as a matter of national pride; when that support ended, financial insecurity followed. The network of ballet schools was disrupted as the different regions of the former Union of Soviet Socialist Republics broke away. Many dancers left for the West, as guest artists or permanently. Beyond Russia, other factors encouraged new flexibility in hiring dancers. In Europe, changes in employment law gave dancers and teachers greater freedom to work in different countries. Schools and companies that had developed during the boom years were now producing their own stars – as well as ambitious young dancers who wanted to try their luck in the older troupes. Japan now has 15,000 ballet schools and more than 100 competitions but – despite a public eager for ballet – Japanese dancers face low pay and very limited opportunity to perform in their own country. Many have found careers overseas. Cuba has become a powerhouse of dance training, exporting many of its dancers;

China, another country with dance and political links to the old Soviet Union, is also establishing itself in the field of ballet.

Instead of drawing on their own feeder schools, companies increasingly took dancers from around the world. A company's unity of style was no longer built into its dancers' training. At the time of writing, the Paris Opéra Ballet is still dominated by its own school, but even the Bolshoi and the Mariinsky – as it is now called again, abandoning the Soviet 'Kirov' – take foreign dancers now. Even if they didn't, there's an increased interest in how other companies dance. In the 1990s, Kirov director Oleg Vinogradov was bowled over by the French star Sylvie Guillem, a tall and highly distinctive ballerina with long limbs and sky-high leg extensions. Suddenly the Kirov's ranks became filled with taller, more flexible women, a generation that was nicknamed 'the basketball team'. Local style was adapted, inspired by the distinctive gifts of a single Western dancer.

Fashions in dance have always changed: Marie Taglioni transformed her generation, too. The changes are now speeded up by technology. When the young Ratmansky was inspired by video footage from other dance companies, he was at the start of a technological revolution: filmed performance available at home. Video was replaced by DVD, which in turn was overtaken by online content. Performances on YouTube can be studied on six continents; points of technique can be copied immediately, though teachers worry that they may not be thoroughly absorbed. With the fast exchange of people and information, ballet's old local accents are becoming less distinct.

In most cases, ballet's identity had been shaped by repertory. This too was becoming more international, through a combination of political change and scarcity. By the 1990s there was an acknowledged choreographic drought. Companies that had been defined by their choreographers seemed to stop producing them. Balanchine died in 1983, a towering genius for whom it was hard to imagine a successor. Ashton died in 1988, after a long semi-retirement. MacMillan, who had moved further away from classical choreography in his later career, and reduced his output due to ill health, died in 1992. New York City Ballet, committed to the new, went on producing new ballets, but with fewer lasting successes. The Royal Ballet was more timid, with fewer new works. (David Bintley, who followed MacMillan as the company's resident choreographer, resigned; his farewell work, *Tombeaux*, was a lament for the lyrical, Ashtonian qualities he feared ballet was losing.) Familiar titles did well at the box office, but it became harder to sell new works. Audiences plumped for the three-act story ballet.

Where had all the choreographers gone? In many cases, they had left ballet. The ballet boom was a dance boom, too, with an explosion of modern and postmodern dance. For many, contemporary dance seemed more immediate and relevant than the formal classicism of ballet. It was also closer to current social dance styles. Until the 1960s, Western social dance was dominated by couple dances, with established steps and patterns – it's easier to dance in step with another person if you already know what moves you plan to make. The couple dance also offered physical intimacy in a more guarded age. Some of ballroom's most popular styles, including the waltz and the tango, were scandalous when they were first introduced. What made them shocking was exactly what made them popular: bodies pressed together, moving in rhythm. Once the rules of sexual behaviour relaxed, ballroom's stylised form of sexual contact lost some of its appeal. A new emphasis on individualism meant that more people danced solo, improvising by themselves on the dance floor.

Throughout its history, ballet has drawn on social dance forms – in the 1960s, Ashton added a *pas de quatre* to *Swan Lake* that included a variation based on the twist. In the later twentieth century, the new freeform social dances were less easily assimilated by ballet, while non-professional audiences had less experience in learning steps. Contemporary dance was experimenting with pedestrian movement and improvisation, but ballet, always a stylised art form, became one step further from average experience. (It's worth remembering that two of the late twentieth century's leading choreographers, William Forsythe and Wayne McGregor, had social dance experience: Forsythe was a high-school rock 'n' roll champion, while McGregor trained in ballroom and Latin American dance as a child.) Ballet's new remoteness was one reason for choreographers to leave. There were others: ballet's formalised gender roles, its sharp male–female divides, could seem out of step with changing social realities. Gay choreographers, such as the Royal Ballet School-trained Michael Clark, turned their back on a form that would keep them dancing heterosexual princes.

With the number of classical choreographers dwindling, ballet turned to creators from other styles. Crossovers were nothing new: Martha Graham had worked with New York City Ballet in *Episodes* in 1959, while Twyla Tharp was already an established name in ballet. The occasional collaborations now became much more frequent, with ballet companies dancing and commissioning works by Tharp, Paul Taylor, Mark Morris and more. When contemporary dance choreographers visit ballet, they can illuminate aspects of style, seeing new things by looking at it from the outside. Modern dance uses weight differently, often working with gravity where ballet tends to defy it. The crossovers have resulted in exciting and much-loved works. But this was one-way traffic, underlining the fact that contemporary dance had no shortage of choreographers. The drought was ballet's problem.

Of course, directors were also on the lookout for new creators within ballet. At the Paris Opéra, which he directed from 1983 to 1989, Rudolf Nureyev was eager to shake up the repertory. As well as staging the classics and creating his own works, he was alert and active in bringing in choreographers from outside. He scored a major hit with William Forsythe.

Born in New York in 1949, William Forsythe was a teenage expert on rock 'n' roll dances such as the twist and the mashed potato, before training in ballet. He danced with the Joffrey and then the Stuttgart Ballet, where he was encouraged to choreograph for the company. In 1984 he was appointed director of another German company, the Frankfurt Ballet. Three years later he created *In the Middle, Somewhat Elevated* for the Paris Opéra, starring Sylvie Guillem and a new generation of Paris Opéra dancers. Forsythe's fractured, post-classical style showcased Guillem's virtuosity to dramatic effect. The dancers combine extreme flexibility and wrenching shifts of balance and direction with catwalk attitude. Both tone and physicality were controversial. Forsythe was hailed as ballet's way forward, and denounced for trashing it – particularly at a time when the pure classical standards of many companies were seen to be under threat. Meanwhile, companies around the world rushed to acquire his ballets.

Forsythe is clearly fascinated by ballet, paying close attention to details of its style – particularly *épaulement*, the changing alignment of the shoulders and waist, which adds internal dynamics to ballet steps. Yet he also looks at ballet with ironic distance. In 1988 he made *In the Middle, Somewhat Elevated* the centrepiece of an evening-length work called *Impressing the Czar*. 'It's a fake full evening ballet,' he said in an interview for Sadler's Wells:

> It looks and acts like a full evening ballet, but it's not. The full evening ballet has some sort of story about human passions and death and love and all these things that full-length story ballets are supposed to have, and kidnapping and pirates and slaves and oh, just the whole nine yards. Since that's not possible any more, how do you make a full-length ballet? You make something that *looks* like a full-length ballet![3]

For Forsythe, ballet's established norms were out of the question: 'You can't make a full-length ballet any more, because that's something that was made in another era.' His description suggests the bind that ballet choreographers were finding themselves in. Ballets on traditional lines seemed dated, while postmodern or contemporary takes often left ballet behind altogether. With his own company, Forsythe moved away from 'ballet ballets' towards contemporary dance and conceptual art. He may come back: having stepped down as director of The Forsythe Company in 2014, he became associate choreographer at the Paris Opéra Ballet, planning a new work for the 2015/16 season.

One answer to the problem of repertory was to look to the ballets that really were made in another era. Ballet has always been a fragile art, living in performance and losing many of its greatest works. Since the 1980s it's been working furiously to record and recover them.

Balanchine's death, and the working out of his will, helped to prompt a new approach. In 1976 copyright protection in the United States had been extended to cover ballets. In 1983 Balanchine left his ballets to his friends and colleagues. Many of them deposited their rights into The Balanchine Trust, a body that organises the licensing, promotion and staging of the ballets. It has a special agreement with New York City Ballet, Balanchine's own company; when other companies apply to dance ballets, they must meet the Trust's requirements. Authorised stagers teach and coach the works, while the choreographer's style and technique have been trademarked. The George Balanchine Foundation records and documents works, and attempts to recover ballets that have fallen out of performance. Balanchine had compared ballets to butterflies, beautiful today, but not here forever. In practice, his has become the best-protected and best-preserved legacy in dance.

Other choreographers are more vulnerable, but they too are being brought back from the brink. Frederick Ashton's *Sylvia* was created for Margot Fonteyn in 1952, but fell from the repertory without her. In 2004, after almost forty years, it was successfully restaged by The Royal Ballet, in a production that has since been danced by American Ballet Theatre, the Staatsballett Berlin and the Mariinsky Ballet. An abandoned, almost lost work has sprung back into life, now danced more widely than at any time in its history. *Sylvia* is arguably a bigger hit as a retro discovery than it was as a new ballet.

Sylvia has the advantage of being an evening-length, nineteenth-century-style ballet. Since evening-length classics have become the backbone of the repertory, there's a strong urge to find more of them – and if they're not being created new, they can be rediscovered. In the 1990s *Le Corsaire* suddenly became popular in the West, with multiple productions springing up after the success of the Kirov's 1987 production on tour. It's also precisely the 'kidnapping and pirates and slaves' kind of ballet that Forsythe argued couldn't be done any more. As a ballet, *Le Corsaire* is much weaker than, say, *La Bayadère*: the story is foolish, while the choreography has nothing to compare with the hypnotic beauty of *La Bayadère*'s Shades scene. Its success depends on exotic spectacle and the dancers' virtuosity, but these have been enough to win it a place in the repertory of many companies. The drive to find new nineteenth-century ballets peaks with the work of Pierre Lacotte, who has staged old ballets with new choreography. In 1972 he created a version of *La Sylphide* in the manner of Taglioni; he went on to recreate other hits of the nineteenth century, such as *Marco Spada* and *The Pharaoh's Daughter*.

Ballet could expand its repertory by importing choreographers or looking to the past, but neither suggest an art form in peak condition. Successful new works from within ballet's academy were much rarer, and choreographers who could create them are in demand worldwide – leading to careers that are also more international.

Born in 1973, Christopher Wheeldon trained at The Royal Ballet School, joining the company in 1991. Two years later, he saw a Hoover sales promotion that offered a free flight to New York with every vacuum cleaner purchased. While in New York, he joined New York City Ballet, becoming the company's artist in residence – a position specially created for him – in 2000. With British training and American experience, Wheeldon was already a transatlantic choreographer, making ballets in New York and London in the 1990s. In 2001 he created his breakthrough work, *Polyphonia*, a sleek leotard ballet to complex music by Ligeti.

Given the worldwide shortage of ballet choreographers, Wheeldon's clear talent pitched him into the spotlight, cast as ballet's next great hope. It led to a great many commissions and considerable pressure. Although Wheeldon has stepped outside ballet to work in musical theatre, he initially showed naïvety in connecting with mainstream theatre. Morphoses, the transatlantic ballet company that he founded in 2006 but left in 2010, launched with comparisons to the Ballets Russes but came across as the product of a sheltered ballet world. Wheeldon's more recent big productions have shown greater theatrical fluency, with an increase in confidence and ambition shown in the 2014 ballet *The Winter's Tale*.

The career of Alexei Ratmansky exemplifies many of the changes that faced ballet in the later twentieth century. Born in St Petersburg in 1968, he trained at the Bolshoi Ballet school, graduating in 1986 – just as the Soviet

Union showed the first signs of breaking up. After dancing with Ukrainian National Ballet, Ratmansky moved to the West, dancing with the Royal Winnipeg Ballet and the Royal Danish Ballet. He emerged as a choreographer in the late 1990s, with works created for the former Bolshoi ballerina Nina Ananiashvili.

Trained in the Soviet tradition before discovering Western ballet, Ratmansky shows a hyper-awareness of ballet's history. He was appointed director of the Bolshoi Ballet after the huge success of *The Bright Stream* (2003), which reimagined a lost ballet of the Soviet period. It's a characteristic work in several ways. It fills in a missing section of ballet's past – and a specifically Soviet past, with a Shostakovich score from the era of Stalin's terror. Ratmansky has returned to Shostakovich again and again, using the composer to explore and come to terms with the past, from the cheerfulness of the ballet *Concerto DSCH* to the images of repression in his Shostakovich trilogy. Finally, *The Bright Stream* revealed Ratmansky's love of classical dance steps, his ability to use traditional vocabulary to make ballets of today. His engagement with the past is neither pastiche nor nostalgia: it works to make sense of present-day identity.

In the same spirit, Ratmansky's modernising directorship of the Bolshoi involved looking back to the company's history. Some past works were brought back in revised, reframed form, such as *The Flames of Paris*; others were careful historical reconstructions, such as his staging of *Le Corsaire*, or Diaghilev-era works that had not been seen in Moscow: he's shown a particular loyalty to Massine. He moved the company away from its Yuri Grigorovich tradition, leading to clashes within the company. Ratmansky left the Bolshoi in 2008, moving back to the West to focus on choreography. The divide between the modernising and Grigorovich factions continued at the Moscow theatre, with tensions culminating in the horrific acid attack on director Sergei Filin in 2013.

After leaving the Bolshoi, Ratmansky created ballets for New York City Ballet before unexpectedly switching to American Ballet Theatre, where he became artist in residence. He has continued to make works for many other companies, including more restagings of 'lost' works. As well as demonstrating a brilliant approach to classical dancing, he shows a stubborn readiness to rethink ballet's own narrative, to ignore current fashions in genre. In Russia he confronted the Grigorovich tradition head on; in America, where Balanchine's pure-dance aesthetic dominates, he's shown a loyalty to his Soviet roots; and he has succeeded in taking dancers, audiences and critics along with him.

Glass Pieces

Choreography: Jerome Robbins
Music: Philip Glass, *Rubric* and *Façades* from *Glassworks*, excerpts from *Akhnaten*
Set: Jerome Robbins, Ronald Bates
Costumes: Ben Benson
Premiere: 12 May 1983, New York City Ballet, New York State Theater, New York
Original cast: Heléne Alexopoulos, Peter Frame, Lourdes Lopez, Joseph Duell, Lisa Hess, Victor Castelli, Maria Calegari, Bart Cook

Long before *Glass Pieces*, Jerome Robbins and Philip Glass had been looking for an opportunity to work together. Glass had hoped that Robbins would direct his opera *Satyagraha*; when that fell through, they worked together on the early stages of the opera *Akhnaten*. When Balanchine fell ill, Robbins withdrew from *Akhnaten* to focus on his work with New York City Ballet, but he had already decided to make a ballet to Glass' music, in preparation for directing the opera. In *Glass Pieces* he uses Glass' characteristic repetitions to set a large ensemble moving, then cuts across it with superhuman soloists. It was the first new work presented by New York City Ballet after Balanchine's death.

Glass Pieces is in three sections. In *Rubric* the *corps de ballet* dancers cross the stage like busy pedestrians, each walking quickly along his or her own path. They're dressed in varied, brightly coloured practice clothes, the dancer's equivalent of everyday dress. Behind them, the backdrop looks like yellow graph paper, underlining the mathematical qualities of the steps and music. Then soloists break into the crowd – first one, then two, then three couples, dancing athletic classical steps in shiny body tights. 'I want you to be a steel angel from outer space,' Robbins told the dancer Heléne Alexopoulos.[4]

In *Façades* the women of the *corps* form a silhouetted frieze along the back of the stage, walking in steady rhythms with varied moves: changing places, facing forwards or turning to the side, changing arm positions. In front of them, a couple dance together, responding to Glass' clarinet line. Robbins makes the regular beat of the *corps* as gripping as the melody represented by the couple.

The final section is danced to the funeral march from *Akhnaten*. Three men move quickly across the stage, doubling in number, then doubling again. They move in athletic jumps and stamps, recalling the energy of Robbins' own *West Side Story*; the women wind through sinuous lines.

Groups form and break up, building waves, lines and circles to Glass' driving rhythms, fast, urgent and exhilarating.

Artifact

Choreography, stage design, lighting, costumes, text: William Forsythe
Music: Parts I and IV: Eva Crossman-Hecht; Part II: Johann Sebastian Bach, Chaconne from Partita No. 2 in D minor for solo violin; Part III: sound collage by William Forsythe
Premiere: 5 December 1984, Frankfurt Ballet, Frankfurt
Original cast: *Person in Historical Costume* Anne Maree Bayard; *Person with a Megaphone* Nicholas Champion; *The Other Person* Alida Chase; Elizabeth Corbett, Jeppe Mydtskov, Gisela Schneider, Andrew Levinson

Artifact was the first work William Forsythe made as director of Frankfurt Ballet. A large-scale ballet in four acts, with more than thirty dancers, it's a self-aware response to ballet's history. 'Step inside,' says the Person in Historical Costume – she's dressed in a grand baroque dress and wig, evoking ballet's roots in the sixteenth and seventeenth centuries. 'Welcome to what you think you see.'

The stage is stripped back, with no wings or backdrop: Forsythe won't be providing the audience with any context for what he shows us. The music is built around Bach's Chaconne, played straight in the second act. Eva Crossman-Hecht, a composer and concert pianist who worked as Forsythe's rehearsal pianist at Frankfurt Ballet, created improvisations on Bach that became the basis of the piano score. A large *corps de ballet* builds intricate patterns from basic ballet positions, while soloists push this vocabulary into extreme lines.

Forsythe evokes ballet's traditional steps and hierarchies, before subverting them. 'It references Balanchine, whom I am so indebted to,' Forsythe told dance critic Gabriella de Ferrari in 2006. 'It's like a thank you note to him for everything I've learned by watching his work. And it reflects both my love and my doubts: on one hand, it's reverent; on the other hand it acknowledges the epoch he worked in as something bygone.'[5]

Synopsis

Act I. The Person in Historical Costume welcomes the audience in. She keeps up a fluent babble about perception and memory, her words variations on a set of concepts: 'When I stepped inside, I remembered what I should have seen.' At one point, she tells another dancer, 'I forget the story about you.' She claps her hands to interrupt the music and dancing, like a *répétiteur* in a ballet rehearsal. A second character, a Person with a Megaphone, walks slowly across the stage. Laconic where the woman is fluent, he mutters about rocks, dust and sand. A third character, the Other Person, is barefoot and grey all over. The man and the woman peer into a trapdoor, from which the Other Person emerges. She demonstrates arm movements that are sometimes copied by a large *corps de ballet* of men and women, dressed in leotards. Crossman-Hecht's piano themes are relentlessly repeated.

Act II. This act is pure dance, set to Bach's Chaconne and bathed in golden light. It has the structure of a classical set piece, with the *corps de ballet* framing duets for two couples. These are fast and angular, dancers extending and distorting lines, pushing themselves off-balance. The dancing is constantly interrupted by a curtain coming down with a crash – it's weighted so that it lands heavily and noisily. When the curtain rises again, the dancers have regrouped. The interrupted flow wrong-foots the audience, though Forsythe has argued that it's timed to changes in the music.

Act III. The ballet's elements are recycled in chaos. The Chaconne is played very fast, while the Person in Historical Costume gabbles at double speed, so fast she almost runs out of breath. She has lost her skirt, and argues with the Person with a Megaphone. Panels with line drawings on them are set up at the back of the stage, collapsing to reveal a woman standing behind them. Dancers rush on and collapse.

Act IV. The panels have been set up again, lit at the back of the stage. In front of them, the *corps de ballet* moves in silhouette. The man and the woman wander through, still debating their own meanings. As the lights come up, the *corps* dances in groups, lines and rows, returning to classical building blocks and to Forsythe's evolutions of them. Circling their arms and legs through ballet's basic positions, the dancers define circles of space around themselves. The ballet ends when the Woman in Historical Costume invites the audience to 'step outside'.

In this early Forsythe work, several characteristic themes are already in place: the fast, fractured style of the duets, the mix of pure dance with speech and everyday movement, the outbreaks of apparent disorder, the stark lighting and stagecraft, the way the work comments on itself and on the history of art. These elements are combined less abrasively than in later

Forsythe pieces; though the dancers exaggerate lines and positions, they're not yet doing so with slamming force.

The *corps* dancing insistently defines both stage and personal space. The circling arms recall Leonardo's drawing of Vitruvian man, drawing arcs in space. The dancers walk in lines, sometimes clapping their hands, or move in block formations. Praising the ballet's architecture, Forsythe dancer Kathryn Bennetts remembered that 'The lights he used, there's lots of diagonal long beams – it's very architectural, so the dancers are also making those shapes. When we performed it a lot in Paris in the nineties, groups of architects were always waiting at the stage door afterwards.'[6]

A ballet stuffed with variations and reworked material, it now has its own variations. Forsythe has staged different versions of *Artifact Suite*, a group of dances from the full-length work. His 1985 ballet *Steptext*, a smaller-scale work, also draws on material from *Artifact*.

Steptext

Choreography, stage design, lighting, costumes: William Forsythe
Music: Johann Sebastian Bach (Chaconne from Partita No. 2 in D minor for solo violin)
Designs: Raymond Dragon Design Inc. and William Forsythe
Premiere: 11 January 1985, Aterballetto, Teatro Ariosto, Reggio Emilia, Italy
Original cast: Elisabetta Terabust, Mauro Bigonzetti, Marc Renuard, Alessandro Molin

Steptext is danced by a woman in a scarlet leotard and three men in striped grey. Like Act II of Forsythe's *Artifact*, created the previous year, it uses Bach's Chaconne and a disrupted theatrical experience. (Even the panel that forms the set is familiar from the earlier ballet.) The mood is different; this is a much more aggressive, more defensive work. Between dances, the performers stay onstage, catching their breath, avoiding each other's gaze. In duets, they lean away from each other, testing and shifting their weight and balance as they push to the limits of their own flexibility

It's a splintered performance. The dancing starts before the house lights go down, as the audience is still coming into the auditorium. The music is a recording, which stops and starts abruptly, sometimes playing snatches of only a few seconds. The performers keep dancing in silence, or break off while the music is still playing. The lighting is equally unpredictable, with sudden blackouts, while the house lights go off and on.

In the Upper Room

Choreography: Twyla Tharp
Music: Philip Glass
Costumes: Norma Kamali
Lighting: Jennifer Tipton
Premiere: 28 August 1986, Twyla Tharp Dance, Ravinia Festival, Highland Park, Illinois
Original cast: Jamie Bishton, John Carrafa, Richard Colton, Erzsebet Foldi, Stephanie Foster, Julie Nakagawa, Kevin O'Day, Cathy Oppenheimer, Kevin Santee, Karen Stasick, Ellen Troy, Shelley Washington, William Whitener

In the Upper Room mixes high-energy dancing with a relentless Philip Glass score, layering ballet and modern dance across nine movements. As ballet turned to contemporary dance, contemporary choreographers were also influenced by ballet: Tharp created In the Upper Room, pointework and all, for her own company.

Jennifer Tipton's spotlights and smoke effects make it impossible to see where the stage ends. It's a brightly lit vacuum, dark and light at once. The dancers emerge from the smoke or vanish into it. Norma Kamali dresses them in striped grey shirts, trousers or dresses, like pyjamas, with touches of vivid red.

In the Upper Room starts with two women, moving in mirror image. They catch one foot, pull it behind them and let go. This tips them off balance, which they recover by spinning, before jogging backwards in a circle. In a BBC documentary Tharp described this pair as:

> custodians of the space, like Chinese watchdogs ... by starting both sides of the phrase simultaneously but on opposite sides, the phrase will define an arena for the dance to come.
>
> Now the men enter, with the second phrase. They dance this in a triangular formation, the downstage man inverting the phrase so that the same movement is seen moving both forwards and backwards. As the men and women perform the two phrases together, you see forward and back, right and left, circular and vertical, male and female, thus making it clear that In the Upper Room is about opposing forces held in balance. Old and new, modern and classical.[7]

Tharp's description of the ballet's first minute underlines just how highly organised In the Upper Room is, its patterns tight and ruthlessly controlled.

Her cast of thirteen is divided between ballet and modern dance: there are six dancers in sneakers and seven who move balletically – though one woman switches sides. Nicknamed 'stompers', the dancers in sneakers sprint through the ballet. They have a loose, jazzy way of moving, matched to a driving turn of speed. On the ballet side, two women in bright red *pointe* shoes have been nicknamed the 'bomb squad', perhaps for the sheer attack of their dancing.

In the finale, the whole cast appear, dancing in high-speed variations of the work's motifs. The dancers vanish into darkness, leaving the two women who began the piece. They pull down their hands sharply, ending the work.

In the Upper Room is a marathon of a ballet, both celebrating the dancers' strength and stamina and underlining the demands it makes of them. As the work goes on, they shed layers of clothing, revealing bright-red leotards and hard-working bodies under the baggy, striped costumes.

The title comes from a song sung by Mahalia Jackson. The score was commissioned: after years of improvising to music by Glass, Tharp decided that this work needed a score by him. 'Now, Philip Glass is always very busy, probably booked for years,' Tharp remembered, 'but I say, "Look Phil, just a little music after breakfast every day."'[8] She got her score.

In 1988, Tharp became an artistic associate of American Ballet Theatre. She disbanded her own company and brought seven of her dancers with her to ABT, where they danced in her works – including *In the Upper Room* – and in other ballets.

Sechs Tänze (Six Dances)

Choreography: Jiří Kylián
Music: Wolfgang Amadeus Mozart, German Dances, KV 571
Designs: Jiří Kylián
Lighting: Jiří Kylián, realised by Joop Caboort
Premiere: 14 October 1986, Nederlands Dans Theater, Het Muziek-theater, Amsterdam

Six Dances is the earliest of Kylián's 'Black and White' dances, named for the colour of their costumes. (The others are *No More Play, Petite Mort, Sweet Dreams, Sarabande* and *Falling Angels*.) With this group of dances, Kylián moved on from the folk-inflected imagery of his early works, showing a new focus on sexual politics. Several of the 'Black and White' dances use eighteenth-century music and imagery, particularly grand baroque dresses, with full skirts and fitted bodices, mounted on rollers. Kylián also adds surreal touches, such as soap bubbles or unexpected use of the dresses on rollers. The dances have been staged as a complete evening or separately, *Petite Mort* and *Six Dances* being particularly popular with ballet companies.

Six Dances is performed by eight dancers in eighteenth-century underwear – bodices and petticoats for women, knee-length drawers and powdered wigs for men. Both sexes wear chalky white make-up, with red lips and dark eyebrows, suggesting both powdered eighteenth-century aristocrats and circus clowns. The performance style is self-consciously broad and zany, with pulled faces and slapstick.

In his notes on the ballet, Kylián reprints a comic, scatological letter from Mozart to his cousin Maria Anna Thekla Mozart, adding that 'Mozart understood life in all its richness, fantasy, clownery and madness. It is his spirit, and his acceptance of the fact that our life is not more than a masquerade or a dress rehearsal for something deeper and much more meaningful, which has inspired me to make this work.'[9]

The dancing is fast-paced, with pointing gestures, pattacake hands, little hops and skips. Men partner women by holding onto their skirts, and sometimes, more disturbingly, by holding their necks.

The full-skirted dresses glide past, with women lying horizontally across the panniered skirts rather than wearing them. Men stand inside the dresses with fencing foils between their teeth. Stabbings and a beheading are mimed. Clouds of powder fly up from tapped wigs, while soap bubbles float down from above. The dance seems to end with a shrug, but the dancers twitch nervously afterwards.

In the Middle, Somewhat Elevated

Choreography, lighting: William Forsythe
Music: Thom Willems in collaboration with Leslie Stuck
Design: Michael Simon
Costumes: William Forsythe, Férial Simon
Premiere: 22 May 1987, Paris Opéra Ballet, Paris
Original cast: Isabelle Guérin, Sylvie Guillem, Laurent Hilaire, Manuel Legris, Fanny Gaïda, Karin Averty, Nathalie Aubin, Virginie Rousselière, Lionel Delanoë

With *In the Middle, Somewhat Elevated*, William Forsythe burst onto the international scene. The ballet was promptly taken into the repertory of companies around the world, influencing a whole generation of younger choreographers. Forsythe later made this work the centrepiece of the evening-length ballet *Impressing the Czar*, but it's *In the Middle*, the pure-dance suite, that remains the work most identified with Forsythe. Many of its qualities would reappear in other Forsythe ballets: the extreme poses, the drastic approach to classical technique, the dancers' air of supermodel disdain, harsh overhead lighting and even Thom Willems' crashing electronic score.

The ballet starts with two women standing in the middle of the stage, testing their *pointe* shoes and gazing up at a pair of golden cherries that hangs overhead. One walks off, a man joins the other and they launch into dance, moving in unison with aggressive speed and force. Thom Willems' music crashes in, with ticks and thwacks in insistent patterns.

In the Middle, Somewhat Elevated is a theme-and-variations ballet. It's built around a sequence that is danced by the lead ballerina, while the other eight dancers perform sections of it. Every dancer has a solo and a *pas de deux*. Dancers will dance flat out, then break off and stroll away. Others watch from the shadows at the edges of the stage, or dance solo or group dances there before claiming centre stage. The costumes are teal green: unitards for the men, leotards with black footless tights and *pointe* shoes for the women.

Forsythe's steps deconstruct the classical vocabulary. When he was making the first theme, he explained in an interview for Sadler's Wells, 'I did a *pas de chat* forward, and then I moved it backward at the same time . . . Isabelle Guérin, one of the two, the main ballerinas in the piece, burst out laughing, and said: "You can't do that." I said, why not? And she said, "It doesn't exist!" And I said, "Now it does." ' Forsythe points out that 'everything was legal': the different parts of the step came from academic classicism, put under pressure by being pulled in different directions at the same time. Guérin recognised the departure, Forsythe remembered: 'She immediately analysed it and said, well, it doesn't follow the rhetoric of ballet. I guess that was a turning point . . . Then I really went for it.'[10]

It's no accident that Forsythe created *In the Middle* for the Paris Opéra, with its long history and strict hierarchies. The critic Roslyn Sulcas points out Forsythe's

> canny understanding of the culture of the Paris Opéra Ballet, with its formal hierarchies of grades and its deeply rooted competitiveness, which begins at the Paris Opéra Ballet School, where students are ranked from top to bottom each year.
>
> This ranking continues through their professional life – once in the company, promotion can be achieved only through an annual competition. *In the Middle* perfectly captures the intimate, prickly, ambiguous

relationships of dancers who grow up together but must never forget that their friends are also their rivals . . . Even during the solos of *In the Middle*, there is always another dancer, or several, to the side or back of the stage. Moving slowly through formal ballet poses, they are waiting, by implication, to replace whoever is dancing.[11]

In the Middle was the second ballet Forsythe made for the Paris Opéra: Rudolf Nureyev, working to update and open up the company, had commissioned *France/Dance* from him in 1983. This time, working with a young cast, Forsythe created a huge hit, showing off a new generation of stars. The most famous was Sylvie Guillem, whose extraordinary technique and flexibility became a new balletic ideal. Ballet directors across the world began looking for tall, long-limbed dancers with sky-high extensions; dancers strove to match Guillem's 'six o'clock' legs.

The ballet's name comes from its only piece of decor, two golden cherries hung over the stage. Forsythe's original plan was to have many golden objects, reflecting the gilded stucco of the theatre itself. However, *In the Middle* had its premiere as part of a mixed bill that also included a Karole Armitage ballet with an immensely complicated set. At technical meetings, Forsythe realised there wouldn't be time to hang all his golden objects. Instead, he picked just one item, the pair of cherries, and asked whether they could be hung 'in the middle, somewhat elevated'.

Impressing the Czar

Choreography: William Forsythe
Music: Ludwig van Beethoven, Leslie Stuck, Thom Willems, Eva Crossman-Hecht
Stage design: Michael Simon and William Forsythe
Lighting: William Forsythe and Michael Simon
Costumes: Férial Simon
Text: William Forsythe, Richard Fein, Kathleen Fitzgerald
Premiere: 10 January 1988, Frankfurt Ballet, Frankfurt
Original cast: *Agnes* Kathleen Fitzgerald

Having created *In the Middle, Somewhat Elevated* for the Paris Opéra, Forsythe decided to expand it to an evening-length work for his own Frankfurt Ballet, something on the lines of *Artifact*. *Impressing the Czar* is an elaborate evening of postmodern whimsy – a quality you may find playfully clever or repetitive and arch.

A discussion of art history runs through the ballet, prompted by the way Forsythe and designer Michael Simon expanded the stage design of *In the Middle*, which hangs a pair of golden cherries overhead. They trawled through Western paintings, looking for cherries. 'We went through, and we looked for where we could find cherries,' Forsythe said, continuing:

And we found them in every conceivable corner of the history of art. So we sort of tried to build this fictive context for what would be the sole piece of decoration in the second act. And somehow, I guess a lot of the iconography of the painting was religious. There were saints, and people being shot, and . . . paintings about the history of painting – the Dutch paintings of these tremendous galleries of paintings which the collector had commissioned . . . We basically made a context out of the context. And because of the religious iconography, we ended up with these Catholic schoolgirls . . . [The first-cast Agnes] Kathy Fitzgerald, was brought up as a devout Catholic, and had with her the book of the saints, and was a tremendous resource![12]

Synopsis

Part I: *Potemkins Unterschrift* (*Potemkin's Signature*). The opening section is a jumble of symbols. A slanting chessboard platform covers part of the stage, with gilded objects laid out on its squares. The music includes snatches of Beethoven string quartets, repeated and distorted. Dancers in black or bronze-coloured skirts perform courtly steps or traditional balletic mime scenes. Painted canvases are unrolled and draped around dancers. One man takes up Saint Sebastian poses. Agnes, a woman in a crinoline, wanders through the action, commenting by radio link to her colleague Roger. She tells him about her location 'within the composition', describing the action around her or discussing the character Mr Pnut.

Part II: *In the Middle, Somewhat Elevated* (see entry above).

Part III: *La Maison de Mezzo-Prezzo*. Agnes auctions off her fellow dancers, who are wrapped up in gold tinsel. (In revivals, Agnes' auction-house chatter is adapted with local and recent references, mocking consumerist attitudes to art.)

Part IV: *Bongo Bongo Nageela*. Hordes of dancers appear, men and women dressed as schoolgirls in pleated skirts, knee-socks and bobbed wigs. They dance in a huge circle around Mr Pnut, who lies in the centre, posed like Saint Sebastian with an arrow in his chest. In *Mr Pnut Goes to the Big Top*, the last section, he rises from the dead.

Drink to Me Only With Thine Eyes

Choreography: Mark Morris
Composer: Virgil Thomson, from *Nine Etudes* and *Ten Etudes*: 'Chromatic Double Harmonies', 'Repeating Tremolo', 'Fingered Fifths', 'Doubled Glissando', 'Oscillating Arm', 'Pivoting on the Thumb', 'Alternating Octaves', 'Double Sevenths', 'Broken Arpeggios', 'Parallel Chords', 'Ragtime Bass', 'For the Weaker Fingers', 'Tenor Lead'
Costumes: Santo Loquasto
Lighting: Phil Sandström
Premiere: 31 May 1988, American Ballet Theatre, Metropolitan Opera House, New York (excerpt first performed on 10 October 1987 at the Dancing for Life Benefit, New York State Theater, New York)
Original cast: Mikhail Baryshnikov, Shawn Black, Julio Bocca, Isabella Padovani, Robert Hill, Susan Jaffe, Carld Jonassaint, Lucette Katerndahl, Kathleen Moore, Martine van Hamel, Robert Wallace, Ross Yearsley

Born in 1956, Mark Morris came to ballet after a meteoric rise as a modern-dance choreographer. After a contemporary-dance generation that had pursued minimalism and austerity, Morris embraced low and high culture, theatricality and, above all, music. His choreography for his own company recalls the runs and skips of early modern dance, with juicy, muscular phrasing and extraordinary musicality, responding to the formal structure and individual phrasing of music from baroque oratorios to Indian pop songs.

In 1988, Mikhail Baryshnikov invited him to create a work for American Ballet Theatre. *Drink to Me Only With Thine Eyes* is a fresh, bright and demanding dance for six men and six women. It's almost a classroom ballet, but one that plays games with rhythm, timing and stage space. Santo Loquasto's white costumes suggest 1980s dancewear, the men in tops and trousers, the women in white jersey dresses over knee-length leggings. Virgil Thomson's piano studies are full of danceable rhythms – ragtime, tango – that also, in this context, have ballet-class overtones. Where space permits, the piano is placed onstage. The title comes from Ben Jonson's poem 'To Celia', written in 1616 and later set as a song. Thomson's 'Tenor Lead', the last of the studies played in the ballet, uses the song's melody.

Morris uses academic classical steps, given a twist with tilted torsos, changed arm positions, adjusted angles. In one trio, three women move in and out of unison – sometimes variations on a theme, sometimes in cheerful counterpoint. The overlapping patterns are funny as well as airy: in the final pose, one woman crouches to support the central woman, while the third helpfully supports her raised leg.

Group dances are often at the heart of Morris' works, where ballet tends to have hierarchies of soloists and *corps*. Working with a ballet company, Morris tends to push at those divisions. According to his biographer, '*Drink to Me*, like so many Mark Morris works, was a group piece – twelve dancers, no stars – the joke being that hidden in the group was the biggest ballet star in the world, Mikhail Baryshnikov.'[13]

Company B

Choreography: Paul Taylor
Music: Songs by the Andrews Sisters: 'Bei Mir Bist du Schön', 'Pennsylvania Polka', 'Tico-Tico', 'Oh Johnny, Oh Johnny Oh!', 'I Can Dream, Can't I?', 'Joseph! Joseph!', 'Boogie Woogie Bugle Boy (of Company B)', 'Rum and Coca-Cola', 'There Will Never Be Another You', 'Bei Mir Bist du Schön' (reprise)
Costumes: Santo Loquasto
Lighting: Jennifer Tipton
Premiere: 20 June 1991, Kennedy Center for the Performing Arts, Washington DC

Born in 1930, Paul Taylor is one of modern dance's most influential chore-ographers. After dancing with Martha Graham and Merce Cunningham, his first works were avant-garde. The 1957 *Epic*, an almost motionless dance performed to telephone time signals, was reviewed by Louis Horst with a blank page. Taylor then returned to music, with an open, neo-classical performance style that has been taken up by ballet companies.

In *Company B*, Paul Taylor evokes 1940s America, from bobby-soxers to the gunfire and deaths of wartime. The work has become a staple of Taylor's own company, but it had its premiere with Houston Ballet, and is danced by other ballet troupes.

It's danced to nine songs by the Andrews Sisters, a close-harmony singing trio who were America's most popular female singing group in the 1940s. Taylor chooses a range of their songs – lots of upbeat numbers, a couple of ballads. He also shows the variety of ethnic song types the sisters sang and popularised: Yiddish songs, polka, Latin rhythms. Like the film star Betty Grable, the Andrews Sisters had a girl-next-door quality that was particularly popular in wartime. Taylor catches that bright energy and optimism, while acknowledging the death and loss of the era.

Santo Loquasto's costumes are in beige and green: the men's shirts and trousers suggest khaki uniforms. Most of the women wear knee-length skirts with ankle socks and soft slippers; a couple wear trousers. Taylor's choreography mixes speedy social dance, light balletic jumps and a modern-dance sense of gravity. There are lots of falls in this ballet, dancers dropping to the ground and using the floor.

Synopsis

In the opening number, 'Bei Mir bist du Schön', the dancers emerge in silhouette, springing into carefree dances, from perky polka couple dances to winding lines and circles. Taylor's blithe choreography catches the lilting rhythms: as the sisters sing 'HOW grand you are,' everyone swings a leg up at once. During the dance, one of the men falls, apparently dead.

In 'Pennsylvania Polka', a couple prance through polka steps in the foreground. At the back of the stage, a file of men crouch to fire, march, stagger and fall. Taylor balances these images with great lightness of touch. The wartime imagery doesn't devalue or mock the exuberant polka, it coexists with it: they're part of the same wartime world.

'Tico-Tico' shows off an energetic male soloist. In his triumphant dance, he turns a circle of balletic jumps before dropping to the floor, rolling quickly along it and springing back up again. 'Oh, Johnny, Oh Johnny Oh!' has a happy bespectacled man chased by seven women: he catches three of them at once, all clinging to him with arms and legs, while the others flap their hands in delight. 'I Can Dream, Can't I?' is a ballad for a whirling, soaring female soloist, while the scampering groups of 'Joseph! Joseph!' end with a woman grieving over a fallen body.

The ballet's title comes from 'Boogie Woogie Bugle Boy (of Company B)'. The man playing the virtuoso bugler dances exuberantly for the whole song (two and a half minutes, so it's tireless as well as high-spirited). He throws us a final salute and marches off – and is shot, falling dead on the last note.

Left lying on the ground, he becomes one of the very-much-alive men swooning over the heroine of 'Rum and Coca-Cola'. The Andrews Sisters naïvely missed the song's implications of prostitution ('both mother and daughter working for the Yankee dollar'). Taylor's dancing woman is a wholesome vamp, while the song's lyrics hang in the air.

The female soloist in 'There Will Never Be Another You' dances around her partner as much as with him; he's as much a memory as a person. The ballet ends with a reprise of 'Bei Mir Bist du Schön', with the dancers fading back into the shadows.

Petite Mort

Choreography: Jiří Kylián
Music: Wolfgang Amadeus Mozart: Adagio from Piano Concerto in A major (KV 488), Andante from Piano Concerto in C major (KV 467)
Decor: Jiří Kylián
Costumes: Joke Visser
Lighting: Jiří Kylián, realised by Joop Caboort
Premiere: 23 August 1991, Festspielhaus, Salzburg
Original cast: Elke Schepers, Jorma Elo, Lorraine Blouin, Nancy Euverink, Davide Luca, Martino Müller, Sol León, Cora Kroese, Paul Lightfoot, Johan Inger, Jennifer Hanna, Bruce Michelson

Another of Kylián's 'black and white' dances, *Petite Mort* was choreographed for the Salzburg Festival, marking two hundred years since Mozart's death. Choreographed for six men, six women and six fencing foils, the work also uses the baroque dresses on rollers that feature in *Six Dances* and some of the other 'black and white' ballets. The title is a French phrase for orgasm, and the ballet has a focus on sexual politics. Joke Visser's costumes – leotards for women, underpants for men – have a suggestion of corset lacing, evoking the eighteenth century.

Six men pose with fencing foils: swishing them, testing them, letting them fall and picking them up with their feet, bending and manipulating them around their bodies. Running to the back of the stage, they pull a billowing swathe of fabric down to the footlights. When they pull it back again, they uncover six women.

The ballet is full of couple dances: a dance for a couple with a foil, the man curling his blade around his partner, or dances for the whole cast. All twelve dancers fall to the floor, lifting opened arms and legs into the air – a splayed, arched-back position that Kylián uses in several of his works. Women lie on their backs, tucking up their knees when the men move onto them – so they both hold the men off, and hold them up in the air. The baroque dresses are trundled through, the women stepping in and out of them, as if trying on identities.

Carmen

Choreography: Mats Ek
Music: Georges Bizet, arranged by Rodion Shchedrin
Designs: Marie-Louise Ekman
Lighting: Göran Westrup
Premiere: 13 May 1992, Cullberg Ballet, Norsborg, Stockholm
Original cast: *Carmen* Ana Laguna; *Don Jose* Marc Hwang; *M* Pompea
Santoro; *the Toreador* Yvan Auzely

Where Roland Petit's *Carmen* was both explicit and chic (see chapter 5),
Mats Ek's retelling is ribald and cartoonish. Both ballets use music
from Bizet's opera; Ek uses Rodion Shchedrin's irreverent arrangement,
originally created for his wife, the ballerina Maya Plisetskaya, in 1967.
Shchedrin had intended to create a new score, but found Bizet's tunes
running in his head. Scored for strings and extravagant percussion, his
version is full of musical jokes. For one section of the 'Toreador's Song',
for instance, he sets up the familiar accompaniment, then leaves out
the big melody – it's so famous that audiences will fill in the gap. The Soviet
authorities were shocked by what they saw as an insult to Bizet, and the
work was briefly banned, but it has since become Shchedrin's most popular
score.

Ek's 1992 staging draws on both Bizet and his source, the novel by
Prosper Mérimée. It uses a flashback structure – the story flashing before
Don José's eyes as he faces a firing squad. The ballet focuses on the differences between Carmen and Don José: she is an independent, cigar-smoking,
'masculine' figure, while he is feminised, desperate to settle down. Ek
combines Don José's fiancée Michaela and his mother into a single character, 'M'. She reappears throughout the ballet, as if commenting on the
action, symbolising the voice of motherhood. Marie-Louise Ekman's
designs are colourfully non-naturalistic, with polka-dot backdrops, metallic
gowns and symbolic objects.

Synopsis

Don José sits on a large ball, awaiting his execution. An officer stands beside
him, while M dances a quirky lament around them. He's led to the firing
squad, but instead of bullets, the music crashes in, bringing him back to the
start of the story.

Crowds celebrate, with women in ruffled metallic dresses dancing for
the men. Carmen enters, dressed in red, smoking a large cigar. Don José

watches, fascinated, as she dances and fights with her lover, shouting and stuffing a scarf in his mouth. She puts her cigar into Don José's mouth and leaves. M circles him, cradling him like a mother.

Don José joins a group of soldiers. Carmen dances among the men, who light and smoke cigars as she dances between them. After a dance with other women, she is arrested. In prison, she pummels the walls in frustration, then seduces her guard Don José: she draws a red scarf from his breast pocket, pulling out his heart. He lets her escape.

After a lament by M, the ensemble celebrates Escamillo the toreador. Carmen reappears, smoking her cigar: this time, she pulls a pink scarf from the zip of Escamillo's trousers.

In prison, Don José dances romantically with a dream Carmen. They pose arm in arm – he holding a bunch of flowers, she smoking her cigar.

Escamillo prepares for the bullfight. Don José becomes increasingly frantic, obsessed with Carmen. His fight with Escamillo is staged as a bullfight, with a cape. When Carmen enters, she wears a dress with a very long train, which she pulls between her legs – and produces a cigar from under it, puffing defiantly. Don José stabs her. Another lover drags her body away, and Don José faces the firing squad.

Other Stagings

Carmen Suite, the first version of Shchedrin's score, was created by Alberto Alonso in 1967. It was staged for the Bolshoi with Plisetskaya and, the same year, for the Cuban National Ballet with Alicia Alonso in the title role. Alonso's scenario focuses on Carmen, Don José, Escamillo and a new character, Fate, a ballerina dressed in black who represents Carmen's alter ego. Boris Messerer's designs place the ballet in a stylised bullring.

Herman Schmerman

Choreography, stage design: William Forsythe
Music: Thom Willems, *Just Ducky*
Lighting: Marc Stanley
Costumes: Gianni Versace
Premiere: 28 May 1992, New York City Ballet, New York State Theater, New York
Original cast: Kyra Nichols, Margaret Tracey, Wendy Whelan, Jeffrey Edwards, Ethan Stiefel
The *pas de deux* premiere was on 26 September 1992, when it was danced by Tracy-Kai Maier and Marc Spradling.

Created for New York City Ballet's Diamond Project, a platform for new choreography, *Herman Schmerman* is Forsythe in a lighter mood. The title comes from a line spoken by Steve Martin in the 1982 film *Dead Men Don't Wear Plaid*. 'I think it's a lovely title that means nothing. The ballet means nothing, too. It's a piece about dancing that will be a lot of fun. It's just five talented dancers dancing around – and that's good, isn't it?'[14] There's a pop quality to Thom Willems' electronic score, which has perky, casual lines rather than the driving attack of *In the Middle, Somewhat Elevated*.

Reviving the work for his own Frankfurt Ballet, Forsythe added a new *pas de deux*. Since the New York City Ballet revival of 1999, Forsythe has chosen to present the *pas de deux* alone.

In the *pas de deux* version, a man and woman stroll onstage. They dance separately and then together, breaking off and returning, with a rehearsal-room sense of dancers trying out moves. The duet is full of tests of balance, the man taking the woman's weight as she tilts away. Halfway through, she leaves to put on a pleated yellow skirt; he does likewise. (She wears hers over her leotard, he wears his with bare chest and legs.) The duet finishes with a formal classical finger turn, going back to ballet's academic roots as the lights go down.

Gianni Versace dresses the woman in a leotard with a sheer top. Dancers choose whether to wear black underwear, or to leave their breasts visible.

Le Parc

Choreography: Angelin Preljocaj
Music: Wolfgang Amadeus Mozart: Adagio from Symphony No. 36 'Linz' in C major, K. 425; Adagio and Fugue in C minor, K. 546; Six German Dances, K. 571 (except No. 4); Andantino in B flat from Piano Concerto No. 14 in E flat major, K. 449; Rondo from Eine Kleine Nachtmusik, K. 525; Andantino in A from Divertimento No. 11 in D major, K. 251; Presto from the Musical Joke for strings and two horns, K. 522; Andante in B flat from Piano Concerto No. 15 in B flat major, K. 450; Adagio in F major from Adagio and Fugue for strings after J. S. Bach, K. 404a; Allegro from Divertimento in B flat major, K. 137; Adagio from 'Haffner' Serenade in D major, K; 250; Adagio in F sharp from Piano Concerto No. 23 in A major, K. 488
Sound design: Goran Vejvoda
Sets: Thierry Leproust
Costumes: Hervé Pierre

Premiere: 9 April 1994, Paris Opéra Ballet, Opéra Garnier, Paris
Original cast: Isabelle Guérin, Laurent Hilaire

Le Parc is a very French game of love, a three-act ballet exploring the codes, games and laws of attraction in a formal, eighteenth-century garden. Born in Paris, Preljocaj studied ballet before changing to contemporary dance. He studied in New York and in France before founding his own company in 1984. He has returned to ballet with commissions from companies including New York City Ballet and the Bolshoi Ballet. *Le Parc*, his first work for the Paris Opéra, is perhaps his best-known and most popular ballet. It particularly suits the chic elegance of Paris Opéra style.

It's inspired by an aristocratic French tradition of literary love games, stretching from the 'précieuses' of the 1650s and the restrained loves of the novel *La Princesse de Clèves* (1678) to the more explicit, and crueller, intrigues of Pierre Choderlos de Laclos' *Les Liaisons dangereuses*, published in 1782. The 'précieuses' of the French court held salons and wrote novels debating questions of love. Madeleine de Scudéry's novel *Clélie* (1654) included an allegorical 'Carte de tendre', a map of the affections in which lovers can find different routes to happiness – quickly, along the river of Inclination, or more slowly through the villages of Love Letters and Little Gifts. The précieuses and their elaborate language were roundly mocked by the playwright Molière in *Les Précieuses ridicules* (1659), but the idea of intricate, aristocratic games of love lived on in French literature.

The ballet is set in a formal French garden, given an industrial edge by the geometric metal trees of Thierry Leproust's set design. Eight couples flirt with and seduce each other to music by Mozart, backed by a *corps de ballet* of fifteen women. Four modern 'gardeners', wearing dark glasses and moving to electronic sounds, observe or direct events. *Le Parc* is divided into three acts, each ending with a duet for the leading couple, but is performed without an interval.

Synopsis

Act I. The gardeners appear in the park, ready to observe events. Aristocrats gather in the gardens in daylight. Both men and women wear breeches, coats and embroidered waistcoats as they play games with chairs. In their first *pas de deux*, 'Rencontre' (meeting), the leading couple dance separately but are very much aware of each other. After he first approaches her, they dance in unison, though still apart; he keeps advancing, touching her ankle or briefly lifting her. At last he kisses her; she withdraws.

Act II. The trees move to centre stage, evoking a maze, while the lighting suggests night is falling. The women wear extravagant period dresses, or strip to their underwear, bodices and short petticoats with bare feet. In their second *pas de deux*, 'Résistance', the man pursues the woman, kneeling at her feet or moving very close to her body, not quite kissing her. He catches hold of her repeatedly, but she holds back.

Act III. Night. The seven couples succumb to love, casting off restraint, leaving only the leading couple. The leading woman appears, wearing a spectacular red dress. The gardeners undress her, leaving her in a night-dress with her hair loose. In the ballet's most famous moment, she kisses her lover, her arms tight around his neck. He responds by turning, spinning until her body swings straight out. After the duet, the gardeners return to end the ballet.

Preljocaj's ballet mixes academic steps with more naturalistic moves, such as crouching or nuzzling. It's a small and repetitive vocabulary, coloured by the changing responses of the leading couple and the dancers' own refined, formal bearing. Preljocaj makes the most of Paris Opéra dancers' chic, the stylish way they wear costumes, from the page-boy outfits of the first act to the grand-period dresses worn later in the ballet. Dancers make elaborate formal gestures, circling their wrists, or practise swooning to a soundtrack of giggles.

Bella Figura

Choreography: Jiří Kylián
Music: Giovanni-Battista Pergolesi, Alessandro Marcello, Antonio Vivaldi, Giuseppe Torelli, Lukas Foss
Sets: Michael Simon
Costumes: Joke Visser
Lighting: Jiří Kylián, realised by Tom Bevoort
Premiere: 12 October 1995, Nederlands Dans Theater, AT&T Danstheater, The Hague
Original cast: Brigitte Martin, Stefan Żeromski, Philippa Buckingham, Joeri de Korte, Elke Schepers, Ken Ossola, Lorraine Blouin, Johan Inger, Megumi Nakamura

The punning Italian title means both 'beautiful body' and 'putting on a brave face', in a work that explores ideas of performance and reality.

Bella Figura sets a series of images, often picked out by spotlights or framed by curtains, to a patchwork of baroque and contemporary music. Where William Forsythe uses curtains abruptly, cutting off our view of the action with a thump, Kylián's curtains fall softly, reshaping the performance space, draping the performers or echoing their movements. Although Kylián's dancers sometimes swing their legs high or wide, the attack is even, rather than making the movement jarring or drawing attention to its contrasts. Similarly, the musical transitions are smoothed over.

The ballet starts with the nine dancers getting into position, dancing different steps like an orchestra tuning up, then freezing as a curtain falls. In one square space, we see a man twisting into a shoulder-stand. On the other side of the stage, an apparently naked woman is wrapped in the curtain, framed by its graceful folds as she is lifted by invisible partners.

The work continues in glimpses, the curtains opening for dances that fill the whole stage, or drawn to mark out narrow performance spaces. A duet becomes a trio when a second man sprints in to join it. Two dancers cross the stage in unison, pursued by the curtain, which is drawn slowly behind them. A woman prowls on hands and feet, like a cat, while her male partner keeps his hand on her curved back. Dancers rush in and slide to a stop, without appearing ruffled.

Joke Visser's costumes are a mix of leotards, underwear and tights in black mesh, flesh colour and red, and full red skirts, worn by bare-chested women and men. In Bella Figura's best-known scene, two women kneel facing each other, torsos and flowing skirts rippling as they sway and reach towards each other, almost caressing but never quite touching. The ballet ends with a series of male-female duets, using the full stage space which is lit by two cauldrons of real flame.

The Vertiginous Thrill of Exactitude

Choreography, stage design, lighting: William Forsythe
Music: Franz Schubert: finale of Symphony No. 9 in C Major, D 944 ('The Great')
Costumes: Stephen Galloway
Premiere: 20 January 1996, Frankfurt Ballet, Frankfurt
Original cast: Laura Graham, Francesca Harper, Helen Pickett, Noah D. Gelber, Desmond Richardson

The Vertiginous Thrill of Exactitude was presented, along with Forsythe's *Approximate Sonata*, as 'Two Ballets in the Manner of the Late Twentieth Century'. With its stylised tutus, nineteenth-century music and pure-dance format, *The Vertiginous Thrill of Exactitude* has proved very popular with ballet companies, and is danced much more widely than its companion piece.

Both of these works approached nineteenth-century music from a different angle. Whereas *Approximate Sonata* was choreographed and rehearsed to the music of Beethoven, then danced to electronic music, *The Vertiginous Thrill* is usually performed to a recording of Schubert, with a tinny effect of amplification. The women's mustard-coloured tutus are as stiff as plates, a single layer of flat skirt with no net underfrills. Like the ballet itself, the tutus refer to ballet's classical tradition while actually updating it. The men wear ketchup-coloured short leotards.

'A ballerina at the San Francisco Ballet said she would rather give birth again than dance *Vertiginous Thrill*,' Forsythe remembered:

> Apparently, it has a reputation of being extremely difficult to dance. But then again, dancers do like challenge. I made it for that reason, to exploit the talent that I had at that time. . . . One of the really important things is for people to pay attention to the music. People get involved with the steps, which are finally of absolutely no value without musicality. I think that I'd left a lot of the musical nuance over to those dancers because they were so skilled. Then you go back, and you're going, 'Okay, what was it exactly?' You thought it was somehow all your own craft, and it wasn't, it was actually their incredible artistry.[15]

In solos, duets, trios and group formations, the three women and two men perform academic steps at driving speed. Leg extensions are high, but lines are not fractured. The performance style looks back to the graciousness of nineteenth-century tutu works, while moving at a walloping pace.

Por vos muero

Choreography: Nacho Duato
Music: Venegas de Henestrosa, Pedro Guerrero, Diego Ortiz, Pedro Rimonte, Antonio Martín y Coll, Juan Vásquez, Cristóbal de Morales, traditional
Premiere: 11 April 1996, Compañia Nacional de Danza, Teatro de Madrid, Madrid

Born in Valencia in 1957, Nacho Duato started dance training at the age of sixteen, studying at the Rambert School, at Béjart's Mudra School in Brussels and at Alvin Ailey American Dance Theatre, before dancing with Cullberg Ballet and then Nederlands Dance Theater. His choreography reflects these modern dance influences, especially those of Jiří Kylián and Mats Ek.

In 2011, Duato became director of the Mikhailovsky Ballet in St Petersburg, where he staged his own works alongside the company's classical revivals, and created his own, largely traditional, version of *The Sleeping Beauty*. In 2014 he became director of the Staatsballett Berlin.

Por vos muero was created for the contemporary-dance Compañia Nacional de Danza, but has been taken into the repertory of many ballet companies. It is set to a poem by the sixteenth-century Spanish poet Garcilaso de la Vega, spoken in voice-over, and a selection of Spanish music from the same period. It opens with dancers in flesh-coloured leotards, their backs to the audience, running away in slow motion, When baroque music starts, the dancers spring into action, moving one by one into dips, *pliés* and duets.

The stage clears, and couples return wearing stylised Renaissance costume, dancing with a mix of athletic partnering and formal gesture, recalling period court dances. In the ballet's second half, Duato adds props: women appear with masks on sticks, while men swing incense burners to religious vocal music. At the end of the ballet, the dancers return to their flesh-coloured leotards for a series of more duets, alternating between period costume and modern undress.

Remanso

Choreography, designs, lighting: Nacho Duato
Music: Enrique Granados, *Valses Poéticos*
Premiere: 5 November 1997, American Ballet Theatre, City Center, New York
Original cast: Desmond Richardson, Parrish Maynard, Vladimir Malakhov

Remanso was created to show off a strong male cast. Since the ballet boom of the 1960s, male dancers have become more prominent. With a strong roster of men, American Ballet Theatre has both expanded male roles within traditional ballets such as *Swan Lake*, and commissioned all-male or male-dominated ballets. *Remanso* has been danced by many other companies, and also features in the repertory of male-dance showcases, such as Kings of the Dance.

In *Remanso* ('haven' in Spanish), a single panel is placed at the back of the stage. An arm reaches around it, holding a rose, while three men stand lined up at the side. As the arm slowly withdraws, the three men perform a trio with jumps, dips and crouches. Retreating behind the panel, they step out and are pulled back. In a series of solos, Duato blends balletic jumps and spins with Mats Ek-influenced deep *pliés* in second and nervous gestures.

The dancers use the panel to make entrances and exits. Arms continue to reach around it. One man climbs over it to join a duet. Another holds an *arabesque* against it, his arms stretched wide to join hands with unseen companions. In a trio, all three pile themselves against the wall, before a dance full of 'blindfolding' gestures. One man dances with a rose between his teeth, and is lifted to hang upside down from the panel wall, his companions grouped around him.

The Pharaoh's Daughter (La Fille du Pharaon)

Choreography: Pierre Lacotte
Music: Cesare Pugni
Designs: Pierre Lacotte
Premiere: 5 May 2000, Bolshoi Ballet, Bolshoi Theatre, Moscow
Original cast: *Aspicia, the Pharaoh's Daughter* Nina Ananiashvili; *Taor/ Lord Wilson* Sergei Filin; *Ramze, Aspicia's servant* Maria Alexandrova

In 1862, *The Pharaoh's Daughter* was Marius Petipa's first big hit, an extravaganza packed with dancing and exotic spectacle. Petipa created the libretto with Vernoy de Saint-Georges, who had worked on the story of *Giselle* with Théophile Gautier. For their new story, Petipa and Saint-Georges turned to Gautier again, basing *The Pharaoh's Daughter* on his *Roman de la Momie* (*The Mummy's Tale*). It was performed up until 1926, then fell from the repertory. In 2000, Pierre Lacotte created a new production in the style of the original. The new ballet is a leisurely affair, stuffed with parades, dances, lavish scenery and wild animals. The characters encounter lions, a real horse, a fake monkey (a role once danced, in the Petipa staging, by a very young George Balanchine) and a glove-puppet cobra.

Synopsis

Act I. Scene 1. Lord Wilson, an English traveller, is in Egypt with his servant, John Bull, seeing the ancient monuments. By a pyramid, they meet a group of Arab merchants, who invite them into their tent. When a storm suddenly rises, everyone takes shelter inside the pyramid.

Scene 2. Inside the pyramid, a guide points out the grand tomb of Aspicia, the daughter of a powerful Pharaoh. The travellers settle down and light opium pipes. As clouds of smoke fill the stage, Lord Wilson falls asleep and begins to dream. The mummies climb from their sarcophagi, including Aspicia, who lays her hand on Lord Wilson's heart. Lord Wilson and John Bull are magicked back to Ancient Egypt, where they become Taor and his servant Passiphonte. Taor tries to follow the beautiful Aspicia, but she vanishes. The scene changes.

Scene 3. Aspicia is out hunting with her attendants. After a dance with bows and arrows, including solos for Aspicia and her slave Ramze, Aspicia lies down to rest. Taor and Passiphonte arrive, searching for Aspicia. After encountering a playful monkey, Taor finds Aspicia asleep on a rock, and wakes her. They fall in love.

At the sound of hunting horns, Aspicia asks Taor to hide. Ramze tries to persuade her mistress to leave. The hunters arrive, warning Aspicia that there is a lion in the forest. It emerges from the rocks, about to attack the princess. Just in time, Taor seizes a bow and shoots an arrow into the lion's heart, saving Aspicia. She swoons, but Taor catches her.

The Pharaoh enters in a horse-drawn chariot, with a host of attendants. He is furious to see his daughter in the arms of a stranger, and orders that Taor should be arrested. When Aspicia wakes, she explains that he saved her life, and should be rewarded. Now grateful, the Pharaoh frees Taor and invites him to his palace.

Act II. Scene 1. Taor visits Aspicia's living quarters and tells her he loves her. The Pharaoh enters with his train, followed by the King of Nubia, who hopes to marry Aspicia. The Pharaoh agrees to this diplomatic marriage, and the two rulers sign a treaty. Hearing this, Taor despairs, but Aspicia promises she will never love anyone else. The Pharaoh orders festivities for the wedding of Aspicia and the King of Nubia, and the lovers decide to run away.

Scene 2. During the wedding celebrations, the couple escape from the palace through a secret door. The angry Pharaoh orders that the runaway couple must be stopped. Spotting the secret door, the King of Nubia and his bodyguards pursue the lovers.

Act III. Scene 1. Taor and Aspicia are hiding in a fisherman's hut on the banks of the Nile. As night falls, Taor agrees to join the fishermen at work, but Aspicia is tired and decides to stay behind. When she is alone, the King of Nubia and his bodyguards enter the hut. To escape him, Aspicia runs to the window and throws herself into the Nile. Taor and Passiphonte return, and are seized by the vengeful King of Nubia.

Scene 2. In the depths of the river Nile. Suspended on wires, the ballerina playing Aspicia is lowered to the bottom of the river, where the God of the Nile, the ruler of the underworld, welcomes her. Recognising her as a princess, he entertains her with a grand ballet performed by the rivers of the world. At the end of the dance, Aspicia asks to see Taor again. The God of the Nile shows her visions of her beloved – on top of a cliff, in a waterfall. Aspicia begs the God of the Nile to send her back to dry land in search of Taor. He agrees.

Scene 3. In his palace, the Pharaoh is frantic over his missing daughter. He threatens to kill Taor if he won't tell him where Aspicia is hiding. Since Taor doesn't know, he is condemned to death, to be bitten by a sacred snake. A joyful march is heard in the distance: the fishermen have found Aspicia and are bringing her back to the palace.

Aspicia throws herself into her father's arms, telling him that she loves Taor and jumped into the Nile to escape the King of Nubia. The Pharaoh tears up the treaty of friendship and orders the King of Nubia to leave. When Aspicia begs for Taor's freedom, however, the Pharaoh refuses: he has abducted a princess, and must die. Aspicia declares that she will die with Taor, and offers her hand to the sacred snake. The Pharaoh prevents her and, moved by her love for Taor, gives the couple his blessing. During the celebrations, clouds of smoke fill the stage.

Scene 4. The scene changes from the palace to the pyramid. Lord Wilson wakes up and looks around in amazement. When he sees Aspicia's tomb, he smiles at the memory of his extraordinary dream.

In staging *The Pharaoh's Daughter* for the Bolshoi Ballet, Lacotte chose to 'remodel and shorten' the ballet: it's a pastiche 'in the style' of Petipa, rather than a reconstruction such as Vikharev's revival of the 1890 production of *The Sleeping Beauty*. Like the 1890 *Beauty*, *The Pharaoh's Daughter* was notated. After consulting specialist Doug Fullington, Lacotte chose to create his own dances, believing that those created from notation weren't detailed enough. (Two 'River' variations were reconstructed from Stepanov notation by Fullington and staged in the new version.)

Lacotte aims to evoke 1860s style, drawing on his own training at the Paris Opéra, and his work with ballerinas Carlotta Zambelli and Lubov Egorova. For *The Pharaoh's Daughter*, he also consulted Marina Semyonova, who danced the heroine in the 1926 revival when she was just seventeen. His new dances emphasise small, fast steps with lots of beats. As director of the Bolshoi, Alexei Ratmansky praised the work as 'a very good school for our dancers. It gives them *batterie* [beaten steps], transitions between the big steps – something that they had paid less attention to, because they're trained in the choreography of Grigorovich, which is very big and dynamic.'[16]

Lacotte's designs also evoke the grand spectacle of the original, with palaces, temples and forest scenes. The women wear tutus with 'Egyptian' detailing, such as lotus patterns around the skirts. Shockingly, the production also features blacked-up 'slave' characters: some *corps de ballet* dancers wear caricatured blackface, while Aspicia's servant Ramze is painted brown.

A Million Kisses to my Skin

Choreography, concept and staging: David Dawson
Music: Johann Sebastian Bach, Piano Concerto No. 1 in D minor
Sets: David Dawson
Costumes: Yumiko Takeshima
Lighting: Bert Dalhuysen
Premiere: 15 June 2000, Dutch National Ballet, Het Muziektheater, Amsterdam
Original cast: Sofiane Sylve, Gaël Lambiotte, Kumiko Hayakawa, Raphaël Coumes-Marquet, Charlotte Chapellier, Megumi Eda, Marisa Lopez, Denise Kromopawiro, Britt Juleen, Igone de Jongh, Sarah Fontaine

The title of David Dawson's ballet evokes the feeling of bliss in dancing. 'I had it a couple of times on stage, and it feels just like that – a million simultaneous kisses to your skin', the choreographer remembered.[17]

Born in London in 1972, Dawson trained at The Royal Ballet School and danced with Birmingham Royal Ballet and English National Ballet before moving to Dutch National Ballet in 1995. *A Million Kisses to my Skin*, his breakthrough work, was also his farewell to Dutch National Ballet; he left to join William Forsythe's Frankfurt Ballet. Dawson has called the work 'kind of my goodbye to my classical career . . . it was important for me to create this piece using classical steps, but also to create a ballet that was about individuality and freedom'.[18]

The ballet is performed on a bare stage, with a white floor and a backdrop of blue panels framed in black. The dancers wear paler blue – leotards and *pointe* shoes for the women, blue tights and lighter T-shirts for the men. As the curtain goes up, a solo woman strolls forward into a speedy solo. She's joined by a second woman, moving in and out of unison, then by the rest of the cast. Dawson uses academic vocabulary with spiky touches: off-balance turns, upflung arms and legs. In the duets, women will dip into deep lunges or be swung into the air. Dancers come and go at high speed, while both men and women lift their legs into high extensions. There is also a slow *pas de deux* for a leading couple, but the ballet's general mood is fast-paced and energetic.

The music is J. S. Bach's first keyboard concerto (written for harpsichord, but now played with a piano soloist). 'The concerto's three movements reminded me of my whole experience as a dancer,' Dawson remembered: 'a serious beginning and a definite ending.'[19] In 2014 he revised the ballet for a Dutch National Ballet revival, staging it with nine dancers rather than fourteen.

Polyphonia

Choreography: Christopher Wheeldon
Composer: György Ligeti: 'Désordre' and 'Arc-en-ciel' from *Études pour piano, premier livre*; 'No. 4 Tempo di Valse' from *Musica Ricercata*; *Invention*; 'No. 8 Vivace energico' from *Musica Ricercata*; 'No. 2 Hopp ide tisztán' from *Three Wedding Dances*; 'No. 7 Cantabile molto legato', 'No. 3 Allegro con spirito' and 'No. 2 Mesto, rigido e cerimoniale' from *Musica Ricercata*; *Capriccio No. 2 – Allegro robusto*
Costumes: Holly Hynes
Lighting: Mark Stanley
Premiere: 4 January 2001, New York City Ballet, New York State Theater, New York
Original cast: Wendy Whelan, Jennie Somogyi, Jennifer Tinsley, Alexandra Ansanelli, Jock Soto, Edwaard Liang, Jason Fowler, Craig Hall

With *Polyphonia*, Christopher Wheeldon became one of the ballet world's most in-demand choreographers. Set to ten of Ligeti's piano pieces, the ballet makes lucid dances out of complex music. As they fold up, drop to the floor and coil into intricate lifts, the dancers look etched in space.

This was the first work Wheeldon made as artist in residence with New York City Ballet, following his own retirement from dancing with the company. It was also the first of a trio of Ligeti ballets: *Continuum* (created in 2002 for San Francisco Ballet) is a close companion, with more piano music, while *Morphoses* (created in 2002 for New York City Ballet) is a work for four dancers to the composer's first string quartet. *Polyphonia* is a confidently transatlantic ballet. Balanchine's leotard ballets are clearly an influence, while Wheeldon's British training is evident in his care for upper-body detail. The influences are lightly worn: in *Polyphonia*, Wheeldon showed his own distinctive voice.

Polyphonia opens with its four couples in a line, dancing simultaneous duets. Having started in unison, they peel off into different steps – in fact, it's the same group of steps, but each couple dances them in a different order. The couples spring quickly from one shape to another, the motifs standing out clearly before vanishing again. Sometimes the patterns overlap, sliding in and out of sync, before the section with a return to unison movement. This opening is danced to a piece called 'Désordre', but the dancers help an audience to see the order in Ligeti's dense, chaotic rhythms. As motifs return, you can recognise a pattern, even as it's shaken up. Mark Stanley's lighting casts the dancers' shadows on the backdrop, as if the patterns were even more complicated, with even more dancers.

This opening is followed by solos, duets and more group dances. In 'Arc-en-Ciel', a ballerina winds over and around her partner, carried through arcs and turns. Another pair waltz together before being joined by two other couples. Three women fold into angles, hands to the floor before picking up and then straightening one leg. One woman floats and spins through a solo before being joined by her partner. In the penultimate piece, 'Mesto, rigido e cerimoniale', the 'Arc-en-Ciel' couple returns for an even more intricate duet that includes what may be *Polyphonia*'s most famous image: the woman curved over her partner's back, her bent legs scissored. The ballet ends with another ensemble.

Gong

Choreography: Mark Morris
Composer: Colin Carhart McPhee, *Tabuh-Tabuhan*
Costumes: Isaac Mizrahi
Lighting: Michael Chybowski

Premiere: 1 May 2001, American Ballet Theatre, Metropolitan Opera House, New York

Original cast: Erica Cornejo, Susan Jaffe, Anna Liceica, Amanda McKerrow, Michele Wiles, Angel Corella, Robert Hill, Giuseppe Picone, Isaac Stappas, Sean Stewart

Gong draws on both Western and Balinese classical arts. Colin McPhee's 1936 score evokes the chiming, reverberant sound of the gamelan, though it's scored for a Western orchestra, plus two Balinese gongs and cymbals. Similarly, Morris' ballet evokes both classical ballet and Balinese dance – one sequence is lit so that the dancers cast huge shadows, suggesting Indonesian shadow puppetry.

The work is danced by five couples and five *corps* women. The fashion designer Isaac Mizrahi, a frequent Morris collaborator, dresses the dancers in different jewel-bright costumes: when they line up they create rainbow patterns of saturated colour. Men and women wear bright gold earrings and anklets. The women have stiff tutu skirts, worn low on the hips – big skirts for the soloists, shorter ones for the *corps*.

The dancing has a ceremonial air, with ballerinas tilting from side to side or walking in crouches. In works for his own company, Morris has shown an interest in Indonesian dance and in gamelan music. In *Gong* he adds Balinese-style hand gestures to ballet steps, with stretched-back fingers and hands touching foreheads. Characteristically for Morris, the group dances dominate, with patterns heightened and underlined by Mizrahi's bright colours. The ballet also includes two duets danced in silence.

Clear

Choreographer: Stanton Welch
Music: J. S. Bach, Concerto for Violin and Oboe in C minor, first and second movements of the Violin Concerto in G minor
Costumes: Michael Kors for Céline
Lighting: Lisa J. Pinkham
Premiere: 25 October 2001, American Ballet Theatre, New York City Center, New York
Original cast: Julie Kent, Angel Corella, Maxim Belotserkovsky, Marcelo Gomes

The son of leading Australian dancers Garth Welch and Marilyn Jones, Stanton Welch fell in love with ballet after working backstage as a dresser in his teens. He started training late, studying at the San Francisco Ballet School before joining The Australian Ballet in 1989. Two years later, he created his first big work for the company, *Of Blessed Memory*, and went on to an international career as a choreographer. He became director of Houston Ballet in 2003.

Clear, one of his most popular works, is a showcase for seven men and one woman. Rehearsals for the ballet started weeks after the terrorist attacks of 9/11, and it reacts to those events. The music is from two Bach concertos – both originally written for harpsichord soloists, but since transposed for violin and oboe and for violin. Fashion designer Michael Kors dresses the cast in flesh-coloured trousers, with a cropped top and *pointe* shoes for the one woman.

The ballet opens with its seven men in a symmetrical line-up, the outer pairs and the centre man jumping in alternation. In *Clear*, Welch employs an academic vocabulary of jumps and turns, adding gestures such as slapped chests, waggled heads and hands lifted to cover the face. The formation pattern runs through the ballet.

In the second movement, the woman dances alongside the men before emerging for her own solo. The men get most of the ballet's energy, with the woman in a calming role. 'In a time of tragedy, what is the clearest thing that occurs to people? What is the common thread? To me it's love and family,' Welch said. 'In *Clear*, the woman brings clarity to the seven men in the ballet. She represents the thing that leads you home and out of the mess you're in.'[20]

Three men dance an energetic trio to the third movement of the oboe concerto, jumping and spinning in canon and in unison. Two men dance an *adagio pas de deux*, in which one man echoes the other. The ballet's 9/11 theme is most obvious in the final male-female *pas de deux*, which includes lamenting gestures and embraces.

The Bright Stream (also called The Limpid Stream)

Choreography: Alexei Ratmansky
Libretto: Adrian Piotrovsky and Fedor Lopukhov
Music: Dmitri Shostakovich
Designs: Boris Messerer
Premiere: 18 April 2003, Bolshoi Ballet, New Stage, Moscow
Original cast: *Zina, the morale officer of the Bright Stream collective farm*
Inna Petrova; *Pyotr, her husband* Yuri Klevtsov; *the Ballerina*
Maria Alexandrova; *Her Partner*, Sergei Filin; *The Accordion Player,*

Gennady Yanin; *an Old Dacha-Dweller* Andrey Melanin; *his Wife, who is anxious to appear younger than she is* Lyobov Fillipova

The Bright Stream is a gleeful romp, a romantic comedy in two acts that combines virtuoso display for soloists and *corps de ballet* with broad comedy numbers and a parade of giant vegetables. At the same time, it reclaims a forgotten part of the Soviet past. In 2004, a year after this immediate hit, Ratmansky became director of the Bolshoi Ballet, a post he held until 2008.

The Bright Stream is based on a lost ballet, a production created by Fedor Lopukhov in 1935. Lopukhov's *Bright Stream* was a popular hit that fell foul of the Soviet authorities (see chapter 6). Lopukhov lost his job as director of the Bolshoi Ballet, while his co-librettist, Adrian Piotrovsky, died in prison. Shostakovich never wrote another ballet.

The scandal of Lopukhov's ballet is part of Ratmansky's production. The new frontcloth is in 1930s propaganda poster style, a globe, a hammer and sickle surrounded by newspaper cuttings – headlines from the articles attacking Shostakovich. Yet the ballet itself is sunny; Ratmansky celebrates Lopukhov, Shostakovich and Piotrovsky's work by recreating it. The entirely new choreography follows the original libretto closely. The collective farm is presented as a happy place, a brightly coloured fantasy world. Boris Messerer's riotous designs frame the action with lush vegetation and the optimistic imagery of 1930s propaganda posters. There are even toy tractors.

Synopsis

Act 1. Scene 1. A country railway station. A troupe of artists is due to visit a collective farm, to celebrate the harvest. Members of the collective, named the Bright Stream, arrive to welcome the guests. They include the heroine Zina (The Bright Stream's morale officer), her husband Pyotr, the activist Gavrilych and the schoolgirl Galya. There are also two middle-class 'dacha-dwellers', an elderly man and his Wife, who is anxious to appear younger than she is.

The troupe arrives, led by a Ballerina, her Partner and an Accordion Player. Zina and the Ballerina recognise each other: they once studied together at ballet school. Reminiscing, they dance a friendly competition, showing who can remember most of their former lessons. Pyotr is dazzled by the Ballerina, and begins to flirt with her. Zina is jealous.

Scene 2. That evening, the field workers make plans for the festival, and dance an improvised celebration with the troupe of artists. The artists have brought presents for the collective's best workers: a gramophone for Gavrilych, a silk dress for a milkmaid. The dacha-dwellers arrive, and dance a comic, outmoded number, full of technical tricks that they can't quite bring off. There is a dance for a group of young girls, and another for the milkmaid, partnered by a tractor driver. The Ballerina and her Partner improvise a dance together. Pyotr's infatuation increases, while the dacha-dwellers are also smitten by the glamorous dancers.

The swaggering accordionist dances a flirtatious number with the shy Galya. Field dancers from Kuban and the Caucasus dance an exuberant folk dance. The Old Dacha-Dweller tries to make an assignation with the Ballerina, while his Wife makes a similar proposal to the ballerina's Partner. Meanwhile, Pyotr goes off with the Ballerina. Zina is distraught, and the young people try to soothe her. The Ballerina returns, reassuring Zina that she isn't interested in her husband. The two friends dance together.

This prompts a new idea. The Ballerina suggests that they all swap clothes. Zina, disguised in the Ballerina's costume, will meet her own husband. The ballerina, in her Partner's clothes, will go to the rendezvous with the dacha-dweller's Wife, while her Partner, also in drag, will meet the Old Dacha-Dweller. All the young people approve of the plan.

Act 2. Scene 1. A clearing in the nearby forest, with convenient bushes to hide behind. The young people assemble. The accordionist tries to make an assignation with Galya, who is taken aback. The Dacha-Dweller, his Wife and Pyotr all remind their 'sweethearts' of their later assignations. The young people quickly change clothes. The tractor driver decides to add to the fun, disguising himself as a dog. When Galya tells them that the accordionist has chatted her up, the tractor driver offers to come to the assignation with her, to protect her. When the accordionist approaches Galya, the dog drives him off. The accordionist realises he is being made a fool of, but agrees to join the main plot.

The Dacha-Dweller arrives on a bicycle, dressed in sporting gear. His Wife turns up, dressed in ballet shoes to impress the male dancer. The dacha-dweller catches sight of a dancer in female costume among the trees. Not realising that this is the male dancer in drag, he pursues him, but the dacha-dweller's Wife is angry and chases her husband away. She in turn is frightened by the tractor driver, still disguised as a dog, riding the bicycle. Appearing in her partner's costume, the Ballerina teases the dacha-dweller's Wife. Finally, they both run off.

Pyotr meets the Ballerina, not realising she is actually his own wife. They flirt and joke together, and he follows her into the bushes. Now the Old Dacha-Dweller comes in with the male dancer, who is still dressed in a romantic ballet dress. Their slapstick dances are a precise parody of the ballet *La Sylphide*, complete with dances on *pointe* for the disguised Partner. The Ballerina, in male clothing, appears and makes a scene, challenging the Dacha-Dweller to a duel. The disguised Ballerina fires, and misses. The Old Dacha-Dweller takes aim, though frightened. Gavrilych hits a bucket, tricking the old man into believing that he has fired. The ballerina's Partner falls to the ground, apparently shot. The Dacha-Dweller flees, leaving the plotters laughing.

Scene 2. The harvest festival. After a triumphant parade of giant vegetables, the whole community assembles for the celebrations. Pyotr, waiting to see the Ballerina, is astonished when two masked dancers rush on stage – Zina and the Ballerina. After their dance, they remove their masks, revealing the plot of the night before. Pyotr begs forgiveness, and everyone is reconciled.

The new *Bright Stream* is full of disguises, intrigues and lively dances. 'When I read the libretto, I thought, this is perfect,' Ratmansky said in 2012:

> Why would you change it? It was very hard for me to convince the Bolshoi administration of the time, and the designer, and the conductor. They said, 'Are you serious? You know the time, with Stalin, the terror.' But I said, 'You don't have that in the music.' Just listen to the score, it's hyper-optimistic. Of course it's a mock optimism, but so what? If there was drama in the music, we would do drama, but it's a game! Everything Shostakovich wanted to say about the subject, he said in the music, so we can just follow him.[21]

The score is full of dance tunes, cheerful waltzes, polkas, foxtrots and more. In the harvest scene, Death appears on stage, swinging his scythe. Other dancers drop down dead, then jump up and keep dancing.

The dances are in a number of styles, from display pieces for the two ballerinas to a drag parody of Romantic ballet. Character dances are broad but still technically demanding. *The Bright Stream* finds plenty of space for dance set pieces, exuberant numbers with intricate footwork. Ratmansky, who clearly loves the traditional academic vocabulary, follows Lophukov in using a mix of character and classical dancing. The complex plot can be hard to follow in full detail, but the thrust of the story is always clear. You may not be able to keep track of the various disguise subplots, but that hardly matters: everyone is plotting, to exuberant comic effect.

Broken Fall

Choreography: Russell Maliphant
Music: Barry Adamson
Lighting: Michael Hulls
Premiere: 3 December 2003, The Royal Ballet, Royal Opera House, London
Original cast: Sylvie Guillem, Michael Nunn, William Trevitt

Russell Maliphant trained at The Royal Ballet School and danced with Sadler's Wells Royal Ballet, before leaving to explore more contemporary work. His movement style is exceptionally fluid, drawing on influences from capoeira to rolfing to create long, smooth movements. He works closely with lighting designer Michael Hulls, who wraps his dances in golden light and shadow. Their work together includes *Two*, a solo framed in a box of light, and dances lit so that moving limbs blur, leaving patterns like vapour trails.

Maliphant has made several works for the BalletBoyz, a company founded by former Royal Ballet dancers William Trevitt and Michael Nunn. First danced at The Royal Ballet, *Broken Fall* was created for the BalletBoyz with Sylvie Guillem. The dancers wear utilitarian shorts and tops, with bare feet and knee-pads.

Two men stand in separate spotlights, swinging their arms, bending into positions or turning on their knees. They're joined by a woman who walks out of a bright light, appearing in blazing silhouette and then almost vanishing as she prowls around them. The three dancers turn and stroll, gradually moving onto low lifts with the woman arching over her partners' backs. These movements develop into more intricate lifts and supported poses, building to high lifts with dramatic drop-catches. The work ends with a spotlit solo for the woman, with the high-swung legs that were Guillem's trademark.

Plan to B

Choreography: Jorma Elo
Music: Heinrich Ignaz Franz von Biber, Prelude, Presto from Violin Sonata No. 1; Violin Sonata No. 2; Violin Sonata No. 81 in A; Violin Sonata No. 3 in F

Costumes: Jorma Elo
Lighting: Pierre Lavoie
Premiere: 25 March 2004, Boston Ballet, Wang Theatre, Boston
Original cast: Sarah Lamb, Larissa Ponomarenko, Joel Prouty, Raul
Salamanca, Sabi Varga, Jared Redick

Born in Helsinki in 1961, Jorma Elo trained at the Finnish National Ballet
School. He danced at the Cullberg Ballet, working with Mats Ek, and at
Nederlands Dans Theater with Jiří Kylián, where he began making dances.
Elo went on dancing after he established himself as a choreographer. After
the success of *Plan to B*, he became Boston Ballet's resident choreographer,
giving up performing.

Danced to virtuosic violin concertos by Heinrich von Biber, *Plan to B*
sets four men and two women moving at great speed. Elo's vocabulary
shows his roots with Kylián and Ek, with sketchy gestures between steps,
but it demands a driving turn of speed from his dancers. In one sequence,
two slide a woman along the floor, then all three snap upright into what is
almost a bathing belle pose, arms bent around the head. As they do this,
another man spins furiously behind them: dancers follow their own trajec-
tories, sometimes overlapping.

Elo designed his own costumes in shades of grey, leotards and soft slippers for the women, tops and trousers with a stripe for the men.

After the Rain

Choreography: Christopher Wheeldon
Music: Arvo Pärt (*Tabula Rasa*, first movement, *Ludus*) and *Spiegel im
Spiegel*
Costumes: Holly Hynes
Lighting: Mark Stanley
Premiere: 22 January 2005, New York City Ballet, New York State
Theater, New York
Original cast: Wendy Whelan, Jock Soto, Sofiane Sylve, Edwaard Liang,
Maria Kowroski, Ask la Cour

After the Rain is best known for its final *pas de deux*, a spare and minimalist
dance with an emotional subtext. This duet was first danced by Wendy
Whelan and Jock Soto, long-term Wheeldon collaborators. Made as Soto
approached retirement, it was the last work Wheeldon made for him. 'What
came through was this love letter, this poem to both of them as artists,'

Wheeldon told critic Joseph Carman. 'It also touched on my personal relationship with Jock and my professional relationship with both of them.'[22] This final part of the ballet is often danced on its own.

The complete ballet opens with Pärt's *Tabula Rasa*, danced by three couples dressed in grey tights and tunics. It's full of bold, unison poses. In the opening image, each man kneels beside his partner, supporting her as she bends forward, swinging her leg high in the air or out to the side, across his shoulders.

Two of the six dancers return to dance the final duet to *Spiegel im Spiegel*. The woman wears a pink leotard, her hair loose, her *pointe* shoes swapped for soft slippers. Her partner is bare-chested, in white trousers. Pärt's music is spare, full of repeated phrases for violin and piano, setting a gentle, melancholy tone.

The dancers stand side by side, at an angle to the audience, shifting and tilting in unison. Then they move into supported *adagio*, the woman leaning against her partner. When she arches back into a crab position at his feet, he picks her up and carries her, her body still arched, her feet still flexed. The duet is full of smooth partnering, the woman lifted, cradled, held overhead. She's also raised from positions on the ground, working into the floor then floating away from it. In the ballet's most famous image, she stands balanced on her partner's braced thigh, supported as she leans forward into space.

Although particularly associated with Whelan, the *pas de deux* in *After the Rain* is popular with many ballerinas, who have found their own approach to it. 'The worst thing you can do with *After the Rain* is to "act" it,' Wheeldon says. 'It's better to settle in and dance it as a piece of movement. When Yuan Yuan [Tan] dances it, it's like a piece of nature, like watching a beautiful piece of willow move. With Wendy, it's very human.'[23]

Russian Seasons

Choreography: Alexei Ratmansky
Music: Leonid Desyatnikov, *Russian Seasons*
Costumes: Galina Solovyeva
Premiere: 8 June 2006, New York City Ballet, New York State Theater, New York
Original cast: *in Orange* Wendy Whelan, Albert Evans; *in Red* Sofiane Sylve, Amar Ramasar; *in Green* Jenifer Ringer, Jonathan Stafford; *in Purple* Abi Stafford, Adam Hendrickson; *in Blue* Alina Dronova, Sean Suozzi; *in Plum* Georgina Pazcoguin, Antonio Carmena

Ratmansky's first work for New York City Ballet was rooted in the Russian past. Leonid Desyatnikov's richly coloured score is a twelve-part set of four violin concertos, on the model of Vivaldi's *The Four Seasons*, with a female singer in five of its movements. There's a folk quality in both music and dance, looking back to peasant Russia – even a touch of Stravinsky's *Les Noces* in Desyatnikov's combination of voice and strings, though Ratmansky's dancers are individuals responding to their situations, rather than being subsumed by the machine of society. Galina Solovyeva dresses the dancers in saturated colours, the men in tunics, trousers and boots, the women in high-waisted dresses (and, at the beginning and end, little pillbox hats).

Ratmansky weaves images of community, love, separation, grief and death into the ballet, life changing as the seasons turn. The dancers shift from classical dancing to casual, everyday movement: in the opening section, men stand about before launching into big double turns. Later, a woman drives through brilliant footwork, then stops to massage and stretch her calf.

There's an explosive, panicky solo for the woman in red, who runs back and forth as the singer describes her fear of being married to an old man. She is surrounded first by clapping women and then by a group of men, before ducking out from under them to escape. Another woman dances with three men in Desyatnikov's 'Song for Ember Days', climbing a staircase of their hands. A third woman plucks imaginary flowers, grieving for a lover who hasn't returned from the war.

As a male soloist whirls through virtuoso spins, and a conga line of women, now in their hats again, prance and dip in lines, men join them to prance in couples, kissing cheeks in a folk celebration. One couple, originally dressed in orange, returns wearing white, the woman with a crown of flowers. In an elegiac ending, they dance a final *pas de deux* while the other dancers watch from the shadows.

Chroma

Choreography: Wayne McGregor
Music: Joby Talbot: *Cloudpark*; '. . . a yellow disc rising from the sea . . .'; *Transit of Venus*; *Hovercraft*, Jack White, arranged by Joby Talbot; 'Aluminum', 'The Hardest Button to Button', 'Blue Orchid' (all three originally by The White Stripes)
Set design: John Pawson
Costumes: Moritz Junge
Lighting: Lucy Carter

Premiere: 17 November 2006, The Royal Ballet, The Royal Opera House, London
Original cast: Federico Bonelli, Alina Cojocaru, Lauren Cuthbertson, Sarah Lamb, Steven McRae, Ludovic Ondiviela, Tamara Rojo, Eric Underwood, Edward Watson, Jonathan Watkins

Born in 1970, Wayne McGregor made his name in contemporary dance, studying at University College, Bretton Hall and the José Limón School. A fast, flexible dancer, he has developed that quality in his own choreography, which is full of slicing limbs yanked into position. McGregor is fascinated by science, by technology and by the mechanics of the body, particularly the body under pressure: his collaborators have included neuroscientists and heart specialists. He founded his own company, Wayne McGregor | Random Dance, in 2002, and has also worked extensively as a freelance choreographer. When he created the dances for the 2005 film *Harry Potter and the Goblet of Fire*, he chose a cast of ordinary London schoolchildren rather than stage school performers, seeking a different kind of movement quality. In 2004 he was a research fellow at the Experimental Psychology department at the University of Cambridge.

He made his first work for The Royal Ballet in 2000. *Chroma* was his second work for the company's main stage, a big, confident ballet that displays its dancers to Joby Talbot's swaggering score. It had a decisive impact on McGregor and The Royal Ballet: shortly after the premiere, he was appointed its resident choreographer, the first to come from outside the company, never mind outside ballet.

Chroma is a plotless work for ten dancers, six men and four women. Moritz Junge dresses them in skimpy camisoles and underwear, in flesh-toned pinks and browns, with soft slippers for both sexes. McGregor points out that 'chroma' can mean intensity of colour, or freedom from white or grey. His dancers are splashes of colour inside a stark set by architect John Pawson, making his debut as a stage designer.

It's a plain white box, with another box within – a raised platform at the back of the stage, set within the frame of the backdrop. Dancers stand in this inner space, often silhouetted by Lucy Carter's lighting, or make dramatic entrances from it, climbing out onto the stage. McGregor plays with space: the opening duet is balanced by a second group of four dancers, who wait at the side, standing at an angle to the action. There are blackouts, and one blaze of light, between different sections of music.

The style has the dancers plunging in and out of extreme poses, with arching spines, jutting buttocks, bobbing heads and limbs swung forcefully high. Dances overlap: those four dancers burst into action before the opening duet is quite over. There is male-male as well as male-female partnering, particularly in a trio for three men. Although there is no *pointe*-work, McGregor uses the strength and articulacy of ballet-trained feet.

'I heard Joby Talbot's *Hovercraft* piece for orchestra and felt its immediate physical impact,' McGregor said, 'visceral, unsettling, hungry and direct.'[24] The score includes Talbot's arrangements of three songs by the band The White Stripes ('Aluminum', 'The Hardest Button to Button' and 'Blue Orchid') with orchestrations by Christopher Austin, and three of Talbot's own compositions. They're full of blaring James Bond brass, dropping to reflective hums.

Hovercraft, the final section, uses the whole cast, with solos, duets and group dances sharing the stage, and women moving from one group to another in dramatic throws and catches. On the last note, the whole cast turn their backs and stand quietly as the lights fade.

Concerto DSCH

Choreography: Alexei Ratmansky
Music: Dmitri Shostakovich, Piano Concerto No. 2 in F major, op. 102
Costumes: Holly Hynes
Lighting: Mark Stanley
Premiere: 29 May 2008, New York City Ballet, New York State Theater, New York
Original cast: Wendy Whelan, Ashley Bouder, Benjamin Millepied, Joaquin De Luz, Gonzalo Garcia

In *Concerto DSCH*, Ratmansky responds to Shostakovich's Second Piano Concerto with changing emotional colour and fizzing virtuoso steps. Although it's a plotless work, the dancers suggest the athletes of the early Soviet period, with mock-heroic poses and truly heroic bravura. The mood can shift from romping camaraderie to quiet tenderness.

The title refers to Shostakovich's musical 'signature', a motif of four notes which, in German musical notation, spell out DSCH, or *Dmitri Schostakovich* (the German spelling of his name). The concerto was written in 1957 as a nineteenth birthday present for the composer's son Maxim. The music – which Kenneth MacMillan also used for his 1966 ballet *Concerto* (see chapter 7) – reveals a mood of new optimism after the repressions of the Stalinist era.

The ballet is led by a couple in green, with a virtuoso trio – two men, one woman – in blue. The seven *corps de ballet* couples wear red and orange. There's a suggestion of workers' dungarees in the leading men's trousers and tops, while the women wear short, simple dresses.

The ballet opens with the *corps* men in a tight circle formation. One by one, the blue trio dancers pop out from the centre of the circle, exploding into dance. The *corps* women enter with the lyrical couple in green. Ratmansky sets the different groups crossing and recrossing the stage, catching different aspects of the speedy, cheerful music. The green couple pose heroically, while the *corps* frames them in respectful circles for a grand fanfare.

Concerto DSCH has a free and easy attitude to its own virtuosity. The athletes in blue streak brilliantly through the first movement – then flop down on the floor to watch everyone else. As the *corps* men spin and dance, one of their number just keeps jumping, so that the repetitions are first funny and then impressive; the straight-legged, flexed-foot jump becomes a motif running through the first movement.

The slow second movement is a flowing *pas de deux* for the couple in green, whose dance is framed by other couples. The women and men embrace and part as if going home to separate dormitories.

The third movement opens with the athletes in blue. The woman bounces between her two partners – and then they switch places so that the men are bounced in turn. The woman whirls off to dance with the man in green, but is brought up short when the ballerina finds them together. All these incidents are fleeting, woven into high-speed, exuberant dancing. In the finale, the speedy blue trio are set against a *corps de ballet* that seems to move in slow motion, before the whole cast runs through block patterns to the final pose.

Concerto DSCH shows Ratmansky's love of classical steps and a fresh sensibility. The dancers' interactions are friendly; he'll use ballet's hierarchies to build a grouping, then slide into something much more democratic. The relations between the sexes are fluid, too. It's easy to read ballet couples as heterosexual love affairs; here, any one of the blue trio might end up with any one of the others.

The ballet was received with rapture. 'As *Concerto DSCH* . . . unfolded at its premiere on Thursday night, you could feel wave upon wave of emotion sweeping across the audience,' wrote the critic Alastair Macaulay:

Wonder, excitement, admiration, affection, hilarity, surprise, exhilaration . . . Again and again, you find yourself thinking, 'I didn't realise this was going to happen after that,' and 'What exactly were those steps that flashed by just now?' Better yet, it's marked by tender pure-dance poetry.[25]

Infra

Choreography: Wayne McGregor
Music: Max Richter
Decor: Julian Opie
Costumes: Moritz Junge
Lighting: Lucy Carter
Premiere: 13 November 2008, The Royal Ballet, Royal Opera House, London
Original cast: Leanne Benjamin, Ricardo Cervera, Yuhui Choe, Lauren Cuthbertson, Mara Galeazzi, Melissa Hamilton, Ryoichi Hirano, Paul Kay, Marianela Nuñez, Eric Underwood, Jonathan Watkins, Edward Watson

Infra is dominated by images of crowds. The first work McGregor created as resident choreographer of The Royal Ballet has no narrative, but adds hints of situation and mood: there are even literal dramatic gestures, a kiss or a cry. In his programme notes, McGregor quotes T. S. Eliot's *The Waste Land*:

Unreal City,
Under the brown fog of a winter dawn,
A crowd flowed over London Bridge, so many,
I had not thought death had undone so many.

Infra is a melancholy ballet, the tone set by Max Richter's mix of murmuring electronica and scratchy string-quartet writing.

The decor, by visual artist Julian Opie, is a wide LED screen hanging overhead, showing electronic figures walking. Although they're round-headed stick figures, they walk with natural, believable body language. Underneath the screen, dancers move through twisting, thrusting moves, rather gentler than the high-definition attack of *Chroma*. Moritz Junge's costumes are black or white dancewear, shorts and tops. McGregor, Richter and Opie all suggest the experience of people-watching. Opie describes watching people in the street as if they were choreographed; Richter's score includes snatches of shortwave radio, hints of voices, 'which for me has a kind of storytelling quality, because there are a lot of voices there, but you don't know whose they are, or when they're from, or where.'[26]

Couples line up in boxes of light, dancing individual duets. Patterns start to emerge, variations and echoes; as more couples arrive, the stage becomes busy with duets.

During one woman's solo, a large cast of people in street clothes cross the stage, living equivalents of Opie's digital crowd. As they walk past, the ballerina sinks to the floor, weeping in silent howls.

Namouna: A Grand Divertissement

Choreography: Alexei Ratmansky
Music: Édouard Lalo
Costumes: Marc Happel and Rustam Khamdamov
Lighting: Mark Stanley
Premiere: 29 April 2010, New York City Ballet, David H. Koch Theater, New York
Original cast: Wendy Whelan, Robert Fairchild, Jenifer Ringer, Sara Mearns, Megan Fairchild, Daniel Ulbricht, Abi Stafford

In *Namouna*, Alexei Ratmansky evokes and jokes about nineteenth-century mythological ballet, with a perfumed French score from 1882 and all the props and situations it suggests. Lalo's music (also used for Serge Lifar's *Suite en blanc*, see chapter 5) was written for an 1882 ballet by Lucien Petipa, in which the sailor hero manages to win the heroine in a bet with a pirate. It was a short-lived work, not least because its music was accused of being too 'Wagnerian' for dancing. Debussy, then aged nineteen, cheered the music so loudly that, he recalled, he was ejected from the theatre for his 'noisy but forgivable enthusiasm'.

Ratmansky's version is, as its title suggests, a divertissement: he kept the sailor hero and the pirate, and even some mime scenes, but there is no actual plot. Instead, there are plenty of situations and even subplots for the large cast of twenty-one women and ten men. In the opening scene, the sailor mimes that he is in love, then encounters three different women. A cigarette-smoking vamp waves away the smoke with a shake of her leg, a move that is echoed by her *corps de ballet*. The second woman, in long white gloves, suggests one of ballet's gypsy heroines, with bounding jumps and backbends. The mysterious third woman is probably Namouna herself, since she's the one who gets our hero.

Marc Happel and Rustam Khamdamov's costumes suggest the 1920s rather than the 1880s, with women in wigs like white Marcel-wave bathing caps or black bobbed hair, like the silent-movie star Louise Brooks. There is a long cigarette-smoking scene, a dance with cymbals and a lullaby in which the *corps de ballet* rocks the hero to sleep.

After its first performance, *Namouna*'s sheer frivolity was criticised; with more performances, and some editing, doubters succumbed to its charms.

Alice's Adventures in Wonderland

Choreography: Christopher Wheeldon
Music: Joby Talbot
Design: Bob Crowley
Lighting: Natasha Katz
Projection design: Jon Driscoll and Gemma Carrington
Puppet concept and design: Toby Olié
Premiere: 28 February 2011, The Royal Ballet, Royal Opera House, London
Original cast: *Alice* Lauren Cuthbertson; *Jack/The Knave of Hearts* Sergei Polunin; *Lewis Carroll/The White Rabbit* Edward Watson; *Mother/The Queen of Hearts* Zenaida Yanowsky; *Magician/The Mad Hatter* Steven McRae; *Rajah/Caterpillar* Eric Underwood; *The Duchess* Simon Russell Beale

Lewis Carroll's *Alice* books are a temptation to choreographers. *Alice's Adventures in Wonderland* and *Alice Through the Looking-Glass* are much-loved titles with celebrated characters and strong visual concepts. The potential stumbling blocks are in the books, too: in the trickiness of Carroll's surreal, episodic narratives and in the focus on wordplay. Neither is an obvious fit for dance. Nevertheless, several ballets have been created on the Alice theme. Glen Tetley's 1986 *Alice*, created for the National Ballet of Canada to music by David Del Tredici, drew on Carroll's relationship with the real-life Alice Liddell, with both child and adult Alices on stage. Prompted by Carroll's interest in photography, Ashley Page's 2011 *Alice* for Scottish Ballet, to music by Robert Moran, used camera imagery.

Christopher Wheeldon's version, a co-production between The Royal Ballet and the National Ballet of Canada, is a big, colourful show that has been popular on both sides of the Atlantic. Using a scenario by playwright Nicholas Wright, Wheeldon tries to develop a dramatic narrative, but the ballet is dominated by spectacular versions of Carroll's familiar scenes, using dancing and elaborate stage wizardry applied with theatrical sophistication. Wheeldon's team for the ballet included many artists associated with Britain's National Theatre, including librettist Nicholas Wright and the actor Simon Russell Beale, who danced the Duchess in the first run.

Wright's scenario frames the book with Carroll's own history. The ballet starts in Oxford, where Carroll was a lecturer in mathematics, and where he befriended the real-life Alice Liddell. These biographical elements have become a familiar part of the *Alice* story. Carroll and Alice have been fictionalised for film, television, the stage and in novels, besides featuring in adaptations of the book itself.

Synopsis

Act I. Oxford, 1862. Henry Liddell, his wife and their servants prepare for a garden party. Their friend Lewis Carroll entertains their three daughters, who include Alice. This naturalistic opening is full of people and incidents that will reappear in the Wonderland scenes. Alice's mother rebukes the gardener's boy, Jack, for including a red rose in a bunch of white roses. He gives the rose to his friend Alice, who gives him a jam tart in return. Alice's mother accuses him of stealing the tart, and dismisses him. Guests arrive, including a magician, clergymen, a woman with a baby and an Indian Rajah. Lewis Carroll prepares to take a photograph, and emerges from the camera cloth as a White Rabbit. He jumps into his camera bag and vanishes. Alice dives after him, falling into Wonderland.

Alice lands in a mysterious corridor full of doors. Through a keyhole, she sees a garden of flowers – played by dancers, who appear around the theatre auditorium. Jack, turned into the Knave of Hearts, rushes through the hall. He is pursued by the terrifying Queen of Hearts (played by the dancer who plays Alice's mother), her guards and the White Rabbit. Alice tries to follow, but the only unlocked door is too small to let her through. She drinks from a bottle labelled 'Drink me', and shrinks; she eats a cake labelled 'Eat me', which makes her enormous. She cries in frustration, and her tears form a lake big enough to swim in. She is joined in the pool by various strange animals. Trying to dry them off and cheer them up, Alice leads them in a race.

The White Rabbit leads Alice further into Wonderland, sailing on a paper boat until they reach the Duchess' cottage, a violent place where the Duchess attends a squealing baby while a threatening Cook makes sausages. A fish-footman brings an invitation to a croquet party held by the Queen of Hearts. The Cheshire Cat, a puppet creation, makes a brief appearance.

The White Rabbit reappears, warning Alice not to follow him to the Queen's garden. The Knave reappears, chased by guards and followed by the Queen and her court. The White Rabbit hides the Knave and Alice. To prevent her following them, the Rabbit and the Knave blindfold Alice.

Act II. Confused, Alice asks the Cheshire Cat for directions, without success. She moves on to meet the Mad Hatter. The Mad Hatter's famous tea party is staged as a performance within a performance, with the Hatter tap-dancing on a raised stage and bouncing on a cake-shaped trampoline. Alice next meets a Caterpillar, who dances a slinky 'exotic' number before giving her a piece of mushroom, which affects her vision. After moving through the hall of doors, she at last finds herself in the flower garden, where she dances with the Knave of Hearts. Their dance is interrupted by the Queen of Hearts.

Act III. In the garden of the Queen of Hearts, gardeners are painting white roses red: the Queen hates white roses. When the Queen arrives, with the King, the court, the Duchess and the Cook, and sees white roses, she orders the gardeners executed. While the Executioner flirts with the Cook, Alice and the White Rabbit help the gardeners to escape.

The Queen dances for the court, partnered by four dancers dressed as playing cards. She and the Duchess pick teams for a croquet match, using flamingos as mallets and hedgehogs as balls. (The flamingos are glove puppets, with the dancer's hand working the head. The hedgehogs are a mix of props and small children in spiny costumes.) As the Duchess and the Queen play and quarrel, Alice meets the Knave behind their backs. He is discovered, and dragged off to be tried for stealing tarts.

A group of playing cards dance an interlude as the scene changes to the courtroom. Alice brings in the witnesses – the characters she has met in Wonderland. Terrified of the Queen, they all accuse the Knave. The henpecked King finally asserts himself and asks the Knave to testify in his own defence. Alice steps up to insist that he is innocent. They win over the court, but the Queen is furious, and snatches up an axe to attack the Knave. In the chase that follows, Alice pushes over a witness – and they all collapse, since they are only playing cards.

Alice wakes up to find herself in present-day Oxford. She has been dreaming over a book, and is relieved to find that she and Jack, her boyfriend, are safe. She asks a passing photographer – who looks very like Lewis Carroll – to take their picture. The curtain falls on Carroll reading the copy of *Alice's Adventures in Wonderland* that she has left behind.

Wheeldon's production is driven and shaped by its stage effects. Alice falls into Wonderland through a mix of puppetry and video projections. (In the Royal Ballet production, she and the White Rabbit dive into a camera bag. When Wheeldon staged *Alice* for the National Ballet of Canada, this effect would not work in all the company's touring venues, and was reworked so that an elaborate jelly served at the garden party became the entrance to Wonderland.) The Cheshire Cat is achieved with bunraku-style puppetry. The cat's head, body, limbs and tail are moved separately, so that – as in Carroll's story – parts of its body can vanish.

Some of the production's effects hark back to the grand spectacles in nineteenth-century ballets: Alice's journey in the paper boat recalls the panorama scene in *The Sleeping Beauty*. The Queen of Hearts' dance with the playing cards is a parody of the Rose Adagio from *The Sleeping Beauty*, with extra cartwheels, pratfalls and partners who are terrified of their execution-happy ballerina. Joby Talbot's commissioned score quotes Tchaikovsky here, echoing the Rose Adagio.

Talbot's music is highly coloured, with extravagant orchestration and distinctive motifs for different characters and scenes, including a ticking-clock motif for Wonderland itself – started when the White Rabbit looks at his pocket watch. The Queen of Hearts is associated with the solo violin, tuned a semitone sharp to suggest her highly strung character.

Although Alice is the ballet's heroine, she is a bystander for many scenes, reacting to the unpredictable characters and events. She is less downright than the Alice of Carroll's books, though the ballet makes the character older and gives her a love story. One of her most characterful dances takes place in the hall of doors: she jumps and jumps as she tries to reach an over-sized handle, and stamps in frustration. Across the ballet, Wheeldon gives her a repeated motif, a flat foot worked along the ground, which recurs in solos and in her dances with Jack. The choreography for Jack casts him as a traditional ballet cavalier, partnering Alice and dancing classical steps.

Dancers can make a stronger impression in the comic supporting roles, especially the Queen of Hearts, who has prominent set pieces, and the Mad Hatter. Steven McRae, the original Hatter, is a gifted tap-dancer, so Wheeldon built this into the role. Later Hatters learned to tap, with some adjustments to the steps.

Viscera

Choreography: Liam Scarlett
Music: Lowell Lieberman, Piano Concerto No. 1, op. 12

Costumes: Liam Scarlett
Lighting: John Hall
Premiere: 6 January 2012, Miami City Ballet, Adrienne Arsht Center for
the Performing Arts, Miami
Original cast: Jennifer Kronenberg, Carlos Guerra, Jeanette Delgado

Born in 1986, Liam Scarlett trained at The Royal Ballet School, where he
won a series of choreographic competitions. He was tipped as a future
choreographer long before he joined The Royal Ballet, and has been fast-
tracked to international attention.

His first main stage work for The Royal Ballet was *Asphodel Meadows*,
with fluent classical dancing to Poulenc's Double Piano Concerto.
Edward Villella, then director of Miami City Ballet, saw rehearsals on a visit
to London, and commissioned Scarlett to create a new work. *Viscera*
was greeted with standing ovations, and has since been taken into the
repertory of The Royal Ballet and the Royal Danish Ballet. In 2012, Scarlett
ended his dancing career, and was appointed The Royal Ballet's artist in
residence.

Viscera is a sleek, plotless work to Lowell Lieberman's energetic First
Piano Concerto: Scarlett has said he wanted to pay homage to Miami City
Ballet's strong Balanchine heritage. He dresses his sixteen dancers in plum-
coloured leotards, their legs bare.

The first movement is fast and confident, sending dancers in waves
across the stage, breaking into solos and group dances. As a soloist
spins, she's joined by a second dancer, so that the two slide into unison
mid-step.

The central movement is a long duet to Lieberman's melancholy piano
lines. It's full of intricate partnering, the ballerina kneeling on her partner's
shoulders and reaching upwards, or diving into an upside-down pose.

The final movement is speedy, with a soloist moving against the tide of
the *corps de ballet*. As she dances, the *corps* dancers move upstage, their
backs to the audience. Then they switch, with the *corps* advancing while the
soloist retreats to the back.

In contrast to his breakthrough plotless works, Scarlett has also shown a
MacMillan influence in his first dramatic ballets, which both feature sexual
violence. *Sweet Violets*, created for The Royal Ballet in 2012, was inspired by
the painter Walter Sickert and the Jack the Ripper murders; *Hansel and
Gretel* set the story in 1950s Americana, with a male, paedophile witch.
Neither won the acclaim of Scarlett's plotless works.

Symphony #9

Choreographer: Alexei Ratmansky
Music: Dmitri Shostakovich, Symphony No. 9 in E flat major, op. 70
Scenery: George Tsypin
Costumes: Keso Dekker
Lighting: Jennifer Tipton
Premiere: 18 October 2012, American Ballet Theatre, New York City Center, New York
Original cast: Polina Semionova, Marcelo Gomes, Herman Cornejo, Craig Salstein, Simone Messmer

Symphony #9 is the first ballet in Ratmansky's 'Shostakovich trilogy', a group of ballets linked by composer, design and apparent themes. Since the early twentieth century, choreographers have used concert music for dancing. Balanchine's pure-dance approach now dominates ballets of this kind, but some of the earliest 'symphonic ballets', particularly those by Léonide Massine, interpreted the music with themes and characters.

'I'm trying to explore this genre of symphonic ballet,' Ratmansky said as he began work on the trilogy:

What does that mean? How can it be put on? I adore Massine's symphonies. And who else does them? Neumeier does a lot of Mahler. But I think it's a very serious, very grand genre. I'd like to explore that direction. I do feel connected to those figures [of ballet's past]. I think I am seeking for some kind of support, maybe. You can't read anything about the craft [of ballet]. You need to reinvent everything yourself. It's silly to be thinking you can reinvent things, everything has been done. So maybe that's also one of the reasons.[27]

Unlike Massine, Ratmansky hasn't spelled out his themes with named characters, but his choice of Shostakovich, a composer who responded to political repression by hiding codes in his music, is telling. The trilogy presents images of repression, of life in a repressive society. In all three ballets, the dancers show a fear of being watched. Jennifer Tipton's lighting casts sinister shadows.

Symphony #9 is led by five soloists – a first and second couple, with a lone virtuoso man – plus eight *corps* couples. It opens with the lone man, joined by other men and a woman, in cheerful dances with a martial air; the woman mimics playing the drums, as if accompanying the music's march. The lone man leaps into the arms of his waiting male comrades. Even in this bright movement, the first couple pause in their duet, as if aware that they are being watched.

The second couple dance a guarded *pas de deux* in the second movement. Meeting her partner, the woman puts her hand to his lips, as if warning him to stay silent. They sink to the floor in stages, folding up. It's a movement that will be repeated by other dancers, across the trilogy. The couple dances to a clarinet theme, which, Ratmansky told the critic Marina Harss, reminded him of the couple in Mikhail Bulgakov's Stalin-era novel *The Master and Margarita*: 'They're outsiders,' he said of Bulgakov's couple, 'living in a little room beneath the level of the street . . . they're protective of each other, not part of the momentum of life. They can't be part of it because they're different.'[28]

In the third movement, the backdrop changes to images of soldiers, planes and red flags; the apparently cheerful finale ends with the single man alone onstage.

Chamber Symphony

Choreography: Alexei Ratmansky
Music: Dmitri Shostakovich, Chamber Symphony for Strings, op. 100a, arranged by Rudolph Barshai
Scenery: George Tsypin
Costumes: Keso Dekker
Lighting: Jennifer Tipton
Premiere: 31 May 2013, American Ballet Theatre, Metropolitan Opera House, New York
Original cast: David Hallberg, Isabella Boylston, Paloma Herrera, Julie Kent

The second ballet in Ratmansky's Shostakovich trilogy, *Chamber Symphony*, comes closest to explicit narrative, with an implied story. Its central figure is an unhappy artist figure, tormented by the trilogy's atmosphere of fear and repression. The music is desolate, repeating the DSCH theme. George Tsypin's backdrop shows a group of faces gazing down: it's based on the Russian artist Pavel Filonov's 1935 work *Eleven Heads*, but these heads have been stripped of colour. Keso Dekker dresses the dancers in dark costumes, with the artist shirtless in a suit.

Ratmansky shows his artist struggling with demons, twisting and crumpling, falling, rising and falling again, watched by a *corps de ballet*. He dances with three different women: one seductive, one tender, one apparently platonic. All three relationships are interrupted and broken off. Men carry the second woman through the air, sweeping her away as the artist reaches for her. The critic Jerry Hochman wrote: 'Based on the way in which the relationships are presented as sequential temptations in the context of unimaginable fear and hopelessness, the segment looks like Balanchine's *Apollo* as choreographed by Kafka.'[29]

The artist-figure's resilience appears at the end, as he turns to the *corps de ballet* and seems to sculpt them into a heroic tableau, creating something new.

Piano Concerto #1

Choreography: Alexei Ratmansky
Music: Dmitri Shostakovich, Concerto No. 1 for Piano, Trumpet and Strings, op. 35
Scenery: George Tsypin
Costumes: Keso Dekker
Lighting: Jennifer Tipton
Premiere: 31 May 2013, American Ballet Theatre, Metropolitan Opera House, New York
Original cast: Diana Vishneva, Cory Stearns, Natalia Osipova, Ivan Vasiliev

The final ballet in Ratmansky's Shostakovich trilogy is the most abstract of the three, and the most apparently positive. Ratmansky changed his mind about the music, switching to the concerto for piano, trumpet and strings at a late stage, having originally planned to end with Shostakovich's First Symphony. They're both early works, from a time when the composer was still in favour with the Soviet authorities.

George Tsypin's backdrop is patterned with bright red shapes, stylised stars and bolts. The leading women wear red leotards, the men in grey, while the dancers of the *corps de ballet* wear grey and red, divided front and back – so that they seem to change colour when they turn.

One leading couple is angular, the other more lyrical. They dance together and individually; after one virtuoso sequence, the two ballerinas stop in fear, one protecting the other. Even in the trilogy's most optimistic moment, fear is not forgotten.

The Winter's Tale

Choreography: Christopher Wheeldon
Music: Joby Talbot

Designs: Bob Crowley
Lighting designs: Natasha Katz
Premiere: 10 April 2014, The Royal Ballet, Royal Opera House, London
Original cast: *Leontes, King of Sicilia* Edward Watson; *Hermione, Queen of Sicilia* Lauren Cuthbertson; *Paulina* Zenaida Yanowsky; *Perdita, Princess of Sicilia* Sarah Lamb; *Polixenes, King of Bohemia* Federico Bonelli; *Florizel, Prince of Bohemia* Steven McRae

Shakespeare's *The Winter's Tale* is a daunting narrative for dance, a story of lost children and lost parents, apparently magic statues, time passing and a very famous bear. Where ballets based on *Romeo and Juliet* and *A Midsummer Night's Dream* proliferate, Wheeldon may be the first to have risked turning this late romance into dance.

In the event, *The Winter's Tale* made the difficult story legible, establishing relationships and changing situations with clarity. The *Alice* design team were reassembled, with the addition of Basil Twist, who created the special effects for Wheeldon's *Cinderella*, to create the bear. Most importantly, where *Alice* is a confident show, *The Winter's Tale* is an assured ballet, its effects rooted in movement and performance rather than relying on stage magic. Critics were enthusiastic, though most preferred either the dramatic first act or the dance-focused Bohemian act (I'm in the second camp). But *The Winter's Tale* is a difficult assignment that worked, suggesting increased maturity for Wheeldon as a choreographer.

Synopsis

Prologue. Two kings, Leontes of Sicilia and Polixenes of Bohemia, are childhood friends who meet again as adults. Leontes marries Hermione, giving her an emerald necklace. They have a son, Mamillius. Polixenes comes to visit his old friend, and stays at his court for nine months. As he prepares to leave, Hermione is soon to give birth to her second child.

Act I. The court of Sicilia. Polixenes prepares to leave. The Bohemian court say goodbye to their Sicilian friends. At Hermione's request, Polixenes agrees to stay for another week. Leontes is suddenly overcome with jealousy, convinced that his wife has been unfaithful, and doubtful whether the new baby is his child: his hand on her pregnant belly becomes twisted and clawlike. He follows Polixenes and Hermione as they walk through the sculpture gallery of the palace. Wheeldon switches between Polixenes and Hermione dancing innocently together, and the scene as Leontes now sees it, where their dance becomes sexual. Leontes attacks Polixenes, who leaves for Bohemia. Leontes publicly accuses Hermione of adultery and treason, and orders her arrest. Their son Mamillius, deeply distressed, falls ill.

In prison, Hermione has given birth to a daughter. Paulina, the head of the royal household, brings the baby to Leontes, hoping that the sight of his child will soften his heart. Instead, he rejects the new baby, ordering Paulina's husband Antigonus to abandon it. As a storm rises, Antigonus sets sail with the baby and some treasure, including the emerald necklace that Leontes once gave Hermione.

At her trial, Hermione pleads her innocence. Leontes, mad with jealousy, refuses to believe her. Frail and ill, Mamillius comes into the courtroom. Seeing his father's rage at his mother, he collapses and dies. Horrified by the death of her child, Hermione also collapses, and her body is carried away. The double tragedy brings Leontes to his senses: he realises what he has done.

The sea coast of Bohemia. Antigonus travels through the storm, coming ashore to abandon the baby princess on the wild coast. He is killed by a bear – a billowing silk wave that comes down to swallow him, with the bear's head and claws painted on the fabric. As day breaks, a shepherd and his son Clown find the baby girl, and take her home.

Act II. A hillside in Bohemia, by a great tree. Sixteen years have passed. Perdita, the daughter of Hermione and Leontes, has been raised by the shepherd who found her. She dances with Florizel, her beloved. He is the son of King Polixenes, but has disguised himself as a shepherd to visit her. The villagers arrive for the annual springtime festival. They hang golden amulets and garlands in the great tree, and prepare to dance.

Polixenes, who has heard that his son has become entangled with a shepherdess, decides to investigate. He and his steward disguise themselves to watch the festival.

Perdita is crowned May Queen. In honour of the occasion, her foster father gives her the emerald necklace he found with her on the beach. Florizel asks Perdita to marry him. Outraged, Polixenes casts of his disguise, and condemns Perdita and her family to death. They all flee by boat to Sicilia, pursued by Polixenes.

Act III. A clifftop in Sicilia. Leontes mourns by the graves of Hermione and Mamillius. Paulina watches over him. They see Perdita's ship approach.

The palace in Sicilia. Perdita and Florizel arrive, and beg Leontes to help them. Reminded of his own lost children, Leontes agrees. When Polixenes arrives, Leontes tries to reason with him. In the struggle, Perdita's cloak falls open, revealing the emerald. Paulina and Leontes recognise her as the long-lost princess. Everyone rejoices.

After celebrations for the wedding of Florizel and Perdita, Paulina brings Leontes to see a new statue of Hermione and Mamillius. In his remorse and grief, he kneels at the foot of the statue. The statue of Hermione moves, stepping down from the pedestal. She is alive, kept in hiding by Paulina for sixteen years. Leontes begs her forgiveness in a duet; she embraces him and then her daughter. The ballet ends with the family happily reunited – but the statue of Mamillius remains onstage, reminding us that some mistakes cannot be undone.

Wheeldon's ballet deliberately changes tone halfway through. The long first act is set in a wintry Sicilia, a court framed by icy white statuary and northern landscapes by the painter Caspar David Friedrich. Joby Talbot's music for this act is cool, efficiently plot-driven, with drum and gong notes heralding Leontes' jealousy. Wheeldon's choreography is also focused on the narrative. Leontes' jealous writhings are strongly influenced by *Mayerling* – Edward Watson, the original Leontes, is an acclaimed Rudolf in MacMillan's ballet. As in his plotless works, some of Wheeldon's duets are over-partnered, women manipulated and turned over in happiness and in jealousy, but the narrative is admirably clear throughout, with character and plot clearly defined. The first act also has fine moments of theatre: as his parents rage, we see the child Mamillius watching them from the top of a flight of stairs, teddy bear in hand.

The second act, set in Bohemia, shows the return of spring. The curtain goes up on Crowley's huge green tree, while an onstage musician plays a hazy, curling solo on the bansuri (Indian flute). Everything relaxes and opens out: there's time for more melody and much more dancing. There are more musicians onstage, playing disparate instruments including accordion and percussion, becoming involved in the action. (They appear briefly with the Bohemian entourage in the first act.) The disguised Polixenes is given a guitar, and for a while there's a real sense that he might be asked to play it.

In Shakespeare's play, Perdita is a difficult role, a static embodiment of various virtues. In dance, as in *The Sleeping Beauty*, her beauty and good-ness become active qualities. Wheeldon's choreography for Perdita and for the ensemble recalls Ashton's joyful dances in *Daphnis and Chloë*, expan-sive and radiant, with virtuoso solos for supporting shepherds. The last act of *The Winter's Tale* combines the two elements, returning to Sicilia with more open musical textures and more time for dancing.

Everywhere We Go

Choreography: Justin Peck
Music: Sufjan Stevens, *Everywhere We Go*, in nine sections: 'The Shadows Will Fall Behind', 'Happiness is a Perfume', 'I Breathe the Air of Mountains and Their Unapproachable Heights', 'To Live in the Hearts We Leave Behind', 'There Is Always the Sunshine', 'Every Flower That Stirs the Elastic Sod', 'I Am In The House And I Have The Key', 'The Gate of Heaven Is Love', 'Thanks to the Human Heart by Which We Live'
Decor: Karl Jensen
Costumes: Janie Taylor
Lighting: Brandon Stirling Baker
Premiere: 8 May 2014, New York City Ballet, David H. Koch Theater, New York
Original cast: Maria Kowroski, Sterling Hyltin, Tiler Peck, Teresa Reichlen, Robert Fairchild, Andrew Veyette, Amar Ramasar

Everywhere We Go is a large-scale, friendly work by Justin Peck, danced to a commissioned score by pop musician Sufjan Stevens. Seven principals and a *corps de ballet* of eighteen move through Stevens' cinematic, sometimes brash score. *Corps* and soloists often overlap, with principals emerging from the group and merging back into it.

Peck and Stevens first worked together on the 2012 ballet *Year of the Rabbit*, set to an orchestration of Stevens' 2002 electronica album *Enjoy Your Rabbit*, based on themes of the Chinese zodiac. The new work is scored for piano and orchestra with plenty of percussion and brass.

The designs, by architect Karl Jensen, are backcloths with geometric shapes cut into them. As they slide past each other, they create changing patterns, sometimes suggesting 3D shapes. Janie Taylor dresses all twenty-five dancers in colour-blocked tights: black with grey tops for the men, white with striped sailor tops for the women, both with a band of red at the waist.

Everywhere We Go is a busy, ambitious work, full of variety and changing moods. In the opening section, 'The Shadows Will Fall Behind', a male duet suggests a man and his shadow: one standing, the other echoing his movements as he lies on the floor. In 'To Live in the Hearts We Leave Behind' a couple dance together but she returns to the ensemble: he keeps coming back for her. This section was choreographed for Robert Fairchild and the taller Maria Kowroski: it's unusual to pair dancers with such a height difference, but Peck puts them together without fuss.

Ballets are often dominated by *pas de deux*, but *Everywhere We Go* emphasises the ensemble, which will interrupt duets or spin its own complex patterns. The title suggests a sense of shared community, which also appears in how the dancers interact. In one of the work's motifs, dancers crumple and fall – and each time, someone is there to catch them.

Peck, who joined New York City Ballet in 2007, started choreographing in 2012. *Everywhere We Go* was his sixth work for the company in just three years. Following its success, he was appointed NYCB's resident choreographer at the age of twenty-six.

Daphnis et Chloé

Choreography: Benjamin Millepied
Music: Maurice Ravel
Decor: Daniel Buren
Costumes: Holly Hynes
Lighting: Madjid Hakimi
Premiere: 10 May 2014, Paris Opéra Ballet, Opéra Bastille, Paris
Original cast: *Chloé* Aurélie Dupont; *Daphnis* Hervé Moreau; *Lycénion* Eleonora Abbagnato; *Bryaxis* François Alu; *Dorcon* Alessio Carbone

Benjamin Millepied's *Daphnis et Chloé* faced high expectations in 2014: it was staged the season before he became director of the Paris Opéra Ballet, starting his tenure with an admired success. Using Ravel's score, spare designs and a cast of twenty-five dancers, it both launched Millepied's new Paris career and reflected his time at New York City Ballet, where he made his first works as a choreographer.

Born in France, Millepied trained at the Conservatoire National de Lyon before moving to the School of American Ballet. He danced with NYCB, where his repertory included roles created for him by Jerome Robbins, Peter Martins, Alexei Ratmansky and Christopher Wheeldon, and he started choreographing in 2001. He was seen as an outsider for the Paris Opéra, but he also brought a touch of transatlantic glamour: he choreographed and appeared in Darren Aronofsky's 2010 ballet movie *Black Swan*, and married its star, Natalie Portman. Millepied has also founded his own company, L.A. Dance Project.

Millepied's *Daphnis* takes a semi-abstract approach to the narrative of Ravel's score, taken from the Greek author Longus. Unlike the first staging, by Mikhail Fokine in 1912, or the later production by Frederick Ashton, Millepied and his collaborators avoid literal scenery. Instead of depicting sacred groves or pirates' dens, the ballet is presented on a bare stage. While it was widely praised, French critics saw it as a conservative work, with classical vocabulary and even *pointe* shoes.

A series of brightly coloured geometric shapes, designed by the artist Daniel Buren, float across the back of the stage, changing the mood and casting reflections on the stage floor. Each is outlined in black and white stripes – a signature feature of Buren's work – and a striped frontcloth is displayed during the overture. Holly Hynes' costumes – tops and knee-length shorts for the men, flowing dresses for the women – are clean and simple in cut. Supporting characters emerge from the *corps de ballet*.

Synopsis

In the first scene, a white-clad *corps de ballet* gathers and dances in pairs, in fluid classical vocabulary with low, skimming lifts. The dancers form lines and friezes behind the flowing dances for Daphnis and Chloé. Lycénion seduces Daphnis in a duet, while Dorcon is a rival for Chloé's affections. A band of pirates, dressed in black and led by the virtuoso Bryaxis, appear and carry off Chloé. The abduction and rescue are non-literal. Instead of the god Pan appearing to save Chloé, the stage lighting blazes red, and the lovers are reunited.

In the final scene, the *corps de ballet* reappears, its dancers now dressed in bold green, red, blue or yellow, for exultant celebration dances with shifting circles, lines and patterns.

NOTES

1 Ballet's Beginnings

1. Mary Clarke and Clement Crisp, *Ballet: An Illustrated History* (London: Hamish Hamilton, 1992), 25.
2. Jean-Georges Noverre, *Letters on Dancing and Ballet*, trans. Cyril W. Beaumont (Alton, Hants: Dance Books, 2004), 9.
3. Clarke and Crisp, *Ballet: An Illustrated History*, 25.

2 The Romantic Ballet

1. Ivor Guest, *The Romantic Ballet in Paris* (Bath: The Pitman Press, 1966), 79.
2. Ibid, 77.
3. Ibid, 73.
4. Ivor Guest, ed., *Gautier on Dance* (London: Dance Books, 1986), 6.
5. Ibid, 70–71.
6. Guest, *The Romantic Ballet in Paris*, 21.
7. Ibid, 209.
8. Ibid, 152.
9. http://www.bournonville.com/bournonville47.html. Accessed 14 November 2014.
10. Guest, ed., *Gautier on Dance*, 94.
11. Guest, The *Romantic Ballet in Paris*, 206.
12. Arlene Croce, 'A New Old Giselle', *The New Yorker*, in Croce, *Going to the Dance* (New York: Alfred A. Knopf, 1982), 373.
13. August Bournonville, *My Theatre Life*, trans. Patricia N. McAndrew (Middletown, CT: Wesleyan University Press, 1979), 88.
14. August Bournonville, *My Dearly Beloved Wife! Letters from France and Italy, 1841* (London: Dance Books, 2005), 89.
15. Ivor Guest, *Jules Perrot: Master of the Romantic Ballet* (London: Dance Books, 1984), 150.
16. Ibid.
17. Ibid, 151.
18. Ole Nørlyng, 'Le Conservatoire: Musical Notes', http://www.bournonville.com/bournonville21.html (accessed 11 March 2015).
19. Jennifer Homans, *Apollo's Angels: A History of Ballet* (London: Granta, 2010), 245.
20. Bournonville, *Theatre Life*, 210.

3 Imperial Ballet

1. Natalia Roslavleva, *Era of the Russian Ballet, 1770–1965* (London: Victor Gollancz, 1966), 21.
2. Ivor Guest, *Jules Perrot: Master of the Romantic Ballet* (London: Dance Books, 1984), 227.

3. Roland John Wiley, ed., *A Century of Russian Ballet: Documents and Eyewitness Accounts, 1810–1910* (Alton: Dance Books, 2007), 235.
4. Ibid, 261.
5. Ibid, 292.
6. *The Times*, 6 March 1876. Cited Jacqueline Banerjee, 'Bertie's Progress: The Prince of Wales in India, 1875–76: Part II, From Delhi to Bombay', http://victorianweb.org/history/empire/india/33.html (accessed 15 November 2014).
7. August Bournonville, trans. Patricia N. McAndrew, *My Theatre Life* (Middletown, CT: Wesleyan University Press, 1979), 582.
8. Alexandre Benois, *Memoirs* (London: Columbus Books, 1988), 143.
9. Roland John Wiley, *Tchaikovsky's Ballets: Swan Lake, Sleeping Beauty, Nutcracker* (Oxford: Clarendon Press, 1985), 101.
10. Mary Clarke and Clement Crisp, *Ballet: An Illustrated History* (London: Hamish Hamilton, 1992), 88.
11. Roland John Wiley, 'Lev Ivanov', *The Nutcracker* (London: Royal Opera House, 2006).
12. Tamara Karsavina, *Theatre Street: The Reminiscences of Tamara Karsavina* (New York: Dutton, 1961), 183–4.
13. Marius Petipa, *Russian Ballet Master: The Memoirs of Marius Petipa*, trans. Helen Whittaker (London: Dance Books, n.d.), 14.
14. Cyril Beaumont, *Complete Book of Ballets* (London: Putnam, 1949), 507.
15. Ivor Guest, ed., *Gautier on Dance* (London: Dance Books, 1986), 39.
16. Wiley, ed., *A Century of Russian Ballet*.
17. Arlene Croce, 'The Return of the Shades', *New Yorker*, 21 June 1982, and in *Sight Lines* (New York, Alfred A. Knopf, 1987) 51.
18. Wiley, *Tchaikovsky's Ballets*, 358.
19. Tim Scholl, *'Sleeping Beauty', a Legend in Progress* (New Haven and London: Yale University Press, 2004), 33.
20. Wiley, ed., *A Century of Russian Ballet*, 390–91.
21. Zoë Dominic and John Selwyn Gilbert, *Frederick Ashton, a Choreographer and his Ballets* (London: George G. Harrap & Co. Ltd, 1971), 223.
22. Wiley, *Tchaikovsky's Ballets*, 221.
23. Ibid, 376.
24. Ibid, 228–9.
25. Mark Morris, Edinburgh International Festival, August 1995.
26. Alexandra Danilova, *Choura* (New York International Publishing Corporation, 1988), 160.

4 The Ballets Russes and After

1. Sjeng Scheijen, trans. Jane Hedley-Prôle and S. J. Leinbach, *Diaghilev: A Life* (London: Profile Books, 2010), 74.
2. Richard Buckle, *Diaghilev* (London: Weidenfeld & Nicolson, 1993), 87.
3. Natalia Roslavleva, *Era of the Russian Ballet 1770–1965* (London: Victor Gollancz, 1966), 169.
4. Isadora Duncan, *My Life* (New York: Liveright, 2013), 141.
5. Mikhail Fokine, *Memoirs of a Ballet Master*, trans. Vitale Fokine (Boston, MA: Little, Brown, 1961), 256.
6. Scheijen, *Diaghilev*, 173.
7. Fokine, *Memoirs of a Ballet Master*, 72.
8. Buckle, *Diaghilev*, 105.
9. Julie Kavanagh, *Secret Muses: The Life of Frederick Ashton* (London: Faber and Faber, 1996), 1–2.
10. Bernard Taper, *Balanchine: A Biography* (New York: Times Books, 1984), 51.
11. Arnold Haskell, *Balletomania: An Updated Version of the Ballet Classic* (Harmondsworth: Penguin, 1979), 26.
12. George Balanchine and Francis Mason, *Balanchine's Festival of Ballet* (London: Comet, 1984), vol. 1, 194.
13. Haskell, *Balletomania*, 112.

14. Mindy Aloff, *Dance Anecdotes* (Oxford: Oxford University Press, 2006), 172.
15. Fokine, *Memoirs of a Ballet Master*, 102.
16. Solomon Volkov, trans. Antonina W. Bouis, *Balanchine's Tchaikovsky* (London: Faber and Faber, 1993), 162.
17. Lynn Garafola, *Diaghilev's Ballets Russes* (Cambridge, MA: Da Capo Press, 1998), 13.
18. John Drummond, *Speaking of Diaghilev* (London: Faber and Faber, 1998), 148.
19. Buckle, *Diaghilev*, 159.
20. Nancy Reynolds and Malcolm McCormick, *No Fixed Points: Dance in the Twentieth Century* (New Haven and London: Yale University Press, 2003), 49.
21. Margot Fonteyn, *Autobiography* (London: W. H. Allen, 1975), 153.
22. Barbara Newman, *Striking a Balance: Dancers Talk About Dancing* (London: Elm Tree Books, 1982), 300.
23. Cyril Beaumont, *Complete Book of Ballets* (London: Putnam, 1949), 716.
24. Drummond, *Speaking of Diaghilev*, 93.
25. Buckle, *Diaghilev*, 180–7.
26. Beaumont, *Complete Book of Ballets*, 721.
27. Drummond, *Speaking of Diaghilev*, 92.
28. Garafola, *Diaghilev's Ballets Russes*, 52.
29. Buckle, *Diaghilev*, 226.
30. Marie Rambert, *Quicksilver* (London: Papermac, 1983), 62.
31. Garafola, *Diaghilev's Ballets Russes*, 64.
32. Richard Buckle, *Nijinsky* (London: Orion Books Ltd, 1998), 269–70.
33. Ibid, 357.
34. Scheijen, *Diaghilev*, 272.
35. Léonide Massine, *My Life in Ballet* (London: MacMillan & Co. Ltd, 1968), 133.
36. Drummond, *Speaking of Diaghilev*, 96.
37. Massine, *My Life in Ballet*, 137–8.
38. Ibid, 142.
39. Buckle, *Diaghilev*, 410–11.
40. Ibid, 411.
41. Igor Stravinsky and Robert Craft, *Expositions and Developments* (Berkeley and Los Angeles: University of California Press, 1981), 118.
42. Ibid, 115.
43. Garafola, *Diaghilev's Ballets Russes*, 129.
44. Nicholas Southon, *Francis Poulenc: Articles and Interviews: Notes from the Heart* (Farnham: Ashgate Publishing Ltd, 2014), 39.
45. Buckle, *Diaghilev*, 420.
46. George Balanchine and Francis Mason, *Balanchine's Festival of Ballet* (London: Comet, 1984), vol. 1, 26.
47. Ibid.
48. Nancy Reynolds, *Repertory in Review: 40 Years of the New York City Ballet* (New York: The Dial Press, 1977), 103.
49. Newman, *Striking A Balance*, 7.
50. Jack Anderson, *The One and Only: The Ballet Russe de Monte Carlo* (New York: Dance Horizons, 1981), 16.

5 National Ballets

1. Bernard Taper, *Balanchine: A Biography* (New York: Times Books, 1984), 151.
2. 'Dame Ninette De Valois', obituary evening, BBC Radio 3, 8 March 2001.
3. Agnes de Mille, *Dance to the Piper* (London: Columbus Books, 1987), 201.
4. Beth Genné, 'Creating a Canon, Creating the "Classics" in Twentieth-Century British Ballet', *Dance Research* 8:2, Winter 2000, 132–62.
5. Lynn Seymour, MacMillan interview series, produced by Lynne Wake, Royal Opera House Collections.
6. Keith Money, *The Art of Margot Fonteyn* (London: Dance Books, 1975), unpaginated.

7. Tyrone Guthrie, *A Life in the Theatre* (London: Readers Union, Hamish Hamilton, 1961), 199.
8. Lincoln Kirstein, introduction to Nancy Reynolds, *Repertory in Review: 40 Years of the New York City Ballet* (New York: The Dial Press, 1977), 5.
9. *Balanchine* (Dance in America, American masters series). Production of Thirteen/ WNET New York. Produced by Judy Kinberg, directed by Merrill Brockway.
10. Robert Gottlieb, *Balanchine: The Ballet Maker* (London: HarperPress, 2006), 78.
11. Deborah Jowitt, *Jerome Robbins: His Life, His Theater, His Dance* (New York: Simon & Schuster, 2004), 144.
12. David Vaughan, *Frederick Ashton and his Ballets* (London: Dance Books, 1999), 93–5.
13. Alastair Macaulay, 'Ashton's Classicism and *Les Rendezvous*', *Studies in Dance History*, vol. 3, no. 2, 12.
14. Vaughan, *Frederick Ashton and his Ballets*, 466.
15. Taper, *Balanchine*, 160.
16. Nancy Reynolds, *Repertory in Review: 40 Years of the New York City Ballet* (New York: The Dial Press, 1977), 37.
17. De Mille, *Dance to the Piper*, 65.
18. Jennifer Dunning, 'Antony Tudor, Choreographer who Transformed Classical Ballet, is Dead', *New York Times*, 21 April 1987.
19. Reynolds, *Repertory in Review*, 133.
20. Vaughan, *Frederick Ashton and his Ballets*, 148.
21. Annabel Farjeon, 'Choreographers: Dancing for de Valois and Ashton' in Alexandra Carter, ed., *The Routledge Dance Studies Reader* (London and New York: Routledge, 1998), 25.
22. Kathrine Sorley Walker, *Ninette de Valois: Idealist Without Illusions* (London: Dance Books, 1998), 196.
23. Lincoln Kirstein, *Thirty Years: The New York City Ballet* (London: A&C Black, 1979), 82.
24. Reynolds, *Repertory in Review*, 64.
25. Gottlieb, *Balanchine: The Ballet Maker*, 103.
26. Ibid, 102.
27. Reynolds, *Repertory in Review*, 68.
28. Judith Chazin-Bennahum, *The Ballets of Antony Tudor: Studies in Psyche and Satire* (New York and Oxford: Oxford University Press, 1994), 114–15.
29. Edwin Denby, 'Fokine's "Russian Soldier"; Tudor's "Pillar of Fire"; Balanchine's "Elephant Ballet"', *Modern Music*, May–June 1942, reprinted in Edwin Denby, *Dance Writings*, ed. Robert Cornfield and William Mackay (London: Dance Books, 1986), 94.
30. Chazin-Bennahum, *The Ballets of Antony Tudor*, 111–12.
31. Interview, *Rodeo*, American Ballet Theatre, 1973.
32. Quoted in Alex C. Ewing, *Bravura! Lucia Chase and the American Ballet Theatre* (Gainesville, FL: University Press of Florida, 2009), 119.
33. Nancy Reynolds and Malcolm McCormick, *No Fixed Points: Dance in the Twentieth Century* (New Haven and London: Yale University Press, 2003), 282.
34. Deborah Jowitt, *Jerome Robbins: His Life, His Theater, His Dance* (New York: Simon & Schuster, 2004), 79.
35. Zoë Dominic and John Selwyn Gilbert, *Frederic Ashton: A Choreographer and his Ballets* (London: George G. Harrap & Co. Ltd, 1971).
36. Vaughan, *Frederick Ashton and his Ballets*, 209.
37. Alastair Macaulay, 'Spring: Ashton's *Symphonic Variations* in America', in Carter, ed., *The Routledge Dance Studies Reader*, 115.
38. Reynolds, *Repertory in Review*, 72.
39. Arlene Croce, 'Momentous', *The New Yorker*, 8 December 1975, reprinted in Arlene Croce, *Afterimages* (London: A&C Black, 1978), 188.
40. Arlene Croce, 'From a Far Country', *The New Yorker*, 22 May 1978, reprinted in Arlene Croce, *Going to the Dance* (New York: Alfred A. Knopf, 1982), 89.
41. Igor Stravinsky and Robert Craft, *Dialogues* (Berkeley and Los Angeles: University of California Press, 1982), 50.

42. Vaughan, *Frederick Ashton and his Ballets*, 221–2.
43. Julie Kavanagh, *Secret Muses: The Life of Frederick Ashton* (London: Faber and Faber, 1996), 356.
44. Vaughan, *Frederick Ashton and his Ballets*, 230.
45. 'Ashton's "Cinderella"', *Ballet*, February 1949, reprinted in Denby, *Dance Writings*, 359.
46. Arlene Croce, 'The Royal Ballet in New York', *Ballet Review*, Summer 1970, reprinted in Croce, *Afterimages*, 378.
47. Reynolds, *Repertory in Review*, 147.
48. Ibid.
49. Leslie Spatt and Nicholas Dromgoole, *Sibley and Dowell* (London: Collins, 1976), 189.
50. Reynolds, *Repertory in Review*, 148.
51. David Nice, 'Would You Give Up *The Ring* for *Sylvia*?', *Sylvia* programme, The Royal Ballet, 2010.
52. Kavanagh, *Secret Muses*, 403.
53. Reynolds, *Repertory in Review*, 116.
54. John Neumeier, *Sylvia* programme note, http://www.hamburg-ballett.de/e/rep/sylvia.htm (accessed 18 December 2014).
55. Paul Parish, 'Who is *Sylvia*, What is She?', *The DanceView Times*, San Francisco Bay Area edition, 30 April 2004, http://danceviewtimes.com/dvw/reviews/2004/spring/sfb5.htm (accessed 18 December 2014).
56. Alexandra Tomalonis, 'Scotch Symphony', in Costas, ed., *Balanchine: Celebrating a Life in Dance* (Windsor, CT: Tide-Mark Press, 2003), 145.
57. Reynolds, *Repertory in Review*, 172.
58. Ibid.
59. Reynolds, *Repertory in Review*, 183n.
60. Reynolds, *Repertory in Review*, 182–3.

6 Soviet Ballet

1. Maya Plisetskaya, trans. Antonina W. Bouis, *I, Maya* (New Haven, CT and London: Yale University Press, 2001), 139–40.
2. Christina Ezrahi, *Swans of the Kremlin: Ballet and Power in Soviet Russia* (Pittsburgh, PA: University of Pittsburgh Press, 2012), 18.
3. Ezrahi, *Swans of the Kremlin*, 20.
4. Bernard Taper, *Balanchine: A Biography* (Berkeley, Los Angeles and London: University of California Press, 1996), 61.
5. Natalia Roslavleva, *Era of the Russian Ballet 1770–1965* (London: Victor Gollancz, 1966), 191.
6. Solomon Volkov, trans. Antonina W. Bouis, *Balanchine's Tchaikovsky* (London: Faber and Faber, 1993), 162.
7. Roslaveleva, *Era of the Russian Ballet*, 194.
8. Elizabeth Souritz, trans. Lynn Visson, ed. with additional trans. Sally Banes, *Soviet Choreographers in the 1920s* (London: Dance Books, 1990), 312.
9. Ezrahi, *Swans of the Kremlin*, 42–3.
10. Roslavleva, *Era of the Russian Ballet*, 199.
11. Mary Clarke and Clement Crisp, *Ballet: An Illustrated History* (London: Hamish Hamilton, 1992), 235.
12. Ezrahi, *Swans of the Kremlin*, 58.
13. Ibid, 62.
14. Barbara Newman, *Antoinette Sibley: Reflections of a Ballerina* (London: Hutchinson, 1968), 67.
15. Angus Macqueen, director, *Dancing for Dollars: The Kirov in Petersburg*, NVC Arts, Telepiu Classica, MIRIS (West Long Brand, NJ: Kultur, 2007). The film was made in 1997.
16. Ezrahi, *Swans of the Kremlin*, 104.
17. Interview for *The Flames of Paris* DVD. © Bel AirClassics, 2010.
18. P. W. Manchester and Iris Morley, *The Rose and the Star: Ballet in England and Russia Compared* (London: Victor Gollancz), 45.

19. Ibid, 46.
20. Interview for *The Flames of Paris* DVD, 2010.
21. Macqueen, *Dancing for Dollars*.
22. Douglas Lee, *Masterworks of 20th-Century Music: The Modern Repertory of the Symphony Orchestra* (New York: Routledge, 2002), 305.
23. Edwin Denby, 'The Bolshoi at the Met', *Hudson Review*, winter 1959–60, reprinted in Edwin Denby, *Dance Writings*, ed. Robert Cornfield and William Mackay (London: Dance Books, 1986), 394–5.
24. Peggy van Praagh and Peter Brinson, *The Choreographic Art: An Outline of its Principles and Craft* (New York: Alfred A. Knopf, 1963), 119.
25. Personal communication, 10 March 2006.

7 The Ballet Boom

1. Nancy Reynolds, *Repertory in Review: 40 Years of the New York City Ballet* (New York: The Dial Press, 1977), 226.
2. Frederick Ashton, 'My Conception of *La Fille mal gardée*', in Ivor Guest, ed., *La Fille mal gardée* (Alton: Dance Books, 2010), 14.
3. Ibid, 13.
4. Nancy Reynolds and Malcolm McCormick, *No Fixed Points: Dance in the Twentieth Century* (New Haven, CT and London: Yale University Press, 2003), 514.
5. David Vaughan, *Frederick Ashton and his Ballets* (London: Dance Books, 1999), 334.
6. Richard Buckle, *The Sunday Times*, 28 March 1965, in Richard Buckle, *Buckle at the Ballet* (London: Dance Books 1980), 168.
7. Barbara Newman, *Striking a Balance: Dancers Talk about Dancing* (London: Elm Tree Books, 1982), 281.
8. Arlene Croce, 'How to Be Very, Very Popular', *The New Yorker*, 11 November 1974, reprinted in Arlene Croce, *Afterimages* (London: A&C Black, 1978), 83.
9. Jann Parry, *Different Drummer: The Life of Kenneth MacMillan* (London: Faber and Faber Ltd, 2009), 300.
10. Ibid, 299.
11. Ibid, 320.
12. Reynolds, *Repertory in Review*, 247.
13. Arlene Croce, 'Free and More than Equal', *The New Yorker*, 24 February 1975, reprinted in Croce, *Afterimages*, 127.
14. Lincoln Kirstein, *Thirty Years: The New York City Ballet* (London: A&C Black, 1979), 194.
15. Reynolds, *Repertory in Review*, 250.
16. John Percival, *Theatre in my Blood: A Biography of Cranko* (New York: Franklin Watts, 1983), 196.
17. Deborah Jowitt, *Jerome Robbins: His Life, His Theater, His Dance* (New York: Simon & Schuster, 2004), 384.
18. George Balanchine and Francis Mason, *Balanchine's Festival of Ballet* (London: Comet, 1984), vol. 1, 159–60.
19. Arlene Croce, 'Balanchine's Girls: The Making of a Style', *Harper's Magazine*, April 1971, reprinted in *Afterimages*, 425.
20. Reynolds, *Repertory in Review*, 267.
21. Ibid, 286.
22. Bernard Taper, *Balanchine: A Biography* (New York: Times Books, 1984), 321.
23. Edmund Lee, 'Dutch National Ballet', *Time Out Hong Kong* online edition, 26 February 2010, www.timeout.com.hk/stage/features/32130/dutch-national-ballet.html (accessed 4 January 2015).
24. Parry, *Different Drummer*, 432.
25. Alastair Macaulay, 'Kenneth MacMillan', *Times Literary Supplement*, June 2003.
26. Parry, *Different Drummer*, 443.
27. Lynn Seymour with Paul Gardner, *Lynn* (London: Granada Publishing Ltd, 1984), 298.
28. Jiří Kylián, programme note, www.jirikylian.com/creations/theatre/sinfonietta/info (accessed 4 January 2015).

29. Jonathan Gray, 'A Dance of Remembrance', Royal Ballet programme note, February 2014.
30. Vaughan, *Frederick Ashton and his Ballets*, 411.
31. Julie Kavanagh, *Secret Muses* (London: Faber and Faber Ltd, 1996), 570.
32. Twyla Tharp, *Push Comes to Shove* (New York: Bantam Books, 1992), 270–71.
33. Lynn Colberg Shapiro, 'Mats Ek, Choreographer, Working at Hubbard Street Dance Chicago', Dance Tabs, 7 December 2012, http://dancetabs.com/2012/12/mats-ek-choreographer-working-at-hubbard-street-dance-chicago (accessed 4 January 2015).

8 International Ballet: Crossing Boundaries

1. Jennifer Homans, *Apollo's Angels* (London: Granta, 2010), xxv.
2. Joan Acocella, 'Dance with Me', *The New Yorker*, 27 June 2011.
3. Interview with William Forsythe, http://www.sadlerswells.com/screen/video/1881622660 (accessed 16 November 2014).
4. Deborah Jowitt, *Jerome Robbins: His Life, His Theater, His Dance* (New York: Simon & Schuster, 2004), 465.
5. Gabriella de Ferrari, 'William Forsythe', *BOMB* 96, Summer 2006, http://bombmagazine.org/article/2839/william-forsythe (accessed 10 October 2014).
6. Kathryn Bennetts interview, Sadler's Wells, 2012, http://www.sadlerswells.com/screen/video/1531641240001 (accessed 8 January 2015).
7. Twyla Tharp interview, 'Class Clips, Dance – Choreography', BBC, 6 October 2010, http://www.bbc.co.uk/education/clips/zx7fb9q (accessed 18 January 2014).
8. Ibid.
9. Jiří Kylián, programme note, *Sechs Tänze/Six Dances*, http://www.jirikylian.com/creations/theatre/sechs_tanze/info (accessed 8 January 2015).
10. William Forsythe interview, Sadler's Wells, http://www.sadlerswells.com/screen/video/25141629001 (accessed 8 January 2015).
11. Roslyn Sulcas, 'Watching Dancers Grow, as Cultivated by a Daredevil', *The New York Times*, 28 December 2012.
12. William Forsythe interview, Sadler's Wells, http://www.sadlerswells.com/screen/video/1881622660 (accessed 8 January 2015).
13. Joan Acocella, *Mark Morris* (New York: Farrar Strauss Giroux, 1993), 201.
14. New York City Ballet, *2013–15 Season: Guide to the Repertory*.
15. Interview with William Forsythe, Sadler's Wells, http://www.sadlerswells.com/screen/video/25139250001 (accessed 8 January 2015).
16. Author interview, 23 June 2004.
17. Ibid.
18. Ibid.
19. Ibid.
20. Programme note, Houston Ballet, http://www.houstonballet.org/Inside-Houston-Ballet/Clear-Info (accessed 8 January 2015).
21. Author interview, 21 December 2012.
22. Joseph Carman, 'Contemporary Classic', *Dance Magazine*, January 2011.
23. Author interview, 21 December 2012.
24. Wayne McGregor, programme note, The Royal Ballet, November 2006.
25. Alastair Macaulay, 'Riding the Emotions of a Ratmansky Ballet', *The New York Times*, 31 May 2008.
26. Max Richter, 'Class Clips, Dance – Choreography', BBC, 6 October 2010, http://www.bbc.co.uk/education/clips/z62ygk7 (accessed 22 February 2015).
27. Author interview, 21 December 2012.
28. Marina Harss, 'Running Like Shadows', *The Nation*, 5–12 August 2013.
29. Jerry Hochman, 'American Ballet Theatre, *The Shostakovich Trilogy*', *Ballet-Dance Magazine*, http://www.ballet-dance.com/201105/ABT31May1Jun2013.html (accessed 22 February 2015).

INDEX OF BALLET TITLES

Page numbers in **bold** refer to main entries.

GENERAL INDEX